PHILOSOPHICAL DIMENSIONS
OF PARAPSYCHOLOGY

Philosophical Dimensions of Parapsychology

Edited by

JAMES M. O. WHEATLEY, Ph.D.

Department of Philosophy
University of Toronto
Toronto, Canada

and

HOYT L. EDGE, Ph.D.

Department of
Philosophy and Religion
Rollins College
Winter Park, Florida

CHARLES C THOMAS • PUBLISHER
Springfield • Illinois • U.S.A.

Published and Distributed Throughout the World by

CHARLES C THOMAS • PUBLISHER

Bannerstone House

301-327 East Lawrence Avenue, Springfield, Illinois, U.S.A.

*With THOMAS BOOKS careful attention is given to all details of
manufacturing and design. It is the Publisher's desire to present books that are
satisfactory as to their physical qualities and artistic possibilities and
appropriate for their particular use. THOMAS BOOKS will be true to those
laws of quality that assure a good name and good will.*

Library of Congress Cataloging in Publication Data

Wheatley, James M O comp.
  Philosophical dimensions of parapsychology.

  Bibliography: p.
  1. Psychical research. I. Edge, Hoyt L., joint comp. II. Title. [DNLM: 1. Parapsychology—Collected works. BF1031 W557p]
BF1031.W48   133   74-13814
ISBN 0-398-03311-0

Printed in the United States of America

CONTRIBUTORS

JOHN BELOFF, Ph.D., Senior Lecturer in the Department of Psychology at the University of Edinburgh, is the author of *The Existence of Mind, Psychological Sciences,* and many articles on a variety of topics. His main area of interest lies in philosophical psychology, but he regards parapsychology as very relevant to the problem of the mind-body relationship. He was President of the Parapsychological Association for 1972.

CARLTON W. BERENDA, Ph.D., has been Professor of Philosophy at the University of Oklahoma since 1946. He has taught physics at various universities and holds a doctorate in philosophy of science. He is the author of numerous articles in philosophical and scientific journals and anthologies.

BOB BRIER, Ph.D., is Assistant Professor of Philosophy at C. W. Post College and a member of the faculty of the New School for Social Research. Formerly a Research Fellow at the Institute for Parapsychology, he is coeditor with J. B. Rhine of *Parapsychology Today* and has published numerous articles in professional journals.

C. D. BROAD (1887-1971) was Knightbridge Professor of Moral Philosophy at the University of Cambridge and one of England's most distinguished philosophers. A twenty-page bibliography that lists his writings through July, 1959, may be found in P. A. Schilpp (Ed.): *The Philosophy of C. D. Broad.* For several years President of the Society for Psychical Research, he was the author of many outstanding articles and lectures on parapsychology. Among his books are *Examination of McTaggart's Philosophy* and *The Mind and Its Place in Nature.*

RÉMY CHAUVIN, DR. RER. NAT. (D.Sc.), is Professor for Experimental Entomology, Nanterre (Paris), and has published over 150 articles in animal behavior. Under the pseudonym "Pierre Duval," he has written several articles and books, including *Nos pouvoirs inconnus* and *La science devant l'étrange*. He is a member of the French Academy of Science and coeditor of the *Journal of Insect Physiology*.

C. J. DUCASSE (1881-1969) was one of America's foremost philosophers and educators. A member of the faculty of Brown University from 1924 until his death, he was the author of many philosophical books and scores of articles, his legionary contributions ranging over most areas of philosophy. He had a deep interest in parapsychology, on which he lectured widely, and held several positions in the American Society for Psychical Research. His last published book was *A Critical Examination of the Belief in a Life after Death*.

ANTONY FLEW, M.A., was educated at St. John's College, Oxford. From 1954 until 1971, he was Professor and Head of the Department of Philosophy at the University of Keele. Currently at the University of Reading, he has taught also at Oxford, Aberdeen, and Calgary. He is the author of numerous books and a large number of articles, besides being a noted editor and lecturer. Three of his books are *A New Approach to Psychical Research, Hume's Philosophy of Belief,* and *An Introduction to Western Philosophy*.

LAWRENCE LESHAN, Ph.D., is currently a full-time researcher in parapsychology as Research Associate, Ayer Foundation. He has taught at Roosevelt University and New School for Social Research. Before assuming his present position, he was Director of a research project on the psychosomatic aspects of neoplastic disease at the Trafalgar Hospital and the Institute of Applied Biology. Coauthor of *Counseling the Dying,* he has also published over fifty articles in professional journals. His most recent book is *The Medium, the Mystic, and the Physicist*.

PAUL MEEHL, Ph.D., holds numerous professorial positions at the University of Minnesota, including those of Regents' Professor of Psychology and Professor at the Minnesota Center for Philosophy of Science. He has published widely in psychology and philosophy. He was President of the American Psychological Association in 1962.

C. W. K. MUNDLE, M.A., is Head of the Department of Philosophy at University College of North Wales, Bangor, a position he held previously at University College (now University of)

Dundee, in Scotland. He is the author of *A Critique of Linguistic Philosophy, Perception: Facts and Theories.* Since 1971, he has served as President of the Society for Psychical Research.

GARDNER MURPHY, Ph.D., is Professor Emeritus of Psychology at George Washington University. He has been Chairman of the psychology department at City College of the City of New York and Director of Research at the Menninger Foundation. His outstanding contributions to psychology and parapsychology are numerous, varied, and well-known. Among the books he has authored or coauthored are *Personality: A Biosocial Approach to Origins and Structure, Human Potentialities,* and *Challenge of Psychical Research.* The American Psychological Association and the American Society for Psychical Research are two of the organizations of which he has been President.

G. C. NAYAK, Ph.D., is Reader in Philosophy at Utkal University in India. Since obtaining his doctorate at the University of Bristol in 1965, he has served as Sectional President for History of Philosophy in a session of the Indian Philosophical Congress and as a visiting lecturer at several universities. He is the author of a forthcoming book on *Evil, Karma and Reincarnation* and numerous articles.

TERENCE PENELHUM, B.Phil., was educated at the University of Edinburgh and Oriel College, Oxford. After a year as English-Speaking Union Visiting Fellow at Yale, he began teaching at the University of Alberta. In 1963, he moved to the University of Calgary, where he is now Professor of Philosophy and Religious Studies and was for three years Dean of Arts and Science. He is the author of *Survival and Disembodied Existence, Religion and Rationality,* and *Problems of Religious Knowledge* and is a frequent contributor to philosophical journals.

H. H. PRICE, M.A., HON. D.Litt., HON. D.C.L., is Professor Emeritus of Logic at New College, Oxford. He is a charter member of the Parapsychological Association and was President of the Society for Psychical Research (1939-41, 1960-61). His published writings include many articles on the philosophical implications of parapsychology, and he is the author of the following books: *Perception, Hume's Theory of the External World, Thinking and Experience, Belief,* and *Essays in the Philosophy of Religion.*

W. G. ROLL, B.Litt., did his undergraduate work in Denmark and at the University of California, Berkeley. At Oxford University, where he was President of the Oxford Society for Psychical Research, he wrote a thesis on parapsychology for which he was awarded his B.Litt. He later joined the staff of the Parapsychology Laboratory of Duke University and was for some years an editor of *The Journal of Parapsychology.* He was President of the Parapsychological Association for 1964 and is the senior editor of the Association's proceedings. Since 1961, he has been Project Director of the Psychical Research Foundation, which engages in research on the question of survival of personality after death. He is the editor of *Theta* and a frequent contributor to other journals.

MICHAEL SCRIVEN, D.Phil., is Professor of Philosophy at the University of California, Berkeley. While attending the University of Melbourne in Australia, where he received his M.A., he founded what is believed to be the first parapsychological research group in the Southern hemisphere and published two research designs for psychokinetic experiments that would yield cumulative results from most types of PK forces. He has published extensively in the fields of philosophy, education, and the social sciences.

KENNETH L. SHEWMAKER, Ph.D., has engaged in private practice of psychotherapy since 1963 and is currently in the Oklahoma City Psychiatric Clinic Complex. He has taught at the University of Oklahoma School of Medicine and elsewhere, and he is the author of journal articles in areas of theory and practice of individual and group psychotherapy.

PETER SWIGGART, Ph.D., has taught literature at Amherst College and the University of Texas and is now in the English department at Brandeis University. His publications include *The Art of Faulkner's Novels* and articles in literary criticism, linguistics, and language philosophy.

CHARLES T. TART, Ph.D., is Associate Professor of Psychology at the University of California, Davis. He has taught at Stanford University and the University of Virginia School of Medicine, and he has conducted research in sleep, dreaming, hypnosis, psychedelic drugs, and parapsychology. His research activities are currently focused in the areas of altered states of consciousness and transpersonal psychology. His scientific publications include *Altered*

States of Consciousness and *On Being Stoned: A Psychological Study of Marijuana Intoxication* as well as more than fifty articles in professional journals.

IRVING THALBERG, Ph.D., has taught at Oberlin College, the University of Washington, and (since 1965) the University of Illinois at Chicago Circle. The essay appearing in revised form here was his first publication. Most of his journal articles, as well as his book, *Enigmas of Agency,* are on philosophy of mind and philosophy of action.

PREFACE

You don't have to be psychic to perceive that interest in paranormal phenomena is mushrooming. Growing attention to them has lately been accompanied by heightened awareness of the importance of parapsychology to our system of knowledge. Not long ago, for example, the American Association for the Advancement of Science recognized it as a legitimate contributor to our understanding of the world by approving the Parapsychological Association's bid for affiliation. And various other signs of the reception of psychical research into the educational framework are highly visible.

Certainly there has been a remarkable increase, at colleges and universities, in the number of courses concerned with parapsychology or the philosophical implications of its findings. Teachers of courses in philosophy of parapsychology, however, have found it hard to provide students with sufficient suitable texts, since much of the material published in the field, excellent though some of it is, is not readily available for classroom use. This book is an attempt to help to meet the need for accessibility.

We have brought together a number of philosophical writings that hitherto have been scattered through the literature of the past thirty-five years. They include searching examinations of parapsychology by Broad, Ducasse, Flew, Price, Scriven, and other distinguished philosophers and scientists, as well as papers by less-known authors. The earliest of the articles was published in 1937, the latest in 1973. Choice of selections sometimes was difficult: a glance through the bibliography will reveal anything but a shortage of material. In many cases, items left out of the book could well have been substituted for ones put in. In some cases, though, deliberation was unnecessary: a few of our choices are "must" selections.

At any rate, we hope that readers will find the present collection well-balanced, exciting, and relatively comprehensive. It is divided into five sections. One of us has written a short introduction to each section, the other a general introduction to the book.

We wish to thank the persons who gave us permission to reprint copyrighted material.

J. M. O . W.
H.L.E.

INTRODUCTION

"Parapsychology" is not easy to define, but it should be remembered that good definitions of "physics," "biology," and "psychology" are not easy to give, either. Still, it must be allowed that attempts to say what parapsychology is are especially controversial. It is less difficult to say what physics is than to say what philosophy is, and in this respect, parapsychology is closer to philosophy than to physics. If we look at the word "parapsychology," we may note that "para" means *beside* or *beyond,* infer that parapsychology is the science beside (or beyond) psychology, and feel a need for more illumination. Parapsychology used to be known as psychical research, which presumably is research into the mind. Why, then, is parapsychology not simply psychology? The answer appears to be that the "mind" with which psychology is concerned is not the "mind" explored by parapsychology. While the former is normal (and, at times, abnormal), the latter is *paranormal.*

Our reflections on "parapsychology" have encompassed a shift, therefore: initially, we took the prefix "para" to qualify the science; now, we see it as qualifying the subject matter of the science. The same shift, in fact, sometimes occurs in discussions where it seems to pass unnoticed; we may do well to remember it. A parastudy of the psyche is one thing, a study of the parapsyche is another. Focus on the former may lead a writer to use the expression "parascience" when referring to parapsychology, but most parapsychologists would think of themselves more as scientists of the parapsyche than as parascientists of the mind. Usually, of course, references are made not to the parapsyche, but to paranormal events, happenings, occurrences, or simply the paranormal.

Extrasensory perception and psychokinesis[1] are commonly cited

---

[1] *The Journal of Parapsychology,* Vol. 37 (1973) pp. 374-375, defines "extrasensory perception" as "[e]xperience of, or response to, a target object, state, event, or influence without sensory contact" and "psychokinesis" as "a direct (i.e. mental but nonmuscular) influence exerted by the subject on an external physical process, condition, or object." Hereafter, I shall use the familiar abbreviations, "ESP" and "PK."

as the primary objects of parapsychological inquiry. What they have to do with either psyche or parapsyche, however, is a potentially entangling question that I shall not examine. Suffice it to say that in some alleged cases of ESP and PK (consider the experiments with rodents, for example), mind seems to enter marginally, at most. Indeed, the reasons for regarding psi (ESP + PK) as necessarily mental are not at all clear. Few would deny, though, that ESP and PK *are* paranormal, and some would contend that parapsychology is preeminently the science of the paranormal. To those who hold this view, Broad's definition of paranormality in terms of what he calls "basic limiting principles" may appear very helpful.

In "The Relevance of Psychical Research to Philosophy," included here in nearly its entirety as the first selection, Broad sets forth several general principles such that if an event is inconsistent with at least one of them, then that event is *paranormal*. The principles have to do with causation in general, the action of mind on matter, the mind-brain relationship, and acquisition of knowledge. Depending on which of the principles a given paranormal event conflicts with, it can be classified as an instance of clairvoyance, telepathy, precognition, or psychokinesis, these being the four principal types of psi, according to standard parapsychological accounts. (The first three are regarded as types of ESP, and capsule definitions of both "ESP" and "PK" have been quoted.[2]) One of the principles, for example, states that it "is impossible for a person to perceive a physical event or a material thing except by means of sensations which that event or thing produces in his mind." An event in conflict with this principle would count as an instance of clairvoyance.

What Broad means by "basic limiting principles," he has written, is a number of "very general principles, mostly of a negative or restrictive kind, which practically everyone who has been brought up within or under the influence of Western industrial societies assumes without question nowadays. They form the framework within which the practical life, the scientific theories, and

---

[2]Corresponding definitions of "clairvoyance," "telepathy," and "precognition" are as follows. *Clairvoyance*: "Extrasensory perception of objects or objective events"; *telepathy*: "Extrasensory perception of the mental state or activity of another person"; *precognition*: "Prediction of random future events the occurrence of which cannot be inferred from present knowledge" *Ibid.*, pp. 374-376.

even most of the fiction of contemporary industrial civilizations are confined."[3]

In brief, it is Broad's view that parapsychology, or psychical research, is the scientific investigation of ostensibly paranormal phenomena or events, i.e. phenomena or events that seem *prima facie* to conflict with one or more basic limiting principles.[4]

"It is the business of psychical research," he states, "to investigate ostensibly paranormal phenomena, with a view to discovering whether they are . . . genuinely paranormal," and to try, if it should be found that there are genuinely paranormal phenomena, "to discover the laws governing them."[5]

There is, to my knowledge, no more adequate definition of "paranormal" than Broad's. It is nonetheless unsatisfactory or defective in some respects. For one thing, the authority and applicability of the principles are none too clear. On what sort of grounds might they properly be argued for, or against? Can they, indeed, be characterized as either true or false? How are they discovered? In his critique (see footnote 3, above), Ducasse sees some of the principles as unproved hypotheses, some as generalizations from experience, and at least one as analytic and hence quite certainly true.[6] Broad himself is inclined to distinguish between basic limiting principles and well-established laws of nature, though he admits that there may be borderline cases: E.g. is the second law of thermodynamics a "law of nature" or a "basic limiting principle"?[7]

This whole difficulty can be summarized: The logical and the epistemological status of the principles remains cloudy. Further, one may well be uneasy about the thrust of "ostensibly" in "ostensibly paranormal." Just what does it mean to say that an

[3]C. D. Broad: *Lectures on Psychical Research.* New York, Humanities, 1962, p. 3. In this work, Broad presents an account differing somewhat, but not essentially, from that in the article reprinted below. For a spirited, sympathetic critique and analysis of the basic limiting principles, see C. J. Ducasse: Broad on the relevance of psychical research to philosophy. In P. A. Schilpp (Ed.): *The Philosophy of C. D. Broad.* New York, Tudor, 1959, pp. 375-410. See esp. pp. 377-381. Part of Ducasse's article is included in Section III.
[4]See Section I and cf. *Lectures on Psychical Research,* pp. 3-5.
[5]*Lectures on Psychical Research,* pp. 5, 19.
[6]*The Philosophy of C. D. Broad,* pp. 377-381.
[7]*Lectures on Psychical Research,* pp. 4-5.

event "seems *prima facie*" to conflict with a basic limiting principle? Seems to whom and in what circumstances? Does one infer that an event is ostensibly paranormal or see that it is?

Such difficulties will no doubt seem academic to those parapsychologists (not yet, I think, more than a small minority) who favor turning away from the idea of the paranormal altogether. Their view is not to be lightly dismissed, but what does parapsychology become if we dispense with characterizing its subject matter in terms of "paranormal phenomena"? As far as I can see, it becomes a sort of ecology, a study of relationships among organisms and between organisms and their environments. While this approach may be promising, it so far leaves us with no working criterion of *which* ecological relationships fall within parapsychology. Moreover, if we reject the idea of parapsychology's being the study of seemingly paranormal phenomena (in such sense as Broad's), is there not a danger that we shall lose sight of the sheer strangeness of the happenings revealed or assumed by the science, strangeness, that is, as judged by everyday experience? The extent to which Broad's definition reflects and directs our sense of such strangeness is a virtue that does much to compensate for the quite possibly remediable defects that have been mentioned.

Provisionally accepting, then, Broad's view of the (present) business of parapsychology, we face the further question whether parapsychologists will *always* be primarily concerned with paranormal events. There is little reason to believe in that outcome. Conceivably, a time will come when no events are paranormal or seem to be so and when parapsychology, therefore, cannot be the study of the paranormal. Would it necessarily have been phased out beforehand? Or would it continue to exist at such a time, as the study of things once, but no longer, paranormal—notably, ESP and PK? While these questions allow no confident response, a tentative forecast of parapsychology's continuation seems reasonable.

Assume for a moment that the year is 2174. There are still, we may imagine, ostensibly paranormal events, but they no longer include ESP and PK, which became "normalized" a hundred years ago. Suitably renamed, though, ESP and PK remain very much a part of the parapsychologist's compass. Parapsychology itself has long since been renamed, yet lines of continuity are such that science S of 2174 can be identified with parapsychology of 1974, as physics of 1974 was identifiable with physics of 1774. But although S, we (now returned to 1974) may suppose, will busy itself two centuries hence largely with normal events, and those events will then be characterized in positive terms unavailable in 1974, we do not now know enough about parapsychology's subject matter to characterize it other than negatively: in terms, that is, of its being paranormal. The link between parapsychology and paranormality is intimate, but not inevitable.

There is another view of psi, discussed in the reflective and provocative paper by Shewmaker and Berenda in Section V, that might at first be confused with Broad's, though really it is basically different. As Shewmaker and Berenda describe it, this is the view that "as we are bound to the . . . abstractions indigenous to our thought forms, we could expect that there would always . . . [be] *inexplicable* events . . . [simply because] of our imposing abstract classes upon the world we experience," and that psi "is the persistent remainder left over from our division of the world into abstract classes."

Two important contrasts between this view and Broad's should be noted. (1) On this view, there could be no conflict between psi and the "abstractions indigenous to our thought forms," as there is conflict between psi phenomena and basic limiting principles. As "the persistent remainder," psi cannot *conflict* with that apart from which it remains. (2) On Broad's view, there is nothing intrinsically inexplicable about paranormal phenomena. Their eventual explanation will indeed require revision of whatever basic limiting principles they happen to conflict with, but such explanation—impossible on the "persistent remainder" view—is something for which we may properly, if optimistically, hope.

Meanwhile, the collective results of parapsychological studies are deeply intriguing. Their philosophical importance is the principal topic of the first set of readings, in which the material is arranged chronologically. Among recent philosophers, no one has contributed more to discussions of the philosophical implications of parapsychology than C. D. Broad, C. J. Ducasse, and H. H. Price. No one else, in fact, has contributed nearly as much, either in volume or in value. All three are represented in this anthology by notable works seeking in one way or another to suggest the significance of parapsychological phenomena and pressing the desirability of philosophical attention to them. In this area, Price is represented by a pioneer article, "Some Philosophical Questions about Telepathy and Clairvoyance," where he scrutinizes the field of parapsychology in general and two types of ESP in particular;[8] Broad by the paper previously referred to, in which he explains the notion of basic limiting principle and discusses the relevance of parapsychology to philosophy; and Ducasse by his contribution to the American Philosophical Association's symposium on psychical research and philosophy, in which he tries to dispel some misconceptions about the philosophical importance of parapsychology and to put that importance in clearer perspective.

In more recent papers, Scriven and Mundle offer philosophic critiques that stress the absence within parapsychology of viable models that would serve to explain the "strange facts," as Mundle puts it, that have been established. Scriven, having drawn some highly interesting contrasts between parapsychology and psychoanalysis, concludes that the former "provides us with . . . a factual basis on which there is yet to be built a great theory." Mundle, while cautioning against inferring from the facts of parapsychology certain metaphysical claims that they are erroneously thought to support, similarly concludes that what psychical research has so far done is to establish the occurrence of various fascinating phenomena "which cannot yet be understood." It seems clear that neither Scriven nor Mundle intends his conclusion to impugn parapsychology's importance for philosophy and that both, moreover, are willing to defend the scientific character of parapsychological research. In the latter connection, their critiques anticipate some of the discussions brought together in the final section of this book.

In Section II, the discussion moves to the relations between ESP

---

[8]Because it relates, to a sizable extent, to the concept of knowledge, we have placed this 1940 article in Section II. It could almost as well have been included in Section I, along with Broad's paper of 1949 and Ducasse's of 1954.

and types of cognition.[9] Both the article by Price already mentioned and my paper on ESP and empiricism deal with knowledge generally, while two short papers by Thalberg and Swiggart are addressed particularly to the problem of knowledge of other minds. Concluding Section II is a seminal contribution by Roll on ESP and memory that surely goes some way toward overcoming the serious and just-mentioned lack of theoretical models.

The basic theme in Section II is knowledge. When it is asked whether ESP can provide knowledge, there are at least two senses in which the question can be taken. In one sense, it means "Can ESP serve as a *source* of knowledge, as sight, for example, can?" In another, it means "Can ESP be employed to *settle* a question of fact, as (again) sight, for example, can?" Roughly, the first question pertains to learning, to getting to know things; the second, to grounds or evidence, to convincing someone that what you claim to know is in fact the case. It may well be that ESP does play a causative role in the acquisition of some of our knowledge, even if we are not able to employ it to justify knowledge-claims. In the literature of psychical research, use of the word "knowledge" is sometimes lax and unclear. This is unfortunate: Its use seems important enough to be undertaken with care. To claim to know that something is the case is to make a rather strong claim. According to one well-known analysis, it amounts to claiming (1) that you are fully confident that what you claim to be the case is the case, (2) that what you claim to be the case really is the case, and (3) that your confidence that it is the case rests on good evidence.

Some philosophers have expressed doubt about the adequacy of this so-called justified-true-belief account of knowledge, but many would defend it—provided it be formulated with considerably more refinement than is necessary here—and it seems to me to be basically sound. Even if it isn't, though, its inadequacy comes from its being too liberal, not too strict. Yet often, it seems, allegations in parapsychological writings that someone knows this or that are indefensible by the justified-true-belief standard. Typically, the

[9]It will be easily noticed that in the selections in this volume, the authors tend to be concerned with ESP rather than PK. This is not a result of editorial bias, but rather reflects the fact that philosophers have not yet explored the implications of PK research nearly as much as they have those of ESP studies. A clear and concentrated examination of the scientific role and philosophical significance of PK is still to appear.

allegations fail because either condition (1) or condition (3), above, proves not to be satisfied. (Indeed, if condition (2) is unsatisfied, the allegations are not apt to be made!) And perhaps the most interesting sense of the question whether ESP can provide knowledge is that in which we ask whether it can provide the good evidence required by condition (3).

Referring, finally, to one form of knowledge not mentioned so far, we can ask a further question that may be equally interesting. We know that sensory perception leads both to knowledge *that* such and such is the case (e.g. knowledge that bicycles were invented before automobiles) and to knowledge *how* to do something (e.g. how to drive an automobile). Can ESP, we may ask, lead to knowing-how, as distinct from knowing-that? For instance, could we learn by ESP how to drive? It has sometimes been suggested that much learning does involve ESP in undetected ways.

The discussion of cognition is followed by discussion of precognition. The first selection on this topic is "Knowing the Future," by Ducasse. Though brief, it raises several basic questions and succinctly gives Ducasse's views on them, which he has developed at length elsewhere. It is succeeded by "The Philosophical Implications of Foreknowledge," a major paper by Broad that is here reprinted in full. It surveys a wide range of philosophic aspects of precognition and discusses in detail three objections that have been made against the possibility of paranormal foreknowledge. These are the so-called epistemological, fatalistic, and causal objections. Of the three, evidently the causal objection is the most intractable. It has to do with the alleged impossibility of an effect's occurring before its cause (which would be backward causation). In the third selection,[10] Ducasse contends that backward causation is indeed impossible—that an effect cannot precede its own cause is, he thinks, *necessarily* true—but he argues that precognition does not entail it. Believing that something is needed to reconcile precognition with the impossibility of backward causation, he proposes an ingenious theory to effect the reconciliation. The theory is not easy to understand and may well be false, but I think that

---

[10]The selection is a portion of Ducasse's contribution to *The Philosophy of C.D. Broad.* See footnote 3.

in trying to understand it, we learn a lot about problems of pre-cognition, causality, and time.

In the final selection on precognition, which was written originally for the present volume, Brier is concerned with the same problem as Ducasse, but he takes a fundamentally different position. "Magicians, Alarm Clocks, and Backward Causation" attempts to show that the causal objection to precognition rests on a misunderstanding, on grounds that it is, after all, entirely possible for an effect to precede its cause.

Even more mystifying than the problem of knowing the future is the problem of the possibility of a future (postmortal) state. John Beloff (author of "Parapsychology and Its Neighbors," in Section V) lately discussed the importance of parapsychology in the following terms. "For a long time to come," he said, "its importance as I see it is neither practical nor in any ordinary sense scientific. It is, rather, metaphysical. By this I mean that parapsychology represents the only body of empirical evidence which has a direct bearing on the traditional mind-body problem."[11] Three philosophical facets of that problem are the nature of mind, the relationship between mental and physical, and the continuity and identity of the self, issues deeply involved in the question of personal survival of bodily death. All of them are critically discussed in the section on psi and survival. Without necessarily going as far as Beloff does in the judgment just quoted, one cannot but be impressed by the extent to which wrestling with the mind-body problem seems to generate a need to deal with parapsychological matters. As for the survival question itself, unless it is simply dismissed as meaningless, a way of disposing of it that would be hard to justify philosophically, it is not only uniquely important. It is evidently the most refractory of all the problems requiring collaboration between parapsychology and philosophy.

In Section IV, survival is examined from various philosophic points of view. Basic concepts are elucidated and questions serving to organize the discussion of survival are framed. As Ducasse says, we have first to inquire whether survival is a *theoretical* possibility, next—if the answer to the first inquiry be affirmative—

---

[11]W.G. Roll et al. (Eds.): *Research in Parapsychology* 1972. (Metuchen, Scarecrow, 1973), p. 117.

to inquire whether it is an *empirical* possibility, and finally—if the answer to the second inquiry be affirmative—to inquire whether it is a reality.[12] Presumably, the first question is amenable to philosophic analysis, the second to a combination of philosophy and science, including parapsychology, while the third is a matter for science alone to decide. In the selections below, emphasis is thus on one or another aspect of the first question. A solution of this problem implies an understanding of one of the most sensitive and divisive issues in the philosophy of survival: Can we conceive of personal existence in a completely nonembodied form? Some philosophers maintain that we can, others advance powerful arguments to the contrary.

It surely is consistent to acknowledge the logical (theoretical) possibility of *survival,* yet to deny that of *nonembodied* survival. To reject the logical possibility of survival is to fly in the face of popular human belief in survival, belief in keeping with philosophical, religious, and social traditions of incalculable age and world-wide dimensions. Such rejection flies in the face of these traditions, moreover, without having the strength of good logic behind it. For denial of the logical possibility of *nonembodied* survival, on the other hand, strong supportive logic can be summoned (see, e.g. Flew's and Penelhum's arguments), *and* the denial is consistent, for the most part, with traditional belief. With respect to that consistency, a comment by Broad is singularly apt. He writes:

> Of all the hundreds of millions of human beings, in every age and clime, who have believed (or have talked or acted as if they believed) in human survival, hardly any have believed in *unembodied* survival. Hindus and Buddhists, e.g. believe in reincarnation in an ordinary human or animal body or occasionally in the non-physical body of some non-human rational being . . . Christians . . . believe in some kind of (unembodied?) persistence up to the General Resurrection, and in survival thereafter with a peculiar kind of supernatural body . . . correlated in some intimate and unique way with the animal body, . . . which has died and rotted away. Nor are such views confined to babes and sucklings. Spinoza, e.g. certainly believed in human immortality; and he cannot possibly have be-

---

[12]See *A Critical Examination of the Belief in a Life after Death* (Springfield, Thomas, 1961), Ch. 7.

lieved, on his general principles, in the existence of a mind without some kind of correlated bodily organism. Leibniz said explicitly that, if *per impossibile* a surviving mind were to be without an organism, it would be 'a deserter from the general order'. It seems to me rather futile for a modern philosopher to discuss the possibility of human survival on an assumption which would have been unhesitatingly rejected by almost everyone, lay or learned, who has ever claimed seriously to believe in it.[13]

Stephen Toulmin's *Human Understanding,* the first of whose planned three volumes has recently been published,[14] is an impressive philosophic inquiry. To introduce the set of problems discussed in our final section, I shall mention one of the concepts that Toulmin analyzes. It belongs in the context of his central account of rational disciplines and has evident application to the case of parapsychology, an application with which Toulmin himself is not concerned. The concept to which we shall attend is that of *would-be discipline,* and hence it is necessary first to cite a summary view provided by Toulmin of the nature of rational disciplines in general, of which the physical sciences, engineering, and law are said to afford prime examples.

Toulmin's theory is that three main conditions must be satisfied for an area of rational endeavor to constitute a *discipline.* We start with a group of people among whom there is widespread agreement about the set of ideals or goals to which they are committed. This is the first condition. Second, their commitment must lead "to the development of [a relatively] isolable and self-defining repertory of procedures . . ." Third, these procedures must be capable of being modified to deal with problems arising because the ideals of the group have not been fulfilled.[15] At an abstract level of discourse, any "collective human enterprise" governed by these conditions can be termed a rationally developing discipline. A further condition must be satisfied if the discipline is to be *scientific*: The ideals or goals to which members of the discipline are committed must be explanatory ideals, as distinct from judicial ideals, for example, or technological ones.

Now consider parapsychology. It is frequently argued that it is

[13]*Lectures on Psychical Research,* p. 408.
[14]London, Oxford U Pr, 1972.
[15]See *Human Understanding,* vol. 1, p. 359.

not really a science, because there is doubt about the genuineness of its phenomena; or because there is no explanatory scheme or model for dealing with the phenomena systematically—they are just floating curiosities that cannot be anchored in a theoretical framework; or because if there is an explanatory model for dealing with the phenomena, there is no way to test it, to verify or falsify it; and so on. Yet, on the contrary, despite such doubts and difficulties, it is perfectly obvious to many students of the field that parapsychology *is,* in some ordinary sense or to some considerable extent, scientific. As a science, it is young, low-level, descriptive, and undeveloped, but nevertheless, successful experiments are conducted, standard techniques of statistics and measurement are employed, hypotheses are framed and confirmed or disconfirmed, and data are collected with all the care and critical-mindedness anyone could wish for. It seems, then, that what we have in parapsychology is not fullfledged science, not nonscience, but something in between; and I think that Toulmin's account of would-be disciplines tells us moderately well what that something is.

A would-be discipline is a subject which aims at disciplinary status but "in which effective disciplinary development has as yet scarcely begun . . ." A would-be discipline may differ from a discipline either methodologically, because of an "absence of a clearly defined . . . reservoir of disciplinary problems, so that conceptual innovations . . . lack any continuing rational directtion"; or institutionally, because of an "absence of a suitable professional organization, so that the disciplinary possibilities . . . are not fully exploited . . ." Would-be disciplinarians "may not merely disagree about their particular observations and interpretations, concepts and hypotheses: They may even lack common standards for deciding what constitutes a genuine problem, a valid explanation, or a sound theory." In a would-be discipline, again, there is "no agreed family of fundamental concepts or constellations of basic presuppositions—no 'paradigm', in Lichtenberg's sense . . ."[16]

---

[16]The quotations in this paragraph are from *Human Understanding,* vol. 1, pp. 379-381. Toulmin points out that G. C. Lichtenberg introduced the term "paradeigma" in the mid-eighteenth century to signify "fundamental patterns of explanation . . ." (p. 106). Readers of the present volume will wish to examine Toulmin's account of disciplines and would-be disciplines. Here, of course, I have only reflected some highlights. Such readers should find the exhibition of present-day psychology as an instance of would-be disciplines especially interesting.

At present, Toulmin believes, while physics is a discipline, psychology and sociology are would-be disciplines. It seems plausible to regard his perception of these not-yet-fullfledged disciplines as decidedly relevant to the current status of parapsychology. Placing parapsychology in that perspective, it could be argued, does justice to both its immaturity and its achievements. On the first side, lie its theoretical shallowness, methodological groping, inability to explain and predict, paucity of full-time practitioners and centers of research, and dearth of educational facilities and training programs. On the second, we can count its general scientific approach to problem-solving, technical advances, experimental ingenuity, active research societies and strong (though small) international professional association, rich assortment of technical literature, including excellent journals, and the quality and volume of data it has amassed through diversified, progressive research.

The first five papers in Section V explore questions about the scientific character of parapsychology and explicate its relations with other subjects and areas of inquiry. The last two papers, by LeShan and Tart, stand as a sort of epilogue to the section and, perhaps, to the whole book. Extending to intriguing lengths lines pursued by the section's earlier papers, they envision some startling possibilities. Essentially, they inquire into the pursuit of science within nonnormal frameworks ("frameworlds"?) in which the objects of investigation, nonnormal themselves from the standpoint of *normal* scientific frameworks, become normal. LeShan, whose idea of individual reality sounds nearly a reprise of the basic-limiting-principle theme with which our selections begin, and Tart, with his concept of state-specific science, both exhibit exciting glimpses of a widened form of science that may be necessary if the new world of the mind is eventually to be scientifically explained in something like its full reach.

To conclude: As the number of parapsychologists is small but increasing, so in the case of philosophers, though comparatively few take up philosophical problems and implications of psychical research, the number who do is also increasing. Journal articles and books in this area, it is reasonable to expect, will become much more a matter of course over the next decade. Of course, as the contents and bibliography of this volume attest, much has already been written. It is notable, also, that while philosophers engaged with parapsychology have been few in number, in more than one era they have included giants of the profession. Seventy-five to a hundred years ago, for instance, William James and Henry Sidgwick were prime movers in a period that produced enduring societies for psychical research; later, near the start of World War I, Henri Bergson and F.C.S. Schiller served as successive presidents of one of those societies; and in our own day, a time of acceleration in parapsychology's scientific growth, the many relevant works of Broad, Ducasse, and Price have reviewed its philosophic bearings and stated them with new precision.

From future intercourse between philosophy and parapsychology, it seems possible for both to benefit further. Heuristic analysis of the latter's main concepts, logical criticism of its method and theory, and philosophical synopsis of its range, all on a larger scale than at present, would flow from increased philosophic attention and might considerably aid parapsychology, especially in its formative stages. For their part, philosophers can find in the young science both challenge and guidance. The following selections give many examples wherein parapsychology, through its varied concerns, may bear instructively on problems of major philosophic import.

Let us now read what recent writers have said in those selections, and so begin to explore the philosophical dimensions of parapsychology.

J. M. O. W.

CONTENTS

Contents   xxix

PHILOSOPHICAL DIMENSIONS
OF PARAPSYCHOLOGY

SECTION I

PSI AND PHILOSOPHY

CHAPTER 1

INTRODUCTION

HOYT L. EDGE

A PROBLEM FOR PARAPSYCHOLOGY, as for every developing discipline, is to formulate a satisfactory definition of itself. Probably the most thorough and satisfactory attempt at giving us an adequate definition for this elusive field is that provided by C. D. Broad, who draws our attention first of all to what he calls "Basic Limiting Principles," which "we unhesitatingly take for granted as the framework within which all our practical activities and our scientific theories are confined." He then concludes that "parapsychological research is concerned with alleged events which seem *prima facie* to conflict with one or more of these principles."

There are several interesting points to note about this definition. First, the Basic Limiting Principles are those which Broad says are held by "contemporary European and North American plain men" and, later in the article, by "educated plain men and by scientists in Europe and America." He makes it apparent that these principles are held specifically by educated Westerners and that they may not be held by primitives or Easterners—except perhaps some Eastern scientists who follow the Western scientific tradition. The question, of course, that naturally arises is how provincial are these beliefs? In other words, how limiting are the Basic Limiting Principles in the sense that they limit our ability to observe and understand reality? Interestingly, paranormal events seem to be a more common and accepted occurrence in the East, where the masses of people do not hold to all of the Basic Limiting Principles. Further, can we say that these principles are even becoming more and more inadequate for the contemporary Western

5

scientist, e.g. the theoretical physicist, although still held by the Western nonscientist?

Secondly, the status of the Basic Limiting Principles is difficult to determine. They seem to be the very basis of our *Weltanschauung,* according to Broad, but are they in any way logical principles, such that one would be engaged in a logical contradiction if he failed to accept one of the principles? One could make an argument for this view, as Broad, at one point, refers to some of these principles as "self-evident." Yet, it seems obvious that Broad cannot be and is not saying that these principles are a logical *sine qua non* of rational thinking. If he accepts the existence of events which contradict the Basic Limiting Principles (which he does) and also believes the principles to be a logically necessary condition of our thinking, he would be engaging himself in a logical contradiction. He wants to maintain, however, that it is possible, without logical contradiction, to hold these principles and yet admit that there is empirical evidence which seems to contradict them, i.e. to admit the existence of psi events. Thus, although the Basic Limiting Principles are not logical prerequisites of thinking, it seems obvious that Broad takes them more seriously than just the "run-of-the-mill" empirical statement. The question as to when an empirical statement becomes so assimilated into thought processes that it becomes more than just an empirical statement has been and, of course, remains a problem in the philosophy of science. It is obvious that Broad has not attempted to solve it here, and the status of the Basic Limiting Principles must, perhaps, be grasped more intuitively than deductively.

Thirdly, the definition of parapsychology using Broad's Basic Limiting Principles emphasizes that paranormal capacities are not to be viewed simply as extensions of normal capabilities. A paranormal ability is not a normal ability which simply goes beyond the presently accepted limits of that ability. For instance, the discovery of subliminal perception forced us a couple decades ago to readjust radically our ideas concerning the limits of perception. If ostensibly paranormal events turn out to be comparable to subliminal perception, that is, if they can be explained by taking recognized abilities and simply broadening their scope, then these events cannot be termed paranormal.

It is not difficult, then, to see why parapsychology is of philosophical interest. Ducasse points out that, even if untrue, parapsychology is philosophically interesting, at least for philosophical psychology. However, if we admit the existence of psi, almost all of the traditionally important philosophical problems are confronted again: questions in metaphysics (survival, freedom and determinism, the mind-body problem, space-time, and foreknowledge), in epistemology, in the philosophy of education, in linguistics, in the philosophy of science, and even in ethics. If Broad is right in his definition of parapsychology, the study of this discipline will call into question the very basic principles of our world view and will perhaps require a massive restructuring of our conception of the "world" around us.

Yet, it is also possible, as Ducasse points out, that we will be able in the future to include paranormal events in our scientific theories. What if we find, for instance, that psi is an energy or a set of energies? Even if this should be found to be true, Ducasse argues, we would have to make a distinction between "materialistic theories," in which psi might be included, and "physicalistic theories," which encompass our present theories of matter. In other words, according to Ducasse, even if science can explain psi, it will necessitate such a radical change in our concept of what matter is that we could no longer call matter "physical."*

It is natural, of course, for some people to object to a discipline that calls into question our most deeply held convictions about the world. In his article, Scriven considers two sets of these objections—that the results of parapsychology are insignificant and that they are imaginary. The individual objections within these two large sets, which he tries to meet, are frequently heard against parapsychology. As Scriven points out, by far the most systematic

---

*This is a point that should be considered further in "Psi and Science." Other points of particular interest discussed by Ducasse and others in this chapter that we will find in more detail later are: (1) freedom and determinism—it is obvious that Ducasse is arguing for a soft determinist position as a solution to this problem: (2) survival—can parapsychology prove that a man survives bodily death and what kind of entity could survive?; (3) parapsychology as science—is repeatability of experiments (a problem for parapsychology) a necessary condition of science?; and (4) the theory of collective unconscious—does this theory explain certain problems in epistemology and philosophy of mind, and does Bergson's theory of consciousness make the theory of the collective unconscious more plausible?

objections that have been voiced against the discipline are by C. E. M. Hansel in his book, *ESP: A Scientific Evaluation*[1] in which Hansel concludes that fraud is more likely, however slight the possibility of it, than the existence of any events which so contradict the laws of nature—as psi purportedly does. I am not sure that Scriven's answer to Hansel's argument is sound in its entirety (for instance, is it not the case that Hansel's supposition that psi is incompatible with current physical theory supported, at least indirectly, by a mass of data produced by parapsychologists?). Nevertheless, Scriven makes a seemingly strong point when he contends that Hansel's argument would rule out the possibility of fundamental discoveries ("paradigm switches" in Kuhn's sense) that change our current scientific laws.[2] Scriven's conclusion is that parapsychologists have so far succeeded in providing a factual basis for their discipline but not a theory adequate to bring all of these facts together (while just the opposite is true for psychotherapy).

Finding an encompassing theory to explain psi is precisely what one would think that Mundle would also recommend in an article entitled "Strange Facts in Search of a Theory." Instead, he considers several of the most prominent attempts to make sense of parapsychological data—the theories of dualism, collective unconscious, materialism, and Dunne's theory of time—and rejects them all as being inadequate. His conclusion is that parapsychologists should keep searching for these "strange facts" without worrying at present about a grand explanatory theory because any such theory must seem, at least *prima facie,* to be so absurd (if nothing else because it would probably undercut the Basic Limiting Principles) that it would alienate scientists, from whom we most need assistance in researching this field.

We have attempted in this section to give a general introduction to the philosophical problems of parapsychology: to posit a tentative definition of parapsychology, to show why parapsychology is

---

[1]C. E. M. Hansel, *ESP: A Scientific Evaluation* (New York, Charles Scribner's Sons, 1966).

[2]Hansel's argument is worth reading in greater detail in his book, and with respect to which I would also recommend reading: 1. Stevenson, "An antagonist's view of parapsychology: a review of Professor Hansel's *ESP: A Scientific Evaluation,*" *Journal ASPR,* 61:254-267, 1967.

of philosophical interest, to consider some possible objections to it and what might be said in its defense, and, finally, to introduce the question of developing overarching conceptual models for parapsychology. This should give the reader a general introduction into the problems we will be viewing in more detail in the other sections.

CHAPTER 2

THE RELEVANCE OF PSYCHICAL RESEARCH TO PHILOSOPHY*

C. D. BROAD

I WILL BEGIN THIS paper by stating in rough outline what I con- sider to be the relevance of psychical research to philosophy, and I shall devote the rest of it to developing this preliminary statement in detail.

In my opinion psychical research is highly relevant to philosophy for the following reasons. There are certain limiting principles which we unhesitatingly take for granted as the framework within which all our practical activities and our scientific theories are con- fined. Some of these seem to be self-evident. Others are so over- whelmingly supported by all the empirical facts which fall within the range of ordinary experience and the scientific elaborations of it (including under this heading orthodox psychology) that it hardly enters our heads to question them. Let us call these *Basic Limiting Principles.* Now psychical research is concerned with al- leged events which seem *prima facie* to conflict with one or more of these principles. Let us call any event which seems *prima facie* to do this an *Ostensibly Paranormal Event.*

A psychical researcher has to raise the following questions about any ostensibly paranormal event which he investigates. (1) Did it really happen? Has it been accurately observed and correctly des- cribed? (2) Supposing that it really did happen and has been accurately observed and correctly described, does it really conflict with any of the Basic Limiting Principles? Can it not fairly be re-

*Reprinted from C. D. Broad: *Religion, Philosophy and Psychical Research.* London, Routledge & Kegan Paul, Ltd., and New York, Humanities Press, Inc., pp. 7-16, 19-26. Reprinted by permission of the publishers. (Originally published in *Philosophy,* 1949.)

garded merely as a strange coincidence, not outside the bounds of probability? Failing that, can it not be explained by reference to already known agents and laws? Failing that, can it not be explained by postulating agents or laws or both, which have not hitherto been recognized, but which fall within the framework of accepted Basic Limiting Principles?

Now it might well have happened that every alleged ostensibly paranormal event which had been carefully investigated by a competent psychical researcher was found either not to have occurred at all, or to have been misdescribed in important respects, or to be a chance-coincidence not beyond the bounds of probability, or to be susceptible of an actual or hypothetical explanation within the framework of the Basic Limiting Principles. If that had been so, philosophy could afford to ignore psychical research; for it is no part of its duty to imitate the White Knight by carrying a mouse-trap when it goes out riding, on the offchance that there might be mice in the saddle. But that is not how things have in fact turned out. It will be enough at present to refer to a single instance, viz. Dr. Soal's experiments on card-guessing with Mr. Shackleton as subject, of which I gave a full account in *Philosophy* in 1944. There can be no doubt that the events described happened and were correctly reported; that the odds against chance-coincidence piled up to billions to one; and that the nature of the events, which involved both telepathy and precognition, conflicts with one or more of the Basic Limiting Principles.

Granted that psychical research has established the occurrence of events which conflict with one or more of the Basic Limiting Principles, one might still ask: How does this concern philosophy? Well, I think that there are some definitions of 'philosophy', according to which it would not be concerned with these or any other newly discovered facts, no matter how startling. Suppose that philosophy consists in accepting without question, and then attempting to analyse, the beliefs which are common to contemporary plain men in Europe and North America, i.e. roughly the beliefs which such persons acquired uncritically in their nurseries and have since found no occasion to doubt. Then, perhaps, the only relevance of psychical research to philosophy would be to show that philosophy is an even more trivial academic exercise than plain men had been inclined to suspect. But, if we can judge of what philosophy *is* by what great philosophers have *done* in the past, its business is by no means confined to accepting without question, and trying to analyse, the beliefs held in common by contemporary European and North American plain men. Judged by that criterion, philosophy involves at least two other closely connected activities, which I call *Synopsis* and *Synthesis*. Synopsis is the deliberate viewing together of aspects of human experience which, for one reason or another, are generally kept apart by the plain man and even by the professional scientist or scholar. The object of synopsis is to try to find out how these various aspects are inter-related. Synthesis is the attempt to supply a coherent set of concepts and principles which shall cover satisfactorily all the regions of fact which have been viewed synoptically.

Now what I have called the Basic Limiting Principles are plainly of great philosophical importance in connection with synopsis and synthesis. These principles do cover very satisfactorily an enormous range of well-established facts of the most varied kinds. We are quite naturally inclined to think that they must be all-embracing; we are correspondingly loth to accept any alleged fact which seems to conflict with them; and, if we are forced to accept it, we strive desperately to house it within the accepted framework. But just in proportion to the philosophic importance of the Basic Limiting Principles is the philosophic importance of any well-established exception to them. The speculative philosopher who is honest and competent will want to widen his synopsis so as to include these facts; and he will want to revise his fundamental concepts and Basic Limiting Principles in such a way as to include the old and the new facts in a single coherent system.

The Basic Limiting Principles

I will now state some of the most important of the Basic Limiting Principles which, apart from the findings of psychical research, are commonly accepted either as self-evident or as established by overwhelming and uniformly favourable empirical evidence. These fall into four main divisions, and in some of the divisions there are several principles.

(1) *General Principles of Causation.* (1.1) It is self-evidently

impossible that an event should begin to have any effects before it has happened.

(1.2) It is impossible that an event which ends at a certain date should contribute to cause an event which begins at a later date unless the period between the two dates is occupied in one or other of the following ways: (i) The earlier event initiates a process of change, which continues throughout the period and at the end of it contributes to initiate the later event. Or (ii) the earlier event initiates some kind of structural modification which persists throughout the period. This begins to co-operate at the end of the period with some change which is then taking place, and together they cause the later event.

(1.3) It is impossible that an event, happening at a certain date and place, should produce an effect at a remote place unless a finite period elapses between the two events, and unless that period is occupied by a causal chain of events occurring successively at a series of points forming a continuous path between the two places.

(2) *Limitations on the Action of Mind on Matter.* It is impossible for an event in a person's mind to produce *directly* any change in the material world except certain changes in his own brain. It is true that it seems to him that many of his volitions produce directly certain movements in his fingers, feet, throat, tongue. These are what he wills, and he knows nothing about the changes in his brain. Nevertheless, it is these brain-changes which are the immediate consequences of his volitions; and the willed movements of his fingers, follow, if they do so, only as rather remote causal descendants.

(3) *Dependence of Mind on Brain.* A necessary, even if not a sufficient, immediate condition of any mental event is an event in the brain of a living body. Each different mental event is immediately conditioned by a different brain-event. Qualitatively dissimilar mental events are immediately conditioned by qualitatively dissimilar brain-events, and qualitatively similar mental events are immediately conditioned by qualitively similar brain-events. Mental events which are so inter-connected as to be experiences of the same person are immediately conditioned by brain-events which happen in the same brain. If two mental events are experiences of different persons, they are *in general* immediately condi-

tioned by brain-events which occur in different brains. This is not, however, a rule without exceptions. In the first place, there are occasional but quite common experiences, occurring in sleep or delirium, whose immediate conditions are events in a certain brain, but which are so loosely connected with each other or with the stream of normal waking experiences conditioned by events in that brain that they scarcely belong to any recognizable person. Secondly, there are cases of multiple personality, described and treated by psychiatrists. Here the experiences which are immediately conditioned by events in a single brain seem to fall into two or more sets, each of which constitutes the experiences of a different person. Such different persons are, however, more closely interconnected in certain ways than two persons whose respective experiences are immediately conditioned by events in different brains.

(4) *Limitations on Ways of acquiring Knowledge.* (4.1) It is impossible for a person to perceive a physical event or a material thing except by means of sensations which that event or thing produces in his mind. The object perceived is not the *immediate* cause of the sensations by which a person perceives it. The immediate cause of these is always a certain event in the percipient's brain; and the perceived object is (or is the seat of) a rather remote causal ancestor of this brain-event. The intermediate links in the causal chain are, first, a series of events in the space between the perceived object and the percipient's body; then an event in a receptor organ, such as his eye or ear; and then a series of events in the nerve connecting this receptor organ to his brain. When this causal chain is completed, and a sensory experience arises in the percipient's mind, that experience is not a state of acquaintance with the perceived external object, either as it was at the moment when it initiated this sequence of events or as it now is. The qualitative and relational character of the sensation is wholly determined by the event in the brain which is its immediate condition; and the character of the latter is in part dependent on the nature and state of the afferent nerve, of the receptor organ, and of the medium between the receptor and the perceived object.

(4.2) It is impossible for A to know what experiences B is having or has had except in one or other of the following ways. (i) By

hearing and understanding sentences, descriptive of that experience, uttered by *B*, or by reading and understanding such sentences, written by *B*, or reproductions or translations of them. (I
include under these headings messages in Morse or any other
artificial language which is understood by *A*.) (ii) By hearing and
interpreting cries which *B* makes, or seeing and interpreting his
gestures or facial expressions. (iii) By seeing, and making conscious or unconscious inferences from, persistent material records,
such as tools, pottery, pictures, which *B* has made or used in
the past. (I include under this head seeing copies or transcrip-
tions of such objects.)

Similar remarks apply, *mutatis mutandis,* to the conditions under
which *A* can acquire from *B* knowledge of facts which *B* knows or
acquaintance with propositions which *B* contemplates. Suppose
that *B* knows a certain fact or is contemplating a certain proposition. Then the only way in which *A* can acquire from *B* knowledge
of that fact or acquaintance with that proposition is by *B* stating it
in sentences or other symbolic expressions which *A* can understand,
and by *A* perceiving those expressions themselves, or reproductions or translations of them, and interpreting them.

(4.3) It is impossible for a person to forecast, except by chance,
that an event of such and such a kind will happen at such and such
a place and time except under one or other of the following conditions. (i) By making an inference from data supplied to him by
his present sensations, introspections, or memories, together with
his knowledge of certain rules of sequence which have hitherto
prevailed in nature. (ii) By accepting from others, whom he trusts,
either such data or such rules or both, and then making his own
inferences; or by accepting from others the inferences which they
have made from data which they claim to have had and regulari-
ties which they claim to have verified. (iii) By non-inferential
expectations, based on associations which have been formed by
certain repeated sequences in his past experiences and which are
now stimulated by some present experience.

It should be noted here that, when the event to be forecast by a
person is a future experience or action of himself or of another
person, we have a rather special case, which is worth particular
mention, although it falls under one or other of the above head-

ings. *A* may be able to forecast that he himself will have a certain experience or do a certain action, because he knows introspectively that he has formed a certain intention. He may be able to forecast that *B* will have a certain experience or do a certain action, because he has reason to believe, either from *B*'s explicit statements or from other signs, that *B* has formed a certain intention.

(4.4) It is impossible for a person to know or have reason to believe that an event of such and such a kind happened at such and such a place and time in the past except under one or another of the following conditions. (i) That the event was an experience which he himself had during the lifetime of his present body; that this left a trace in him which has lasted until now; and that this trace can be stimulated so as to give rise in him to a memory of that past experience. (ii) That the event was one which he witnessed during the lifetime of his present body; that the experience of witnessing it left a trace in him which has lasted till now; and that he now remembers the event witnessed, even though he may not be able to remember the experience of witnessing it. (iii) That the event was experienced or witnessed by someone else, who now remembers it and tells this person about it. (iv) That the event was experienced or witnessed by someone (whether this person himself or another), who made a record of it either at the time or afterwards from memory; that this record or copies or translations of it have survived; and that it is now perceptible by and intelligible to this person. (These four methods may be summarized under the heads of present memory, or testimony based on present memory or on records of past perceptions or memories.) (v) Explicit or implicit inference, either made by the person himself or made by others and accepted by him on their authority, from data supplied by present sense-perception, introspection, or memory, together with knowledge of certain laws of nature.

I do not assert that these nine instances of Basic Limiting Principle are exhaustive, or that they are all logically independent of each other. But I think that they will suffice as examples of important restrictive principles of very wide range, which are commonly accepted to-day by educated plain men and by scientists in Europe and America.

General Remarks on Psychical Research

I turn now to psychical research. Before going into detail I will make some general remarks about its data, methods and affiliations.

(1) The subject may be, and has been, pursued in two ways. (i) As a critical investigation of accounts of events which, if they happened at all, did so spontaneously under conditions which had not been deliberately pre-arranged and cannot be repeated at will. (ii) As an experimental study, in which the investigator raises a definite question and pre-arranges the conditions so that the question will be answered in this, that, or the other way according as this, that, or the other observable event happens under the conditions. An extreme instance of the former is provided by the investigation of stories of the following kind. *A* asserts that he has had an hallucinatory waking experience of a very specific and uncommon kind, and that this experience either imitated in detail or unmistakably symbolized a certain crisis in the life of a certain other person *B*, e.g. death or a serious accident or sudden illness, which happened at roughly the same time. *A* claims that *B* was many miles away at the time, that he had no normal reason to expect that such an event would happen to *B*, and that he received no information of the event by normal means until afterwards. An extreme instance of the latter is provided by the card-guessing experiments of Dr. Soal in England or of Professor Rhine and his colleagues in U.S.A.

Intermediate between these two extremes would be any carefully planned and executed set of sittings with a trance-medium, such as the late Mr. Saltmarsh held with Mrs. Warren Elliott and described in Vol. XXXIX of the S.P.R. *Proceedings*. In such cases the procedure is experimental at least in the following respects. A note-taker takes down everything that is said by sitter or medium, so that there is a permanent record from which an independent judge can estimate to a considerable extent whether the medium was 'fishing' and whether the sitter was inadvertently giving hints. Various techniques are used in order to try to estimate objectively whether the statements of the medium which are alleged to concern a certain dead person do in fact fit the peculiarities of that person and the circumstances of his life to a significantly closer degree than might be expected from mere chance coincidence. On the other hand, the procedure is non-experimental in so far as the sitter cannot ensure that the utterances of the entranced medium shall refer to pre-arranged topics or answer pre-arranged questions. He must be prepared to hear and to have recorded an immense amount of apparently irrelevant data, in the hope that something relevant to his investigation may be embedded in it.

(2) It seems to me that both methods are important, and that they stand in the following relations to each other. The sporadic cases, if genuine and really paranormal, are much richer in content and more interesting psychologically than the results of experiment with cards or drawings. In comparison with the latter they are as thunderstorms to the mild electrical effects of rubbing a bit of sealing-wax with a silk handkerchief. But, taken in isolation from the experimentally established results, they suffer from the following defect. Any one of them separately might perhaps be regarded as an extraordinary chance coincidence; though I do not myself think that this would be a reasonable view to take of them collectively, even if they were not supported by experimental evidence, when one considers the number and variety of such cases which have stood up to critical investigation. But, however that may be, there is no means of estimating *just how* unlikely it is that any one such case, or the whole collection of them, should be mere chance coincidence.

Now, if there were no independent experimental evidence for telepathy, clairvoyance, or precognition, it would always be possible to take the following attitude towards the sporadic cases. 'Certainly,' it might be said, 'the evidence seems water-tight, and the unlikelihood of mere chance coincidence seems enormous, even though one cannot assign a numerical measure to it. But, if the reported events were genuine, they would involve telepathy or clairvoyance or precognition. The antecedent improbability of these is practically infinite, while there is always a possibility of mistake or fraud even in the best attested and most carefully checked reports of any complex incident which cannot be repeated at will. And there is no coincidence so detailed and improbable that it may not happen occasionally in the course of history. Therefore, it is more reasonable to hold that even the best attested sporadic cases were either misreported or were extraordinary coincidences than to suppose that they happened as reported and that there was a causal connection between *A*'s experience and the nearly contemporary event in *B*'s life to which it seemed to correspond.'

Now, whether this attitude would or would not be reasonable in the absence of experimental cases, it is not reasonable when the latter are taken into account and the sporadic cases are considered in relation to them. In card-guessing experiments, e.g. we can assign a numerical value to the most probable number of correct guesses in a given number of trials on the supposition that chance coincidence is the only factor involved. We can also assign a numerical value to the probability that, if chance coincidence only were involved, the actual number of correct guesses would exceed the most probable number by more than a given amount. We can then go on repeating the experiments, under precisely similar conditions, hundreds of thousands of times, with independent witnesses, elaborate checks on the records, and so on.

Now Dr. Soal, Professor Rhine and his colleagues, and Mr. Tyrrell, working quite independently of each other, have found that certain subjects can cognize correctly, with a frequency so greatly above chance-expectation that the odds against such an excess being fortuitous are billions to one, what another person *has been and is no longer perceiving,* what he *is contemporaneously perceiving,* and what he *will not begin to perceive until a few seconds later.* This happens under conditions where there is no possibility of relevant information being conveyed to the subject by normal sensory means, and where there is no possibility of his consciously or unconsciously inferring the future event from any data available to him at the time. It follows that the antecedent improbability of paranormal cognition, whether post-cognitive, simultaneous, or pre-cognitive, cannot reasonably be treated as practically infinite in the sporadic cases. These paranormal kinds of cognition must be reckoned with as experimentally verified possibilities, and, in view of this, it seems reasonable to accept and to build upon the best attested sporadic cases.

(3) The findings of psychical research should not be taken in complete isolation. It is useful to consider many of them in connection with certain admitted facts which fall within the range of

orthodox abnormal psychology and psychiatry. The latter facts form the best bridge between ordinary common sense and natural science (including normal psychology), on the one hand, and psychical research on the other. As I have already mentioned in connection with Principle 3, the occurrence of dreams and delirium and the cases of multiple personality would suffice, even in the absence of all paranormal phenomena, to qualify the dogma that, if two mental events are experiences of different persons, they are always immediately conditioned by events in different brains. We can now go further than this. There are obvious and important analogies between the phenomena of trance-mediumship and those of alternating personality unaccompanied by alleged paranormal phenomena. Again, the fact of dreaming, and the still more startling facts of experimentally induced hypnotic hallucinations, show that each of us has within himself the power to produce, in response to suggestions from within or without, a more or less coherent quasi-sensory presentation of ostensible things and persons, which may easily be taken for a scene from the ordinary world of normal waking life. Cases of veridical hallucination corresponding to remote contemporary events, instances of haunted rooms, and so on, are slightly less incredible when regarded as due to this normal power, abnormally stimulated on rare occasions by a kind of hypnotic suggestion acting telepathically. It is certainly wise to press this kind of explanation as far as it will go, though one must be prepared for the possibility that it will not cover all the cases which we have to accept as genuine.

(4) If paranormal cognition and paranormal causation are facts, then it is quite likely that they are not confined to those very rare occasions on which they either manifest themselves sporadically in a spectacular way or to those very special conditions in which their presence can be experimentally established. They may well be continually operating in the background of our normal lives. Our understanding of, and our misunderstandings with, our fellow-men; our general emotional mood on certain occasions; the ideas which suddenly arise in our minds without any obvious introspectable cause; our unaccountable immediate emotional reactions towards certain persons; our sudden decisions where the introspectable motives seem equally balanced; and so on; all these

may be in part determined by paranormal cognition and paranormal causal influences.

In this connection it seems to me that the following physical
analogy is illuminating. Human beings have no special sensations
in presence of magnetic fields. Had it not been for the two very
contingent facts that there are loadstones, and that the one element
(iron) which is strongly susceptible to magnetic influence is fairly
common on earth, the existence of magnetism might have remained
unsuspected to this day. Even so, it was regarded as a kind of
mysterious anomaly until its connection with electricity was discovered and we gained the power to produce strong magnetic fields
at will. Yet, all this while, magnetic fields had existed, and had
been producing effects, whenever and wherever electric currents
were passing. Is it not possible that natural mediums might be
comparable to loadstones; that paranormal influences are as
pervasive as magnetism; and that we fail to recognize this only
because our knowledge and control of them are at about the same
level as were men's knowledge and control of magnetism when
Gilbert wrote his treatise on the magnet?

ESTABLISHED RESULTS OF PSYCHICAL RESEARCH
The Established Results and the Basic Limiting Principles

We are now in a position to confront our nine Basic Limiting
Principles with the results definitely established by experimental
psychical research.

(1) Any paranormal cognition obtained under precognitive conditions, whether autoscopic or telepathic, seems *prima facie* to
conflict with Principle 1.1. For the occurrence of the cognition
seems to be in part determined by an event which will not happen
until *after* it has occurred: e.g. in Soal's experiments the subject's
act of writing down the initial letter of the name of a certain animal
seems in many cases to be in part determined by the fact that the
agent *will* a few seconds later be looking at a card on which that
animal is depicted.

It also conflicts with Principle 4.3. For we should not count the
forecasting of an event as an instance of *paranormal* cognition,
unless we had convinced ourselves that the subject's success could
not be accounted for either by his own inferences, or by his knowl-

edge of inferences made by others, or by non-inferential expectations based on associations formed in his mind by repeated experiences of sequence in the past. Now in the case of such experiments as Dr. Soal's and Professor Rhine's all these kinds of explanations are ruled out by the design of the experiment. And in some of the best cases of sporadic precognition it seems practically certain that no such explanation can be given.

It seems to me fairly plain that the establishment of parai.ormal precognition requires a radical change in our conception of time, and probably a correlated change in our conception of causation. I do not believe that the modifications introduced into the notion of physical time and space by the Theory of Relativity are here relevant, except in the very general sense that they help to free our minds from inherited prejudices and to make us more ready to contemplate startling possibilities in this department. Suppose, e.g. that a person has an autoscopic paranormal precognition of some experience which he will have some time later. I do not see that anything that the Theory of Relativity tells us about the placing and dating of physical events by means of measuring-rods and clocks regulated by light-signals can serve directly to make such a fact intelligible.

(2) Paranormal cognition which takes place under conditions which are telepathic but not precognitive does not conflict with Principles 1.1. and 4.3. But it does seem *prima facie* to conflict with Principle 4.2, and also with Principles 2, 1.3 and 3.

As regards Principle 4.2, we should not count A's knowledge of a contemporary or past experience of B's as paranormal, unless we had convinced ourselves that A had not acquired it by any of the normal means enumerated in that Principle. The same remarks apply *mutatis mutandis* to A's acquiring from B knowledge of a fact known to the latter, or to A's becoming aware of a proposition which B is contemplating. Now, in the experimental cases of simultaneous or post-cognitive telepathy all possibilities of normal communication are carefully excluded by the nature of the experimental arrangements. And in the best of the sporadic cases there seems to be no reasonable doubt that they were in fact excluded. In many well attested and carefully investigated cases the two persons concerned were hundreds of miles apart, and out of reach of telephones and similar means of long-distance communication, at the time when the one had an experience which corresponded to an outstanding and roughly contemporary experience in the other.

If non-precognitive telepathy is to be consistent with Principle 3, we must suppose that an immediate necessary condition of *A*'s telepathic cognition of *B*'s experience is a certain event in *A*'s brain. If it is to be consistent with Principle 2, we cannot suppose that this event in *A*'s brain is produced *directly* by the experience of *B* which *A* telepathically cognizes. For Principle 2 asserts that the only change in the material world which an event in a person's mind can *directly* produce is a change in that person's own brain. If, further, it is to be consistent with Principle 1.3, the event in *B*'s brain, which is the immediate consequence in the material world of his experience, cannot *directly* cause the event in *A*'s brain which is the immediate necessary condition of *A*'s telepathic cognition of *B*'s experience. For there is a spatial gap between these two brain-events; and Principle 1.3 asserts that a finite period must elapse and that this must be occupied by a causal chain of events occurring successively at a series of points forming a continuous path between the two events.

So, if non-precognitive telepathy is to be reconciled with Principles 3, 2 and 1.3 taken together, it must be thought of as taking place in the following way. *B*'s experience has as its immediate concomitant or consequence a certain event in *B*'s brain. This initiates some kind of transmissive process which, after an interval of time, crosses the gap between *B*'s body and *A*'s body. There it gives rise to a certain change in *A*'s brain, and this is an immediate necessary condition of *A*'s telepathic cognition of *B*'s experience. I suspect that many people think vaguely of non-precognitive telepathy as a process somewhat analogous to the broadcasting of sounds or pictures. And I suspect that familiarity with the *existence* of wireless broadcasting, together with ignorance of the *nature* of the processes involved in it, has led many of our contemporaries, for completely irrelevant and invalid reasons, to accept the possibility of telepathy far more readily than their grandparents would have done, and to ignore the revolutionary consequences of the admission.

There is nothing in the known facts to lend any colour to this picture of the process underlying them. There is nothing to suggest that there is always an interval between the occurrence of an outstanding experience in *B* and the occurrence of a paranormal cognition of it in *A*, even when *B*'s and *A*'s bodies are very widely separated. When there is an interval there is nothing to suggest that it is correlated in any regular way with the distance between the two persons' bodies at the time. This in itself would cast doubt on the hypothesis that, in all such cases, the interval is occupied by a causal chain of events occurring successively at a series of points forming a continuous path between the two places. Moreover, the frequent conjunction in experimental work of precognitive with non-precognitive telepathy, under very similar conditions, makes it hard to believe that the processes involved in the two are fundamentally different. But it is plain that the picture of a causal chain of successive events from an event in *B*'s brain through the intervening space to an event in *A*'s brain cannot represent what happens in *precognitive* telepathy. Then, again, there is no independent evidence for such an intermediating causal chain of events. Lastly, there is no evidence for holding that an experience of *B*'s is more likely to be cognized telepathically by *A* if he is in *B*'s neighborhood at the time than if he is far away; or that the telepathic cognition, if it happens, is generally more vivid or detailed or correct in the former case than in the latter.

I do not consider that any of these objections singly, or all of them together, would conclusively disprove the suggestion that non-precognitive telepathy is compatible with Principles 3, 2 and 1.3. The suggested account of the process is least unplausible when *B*'s original experience takes the form of a visual or auditory perception or image, and *A*'s corresponding experience takes the form of a visual or auditory image or hallucinatory quasi-perception resembling *B*'s in considerable detail. But by no means all cases of non-precognitive telepathy take this simple form.

I can imagine cases, though I do not know whether there are any well-established instances of them, which would be almost impossible to reconcile with the three Principles in question. Suppose, e.g. that *B*, who understands Sanskrit, reads attentively a passage in that tongue enunciating some abstract and characteristic metaphysical proposition. Suppose that at about the same time his friend *A*, in a distant place, not knowing a word of Sanskrit, is moved to write down in English a passage which plainly corresponds in meaning. Then I do not see how the physical transmission theory could be stretched to cover the case.

(3) If there be paranormal cognition under purely clairvoyant conditions, it would seem to constitute an exception to Principle 4.1. For it would seem to be analogous to normal perception of a physical thing or event, in so far as it is not conditioned by the subject's own future normal knowledge of that object, or by any other person's normal knowledge of it, whether past, contemporary, or future. And yet, so far as one can see, it is quite unlike ordinary sense-perception. For it does not take place by means of a sensation, due to the stimulation of a receptor organ by a physical process emanating from the perceived object and the subsequent transmission of a nervous impulse from the stimulated receptor to the brain.

To sum up about the implications of the various kinds of paranormal cognition. It seems plain that they call for very radical changes in a number of our Basic Limiting Principles. I have the impression that we should do well to consider much more seriously than we have hitherto been inclined to do the type of theory which Bergson put forward in connection with *normal* memory and sense-perception. The suggestion is that the function of the brain and nervous system and sense-organs is in the main *eliminative* and not productive. Each person is at each moment potentially capable of remembering all that has ever happened to him and of perceiving everything that is happening anywhere in the universe. The function of the brain and nervous system is to protect us from being overwhelmed and confused by this mass of largely useless and irrelevant knowledge, by shutting out most of what we should otherwise perceive or remember at any moment, and leaving only that very small and special selection which is likely to be practically useful. An extension or modification of this type of theory seems to offer better hopes of a coherent synthesis of normal and paranormal cognition than is offered by attempts to tinker with the orthodox notion of events in the brain and nervous system *generating sense-data*.

Another remark which seems relevant here is the following.

Many contemporary philosophers are sympathetic to some form of the so-called 'verification principle', i.e. roughly that a synthetic proposition is significant if and only if we can indicate what kind of experiences in assignable circumstances would tend to support or to weaken it. But this is generally combined with the tacit assumption that the only kinds of experience which could tend to support or to weaken such a proposition are sense-perceptions, introspections, and memories. If we have to accept the occurrence of various kinds of paranormal cognition, we ought to extend the verification principle to cover the possibility of propositions which are validated or invalidated by other kinds of cognitive experience beside those which have hitherto been generally admitted.

The Less Firmly Established Results and the Basic Principles

So far I have dealt with paranormal facts which have been established to the satisfaction of everyone who is familiar with the evidence and is not the victim of invincible prejudice. I shall end my paper by referring to some alleged paranormal phenomena which are not in this overwhelmingly strong position, but which cannot safely be ignored by philosophers.

(1) Professor Rhine and his colleagues have produced what seems to be strong evidence for what they call *psycho-kinesis* under experimental conditions. The experiments take the general form of casting dice and trying to influence by volition the result of the throw. Some of these experiments are open to one or another of various kinds of criticism; and, so far as I am aware, all attempts made in England to reproduce the alleged psycho-kinetic effect under satisfactory conditions have failed to produce a sufficient divergence from chance-expectation to warrant a confident belief that any paranormal influence is acting on the dice. But the fact remains that a considerable number of the American experiments seem to be immune to these criticisms, and that the degree of divergence from chance-expectation in these is great enough to be highly significant.

Along with these experimental results should be taken much more spectacular ostensibly telekinetic phenomena which are alleged to have been observed and photographed, under what seem to be satisfactory conditions, in presence of certain mediums. Perhaps the best attested case is that of the Austrian medium Rudi Schneider, investigated by several competent psychical researchers in England and in France between the first and the second world wars.

We ought, therefore, to keep something more than an open mind towards the possibility that psycho-kinesis is a genuine fact. If it is so, we seem *prima facie* to have an exception to Principle 2. For, if psycho-kinesis really takes place in Rhine's experiments, an event in the subject's mind, viz. a volition that the dice shall fall in a certain way, seems to produce directly a change in a part of the material world outside his body, viz. in the dice. An alternative possibility would be that each of us had a kind of invisible and intangible but extended and dynamical 'body', beside his ordinary visible and tangible body; and that it puts forth 'pseudopods' which touch and affect external objects. (The results of Osty's experiments with Rudi Schneider provide fairly strong physical evidence for some such theory as this, however fantastic it may seem.)

(2) Lastly, there is the whole enormous and very complex and puzzling domain of trance mediumship and ostensible communications from the surviving spirits of specified persons who have died. To treat this adequately a whole series of papers would be needed. Here I must content myself with the following brief remarks.

There is no doubt that, among that flood of dreary irrelevance and drivel which is poured out by trance-mediums, there is a residuum of genuinely paranormal material of the following kind. A good medium with a good sitter will from time to time give information about events in the past life of a dead person who claims to be communicating at the time. The medium may have had no chance whatever to gain this information normally, and the facts asserted may at the time be unknown to the sitter or to anyone else who has sat with the medium. They may afterwards be verified and found to be highly characteristic of the ostensible communicator. Moreover, the style of the communication, and the mannerisms and even the voice of the medium while speaking, may seem to the sitter to be strongly reminiscent of the ostensible communicator. Lastly, there are a few cases in which the statements made and the directions given to the sitter seem to indicate the persistence of an intention formed by the dead man during his lifetime but not carried out. There are other cases in which the ostensible communicator asserts, and the nature of the communications seems to confirm, that action is being taken by him and others at and between the sittings in order to provide evidence of survival and identity.

Some of the best cases, if taken by themselves, do strongly suggest that the stream of interconnected events which constituted the mental history of a certain person is continued after the death of his body, i.e. that there are *post-mortem* experiences which are related to each other and to the *ante-mortem* experiences of this person in the same characteristic way in which his *ante-mortem* experiences were related to each other. In most of these cases the surviving person seems to be communicating only indirectly through the medium. The usual dramatic form of the sitting is that the medium's habitual trance-personality, speaking with the medium's vocal organs, makes statements which claim to be reports of what the surviving person is at the time directly communicating to it. But in some of the most striking cases the surviving person seems to take control of the medium's body, to oust both her normal personality and her habitual trance-personality, and to speak in its own characteristic voice and manner through the medium's lips.

If we take these cases at their face value, they seem flatly to contradict Principle 3. For this asserts that every different mental event is immediately conditioned by a different brain-event, and that mental events which are so interconnected as to be experiences of the same person are immediately conditioned by brain-events which occur in the same brain.

But I do not think that we ought to take the best cases in isolation from the mass of mediumistic material of a weaker kind. And we certainly ought not to take them in isolation from what psychiatrists and students of abnormal psychology tell us about alternations of personality in the absence of paranormal complications. Lastly, we ought certainly to view them against the background of established facts about the precognitive, telepathic and clairvoyant powers of ordinary embodied human beings. There is no doubt at all that the best phenomena of trance-mediumship involve paranormal cognition of a high order. The only question is whether this, combined with alternations of personality and extraordinary but not paranormal powers of dramatization, will not suffice to account for the phenomena which *prima facie* suggest so strongly that some persons survive the death of their bodies and communicate through mediums. This I regard as at present an open question.

In conclusion I would make the following remark. The establishment of the existence of various forms of paranormal cognition has in one way helped and in another way hindered the efforts of those who seek to furnish empirical proof of human survival. It has helped, in so far as it has undermined that epiphenomenalist view of the human mind and all its activities, which all other known facts seem so strongly to support, and in view of which the hypothesis of human survival is antecedently so improbable as not to be worth serious consideration. It has hindered, in so far as it provides the basis for a more or less plausible explanation, in terms of established facts about the cognitive powers of embodied human minds, of phenomena which might otherwise seem to require the hypothesis of survival.

CHAPTER 3

THE PHILOSOPHICAL IMPORTANCE OF "PSYCHIC PHENOMENA"*

C. J. DUCASSE

IN THE TITLE OF THIS PAPER, the words "Psychic Phenomena" are put between quotation marks to indicate disclaim of any intention to beg the reality of the diverse strange kinds of occurrences that have variously been termed "psychic," "metapsychic," "parapsychological," "paranormal," or, more briefly, "Psi" phenomena. The contention implicit in the paper's title is only that the many reports of phenomena of the kinds in view are philosophically important no matter whether the phenomena really occurred as reported, or not.

If they did *not* so occur, then the specificity and numerousness of the reports, and the fact that some of the witnesses, and some of the persons who accepted their reports, have been people of high intelligence and integrity, is exceedingly interesting from the standpoint of the psychology of perception, of delusion, illusion or hallucination, of credulity and credibility, and of testimony. Whereas, if some of the phenomena *did* really occur as reported, they are equally important from the standpoint then of the psychology of *in*credulity and *in*credibility—or, more comprehensively, of orthodox adverse prejudice, such as widely exists among persons having the modern western educated outlook towards reports of psychic phenomena. In this connection, a recent book, *The Nature of Prejudice,* by the Harvard psychologist, Professor G. W. Allport, is not only good reading, but can be also very salutary reading if the insight one gains from it into the determinants of

Reprinted from *The Journal of Philosophy,* 1954, by permission of the editors and Mrs. C. J. Ducasse.

prejudice does not cause one to suppose oneself *eo ipso* free from this malady.

But if some of the phenomena *did* really occur as reported, then there is another reason why they are of great philosophical and scientific importance. It is that those phenomena sharply clash with, and therefore call for revision of, certain tacit assumptions which Professor C. D. Broad, in his recent book, *Religion, Philosophy and Psychical Research,* has termed "Basic Limiting Principles" of ordinary thought; that is, principles "we unhesitatingly take for granted as the framework within which all our practical activities and our scientific theories are confined."

For example, one of the most basic among those limiting principles is that an event cannot cause anything before it has actually occurred; and a phenomenon which would clash with this principle would be, not the inferring, but the *ostensible perceiving,* as for instance in a dream or vision, of an as yet future event of some out-of-the-ordinary kind one had no reason to expect. For then the dream or vision would, paradoxically, be a present effect of an as yet future cause.

The important philosophical problems regarding causality, time, perception, and memory, which a real instance of such so-called precognition would raise, are discussed by Professor Broad with his customary acuteness, thoroughness, and orderliness, in a paper entitled "The Philosophical Implications of Foreknowledge," which deserves very careful study. It appeared in Supplementary Volume XVI of the Proceedings of the Aristotelian Society. A discussion of the paper by Professor H. H. Price follows it, and is itself then commented upon by Prof. Broad.

The interest of the paper, however, is made the greater by the fact that some evidence, both experimental and other, today exists that events—of which precognition is one—sometimes really occur that clash thus radically with one or another of the Basic Limiting Principles of present scientific and commonsense thinking. Moreover, that evidence is both much stronger and more abundant than persons who have not looked it up commonly suspect. Hence the need is correspondingly acute either to explain away the evidence, or else to formulate some conception of Nature capable of including and of uniting both all the facts which the natural sciences have discovered, and the rarer paradoxical and seemingly anarchistic facts with which the parapsychology laboratories and societies for psychical research have concerned themselves, but which scientists and philosophers have so far largely been content either to ignore or to declare impossible on *a priori* grounds.

Moreover, if as I believe in common with Professors Broad and Price among other philosophers familiar with the evidence, it is in some cases too strong to be explained away, then, as Professor Price pointed out in a recent address, philosophers ought to take a hand in devising the needed new conceptual framework; as they did when, in the seventeenth century, a similar need resulted from the new facts which were then being discovered. I am therefore very glad that the Program Committee decided to have a symposium on this general subject and especially that the committee invited Professor Rhine to contribute the first paper; for as the British philosopher, Antony Flew, remarks in his recent book, *A New Approach to Psychical Research,* Rhine's first book, *Extra-Sensory Perception,* published in 1934, is a great landmark, which has given "enormous impetus to experiment, particularly of the 'quantitative' type," in this field. There is no doubt that the energy and resourcefulness which for many years Rhine has given to these studies and to the promotion of them will assure him a permanent and high place in the history of the subject.

I have wanted thus to make clear my high regard for Professor Rhine and my appreciation of the importance of his work because of the criticisms of some of his views which I shall have to make in what follows. Before I turn to them, however, there are two points of terminology which seem to me to call for a few words.

The first concerns the use of such words as "psychical," "psychic," "metapsychic," or "parapsychological," to designate the various kinds of phenomena in view. These terms are appropriate enough to refer to so-called extrasensory perception—that is, to telepathy, clairvoyance, or precognition—and to psychokinesis; but certain other equally strange kinds of phenomena, some of which I shall mention later, seem *prima facie* describable as paraphysical or parabiological, rather than as parapsychological, psychic, or metapsychic. For this reason, it seems to me that the word "paranormal," which begs no questions as to the nature of the operative forces, is preferable when a term broad enough to cover all the diverse kinds of phenomena in view is desired.

The other remark to be made concerns the expression "extrasensory perception." By this time, of course, this name is pretty well established and need not be misleading. But the fact nevertheless is that, because it is somewhat of a misdescription of some of the experiences it designates, it has led some psychologists to believe that it designates nothing real. The word Perception has a variety of usages in ordinary language, but in psychology and epistemology it is usually employed to designate a particular one of the processes by which *knowledge,* properly so called, is gained; and knowing does not consist simply in having or believing an idea which happens to be true, but in believing it because one has evidence that it is true. For instance, if a card—say the ace of spades—is lying face up on the table, *and I look at it,* then *I know,* or more specifically *perceive,* that it is the ace of spades. But if it is lying face down and I guess, or dream, that it is the ace of spades, my guess or dream, although happening to be true, does not constitute knowledge, or more specifically perception, at all. True guesses or visions would have title to the name of perception and of knowledge only if, in their case, the guesser's or dreamer's experience contained some feature—whether sensory or extrasensory—that were a more or less *reliable sign* that the guess or dream is true. But a study by Louisa E. Rhine of more than 3000 spontaneous "precognitive" and "contemporaneous cognitive" experiences, published in the June 1954 issue of the *Journal of Parapsychology,* shows that, in a large percentage of them, no feeling of conviction distinguished the true ones from the false. And, in experimental guesses, it is only very seldom that the correct ones feel any different from the incorrect. Thus, the great majority of so-called extrasensory perceptions are not perceptions at all in the ordinary sense of the term. This, however, should not be permitted to blind one to the real problem, which is to account for the fact that, in for instance certain long and carefully controlled series of guesses, the correct guesses (or with some guessers the incorrect ones) are significantly more numerous than chance would allow for, and moreover, consistently assume certain distinctive patterns.

From these remarks of terminology, I now turn directly to the contents of Professor Rhine's paper. The basic contentions of the first part of it, as I understand them, are that extrasensory perception (ESP) and psychokinesis (PK) have now been experimentally proved to be facts, and that the kind of energy involved in the occurrence of these phenomena has been shown by relevant tests, so far as these have gone, to be unaffected by differences that would affect any known form of physical energy—differences, for example, of distance, of time, of spatial orientation of target cards, or of intervening material obstacles.

That all this is true is likely to be fairly evident, I believe, to anyone who takes the trouble to familiarize himself with the records and who approaches them with an open mind.

The fact that those differences do not affect the phenomena entails, Rhine contends, that in these some non-physical kind of energy operates, which, however, he regards not at all as supernatural, but as perfectly natural in the sense that its operations, like those of physical energy, conform to fixed laws; which, by experimentation scientifically conducted, we may hope to discover eventually.

Certain comments now suggest themselves. The first concerns the term "physical"—and therefore also its contradictory, "non-physical"—employed in the statement of that contention.

Professor Rhine does not formally define the adjective, "physical," but from what he says at various places it would seem that he intends to use it comprehensively as referring not only to the entities and processes studied by physics, but also to those studied by chemistry and the other physical sciences, and also to those which the biological sciences investigate. That is, he apparently uses "physical" in the broad sense in which it means "material"; and, by "physicalism," he means "materialism" rather than what logical positivists nowadays mean by "physicalism."

Now, as Lindsay and Margenau remark in their *Foundations of Physics,* "the physicist has been striving for years to attach a clear meaning to the term *matter,* and undoubtedly we have reason to believe that the concept means much more to us today than to the physicists of fifty years ago." In the modern analysis of it, however, conceptions of space and time enter which are different from those of classical physics. And the atoms, *ex hypothesi* indivisible, which were once believed to be the ultimate constituents of matter, are now known to be more or less complex systems of electrons and protons, not to mention the neutrons, mesons, and other entities of present-day theoretical physics.

The question which these developments thrust upon us, and which is pivotal in the present connection, therefore is, In just what sense are all these atomic and sub-atomic entities and processes *material?* The answer, of course, is that they are so simply in the sense that, although they are not directly perceptible at all, nevertheless they are held to be *constituents* of the publicly perceptible objects—such as stones, water, wood, animal bodies, and so on—which are what the expression "the material world" basically denotes.

But now the question arises whether the presently known subatomic constituents of matter are themselves *ultimate* in the sense of absolutely simple. Will they not perhaps one of these days be in turn analyzed into more nearly elementary constituents? If this should occur, it is safe to say that the latter will have some properties different from those of the sub-atomic entities; just as these have some properties different from those of atoms; atoms in turn, properties different from those of molecules; and molecules, properties different from those of molar masses; for this is the general kind of fact to which the name of Emergence has been given.

Now, certain of the properties of those yet to be discovered but theoretically possible sub-sub-atomic constituents of matter might well turn out to be such as could account for ESP and PK. Even then, however, these constituents and their properties would have the very same title to be called material as have atoms or electrons and their properties; namely, those too, like these, would be constituents of the perceptually public things which the expression "material objects" basically denotes.

We might then, of course—perhaps because of the extreme peculiarity of some of the properties of those sub-sub-atomic entities,— elect to say that, although they are still material for the reason stated, yet they are not "physically" material—reserving thus the qualification "physical" for those levels of material complexity which, however different from one another, nevertheless have to time and space the relations presently described by physics; and qualifying by some other adjective, such perhaps as "psychical" or "paraphysical," those levels of material minuteness at which this ceases to be true.

It is perhaps superfluous to add in this connection that energy well might on special occasions pass from one to the other of those two levels of materiality—the "physical" and the "non-physical" —without, as Professor Broad has shown, any violation of the principle of the conservation of energy (*The Mind and Its Place in Nature*) which anyway, as Professor M. T. Keeton pointed out in the July 1941 issue of *Philosophy of Science,* is not the statement of an empirical fact, but only a defining postulate for the notion of "an isolated physical system."

That matter may have sub-sub-atomic constituents, and that these might have properties capable of accounting for ESP and PK is of course at present pure speculation. I introduce it only to make clear that reality of these and of other kinds of paranormal phenomena would not in principle require abandonment of a materialistic conception of the universe—a type of conception which, of course, has been marvelously fertile—but would only call for a materialism liberal enough to include a level of materiality still more tenuous than the presently recognized sub-atomic one.

This remark now leads me to comment on Professor Rhine's contention that a thoroughgoing materialistic determinism would entail that man could have no "volitional or mental freedom," and that "little of the entire value system under which human society has developed would survive."

This seems to me a completely unwarranted inference, which rests on nothing more solid than failure to distinguish between the axiological and the ontological senses of the term "materialism," or "physicalism"; and similarly of the term "spirit," or "spiritual." The materialism of the natural sciences is ontological, and materialism in the axiological sense is not in the least entailed by it. Rather, if ontological materialism is true, what follows is that even the noblest artistic, ethical, and spiritual achievements of man then were potentialities somehow latent in the particular kinds of matter of which human beings consist. For those achievements are facts of historical record, which would not in the least be obliterated or made less noble by the other fact, if it be a fact, that man has been all along a wholly material being. Moreover, since man, even if wholly material, *did* somehow manage to create those noble values, there would be no reason why he could not go on adding to them in the future.

As regards human freedom, on the other hand, the fact that, under the circumstances existing at this moment, I am free to raise my arm if I will, but am not similarly free to fly through the air like a bird even if I will—this fact remains a fact no matter whether the "volitions" concerned be molecular events in the matter of the brain, or be events of a non-material but in some sense "psychic," "mental," or "spiritual" nature. Moreover, irrespective of whether those volitions were material or non-material events, they had causes sufficient to determine their occurrence—or else they were affairs of pure objective chance, which is something very different from freedom.

The idea that on the one hand freedom of choice, and on the other determinism (in the sense that even volitions have causes), are incompatible is very widespread but quite erroneous. What is incompatible with freedom is not causation as such, but *compulsion,* and causation is compulsion only in cases where what one is caused to will to do is something he *dislikes;* for instance, handing his money to a holdup man who threatens to shoot. But when on the contrary keen appetite causes a person to decide to eat and he *likes* what he eats, he is then correctly said to have decided to eat and to be eating, not under compulsion but *freely.* Furthermore, if, as Professor Rhine's paper apparently but unwarrantedly assumes, determinism inherently constituted compulsion and hence were incompatible with freedom, then this would be so quite irrespective of whether the determining causes happened to be material or nonmaterial. A psychological robot would be just as much a robot as would a physical one; and the two of them together inside one skin, causally interacting with one another, would be a fancier kind of robot, but still only a robot. Freedom of action, or lack of it, is simply a matter of the efficacy, of inefficacy, of a volition to its particular aim. This efficacy or inefficacy is in each case an empirical fact, wholly independent of whether volitions are material events or non-material; and quite independent also of the fact that volitions, like all other events material or mental, themselves have causes of one kind or another, as well as effects.

Lastly, with regard to human responsibility: As soon as moral responsibility is distinguished from historical and from legal responsibility, it becomes evident that without determinism there would be no moral responsibility. For if a person's present volitions were not determined, for example by such causes as memories of praise or blame, of reward or punishment, and of other sorts of consequences of past voluntary acts, and by enticements or threats held out to him relating to similar future voluntary acts, then that person would be termed not morally free but morally irresponsible. This, of course, is the case with infants, idiots, or the insane; and is exactly what we mean when we say that they "do not know what they are doing," or "do not know the difference between right and wrong," and hence are not morally responsible.

The upshot of these various remarks is then that even if, as Professor Rhine quite plausibly contends, paranormal phenomena do depend on a non-physical form of energy, this dependence has no bearing at all either on moral responsibility or on the validity of human values; or on the question of human freedom, which is simple enough when theological preoccupations are left out of it and the few essential distinctions are made; and which, as made clear above, is a semantical question and hence one to which laboratory experiments have no relevance. I therefore much regret that Professor Rhine should have elected to rest the case for the importance of psi phenomena on the implications for human freedom, responsibility, and values, which he believes them to have; but which, if the preceding critique is sound, they do not really have at all. Their true importance, I submit, is of the kinds— scientific and philosophical—which I mentioned at the outset.

There is, however, another sort of importance which certain paranormal phenomena might conceivably have—those, namely, which purport to be evidence of survival of the "spirit" of a person who has died. If it should be concluded that these particular phenomena do prove that the human personality has certain constituents which, even if material, are non-physical in a sense which entailed that death of the human body does not destroy them, then this would establish "survival" *of them.* But, as pointed out by Professor Broad, in *The Mind and Its Place in Nature,* when setting forth his hypothesis of such a surviving "psychic factor," the question would remain as to whether, without its being associated with a living human body, that "psychic factor" could nevertheless still function as an active and experiencing mind or personality. Moreover, even if it still did so function, the fact of its being then discarnate would not entail that its discarnate life is any more moral, beautiful, or intelligent, or has a larger measure of freedom, than was the case during its incarnate life. In this connection, a lecture entitled "Survival and the Idea of Another World," delivered in London a couple of years ago by Professor Price, is exceedingly interesting and well worth looking up in the Proceedings of the Society for Psychical Research (January 1953). And further, even if there is in man a "psychic factor," *and* it survives bodily death, *and* it then still constitutes an actively living mind so that there is a genuine "life" after death—even then, knowledge of this would provide motivation (additional to the earthly motivations) for moral or generous conduct on earth only if one had reason to believe that that future life is one where the many injustices of earth are redressed. But the mere fact of its being a discarnate, "spirit" life would constitute no reason why, in that life, injustices might not go on occurring as merrily as on earth.

The next comment I wish to make concerns the scientific value on the one hand of experimental, and on the other of spontaneous, paranormal phenomena. Professor Rhine holds, I believe, that the latter cannot establish anything, but can only suggest experiments; and that only these, when confirmed under well-controlled conditions, can establish the reality of the kind of phenomenon concerned. Now, I submit that earthquakes, hurricanes, eclipses of the sun and moon, or the fall of meteorites, are phenomena over the conditions of which we have not the slightest control; and yet that their occurrence is completely established. Hence the criterion which Professor Rhine lays down defines not the scientific meaning of "established," but only of the narrower expression "experimentally established."

Of course, for discovery of the conditions on which a given kind of phenomenon depends, experimentation under controlled conditions is highly desirable and often indispensable. But as the examples cited make evident, such control is not indispensable for the purpose of establishing that a given sort of phenomenon *has actually occurred*. Moreover, it is the *reality* of a paradoxical phenomenon—that is, *its having actually occurred*—which establishes the existence of otherwise unsuspected ranges of possibilities; and which, even before these are explored, condemns as provincial any conception of Nature which has no room for that phenomenon.

This leads me now to consider some reports of a spontaneous paranormal phenomenon which illustrates the philosophically important point just made. Moreover, it manifests the greater richness of content which spontaneous phenomena usually have as compared with experimental ones. Another reason for considering it is that the nature and strength of the evidence on record for its occurrence is likely to be something of a surprise to philosophers who have not looked it up. And lastly, the difficulty of explaining away that evidence at all plausibly makes especially pointed the questions I mentioned at the outset concerning the psychology of credulity and incredulity, as contrasted with the logic of rational belief and disbelief.

The phenomenon I refer to is that of levitation; that is, the rising and floating in the air of a human body or heavy inanimate object without action of any of the forces known to physicists. What levitation is reported to be like in the concrete may be gathered from a statement—which I cite for its picturesqueness rather than its evidentiality—made by the Princess Pema Chöki Namgyal of Sikkim to the explorer Fosco Maraini. He quotes it on page 55 of his recent book, *Secret Tibet*. Her statement, which was about her uncle, reads as follows: "Yes. He did what you would call exercises in levitation. I used to take him in a little rice. He would be motionless in mid-air. Every day he rose a little higher. In the end he rose so high that I found it difficult to hand the rice up to him. I was a little girl, and I had to stand on tip-toe. There are certain things you don't forget!"

At least seventy saints or mystics have been reported to have levitated, but where such persons are concerned the testimony is suspect on the ground of religious bias. Yet in a few cases, such as that of the levitations of St. Joseph of Coppertino, the reports are so definite, the witnesses so numerous and some of them so eminent, and their initial biases so diverse, that to dismiss thus *a priori* what they attest is far from easy when one has acquainted oneself with their statements.[1]

But there are other and more recent reports of levitations, of persons who are neither saints nor mystics, but are only so-called "mediums"—a term which was originally intended to mean an intermediary between the living and spirits of the dead; which in the popular mind today connotes little else than charlatanry; but which in psychical research means simply a person in whose presence paranormal phenomena occur with some frequency and on whose presence their occurrence somehow depends. A good deal of evidence exists that there are a few such persons, and that, even if some of the phenomena of some of them have been consciously or unconsciously fraudulent, nevertheless certain others were genuinely paranormal. One of the most famous mediums on record was D. D. Home, of whom many readers of these lines probably have heard, and whose levitations during the second half of the nineteenth century were testified to by numerous distinguished witnesses. Among these was the eminent chemist and physicist, Sir William Crookes, and his testimony is so circumstantial and positive that a sample of it is worth citing *verbatim*.

In an article published in the *Quarterly Journal of Science* for January 1874, Crookes first states that the occurrences now about to be mentioned "have taken place *in my own house, in the light, and with only private friends present* besides the medium." He then writes: "On three separate occasions have I seen [Home] raised completely from the floor of the room. Once sitting in an easy chair, once kneeling on his chair and once standing up. On each occasion I had full opportunity of watching the occurrence as it was taking place." Again, in Volume VI of the *Journal of the Society for Psychical Research,* Crookes states in 1894 that sometimes Home and his chair, with his feet tucked up on the seat and his hands held up in full view of all present, rose off the ground; and Crookes adds: "On such an occasion I have got down and seen and felt that all four legs were off the ground at the same time, Home's feet being on the chair. Less frequently the levitating power was extended to those sitting next to him. Once my wife was thus raised off the ground in her chair." Another levitation

---
[1]See, for instance, Dr. E.J. Dingwall's *Some Human Oddities*, pp. 9-37 and 162-171.

of Home, which like these occurred in Crookes' own house, is described by him in the same report in the following words: "He rose eighteen inches off the ground, and I passed my hands under his feet, round him, and over his head when he was in the air."

An independent account of levitations in the presence of Home is contained in a letter of 1856 from the Earl of Crawford to his sister-in-law. It is presented and its evidentiality minutely dissected by the anthropologist, Dr. E. J. Dingwall, in an article, "Psychological Problems Arising from a Report of Telekinesis," in the February 1953 issue of the *British Journal of Psychology*. Dingwall concludes that neither the hypothesis of fraud nor that of collective hallucination is capable of explaining the facts described by Lord Crawford.

I shall add only two more citations, out of many available. The first is from the testimony of Sir William Barrett, Fellow of the Royal Society, who for many years was Professor of Experimental Physics in the Royal College of Science for Ireland. In a book published in 1918 (*On the Threshold of the Unseen*), he states that in December 1915 he had been invited by Dr. W. J. Crawford (not Lord Crawford mentioned above), who was lecturer on Mechanical Engineering at the Queens University in Belfast, to attend a meeting of a small circle consisting of the family of a seventeen year old girl, Kathleen Goligher, who worked in a local factory and with whom Dr. Crawford had been experimenting. Her mediumship, I may say, seems to have conspicuously degenerated after several years, and perhaps fraud then to have entered. But Mr. Whately Smith, who noticed this after having observed her first in 1916 and later in 1920, stresses in Volume 30 of the SPR Proceedings that no way had ever been suggested in which it would have been possible to produce fraudulently the levitations of 1915 and 1916, such as were witnessed by himself, by Barrett, and scores of times by Crawford.

Barrett, at the place mentioned, states that he and Crawford sat outside the small family circle; and that "the room was illuminated with a bright gas flame burning in a lantern, with a large red glass window, on the mantelpiece. The room was small and as our eyes got accustomed to the light we could see all the sitters clearly. They sat around a small table with hands joined together, but no one touching the table." After describing some of the first phenomena which occurred, he goes on: "Then the table began to rise from the floor some eighteen inches and remained so suspended and quite level. I was allowed to go up to the table and saw clearly no one was touching it, a clear space separating the sitters from the table. I tried to press the table down, and though I exerted all my strength could not do so; then I climbed up on the table and sat on it, my feet off the floor, when I was swayed to and fro and finally tipped off. The table of its own accord now turned upside down, no one touching it, and I tried to lift it off the ground, but it could not be stirred, it appeared screwed down to the floor. At my request all the sitters' clasped hands had been kept raised above their heads, and I could see that no one was touching the table;—when I desisted from trying to lift the inverted table from the floor, it righted itself again of its own accord, no one helping it." Crawford himself, in *The Reality of Psychic Phenomena* (1919), similarly writes that one evening in his own house with the same circle, a table weighing sixteen pounds was levitated many times, and that, during one of these levitations, while "the surface of the table was nearly shoulder-high in the air, I entered the circle and pressed down with my hands on the top of the table. Although I exerted all my strength, I could not depress the table to the floor. A friend who is over six feet in height then leaned over the circle and helped me to press downwards, when our combined efforts exerted to the limit just caused it to touch the floor."

Now, do I believe that these various levitations really occurred as reported? This, of course, is a merely biographical question and as such unimportant. Nevertheless, I shall answer it by confessing to a slight case of dissociated personality! My habit-begotten and habit-bound, adversely prejudiced, conservatively practical self finds levitation as hard to believe as probably does any reader of the preceding citations. On the other hand, my rational, philosophically open-minded, scientifically inquisitive self notices several things.

One is that the experimental demonstrations of telekinesis by statistical treatment of long series of carefully controlled and recorded dice-castings, made in Rhine's Laboratory and elsewhere, immediately decrease the antecedent improbability of levitation;

although I must say that if I were told—let us suppose by the chairman of our Program Committee, Professor Farber—that, in his own dining room and in good light, he had seen Professor Rhine rise eighteen inches in the air, and that, as Crookes did with Home, he passed his hand under, above, and around Rhine and found nothing, then such a report would be to me even more convincing both psychologically and rationally than are the reports of the results of the dice-casting experiments. And I have no reason to suppose that Crookes was a less competent observer, or less truthful, than Professor Farber would be.

Secondly, although this would be a contemporary report, whereas those of Crookes and the others are old, the fact is that the age of a piece of circumstantially stated, intelligent, and sincere testimony has no logical bearing on its force unless the testimony was biased by beliefs commonly held in the days of the witness but since proved to be groundless or false; or unless some normal explanation of the events judged by him to have been paranormal has since been discovered. But neither of these sources of weakness exists in the testimony quoted.

Thirdly, assertions of antecedent improbability always rest on the tacit but often in fact false assumption that the operative factors are the same in a presented case as they were in superficially similar past cases. For example, the antecedent improbability of the things an expert conjurer does on the stage is extremely high if one takes as antecedent evidence what merely an ordinary person, under ordinary instead of staged conditions, can do. The same is true of what geniuses, or so-called arithmetical prodigies, can do as compared with what ordinary men can do. And that a man *is* a genius or a calculating prodigy is shown by what he *does do, not* the reality of what he does by his being a genius or prodigy. This holds equally as regards a medium and his levitations or other paranormal phenomena. The crucial question is therefore not whether paranormal levitations are frequent, or happen to ordinary people, but whether they ever actually have occurred. If even only once, this is enough to show that some force as yet not understood by us exists.

Thus, the philosophically open-minded, critically rational part of the dissociated personality to which I have confessed finds, as standing in the way of acceptance of the clear cut testimony quoted, little else than the naive tacit assumption that if the knowledge possessed by physicists as of December 1954 cannot explain levitation, then levitation is impossible!

CHAPTER 4

THE FRONTIERS OF PSYCHOLOGY: PSYCHOANALYSIS AND PARAPSYCHOLOGY*

MICHAEL SCRIVEN

I T SEEMS TO ME (as it does to most of the participants in this program) of the greatest importance that a philosopher of science should be able to make some substantial contribution to the work of practicing scientists, either empiricists or theoreticians.

Here, I shall be discussing in some detail, at a level which is very close to that at which subjects are discussed in the relevant technical journals, two topics which are very close to what I have called the "Frontiers of Psychology." In Part II of this Essay I shall be taking up topics which are of a much more philosophical nature; and I want to begin here by giving you some idea of how I intend to relate these analyses.

KINDS OF FRONTIERS

There are, it seems to me, three kinds of scientific frontiers; and it will be helpful for us to consider a geographical analogy. At the moment there are three different kinds of geographical frontiers. Let us take as examples the following three places: first, Antarctica; second, the Moon, and third, the Andromeda Nebula. If we were speaking in the middle of the past century instead of the middle of this century, the first item could be the West, the second Antarctica, and the third the Moon. Now the distinction that I have in mind is this. When we refer to the coastal areas of Antarctica today or to the

*Reprinted from FRONTIERS OF SCIENCE AND PHILOSOPHY edited by Robert G. Colodny, Volume I of University of Pittsburgh Philosophy of Science Series by permission of the University of Pittsburgh Press. Copyright 1962 by the University of Pittsburgh Press.

West as it was in the eighteen-forty's as "frontiers," we think of them as the boundary of current civilization, everything this side of such a point being more or less within the orbit of regular commerce, and everything beyond it being beyond that orbit, while the place itself is—with hardship—inhabited.

The moon, on the other hand, represents for us, at this stage, the boundary of current technical possibility. We have no permanent installations on the Moon, though there are a number of small metal tags up there with the Hammer and Sickle or Stars and Stripes on them, but it is nevertheless clear that, given the sociological and financial incentives, we can place men on the Moon; and it is only a matter of time before we do that, and so expand to new frontiers. Nevertheless, in a very important sense, it is a problem of a kind quite different from that of placing men in Antarctica, where we can go and live uncomfortably tomorrow by simply chartering a plane or boat today.

The third of my examples, the Andromeda Nebula, raises quite different questions and only in a very different sense can it be called a "frontier." It is a frontier in the sense that I shall be talking about in Part II, a last frontier, perhaps, because in connection with the settlement of the planets of other stars in other galaxies there arise extremely serious questions of technical possibility, so serious, indeed, that there are plenty of people today who are willing to argue that it is not physically possible we shall ever succeed in doing this. And they say this not because it is obviously a long way, but for much more interesting reasons, such as the upper limit on the possible velocity of travel, and the length of time it would take to get there, traveling at that rate, relative to our own earth time, of course; and the problems that would arise in passing through clouds of cosmic dust traveling at *that* kind of velocity, and so on. These difficulties are not as simple as those which face us in putting men on the Moon. It is by no means certain that money will solve these difficulties at any stage.

Now in terms of the field of scientific investigation, and in particular in the field of psychology, it seems to me that a reasonable analogy can be drawn in the following way: a frontier in psychology, in the sense in which Antarctica is today a frontier for us geographically, is the area studied by any current research problem in recognized fields of psychology. For example: the study of the effects of beliefs on perception; of drugs on performance and on feelings, and so on. Now we need something that stands in the same relationship to intellectual exploration as the Moon does to geographical exploration, that is, at the point where the limits of our current technical capacity are strained but there seems to be in principle no impossibility about the investigation. Here we have a series of topics in psychology and related fields, such as psychoanalysis (about which I shall talk first); the nature of hypnosis (where there arise questions about, for example, the possibility of the self-induction of hypnotic states, which, of course, is of great practical importance in introducing anaesthesia after a serious wound); infant learning of complex languages (the work which has been going on at Yale, attempting to get the normal three-year-old to speak, write, and explain himself in English, and do arithmetic); psychosomatic effects of various kinds (that is, the area where we are studying not the therapeutic effect of drugs operating through physiological mechanisms, but the effects of, for example, the laying on of hands—or the "laying on of drugs," where, in fact, we think there is no physiological mechanism at work). The placebo studies, for example, supply an excellent example of the beginning of this. These are all areas which do not fit into the regular run of current psychological investigations, but they are not so far beyond us that we would want to deny they are appropriate subjects for scientific study today.

I have so far said nothing about parapsychology. Let us first look at the third category of frontier, the ultimate boundaries for psychology, the "last frontiers" beyond which there will, in fact, so it is alleged, never be scientific progress. Here we are concerned with such a barrier to the possibility of total prediction of human behavior as is supposedly provided by the existence of free will in man, and such barriers to the total description of human behavior as are provided by the existence in men's conceptual schemes of *values,* which are in certain respects impractical subjects for scientific investigation and description. Other supposedly insurmountable difficulties are provided by man's possession of a soul, his life after death, and the uniqueness of the individual. All these are hoary puzzles, long discussed amongst psychologists and philosophers; all of them recognizable as candidates for a "last frontier," candidates for an ultimate limit to psychology.

Parapsychology has been thought by some to lie in this third category, to be a discussion of something which it is essentially impossible or improper for science to handle. It has been thought by others to lie within the realm of proper, though very little practiced investigation, that is, the second category. Those who think there is nothing to the phenomena will think it entirely proper that there is relatively little active research in the area. Others will think it a sign of the excessive conservatism of a newly-independent and insecure discipline. I shall leave the decision as to the category until after I have said something about the subject. One category or another, however, it qualifies as a frontier area.

. . . I shall begin by attempting to relate the fields of parapsychology and psychoanalysis. First of all, we must ask, "What are the claims of these fields?" and in particular, "What claim can we take as representative of these fields in order to discuss the question of whether, in fact, these subjects have or could be scientifically investigated?" In the case of parapsychology I shall take the basic claim to be the assertion that some people can acquire information about states of affairs which they are not able to perceive by means of the normal senses, nor able to infer from any data that are available to their senses. The claim then is the claim that *some* people have the power that is sometimes popularly referred to as "extrasensory perception." Notice that I am not considering the claim that everybody can, nor the claim that there are some people who can *always* do this. There are in fact *many* claims I am not considering which have on occasion been made by parapsychologists. It is unnecessary to stick out one's neck any farther than with the more modest claim. I wish to confine our attention precisely to this claim.

Now the nature of this claim deserves a moment of prior consideration. Suppose that it is disputed; what kind of objection is likely to be raised? There are two importantly distinct objections.

It might be argued in the first place that the conditions referred to in the definition do not apply; that, in fact, it is possible in the experimental situations for ordinary sensory information to be received by the subjects in the study. That would be an attack upon the question of whether the conditions have been met. Now, what are the conditions? It is stipulated that the subjects are not able to gather the information they acquire by means of the normal senses, nor able to infer it from any data that is available to their senses. You cannot perceive that it is going to rain tomorrow, but you may be perfectly able to infer this from available meteorological data, and we wouldn't, of course, call that "extrasensory perception." Now the trouble with this statement of conditions is that it is negative. It says that a certain procedure or normal perception is ruled out, is not possible in the conditions mentioned. It is not easy to establish a negative condition, and it is because of that logical feature of the claim that some of the difficulties arise. The claim is, in fact, a negative causal claim; it is the claim that the transfer of information, if it occurs, is not due to ordinary sensory perception. And that is always much harder to establish than a straightforward positive causal claim, such as that caffeine induces insomnia.

The second kind of objection that may be raised in a particular case of alleged extrasensory perception is a doubt whether the effect actually does occur. The first is whether the conditions are met, for the alleged transfer of information; the second is whether or not there is a transfer of information. This matter is not as easily settled as you might think because, in almost all cases, the transfer is statistical in nature, and not absolute in nature. It is not like the case where I transferred to you a second ace of spades from the bottom of the pack, a fact that we can very readily disclose by a suitable examination; it is much more like the case where you are unable and I am able to give the correct description of certain objects at some distance through a slight fog. I do not always get them right, but I get them right a little more often than you, and that suggests that I have in that particular case, better fog sight than you, or else that I have been making lucky guesses. In the extrasensory case, success suggests the same; it might be skill or it might be luck. So *we have a special kind of difficulty in handling the extrasensory work, that of demonstrating the improbability of coincidence.* These are the two features of the claim that lead into certain difficulties for the experimenters.

Now, what about psychoanalysis? The term is used to refer to many things, including a particular kind of psychotherapy, and theories about the development of man in his own lifetime and in the course of history. These involve at least two very distinct kinds of claim, customarily referred to as "process hypotheses" and "outcome hypotheses." A process hypothesis in psychoanalysis is a hypothesis about what goes on "within" people: for example, the hypothesis that someone who had a certain dream was representing his father by the masked figure in the dream, or the hypothesis that successful therapy involves countertransference, i.e. a stage involving a reversal of the affectual attachment to the analyst of the patient. Any hypothesis about what happens during the psychoanalytic therapy, or during any normal living situation which is subjected to psychoanalysis, is said to be a "process hypothesis." I am particularly interested in those that refer to therapy.

The second kind of hypothesis is an "outcome hypothesis," and here we have a relatively simple and distinct kind of hypothesis, the hypothesis that people are "better" after having psychoanalytic therapy. In particular, people of a certain kind that is not too easy to specify, the so-called neurotic.

Now I cannot discuss, in the space at my disposal, both claims. I shall therefore make the following comment on them and then concentrate on an "outcome" study. The comment is, that, essentially similar features must be involved in both types of study. This is generally disputed by analysts. It is often said that hypotheses about what goes on in the patient's mind, his unconscious mind, during the course of therapy can really only be studied by the words that are produced and the affectual indications that are available to the analyst. They cannot be studied by the use of control groups, by the use of any kind of objective "test" which involves verbal responses to some test by the patient, which could be scored by any judge. They cannot, in fact, be done in any way except by the use of free association and the standard techniques of psychoanalysis.

I am not going to concern myself much with the question of how to meet these comments, these complaints. They are relatively easy to meet and involve both plain confusions and more complicated question begging. I make the claim then that both types of study—although importantly different, since one is about the efficiency of therapy, the other is about what happens psychologically inside a person—are, from the methodological point of view, very similar.

I shall now concentrate on the second. I do that rather than concentrating on the first because it seems to me that this is the fundamental claim in the moral and social sense the psychoanalyst has to make. It seems to me of the very greatest importance, in fact, of the first importance, that we get to work on the question of whether we can help those people who are seriously ill, psychologically speaking, and who fall into the category which an analyst claims he can help. This is, very roughly speaking, the wide-ranging category of neuroses, a certain range of psychosomatic disorders, and a certain range of character disorders. There is great disagreement about what this exact range is; but there are certainly some cases which are clearly claimed by analysts to be such that their techniques will be a help.

I remind you, then, that I am here concerned with dynamic or process hypotheses, and I am here not talking about the question of whether other medical disciplines are superior to or worse than psychoanalytic theory in therapeutic efficiency. I certainly do not wish to imply this last in what follows, which will involve some pretty solid criticisms of psychoanalysis and psychoanalytic therapy. I do mean to imply that it is not at all clear that psychoanalytic therapy is much good, that this is a pretty serious complaint and that it should be met as immediately as possible by bringing to bear a great deal of research, interest, and backing. I intend to outline in some brisk detail how to do that.

Let us look at the logical features of this particular claim, the claim that a substantial portion of people with certain kinds of psychological malady can be significantly improved by psychoanalytic therapy. The conditions are vague, that is, the exact specifications of the people we are intending to study is not too clear; that is not a serious drawback, since we can usually agree on some of them and we can study the effect on these. The important issue is then two-fold. "Does the improvement take place, (however improvement may be defined)?" and, secondly, "What is it that produces this improvement?" So this is a *direct* causal claim. The extrasensory claim is a claim that something happens under certain conditions which exclude certain causes. The psychoanalytic claim is the claim that: (a) something happens, and (b) something specific causes it, namely, the psychoanalytic therapy.

I am going to begin by looking at psychoanalysis because the contrast is better drawn in this way for reasons that you will see in the course of the description.

The basic phenomenon that we are investigating is this: "At a certain time the patient is in a certain condition C^1; from that time till a certain second time he undergoes a treatment called "T", and he is then in condition C^2. C^1 may or may not be the same as C^2."

In these terms there are two claims to investigate. The first is the claim that C^2 is a "better" state than C^1, whatever this is going to turn out to mean; that is, the claim that the patient is somehow improved. It is not the claim at all that the patient is cured. Analysts are extremely cautious and sensible about that claim—and so are doctors in general about claims with that kind of strength. If there is not any improvement at all, then, of course, it is very difficult to see how one would justify psychotherapy. There is, however, a possible exception to that conclusion. Supposing that you could prove that the patient would have gotten worse if he had not had analysis, then the fact that C^2 is no better than C^1 does not show that psychoanalysis did not help. It shows that it prevented things from getting worse and that is always a gain in this world! So the first claim is that C^2 is better than C^1. The second part of the claim, the tricky part, is the claim that the change is due to a particular feature of the patient's environment, viz. "T."

I am going to discuss the claim by raising a series of questions that a skeptic might raise about psychoanalytical therapy and then produce the kind of response that scientists trying to support the claim or, at any rate, trying to find out the truth about it, could give in reply. These questions may bear on one or the other of the two elements in the "outcome" claim.

Suppose that we begin with the remark which one often hears from people whose friends have been analyzed, "There really isn't any difference at all about him afterwards." That is a plain denial that C^2 is any different from C^1. A number of comments have to be made about that. The first one is—it is totally improbable, since the individual is two or five years older; and if he has not changed at all, then he is very unlike a normal human being. Therefore, it is extremely likely that there was something of a change in him. When the critics say there was really no change, they are not denying that he has lost some more hair, they are, of course, referring to a change in the relevant neurotic symptoms. For us that raises the difficulty, a very serious one, of identifying the neurotic symptoms, as distinct from the symptoms of aging, incidental illnesses and accidents, emotional traumas due to death of spouse or relatives. There are other changes that indisputably occur in many, though perhaps not all individuals, who have completed analysis. In the first place, they are almost certain to have a different vocabulary for describing their difficulties. It is very rare that one cannot make some reasonable estimate of the likelihood that somebody has had analysis, or has not had analysis, from their vocabulary when they are talking about mental stress of various kinds. It is not infallible, but there is at least likely to be a difference in their vocabulary; and we have no hesitation in saying that the analyst is responsible for that. There will be occasions when he is not; but it is very rare and we can reasonably give him credit for that. But it is not *this* kind of change we care about. The question we have to ask ourselves is whether, and to what extent, differences in the appropriate and interesting dimension, the dimension of neurotic symptomatology, are due to the analyst. A third kind of reported difference that will be noticed is the subjective account given by the ex-patient. It is often the case that the patient, or the ex-patient, will describe himself as very much better. This is obviously more relevant than the changes discussed earlier. But the skeptic may still have some comments. He may say that even though the patient *thinks* he is better, in fact there is no difference. To that we reply, "There certainly is a series of differences of a fairly readily identifiable kind, including a difference in how he feels about himself." Now then, he makes his complaint a little more interesting. The second comment is, "All right, so there are these differences, but they are not really improvements. Sure he can talk about his troubles now, and now he knows that he is arrested in a pregenital phase and this makes him feel better about being a homosexual (or perhaps it doesn't) but the fundamental fact remains that he still is a homosexual, (or impotent, or claustrophobic)."

Thus we are unavoidably brought to the problem of defining

improvement. It is very interesting to read through the psychoanalytic literature, looking for a discussion of what is called the "Goal of Therapy." These begin at one extreme with something produced not long ago by Szasz. In an extremely sophisticated article, he announced that, so far as he could see, the proper goal of therapy was teaching the scientific method. Now it seems to me that this is an admirable aim; but it is not clear to me that the patient is, in fact, expecting this; nor whether, in fact, for $25.00 an hour he might not be able to get it a little more quickly. At any rate, I first wish to distinguish the people who explicitly reject any claim to producing improvement, of which he is one.

Then you get views of a slightly different kind, e.g. "The goal of therapy is better self-understanding." Now immediately one asks this question, "How do you know that it is really better self-understanding and not simply a new vocabulary for talking about his problem?" For I can easily give you an astrological jargon with which to talk about your problems and the question will then still arise as to whether you understand your problems any better. Now the same problem arises about psychoanalysis, and I answer it perfectly straighforwardly, saying it has to be *shown* that the patient's hpyotheses about his own behavior are correct, and that means substantiating process hypotheses, so you would immediately have to do both studies to handle an assessment of therapy, if we took this as the goal.

There is, on the other hand, the possibility which I think most therapists are interested in, that the increased "self-understanding," real or not, actually leads to a real improvement in the ordinary sense; for example, to the reduction of anxiety in the patient. Perhaps he feels less shocked by his behavior pattern; he feels that he can now fit it into the story of the things that have happened to him over which he had no control, and he therefore sees this as something which is in a way a justification for him, and he feels less uneasy. There are various ways in which that might occur, but if there is any such improvement, we ought to be able to detect that directly. So I then move on to the straightforward claim that there is a genuine gain of the ordinary kind in the patient.

Now, what enters into the ordinary claim that there is an improvement? There are a number of factors: First, and often thought to be the only matter of concern, is the question of the patient's objective report about himself. It is certainly important in assessing improvement that we take account of that kind of improvement. On the other hand, there are many situations well known to therapists where the subject reports that he is much better, whereas the study of his family relationship shows that this subjective gain has been obtained by transferring his aggression from himself, where its impact made him feel bad, to his children, which makes *them* feel bad, but makes him feel good. It would then hardly be appropriate for us to regard the subject's feeling of improvement as equivalent to improvement in all cases. The analyst is, of course, often in a difficult situation about evaluating the impact of this particular kind of a point because he is not always (though he is sometimes, and increasingly so in recent years) discussing matters with others in the family, concurrently with the patient. To make an assessment of improvement, therefore, we must take account of social relations and social behavior, as well as the subject's report. We shall have to do this with the aid of field investigators interviewing those in social contact with the patient.

Next, there are the psychosomatic symptoms. Regardless of whether there are any social gains, regardless of whether the patient reports feeling better or does not, there is the question of whether paralysis has vanished; whether a particular kind of tic stopped; whether other sorts of behavioral peculiarities supposedly due to the psychological conditions of the patient have diminished, vanished, or begun.

Next, there is the question of whether his objective judgment, his rational capacity for insight into material affairs and personal relationships has improved. This is quite separate from the previous things and will, of course, need an independent kind of assessment.

Possibly, in addition to these, there is the problem of whether his moral judgment and his moral forms of behavior have changed. This raises a lot of interesting and difficult problems. I want to make it perfectly clear that I am not ruling it out in the way the definition has been given. Suppose we found a man who was feeling worse, behaving worse toward his family; his judgment of the attitudes of his neighbors had become almost paranoid, but he was now able to stand up in the cause of integration in a Southern community where previously he could not, and as a result, feels that he is doing the right thing and is rewarded by that fact; then it would be possible to argue that he has not improved in any respect, if we only take account of the things I have mentioned so far. Thus, it seems not to be possible to rule out consideration of the morality of his behavior, when you are assessing improvement. Whatever you do, however, you cannot rule out the preceding four considerations. Those are difficult things to evaluate, as difficult as anything there is to evaluate about a person, but I do not introduce them as a kind of burden to place on the shoulders of the analyst; I introduce them as necessary parts of what must be meant by someone who claims that psychoanalysis does improve the people whom it treats. If this could not be said, if that claim could not be made to stick in terms of the definition given, then the analyst's therapeutic claim is in doubt and, of course, it would require a very substantial investigation to determine whether these things do apply.

Having given an account of improvement, which I have been obliged to construct since no explicit account of this kind is available in the literature, we pass to the third complaint which is: "All right, so now there is a *difference,* and we have an idea of what *improvement* means, but how are we ever going to judge those differences as improvements?" The judgment of improvement is hopelessly subjective, it is suggested; it is hopelessly subjective for a reason which provides the experimenter with an unsolvable dilemma. Either he asks the analyst himself whether the patient is better, in which case, of course, the judgment is hopelessly biased, or he does not ask the analyst. In the latter case, you apply these tests for improvement quite independently of the analyst's judgment of improvement, in which case it could be said it is a hopelessly unsatisfactory judgment and could be said to be a judgment by some ignorance, rather than anything else. It would be argued that the most important material of all is revealed only in the analyst's sessions, and without his insights we are without the best based judgment of all.

There are a number of replies to this. I will only mention them. The first is the use of what is called "uncontaminated judges," a nice phrase, which means judges who do not know whether the person they are judging for improvement has actually undergone psychoanalytic therapy or not. That is, they do not know whether he is a member of the control group, or whether he is a member of the experimental group, the group that received the treatment. There are extremely difficult problems that have to be met here. There is the problem of whether the vocabulary he uses provides an index to which group he was in, so that the judges' prejudices in favor of or against psychoanalysis would be able to operate. There are ways of handling this that are not *completely* satisfactory, but, using this panel, and the analyst's own report, and studying further cases of discrepancy between them, we have a study which is well worth doing, since until we have done it we do not know whether even a possibly—slightly—biased judgment of improvement exists. We, of course, know that the analyst, who simply sees the analysis of his patient, very often says that there was some improvement as a result of the therapy, but we do not know whether it is true, nor can he. We, therefore, have got to have some attack on the problem of objective evaluation, before and after, of the patients who go through. Remember, that if the difference in the patient is not detectable to other people, then it is not going to be the kind of improvement we primarily desire. It would not be very much good if the analyst always said, "Yes, he is better," but nobody else could see any improvement at all and neither could the patient.

Now the fourth point: Supposing all this is said and done, the above points are all met, the suggestion might still be made that the improvement is only *temporary*. It might even be suggested that the termination of the therapy will actually lead to a collapse on the part of the patient who has become dependent on the analyst. Of course, a standard point of psychoanalytic therapy is that this possibility be meticulously investigated and carefully avoided. However, an unfortunate feature of the standard arrangement is that there is no good way of telling whether it *was* avoided, because if the patient, having been through five years of analysis, terminating with a judgment of improvement by the analyst, then finds himself falling in the same neurotic depression that he was previously subject to, he is rather less than likely to go back to the same individual. We therefore require what is known as a follow-up, i.e. a repetition of the evaluation tests some time after the conclusion of therapy, and we have got to apply this again at various intervals after the conclusion of therapy in order to see whether the improvement, whatever it may be, is relatively permanent.

Supposing now that we are satisfied that there has been a change for the better, and that it is a relatively permanent one; the fifth question arises, whether the patient would not have improved anyway.

Five years is a long time in the life of a neurosis, and the evidence that we have, inadequate as it is, suggests that there is a tendency for neuroses to get better in the course of time, without therapy, in approximately two-thirds of the cases accepted. Now the question is, "Just how much more than two-thirds of his patients is the analyst helping?" To discover whether the figure is two-thirds, *and* whether the analyst is doing better than the great healer Time, we need a control group. Suppose he judges that out of a number of people that come to him for help, and perhaps after a number of diagnostic interviews, he could help a certain group of them, we then take that group, split it in half randomly, and give him half. Now then, what are we comparing? We are comparing the control group, the people he thought he could help, though we do not allow him to help them, with the people he thought he could help, whom we do allow him to try to help. If there is no significant difference between these groups at the end of therapy with the group he does treat, it is going to be very difficult to support the claim that he really did help them.

Might it not be that he gets all the really hard cases in his group? If we use a very large number of individuals in these groups, we can take care of such as possibility. Moreover, supposing it is said, for example, that obviously when there is a difference of sex, there must be a completely different method of treatment, perhaps owing to the special role of the Oedipus relationship in male development. Then it must be replied that we can match perfectly well for sex, that is, we can arrange that there will be exactly the same number of women in the control group as in the experimental, and so on. Any feature that is said to be relevant to the method of treatment can immediately be matched. Now, supposing that there turned out to be an indefinite number of these. It might be said that every respect in which a patient had childhood experiences of a particular kind is relevant to therapy and, therefore, we must, in fact, match with this. Obviously we would be getting an experimental group running several thousand people. However, this line of attack on an experimental study only raises a problem for the analyst, who often suggests it. The problem is this: If there are that many relevant variables, how did the therapist ever learn which ones to treat, since he has never had that many patients? Hence, there is a point at which we can turn the proliferation of relevant features into a complaint about the therapist's own claims.

We now turn to the last three questions, which provide many difficulties. It might be argued that, although the analyst's group should show a substantial gain over the control group, it was not the psychoanalysis that cured the patients, but the experience of discussing their problems with somebody who is not going to rattle off a lot of complaints about immoral behavior. There are a number of other factors that have been suggested as being the truly curative element in psychoanalysis. True or false, the loophole must be closed. It immediately introduces the necessity for *several* control groups. We have got to have other control groups in which an attempt is made to match for these things which might be curative. For example: We could have one group which is referred to a "naïve" (of Freud) graduate student who interviews the patients (naïve means graduate student in geology, for example). We take great care that he knows nothing about psychoanalysis, or as near as can be to nothing, and we give him a free hand to discuss the problems which the patient has. We prefer him with a beard and so on. We match with as many of these factors (which the analyst says are *not* the crucial therapeutic elements in his treatment) as we can, and we then see whether there is still a significant difference.

Suppose that there is a significant difference, we then come to the last two difficulties. Suppose that it is still the case that the analyst, in fact, is doing better than the other groups. The difficulty still remains that the analyst has, in the contacts with the patients that come to him, a tremendous advantage over the bearded Greek graduate student, and that is that they are talking Freudian talk, and that the patient came to you for Freudian analysis (or some other kind). It is, therefore, perfectly clear to the patient that he is in one case getting and in the other not getting what he came for, and since he most likely believes in the therapeutic power of what he came for, or he would not have come for it, the analyst still has up his sleeve a trick which has nothing to do with psychoanalytic theory as such, but has a great deal to do with the prestige of psychoanalytic theory.

Finally, there is the possibility that the analysts select from the applicant group just those people with whom they personally interact well and then success is due entirely to a personality interaction, the psychoanalytic terminology and rituals being essentially or largely irrelevant. Again it is possible to match, in order to eliminate these possibilities, and without matching we shall simply never be able to answer the question whether psychoanalysis helps neurotics. There is no substitution for a study that involves all of those features; without them, other highly probable interpretations will still be possible. And they may not be exhaustive. What is absolutely certain is that no study has ever been done which takes account of half of these points. It would be expensive to answer this question about psychoanalysis, but important: less expensive and more important than one B-58 bomber.

An interesting moral problem that arises in the course of all this is the question of whether one should say these things to people who might need to get analyzed, namely the readers of this essay. However, I will leave that to one side and try and stick to the question—whether you should.

Now remember these points in closing on that subject; it does not follow from the fact that no study that remotely meets the conditions I've mentioned has been done, that a psychoanalyst has no therapeutic effect. Of course, he may well have a therapeutic effect; he is a person with prestige, listening to your problems, willing to discuss them with you, willing to help you with them. It is quite likely that he does for many reasons. But we have been raising the question about whether psychoanalysis as such has any therapeutic efficacy and that is, in the long run, the important question; because if the other factors are doing it we can easily produce the other factors. It will then be a relatively inexpensive kind of therapy, and it will not mean that people will have to put in seventeen years' training to do it. So I am not arguing that going to an analyst is silly. I am arguing that it is impossible to claim that it is the psychoanalytic part of what he says that is responsible for the improvement, if any, and we do not *know* whether there is any. There may be some; and it is quite clear that if you feel sick (psychologically sick); you can afford it; you dislike burdening friends with your troubles; you are an atheist, (and, therefore, do not want to go to a clergyman) and you believe in Freud; then you should go to an analyst. Why? Because there is nothing else you can go to and there is no good reason for supposing this will not help. But do not make the claim that psychoanalysis as such cured you, unless you have got better evidence than the sequence of events, neurosis, psychoanalysis, no neurosis.

I am usually asked at this stage, or shortly after such discussion, whether I have been analyzed or whether I have been run over by an analyst or whether my father was an analyst. Well, those considerations are irrelevant to the truth of my comments and so we will leave them open. If you can meet these objections logically, that is fine—if you cannot, it will not help you to know what I was or was not.

Now let us turn to parapsychology. We are here considering a different claim, a negative claim. We are considering a claim that a particular thing is happening and it is *not* due to this, this, and this—the normal sensory processes. We need to set out a situation in which no sensory communication or inference is possible. Now the standard situation in extrasensory perception experiments is a very simple one. An individual in one room, supervised by an experimenter in that room, and called the "agent," looks at a pack of cards that have been randomly shuffled and have on them certain very simple designs, perhaps numbers, perhaps letters, perhaps colored pictures, animals—a number of items have been used. In another room or another house at the other end of the street or in another country, depending on the study, somebody else—the subject supervised by another experimenter—attempts to write down on a list the order of cards that the first individual is looking at. You can see that the elimination of sensory communications is pretty direct.

Let us take one of the standard cases in which one of the best subjects that has worked in this area was used. This was Mrs. Stewart, who kept going for a number of years, producing scores at a very even level, as high as forty or fifty percent better than chance expectations, depending on the agent. In one series she was set up in Belgium; watches of the two experimenters were synchronized; and the "agent" (Mrs. Holding) was set up and supervised in London. It is very difficult to explain how they would have communicated using the ordinary senses. They did not communicate using the telephone, which would of course be physically possible, nor radio. We have a number of supervisory reports about this. All that happened was that on the BBC seven o'clock time signal they started, and every three seconds the agent would turn over a card and look at it, while at the other end, every three seconds, the subject would write down another response. The results were then sealed by the separate experimenters and given to another investigator for tabulation, and it turned out that Mrs. Stewart was able to score, as I said, about forty or fifty percent above chance on this. There was an expectation that she would get five right by just guessing, and in fact most people do—many studies have been done to see whether they, in fact, do. She was getting seven, better than half right, and in financial terms, of course, that is a very profitable arrangement and would rapidly accumulate for her a disproportionate amount of money in a betting game. It seems reasonable to conclude that extrasensory perception is hereby demonstrated.

That is a standard kind of experiment that has been done by a number of people with a good many subjects and it is substantially similar in each of them. Now, let us use the same procedure we used with the psychoanalysis study: Let us consider some possible objections. First, it is done with secret signals. I have explicitly described the experiment in such a way that it is very difficult to see how that could be. On some of the other ESP experiments it is possible to see how it *could* be done, but we have people there watching for it to be done who cannot detect it being done. One very interesting maneuver came out of a recent series involving two boys as subjects. The possibility arose that they were using a hypersonic whistle, to which, of course, their ears are sensitive, whereas the ears of the older experimenters would not be sensitive. It is an interesting hypothesis, and the experimental design was such that it is not possible to rule it out, and the experiments must therefore be completely disregarded. It is a rare occasion in the recent history of this type of investigation, because most of these traps have been thought out so thoroughly now that it is very unusual for anybody even to bother with an experimental design that does not rule them out. Ordinary suggestions about whispered messages and subvocal remarks and so on are quite easily met by separating the subject from the agent by greater distance and more closed doors.

The second possibility is recording errors made unconsciously due to motivation to produce exciting results. The man who compares the subject's results with the original card order is presumably anxious to see success or he would not be in the business of investigating this, and it is relatively easy when you are checking off these long columns of paired symbols to make errors. This point is readily met by using photographic recording techniques or keeping the record for independent check, which has been done with all the major series. They are available for inspection, and the study of them shows an occasional recording error, but they work out very nearly equal in both directions: sometimes a "hit" is actually scored as a "miss" and sometimes the other way around. But this does not turn out to be a very significant fact and it is always open to subsequent inspection.

Third objection: These studies are not repeatable. Telepathy is not a truly scientific effect, according to this suggestion, because these results cannot be reliably produced by anybody that sets up this kind of an experiment. This complaint is based on a simple misunderstanding of the requirements of scientific experiments. We cannot repeat the study of the eclipse that was made three years ago and there are important respects in which each eclipse is different—for example, the solar flares that occur on these occasions are unique—and these are respects in which we are quite clear significant scientific information resides.

Repeatability is not a requirement unless the claim made is of a very strong kind. If I make the claim that a certain kind of drug will cure diabetes, administered in a specific way, then I expect when I administer it in this way to find this result. That is not the kind of claim that is being made here. The claim that is being made here is that *some* people have a certain *capacity*. The appropriate comparison is with claims about individuals who are alleged to be calculating prodigies or eidetic imagers. The calculating prodigy is a very good case for comparison.

The prodigy is often a poor shepherd boy or peasant child who has had no formal education but can perform miraculous calculating feats using a kind of mental imagery that they find very difficult to explain. Such children often are taken in hand, after having been exhibited publicly for some years, by some kind patron who then gives them a formal education. Towards the end of this they frequently lose their capacity for lightning calculations. There have been some important exceptions to this, of course, some of the great mathematicians amongst them, but there are on record a considerable number of cases of the sort that I have described. These are cases which have been very thoroughly investigated; there is no possibility of straightforward fraud here. But when one makes the claim that such skills exist, one does not thereby guarantee that they will be discovered in every child, nor indeed in children selected by any particular method of selection except direct test on the kind of task which the prodigy performs. The only repeatability to which one is committed extends over the active life span of the calculating skill in a particular individual; that is, one makes a claim about him very like the claim one might make about a child to the effect that he can hear notes of a frequency of 20,000 cycles per second. For a certain span of his life this will be true, and he will repeatedly perform tasks which are dependent upon this skill. Exactly the same kind of repeatability is both required of and constantly evidenced in the ESP work.

The next sceptical move about ESP consists in the suggestion that it is nothing more than a kind of mental radio—simply another electro-magnetic phenomenon. Now it is important to notice that even if this were true, it would hardly result in a serious weakening of most of the ESP claims because it would demonstrate a hitherto completely unrecognized sensitivity by means of which information is indeed passed from individual to individual other than by means of the usual senses. In point of fact, however, several studies have been made where the subjects were separated from the agents by a substantial thickness of lead, without noticeable diminution in the ESP performance. Moreover, on independent grounds, the estimates we have of the extent of the electrical activity in the brain make it clear that telepathy across the English Channel from London to Belgium would be incompatible with our current electro-magnetic theory, if for no other reasons than from considerations of the impossibility of exhibiting the degree of sensitivity and selectivity required. In general, we have no evidence which would enable us to say that there is a falling off in ESP performance with distance, though this is by no means decisive in attempting to determine whether it is a signal propagation procedure which obeys an inverse square law.

We now come to some more fundamental suggestions. Surely, it has been said, you will get this kind of effect sometimes, if you look long enough. Indeed, it is true that if you were to make a very large number of investigations into the success with which people guess, say, the outcome of horse races, you would expect to find a number of individuals whose performance was substantially better than average. And the longer you looked, the more likely it would be that you would find some really remarkably successful guesses. In fact, unlike previous considerations, this criticism does not rest on some kind of intrinsically fallacious hypothesis. Its only defect, albeit a fatal one, is that it is quantitatively hopeless. That is, the odds against a chance explanation of the results that were obtained in Soal's basic series of experiments are about 10^{70} to one, and there is no significant chance at all that we would come across scoring of this degree of success, however long we or other people looked. To back this up, imagine that the entire series of his experiments, which ran for a period of some years and involved 37,000 separate trials, had been performed every minute throughout the entire history of the earth back to the days when it was a cloud of gas, i.e. for about three thousand million years. In the course of all *that* searching, what would be the chance that we would come across someone who performed so well? It would be about one chance in 10^{54}, i.e. still completely negligible. So the argument that the ESP results are based upon counting the positive instances and ignoring the negative ones is hopeless because even the most absurd assumptions about the number of negative ones still leaves us with a staggering preponderance of successes in this area—far too large to be accounted for by chance alone. When the roulette wheel keeps coming up on the number three, time after time, no matter how we spin it, we must eventually take seriously the hypothesis that it has jammed, or that someone is jamming it. The same applies when we find someone who can guess at a rate 50 percent better than chance, and keep it up for years.

Having considered an attempt to dismiss the results as insignificant, it is now appropriate for us to look at the suggestion that the results were imaginary.

It has been suggested on a number of occasions that the ESP work is a gigantic fraud, involving deliberate deception by a considerable number of people of great professional eminence in several countries. There is absolutely no doubt that this is possible, and there is absolutely no way to calculate the odds of it being true. Hence we cannot demonstrate, as we did in connection with the last difficulty, that there is a gross divergence between the suggested hypothesis and the actual quantitative evidence. One can only make an attempt to weigh the imponderables, such as the tremendous risk to a professional career that results from getting involved in parapsychological work. These considerations by no means rule out the possibility, of course, and the sceptic who takes this line must follow it up making a serious attempt to attend the sessions of the experimentalists whose honesty he is impugning, by examining their records for the kind of slip that fraudulent manipulation would undoubtedly reveal sooner or later, and by attempting to perform experiments of a similar kind himself. This is not an issue which can be settled by any *a priori* considerations. It is not only pointless but immoral for critics to suggest dishonesty amongst their colleagues unless they are prepared to substantiate this or apply it to other scientists producing wholly novel claims, as a result of which large sections of earlier physics or chemistry are overthrown.

The scientific attitude indeed requires that we remain perpetually aware of and seriously prepared to consider claims of dishonesty just as we should have this attitude towards claims of startling discoveries. Neither claim should be accepted without supporting evidence, and until very recently, in the present dispute the evidence was all on one side. A forthcoming book by C. E. M. Hansel will contain the most serious attempt—indeed one might say, the only really serious attempt—so far. Judging its contents from points made in correspondence and earlier papers by Hansel, one can only say that he has made the possibility of a rather complicated deception much more significant, though in my judgment still not as probable as the alternative.

It is commonly argued in discussions of the fraud hypothesis that no matter how unlikely fraud may be, it is still far *more* likely than the alleged extrasensory phenomena. George Price put this as a form of Hume's argument against miracles; miracles (or extrasensory phenomena) are incompatible with the laws of nature as we now understand them; the latter are supported by a gigantic body of evidence, hence this same evidence counts against the possibiltiy of miracles (or ESP) and far outweighs the probability of an alternative explanation of the effects. In short, if we have to choose between the evidence that fraud took place, admittedly slight, and the evidence that the laws of nature are false, then, since they are supported by so much evidence, the latter probability is far lower than the former. The main weaknesses in this argument are that it supposes the laws of nature to have been established in the region where extrasensory phenomena apply, and that it supposes a fundamental incompatibility between ESP and current physical laws. The argument suffers from another weakness, not specific to its application to ESP, and that is—it is too strong. If valid it would constitute an *a priori* disproof of any fundamental discovery that threatened previously established scientific systems—one thinks of Leverrier's observations on Mercury, for example. I have argued elsewhere that the relationship between current physical laws and extrasensory phenomena is that if accepted, the latter would require that the former be viewed as having a slightly more restricted range than one had carelessly supposed. It is only when the laws are extrapolated from the regions in which they have been directly supported by experimental evidence that they could come into conflict with ESP. Such an extrapolation is tempting, and appropriate enough in the absence of contrary evidence, but so weak that here—as so often before—the first well-substantiated counterclaims in the extended range cannot be dismissed as having high antecedent improbability, though it is true that the evidence for the present laws of nature supports them in a range where they are not jeopardized by the new results. There are, in addition, some grounds for doubting whether any laws of nature are in any way jeopardized by the new results. It is true that certain vague general principles which characterize many of our laws are rejected by ESP supporters, but I would class these general principles as being at the level of philosophical rather than physical insights, and consequently even more readily subject to reformulation.

I now turn to a criticism that has been made of the experiments on statistical grounds. This is the so-called "optional stopping!" The argument goes as follows. It is a theorem in statistics that if one proceeds long enough with a random series one will be able to find a point at which the deviation from chance of the results so far is as unlikely as one wishes. This is a much more sophisticated kind of criticism than the "what about the negative cases?" criticism. It rests on a theorem which is regarded as counter-intuitive by many well trained mathematicians. It is not the theorem that sooner or later in a random series one will find a sequence of the most unlikely kind—for example, sooner or later in throwing an unbiased die one will come across a run of 600 sixes. It is a theorem that has the consequence that sooner or later in throwing an unbiased die the average number of sixes thrown will diverge from one sixth of the total number of throws by enough to make the divergence as unlikely as one likes. The application of this theorem to ESP work is as follows: It is suggested that the basic experiments proceed up to the point where this extremely improbable divergence is observed and shortly thereafter are terminated, on the grounds that the subject is "losing his power." In reality, the subject is undergoing the to-be-expected drop back to his normal scoring rates. The reputation of this criticism is roughly that it cannot explain why the successful subject's performance is high at the beginning and continues at the same level throughout until the final terminating period. Subjects are not persisted with unless their initial performance is good. There is no policy of extensive testing of subjects who begin poorly, in the hope that they will ultimately turn in significantly deviant scores. Now the likelihood that a subject will *consistently* score at the level above chance that Mrs. Stewart achieved is not made any higher by the theorem. Hence we are correct to suppose that its improbability is so large as to require some alternative explanation.

The third kind of attack on the statistical theory involved in the interpretation of the results of the ESP tests is of an extremely fundamental kind. It involves nothing less than an attack on the meaningfulness of the concept of randomness itself. Whenever we interpret an ESP test, or any of a wide range of tests of the efficiency of fertilizers, the rate at which mathematics is learned, the reliability of the manufacturing process and so on, there is a stage at which we say "it is extremely unlikely, to such and such a degree, that the results observed could have come about by chance." If the degree mentioned is sufficiently high, then we commonly regard the case as proven for the existence of a significant and perhaps novel effect. The criticism now under consideration, put forward in its most widely-known form by Spencer Brown, suggests that this stage of the argument is faulty. No less an authority than R. A. Fisher gave this approach the sanction of his support at one stage. Now it *is* perfectly true that the concept of randomness is a rather elusive one, logically speaking. Moreover, and rather excitingly, Spencer Brown was able to uncover peculiarities in the tables of random numbers that experimenters usually employ to give their cards an unbiased sequence. These turned out to be due to the interference by the individuals responsible for publishing the tables, with the output of whatever device they were employing to give them a random sequence. This interference was prompted by the feeling that the sequence as it came from the apparatus was biased, e.g. because it had too many nine's in it. Hence the tables of "random numbers" were actually tables of mechanically produced sequences which looked random to their transcribers, a rather intuitive criterion.

However, to be practical about the matter, the logical difficulties do not have insuperable consequences for the practicing scientist and the weaknesses in the tables are rather slight, and corrections can be applied to the interpretations based on them which adequately compensate for the degree of bias introduced by the touchiness of the various compilers. There are three other crushing arguments against viewing this kind of attack as constituting a serious difficulty for the ESP work.

First, exactly the same statistics are used in the analysis of this work as elsewhere in science. And the use of these simple statistics in developing better hybrid corns, and better stamping machinery and vaccines, has for a long time borne so much fruit in practical benefits that we can have great confidence in its overall reliability. This rebuttal would not be satisfactory if the effects in question were of a very marginal kind. But they are, on the contrary, of a very clear-cut kind, at least as significant as any of the results uncovered in ordinary statistical experimentation.

Second, we need not rely in any way on an abstract analysis of randomness, nor on the use of random tables. We may just set to work and find out how often one pack of cards will match another pack of cards. This is a case when nobody is making a guess, and where we may set about finding out what happens when there is no intention to make a telepathic or clairvoyant perception. Half a million cards have been matched in this way, in one of the major investigations, and the results are absolutely indistinguishable from those which our usual theory of probability leads us to expect. Yet when one of the gifted subjects in these experiments attempts to set down a list of cards to match a hidden pack, the results are quite different. We can only conclude that this difference is due to some special feature of the experimental set-up, and in the reliable designs it appears that the only real difference is the telepathic intent.

Third, there is an internal feature of the results in the classic series that annihilates any kind of attack on these statistics. During the course of an experiment, and without informing the subject, the conditions were radically changed; instead of there being an agent who was examining the cards at the same time the subject was attempting to guess them, the agent would simply pass them from one pile to another without looking at them. Hence there was no opportunity for telepathy to occur. What was the effect on the scores by the subject at such times? The effect was striking and significant; the subject's scores would drop to the chance level whenever the conditions were changed in this way. That is, the subject was able to apprehend successfully the card on many occasions when there was somebody else in a distant place who knew what it was, but was not able to do this when there was no such person. Yet the same statistics apply whether or not someone is looking at the card. The *difference* between the subject's score when telepathy is possible and when it is not cannot therefore be explained by any feature of the statistical analysis. There is really a fourth weakness in this kind of an attack. The suggestion is that statistical analysis is absolutely indispensable to getting these startling results. It is not. There was a memorable occasion in the Soal series where R.H. Thouless suggested stacking the deck, again without informing the subject. The first twelve cards of the twenty-five were arranged to be the same and the next thirteen were arranged to be the same, though different from the first twelve. Under these conditions, we have the equivalent of what the communications engineer does when faced with the necessity for getting a message through a noisy line. He simply repeats the message a number of times, and the recipient picks out the most frequent symbol from each group of repetitions. In the experiment we are talking about, the results were unmistakable, and absolutely no use of statistics was involved. On each occasion where twelve or thirteen repetitions of the same signal were "sent," one symbol and only one occurred predominantly in the subject's responses. And this symbol was always the symbol that the agent was thinking about. It is worth adding that the conditions of this experiment were such as to bias it strongly against success. For the subject believed that she was guessing at a randomized pack, and was thus strongly motivated against producing multiple recurrences of the same "guess." Hence she was biased against uttering what was in fact the truth. The question is often asked why, if telepathy is possible, ordinary messages are not sent and received instead of these symbol codes. The answer is that it would be much easier to send them, and moreover in their most difficult form they have already been sent.

SUMMARY

I have now completed my listing of the criticisms that a thoughtful person would wish to hear answered before he would be satisfied to accept certain rather elementary claims of psychoanalysis and parapsychology—namely the claims that psychoanalysis does some good and that parapsychology studies something that exists. It is proper to be sceptical about the claims of these subjects if these criticisms cannot be met. It is not proper to suppose that because one does not know the answers to them oneself, the answers do not exist; a dull remark, but one which is really heated in these areas.

Now, what is the state of these two subjects in the light of the criticisms raised above? It seems perfectly clear that psychoanalysis has not met the appropriate objections, whereas parapsychology has met them. There is a brilliant paper in the literature which provides a detailed documentation of the parallelism between psychoanalysis and phrenology. I have here been concerned to stress the differences between psychoanalysis and another of the "disreputable subjects." I would sum up my conclusions in this way: psychoanalysis provides us with a great theory without a factual foundation; parapsychology, a factual basis on which there is yet to be built a great theory. I leave it to you to draw your own conclusions as to the scientific merits of these two conditions.

POSTSCRIPT

1. There are many cases of supposed extrasensory capacities on the part of animals. A number that have been carefully investigated turned out to be demonstrations of extreme sensory acuity, often on the unconscious level as far as the animal's owner was concerned. But there are areas—such as the homing of pigeons—where we have by no means eliminated the possibility of ESP as an explanation.

2. There is no strong evidence at the present moment for a correlation between extrasensory capacity and intelligence.

3. There is no strong evidence that ESP powers increase in individuals with any particular kind of brain damage. The evidence is slightly better for the improvement of ESP powers under certain kinds of relaxing treatment e.g. drugs, alcohol, and hypnosis.

4. The discovery of fraud on the part of a medium in the conventional seance phenomena is not adequate ground for supposing that she is capable of nothing but fraud. Any professional medium is under considerable pressure to produce phenomena on schedule. It is extremely unlikely that the kinds of phenomena we are concerned with can be produced on demand, hence it is extremely likely that a medium if she did have significant ESP powers would be constantly failing unless she were to "help them out" somewhat on some occasions. Of course one likes to breathe a sigh of relief when one uncovers fraud in these cases, but honesty requires a perpetual willingness to return to the investigation if any possibility

of genuine phenomena still exists, in the light of the consideration I have just mentioned.

5. ESP could be regarded as action at a distance; and so could electro-magnetic phenomena. On the other hand, both can be regarded as action through the medium of the field. The difference seems to me to be largely verbal, in the present state of the evidence. It is sometimes said that the velocity of propagation must be infinite for a phenomenon to constitute action at a distance. But the velocity of propagation of eletro-magnetic phenomena from the frame of reference of the signal itself is infinite (in the sense that no time passes, though distance is covered) and I rather think that is the crucial frame of reference for this issue.

6. We have no grounds for saying that telepathic propagation operates according to an inverse square of the distance law, but we also have no grounds for saying that it does not. The effects so far could be quite well explained by supposing that there is an inverse square law but that the receptor sensitivity is extremely high, just as they could be quite well explained by supposing that there is no fall-off at distance. Pratt's recent work has suggested that taking all the distance studies together one does find some support for an inverse square law.

7. The evidence for precognition seems to me substantially weaker than the evidence for telepathy or clairvoyance. The evidence for psychokinesis seems to me very much less satisfactory than for precognition. Propagation hypotheses that can handle precognition are of course extremely tricky.

8. When I say that psychoanalysis is a theory without a factual foundation, I do not intend to suggest that it is a theory without any facts to explain. It is indeed a theory about certain kinds of facts, notably facts about the behavior of children and neurotics, and about our own aberrant behavior, as well as about normal adult behavior. But having facts to explain is not the same thing as having facts to support a theory. The facts which are supposed to support the claims of therapeutic efficacy on the part of psycho-analysis are at the moment more readily explicable in terms of less novel hypotheses. The various hypotheses in psychoanalysis that are concerned with process rather than outcome have not been discussed in this paper, and provide a very much more complicated

problem. It must be stressed that the correctness of psychoanalytic process hypotheses would lend almost no support to the claim of psychotherapeutic efficacy, *and vice versa*.

CHAPTER 5

STRANGE FACTS IN SEARCH OF A THEORY*

C. W. K. MUNDLE

THE PHENOMENA INVESTIGATED by our Society have included spirit lights seen at seances. I shall start by quoting a case from the Scottish highlands illustrating belief in spirit lights of a different type. A doctor was called out at night to attend a confinement in a remote croft. Knowing it to be lit only by a single oil lamp, he took a powerful electric torch which he gave to the elderly husband to hold during the delivery. After a pair of twins had been washed and swaddled, the doctor announced that there was still another to come. Suddenly the torch was extinguished and the father's arm fell to his side. 'Shine the torch man', the doctor said. 'How can I work without a light?' The father's reply was gruff, firm, and with a deep note of resentment, 'I will do no such thing, doctor. *Cannot you see that it is the light that is attracting them?*'[1]

And now let us be serious. Consider a viewpoint expressed by Professor H. H. Price, who was referring primarily to ESP. He wrote:

> The theoretical side of psychical research has lagged far behind the evidential side. And that, I believe, is one of the main reasons why the evidence itself is still ignored by so many . . . highly educated people. It is because these queer facts apparently 'make no sense' . . . that they tend to make no permanent impression on the mind. . . . If we could devise some theoretical explanation . . . in terms of which the facts did make sense . . . it would be a great

*Presidential Address, 1972, Society for Psychical Research. Reprinted by permission of the Society.
[1]This story is told by Gavin Maxwell in *Raven Seek Thy Brother* (1968), p. 97.

gain. Such an explanation is needed for its own sake; and it is also needed to get the evidence attended to and considered.[2]

Others have endorsed this thesis, but it might have surprised the founders of our Society. Today an outsider might ask 'Why describe card-guessing experiments as *psychical* research?' The answer is that the founders of our Society so described their subject because their concern was to find facts to support a theory which they wished to defend—some form of dualism of mind and matter. In his presidential address in 1900, Frederic Myers described the Society's goal as being to provide 'the preamble of all religions', by making it possible to say to theologians and philosophers: 'thus we demonstrate that a spiritual world exists, a world of independent and abiding realities, not a mere "epiphenomenon" or transitory effect of the material word'.[3] Indeed, he went on to express his conviction that this goal had already been achieved, saying: 'our method has revealed to us a hidden world within us, and . . . this hidden world within us has revealed to us an invisible world without'. Henry Sidgwick, our first president, was more cautious than Myers and less disposed to wear his soul upon his sleeve. For example, he said in his first presidential address that 'any particular investigation that we make should be carried on with a single-minded desire to ascertain the facts and *without any foregone conclusion as 'to their nature'*.[4] He made it clear, however, in his second presidential address that his motivation was much the same as that of Myers. He said:

> When we took up seriously the obscure and perplexing investigation which we call *Psychical Research,* we were mainly moved to do so by the profound and painful division and conflict, as regards the nature and destiny of the human soul, which we found in the thought of our age. On the one hand, under the influence of Christian teaching . . . the soul is conceived as independent of the bodily organism and destined to survive it. On the other hand, the preponderant tendency of modern physiology has been more and more to exclude this conception. . . . We believed unreservedly in the methods of modern science . . . but we were not prepared to bow with equal docility to the mere prejudices of scientific men. And it ap-

---

[2]*Enquiry* (July, 1949), p. 20.
[3]*Proceedings.* XV, p. 117.
[4]*Proceedings,* I, p. 8.

peared to us that there was an important body of evidence—tending *prima facie* to establish the independence of soul or spirit—which modern science had simply left on one side . . . evidence tending to throw light on the question of the action of mind either apart from the body or otherwise than through known bodily organs.[5]

And in his third presidential address, Sidgwick said:

"There is not one of us who would not feel ten times more interest in proving the action of intelligence other than those of living men, than in proving communication of human minds in an abnormal way."[6] It seems fair then to say that psychical research originated as a theory in search of facts which would confirm it; and the phenomena selected for study by the Society's members have been singled out precisely because they have seemed to provide evidence for the theory in question.

When Professor Price wrote that in order to get people to pay heed to the strange facts we need a theory which makes sense of them, he cannot have been referring to the theory which inspired psychical research. For this theory is only too familiar to all people in our culture. We became familiar with it in being taught Christianity and other religions. This theory is, in its essentials, simple, namely that a person's mind, soul or spirit is immaterial and not subject to physical laws, that it interacts with, but does not depend for its existence upon, his body, and that it can survive the death of the body. If we accept this theory, it *does* make sense of many of the strange facts, and it should not surprise us if our minds are, in Sidgwick's phrase, capable of 'action apart from the body'. I suggest that one of the main reasons why many scientifically educated people dismiss or ignore the evidence of ESP is because they reject the dualist theory of human nature, and because so often the strange facts are not only presented as evidence for this theory but are described in language which seems to presuppose its truth. Those who ignore the strange facts might defend their attitude by quoting Professor C. D. Broad. He has said that the facts in question conflict with principles which are 'overwhelmingly supported by all the empirical facts which fall within the range of ordinary experience and the scientific elaborations of it', and notably with

---

[5]*Proceedings,* V, pp. 272-3.
[6]*Proceedings,* V, p. 401.

the principles which Broad presents under the heading 'Dependence of Mind on Brain', namely:

> A necessary, even if not a sufficient, immediate condition of any mental event is an event in the brain of a living body. Each different mental event is immediately conditioned by a different brain-event . . . Mental events which are so interconnected as to be experiences of the same person are immediately conditioned by brain-events which happen in the same brain.[7]

Some philosophers and scientists would consider that Broad's way of decribing the dependence of mind upon brain is too weak. They would claim not merely that each mental event is 'immediately conditioned' by a brain event, but that it is completely determined by brain-processes and has no independent causal efficacy. *(ability to bring things about)* This is the position called 'Epiphenomenalism'. Some contemporary philosophers go even further and adopt what they usually call 'the Identity theory'. They claim that a mental event, e.g. state of consciousness, *is* a brain-process, that it is the subjective aspect of this physical process. According to each of these theories it is misleading to speak, as Broad did, of a mental event producing a change in the brain; for when, as we say, a person's action is caused by his conscious act of choice, it is really a case of *other* physical processes being initiated *by a brain-process,* by one which manifests itself subjectively as a conscious choice. Neither of these materialistic theories can at present be confirmed by experiment, but it is possible that future research might yield facts which would make one or other of them seem well-nigh inescapable. If a person's cerebral cortex is exposed while he is under a local anaesthetic so that he remains conscious, his arm can be made to rise whenever a certain point on his cortex is touched with an electrode, and he experiences such arm-movements as involuntary. But when more is known about the brain and more delicate methods of stimulating it are developed, a brain-surgeon may be able, by titillating a person's brain, to make him have the experience of choosing to raise his arm, and perhaps of choosing to but finding himself unable to do so. Then are we entitled to claim, as Broad has done, that

---

[7]"The Relevance of Psychical Research to Philosophy," *Philosophy* (Oct. 1949), pp. 291-4.

psychical research has 'undermined the epiphenomenalist view of the human mind'?[8]

As the founders of our Society recognised, the only decisive way of refuting epiphenomenalism would be by establishing the continued existence of the minds of deceased persons, on the evidence of communications received through trance-mediums, automatic writing, and so on. In view of the information contained in some such 'messages', there is, on the face of it, a formidable case for concluding that they are what they are presented as being, communications from the spirits of former human beings. But it is now generally recognized that we cannot eliminate an alternative explanation of these facts, namely that this information has been acquired by ESP exercised by the medium and/or other living people. Some critical investigators still hold, however, that the latter explanation is less plausible than the hypothesis of spirit-communication.[9] Their two main arguments are these:

(i) that the alternative explanation requires us to attribute to mediums the exercise of ESP of a kind or a complexity for which we have no independent evidence; 'super-ESP' as Dr. Alan Gauld has called it, because the medium must be supposed to select and piece together information from people whom she has never met and places she has never visited;

(ii) that in some cases, where a spirit-communicator purports to be controlling the medium's body, the medium has impersonated the deceased communicator, speaking in a voice and using phrases and mannerisms characteristic of the communicator and uncharacteristic of the medium herself.

These considerations led Broad to conclude that 'any attempt to explain these phenomena by reference to telepathy among the living stretches the word "telepathy" until it becomes almost meaningless and uses [it] to cover something for which there is no *independent* evidence'.[10]

I think that Broad overstates the case against the super-ESP

---

[8]*Ibid.*, p. 309.

[9]For example, C. J. Ducasse in *The Belief in Life After Death* (1961), C. D. Broad in *Lectures on Psychical Research* (1962) and Alan Gauld in *The Founders of Psychical Research* (1968).

[10]*Lectures on Psychical Research, op. cit.,* p. 427.

hypothesis. The second argument would have considerable weight were it not for the remarkable Gordon Davis case.[11] During some sittings which Dr. S. G. Soal held in 1922 with a 'direct voice' medium, Mrs. Cooper, a new 'communicator', popped up. He called himself 'Gordon Davis', and Soal remembered someone of this name—a boy he had known slightly at school over twenty years earlier and whom he had not met since, except for a half-hour encounter in 1916. Soal recorded at the time of his sittings with Mrs. Cooper that he was much impressed by her 'lifelike reproduction of the mannerisms of speech, tone of voice and accent' of Gordon Davis. Soal then believed that Gordon Davis had been killed during the war. But three years later, in 1925, Soal discovered that Gordon Davis was still alive, so this case undermines the argument that a medium's impersonation of an ostensible communicator need be explained in terms of communication from a departed spirit. It also undermines the other argument for the spirit-communication hypothesis, since what Mrs. Cooper presented as messages from the spirit of Gordon Davis contained some accurate and fairly specific information about the house which Davis was, at the time of the sittings, negotiating to buy, and did later buy and live in; and this information was presumably acquired, *via* telepathy, from Davis himself.* It would appear then that the person sitting with the medium may function as a sign-post directing the medium's telepathic powers to people she has never met. This hypothesis could explain most, if not all,[12] of the so-called proxy sittings,

---

[11]S.G. Soal, "A Report of Some Communications Received through Mrs. Blanche Cooper," *Proceedings*, XXXV.

*Some of Mrs. Cooper's statements seemed to involve precognition, since they described some later contents of the Gordon Davis home, e.g. pictures of the sea which Gordon Davis acquired in 1924 and the 'dickie bird' on the piano. But presumably her ESP would not have become focused upon such things unless she had formed some telepathic rapport with Gordon Davis, mediated by telepathy with Soal. A different interpretation is, however, possible, i.e. that Soal did the precognising and Mrs. Cooper got the information by telepathy from Soal.

[12]It could not explain all of them if decisively significant results should be obtained with the method used by H.F. Saltmarsh in his 'Absent Sitter' experiments, for here both the proxy and the medium knew nothing about the deceased person, D, from whom a message was sought, except that he had owned some small object concealed in a package which the proxy gave to the medium. But this method was strikingly less successful than when the sitter was acquainted with D. (See H.F. Saltmarsh, "Report on the Investigation of Some Sittings with Mrs. Warren Elliott," *Proceedings*, XXXIX, esp. pp. 53-55 and 89-91).

where the sitter is not acquainted with the deceased person from whom a message is sought, and is deputising for those who seek such a message.[13] Admittedly there is no experimental evidence that anyone has employed ESP in quite this way. But this is not surprising, if, as I believe, no one has conducted telepathy experiments in which the subject's task has corresponded to what we are supposing the medium to have done. Some experimenters, however, have reported that their subjects were successful in piecing together information obtained telepathically from two different people, as in Professor Charles Richet's experiments reported in 1884,[14] and the 'Split Agent' experiments which Soal did with Mrs. Stewart.[15] It would not be difficult to adapt Soal's Split Agent experiment to test the sort of hypothesis we are considering.† Until some such experiments have been tried with star subjects, one is not entitled to claim that spirit-communication must be accepted on the ground that the alternative explanation would involve ESP too super to be credible.

It is sometimes argued that, despite the inconclusiveness of the case for spirit-communication, the mere occurrence of telepathy among the living suffices to refute any form of materialism. Professor Price has argued that 'there is no room for telepathy in a Materialistic universe'.[16] Those who argue thus commonly operate with a conception of ESP which presupposes dualism, telepathy being conceived as a direct influence of one mind upon another mind, or as direct cognition of the contents of another person's mind. The public may be given the impression that part of what is *meant* by "telepathy" is that no role is played by cerebral processes in either the agent or the percipient.[17] This is a question-begging procedure. The distinction between telepathy and clairvoyance is

[13]See, for example, C. Drayton Thomas, "A Proxy Case Extending over Eleven Sittings with Mrs. Osborne Leonard." *Proceedings,* XLIII.
[14]"M. Richet's Recent Researches in Thought-transference,' *Proceedings, II.*
[15]S.G. Soal and F. Bateman, *Modern Experiments in Telepathy,* (1954), ch. XIII.
†Part of the information determining the current target would be possessed only by Agent 1 and part only by Agent 2. Agent 1 would be acquainted with Agent 2, but the subject would be acquainted only with Agent 1.
[16]"Psychical Research and Human Personality," *Hibbert Journal,* (1948-1949), p. 109.
[17]Professor A.J. Ayer, for example, has equated telepathy with 'one person's directly inspecting the private experiences of another.' *The Problem of Knowledge,* (1956), p. 231.

normally made by saying that in telepathy the source of the percipient's information is another person's mind and in clairvoyance the source is something physical. But what right have we to assume that, in the cases which we classify as telepathy, the source of the information is the agent's state of mind and not the brain processes which accompany, and for all we know determine, his state of mind? If the source of the information is in fact the agent's brain processes, it is clairvoyance as this term is normally defined. The standard definitions are defective because they make telepathy unverifiable, for we cannot verify that any particular state of mind is *not* accompanied and caused by some brain process. We need to redefine "telepathy". We should not simply define it as 'ESP in which the information originates from another person', for we must allow for the possibility that a person may 'clairvoyantly perceive' another person's overt behavior or utterances and thereby learn about his thoughts or feelings. "Telepathy" should, I suggest, be defined as ESP in which the source of the information is either the private mental states *or* the corresponding brain processes of another person.

Bearing this in mind, the case for Price's conclusion that there is no room for telepathy in a materialistic universe has to be based on the premise that no physical process, analogous to wireless waves, can carry the information from agent to percipient. There is a strong case for accepting this premise. All known forms of physical radiation which might be supposed to fill this bill are attenuated at increasing distances and are absorbed by obstacles like mountains or lead screens, and there is a good deal of evidence that these factors do not affect telepathy. This indicates that we must reject the type of theory of telepathy adopted by Democritus nearly 2,500 years ago. (He ascribed telepathy to transmission of corpuscles from brain to brain.) But does it follow that there can be no theory of telepathy which is consistent with materialism? Some scientists do not think so. Hans Berger, the physiologist who invented the electroencephalograph, recognised that the electrical rhythms which he had thereby detected in the brain are much too weak to transmit telepathic information. He suggested that electrical energy in the agent's brain is transformed into what he called 'psychic energy', which can be diffused over any distance, and can pass through physical barriers, without attenuation; and that, on reaching the percipient's brain, it is transformed back into electrical energy and produces neural patterns and hence thoughts, images or feelings corresponding to those of the agent. But although Berger used the term "psychic energy", he was not a dualist. He conceived psychic energy as one of the forms of physical energy.[18]

(Another unorthodox materialistic theory has been put forward by Mr. Ninian Marshall.[19] Like Berger he accepts epiphenomenalism, but unlike Berger he supposes that telepathy involves action at a distance—that the brain of the agent affects that of the percipient without any intervening process or any transmission of physical energy. To render this idea intelligible, Marshall presents his 'hypothesis of resonance', according to which any two physical things exert an influence upon each other which tends to make them become more alike, the strength of this influence being greater in proportion to (i) the complexity of the structure of the things in question, and (ii) the degree of similarity of structure which they already possess. This hypothetical force he labels 'the eidopoic influence'. He argues that this force has hitherto produced observable effects only in the form of ESP, because the human brain is the most complex physical structure in the world. He predicts, however, that telepathy-type interaction between computers will be detectable if or when such machines are produced which have a complexity comparable to that of our brains.)

There are some experimental results which fit more naturally into Marshall's theory than into any mentalistic theory. For example, Dr. Stephan Figar's experiments using plethysmography,[20] which is a method of measuring involuntary changes in the volume of some part of a person's body associated with changes in the blood-circulation. In Figar's experiment there were two subjects who were screened from each other. We are told that neither subject knew of the other's existence nor was told anything about the purpose of the experiment. Plethysmographic measurements were

---

[18]H. Berger, *Psyche*, (Jena, 1940).

[19]"ESP and Memory: A Physical Theory," *British Journal for the Philosophy of Science,* (1959-60).

[20]"The Application of Plethysmography to the Objective Study of so-called Extra-Sensory Perception," *Journal*, (No. 702, Dec. 1959).

simultaneously made of one hand of each subject and the resulting curves were mechanically recorded in parallel on a single tape. The experimenter periodically showed to subject No. 1 a card on which was written a multiplication problem which he had to solve in his head. The normal accompaniment of such a mental effort is a vascular constriction and this regularly occurred in subject No. 1 while he was calculating. In about 40 percent of the trials the hand of the subject No. 2 showed the same reaction within a few seconds of No. 1 being given a sum to solve. Dr. D. J. West analysed Figar's data, taking into account the records during the rest-periods, and he found that the results were statistically highly significant. Other experimenters have reported positive results using the same method.[21] The Figar-phenomenon does not look like a transfer of what we should normally call 'information'. It suggests that telepathy may be a special case of something more general—a tendency for organisms (of the same species?) so to interact that their physiological responses or rhythms (and hence their behavior) become more similar or better synchronised. Such a tendency might play the role in organic evolution which Sir Alister Hardy has ascribed to telepathy, namely: 'in developing and stabilising [among members of the same species] common behavioral patterns'.[22]

Our theoretical problems would seem manageable, and relatively simple, if only the strange facts could all be analysed in terms of telepathy. Unfortunately the facts are not so obliging. In 1945, Whately Carington expressed the view that the evidence for clairvoyance could be explained in terms of precognitive telepathy.[23] He had, however, overlooked the implications of one of Mr. G.N.M. Tyrrell's experiments.[24] Tyrrell's subject, Miss Johnson, sat beside five small light-tight boxes each containing a tiny electric lamp. Her task was to open the box in which the lamp had just been lit, or would be lit IF she opened the right box. Tyrrell, screened from Miss Johnson, made a lamp light by pressing one of five keys. The electrical connections between keys and lamps were 'scrambled' by

[21]See E. Douglas Dean and Carroll B. Nash, "Coincident Plethysmographic Results Under Controlled Conditions," *Journal*, (No. 731, March, 1967).
[22]*The Living Stream*, (1965), p. 255.
[23]*Telepathy*, (1945), p. 91.
[24]"Further Research in Extra-sensory Perception," *Proceedings*, XLIV, esp. pp. 148-149.

a commutator contained in a closed box. The result for each trial was recorded automatically on a moving tape. One line was drawn on the tape whenever any *one* box was opened. When the correct box was opened a second line was drawn parallel to the other. The crucial point to note is that the record on the tape gave no indication *which* box had been opened at any trial. In view of this, precognitive telepathy could not have helped Miss Johnson. Suppose that she could 'precognise', from the mind or brain of a person who later inspected the tape, that at the next trial she was going to score a hit; this could not help her decide which box to open. This may be described as a pure clairvoyance experiment, and under these conditions Miss Johnson scored at her usual level—nearly 40 percent higher than mean chance expectation.

It looks as if we shall also be obliged to acknowledge the occurrence of psychokinesis; i.e. the ability of a person, simply by willing or wishing, to influence physical processes occurring at a distance from his body. This is alarming because it would reintroduce a kind of magical causation from belief in which science had liberated us. Indeed it would undermine the scientists' experimental methods, for when a scientist seeks by experiment to verify his preferred hypothesis, his hopes would be liable to bias his results, despite all the precautions he might take. According to Sir Ronald Fisher, the results of Mendel's classic experiment in genetics conformed much too closely to his own hypothesis, so closely that Mendel's published figures would be a statistical miracle.[25] If psychokinesis is a genuine phenomenon, this is the sort of thing we should expect, and Mendel or his assistants need not be supposed to have miscounted or cooked the results. But in that case scientists should long ago have noticed a tendency for the same experiment to yield different results depending on whether the experimenter hopes to confirm or to refute the hypothesis being tested. We cannot, however, dismiss the evidence for psychokinesis. Positive results have been reported when people sought, by willing, to influence the falls of dice, the rate of growth of plants, and the movements of animals, including cats and single-celled organisms like the Paramecium.*

---

[25]See Sir Alister Hardy, *op. cit.*, pp. 84-89.

*Where the animals which are influenced are like cats in having a complex central nervous system, we may interpret it either as psychokinesis or as telepathy. But where do we draw the line? Should we speak of telepathy between people and paramecia?

These results cannot be explained in terms of Marshall's 'eidopoic influence', which involves some sort of resonance between things of similar structure. Dice, mushrooms and paramecia are not similar in structure to a human brain, nor indeed to each other. For the same reason Marshall's theory is incompatible with clairvoyance. The physical things, like patterns on cards, to which subjects have responded in clairvoyance experiments are not at all similar in structure to a human brain. Berger's theory might conceivably be adapted to cover psychokinesis, though it seems inconsistent to suppose both that his 'psychic energy' can produce changes in material things *and* that it passes through such things without loss of energy. In any case Berger's theory can scarcely be adapted to cover clairvoyance. We should have to suppose that psychic energy is emitted not only by brains but by Zener cards, electric lamps, and, presumably, by all physical objects. Since the supposed psychic energy is not impeded by physical barriers like lead screens, it must be very different in nature from light-waves. How then could we explain the fact that the information conveyed by clairvoyance commonly concerns the *visible* qualities of things, e.g. their colors? The things which look to us the same color do not have any intrinsic *physical* property in common. It is only relative to the human eye that they have a property in common, a complex causal property—that of reflecting one or other of an infinite number of mixtures of different wave-lengths each of which mixtures stimulates in the same ratio the three cones in a normal human eye. It would be an incredible coincidence if Berger's psychic energy, though physically very different from light-waves, nevertheless transmitted from physical objects some modification from which its source could be identified as red, despite the fact that the things which look red to us have no intrinsic physical property in common.

If you do not follow that abstract argument, just try to conceive a materialistic theory which could explain success in clairvoyance experiments using what Dr. J. B. Rhine calls 'the Down Through method', where the pack of cards lies bunched together and the subject guesses the symbols from top to bottom. How could the subject discriminate physical signals supposedly originating from the different cards? We should expect any such signals to interfere with each other. It seems equally difficult to conceive any materialistic theory which could explain psychometry—the ability to report facts about a person's life by touching or looking at some trinket which once belonged to that person. Should we then conclude, in Myers' words: 'thus we demonstrate that a spiritual world exists'? Well, if materialism is to be rejected in favor of dualism on the ground that materialism cannot explain all kinds of ESP, it needs to be shown that, and how, all kinds of ESP can be explained in terms of immaterial minds. The mentalistic theories (or, if you prefer, the psychic theories) which are on offer are about as vague and general as the materialistic theories of Berger and Marshall. The commonest move is to postulate a common or collective unconscious mind, an idea poetically expressed by William James by saying: "There is a continuum of cosmic consciousness against which our individuality builds but accidental fences, and into which our several minds plunge as into a mothersea."[26] Some of you may feel that we should be content with some such metaphor, perhaps with one which is more simply expressed: "One light, many lamps." But if we ask how such metaphors are supposed to help us to explain ESP, two distinct answers may be given. One was given by Carington who conceived a simple, and in principle readily verifiable, theory of telepathy.[27] His axiom is that if two ideas become associated by one person, P, this increases the probability that, when *any* person, and not just P, thinks of one of these ideas, he will think of the other. This theory led Carington to discover in his own earlier telepathy experiments confirmation of certain sub-laws of the traditional theory of Association of Ideas (the sub-laws concerning recency and frequency of association). The question which then called out for an answer is: *How* can associations of ideas in one mind influence other minds? Carington's last book was an attempt to answer this question.[28] He argued that questions about the transmission of ideas from one mind to another simply do not arise, that the contents of our several minds literally overlap, that each mind is *composed* of ideas (or 'cognita', the term he preferred later) and that most of the ideas which constitute one person's

---

[26]Gardner Murphy and R.O. Ballou (eds.), *William James and Psychical Research*, (1961), p. 324.

[27]*Telepathy, op. cit.*, ch. VI.

[28]*Matter, Mind and Meaning*, (1949), esp. pp. 203 ff.

mind are, not just similar to, but numerically identical with ideas which are also constituents of other people's minds. Carington did not go so far as to postulate a cosmic consciousness or an all-embracing collective unconscious. He supposed rather that there is a collective unconscious, or 'group mind', for each species of living animal, including the human animal. He conceived a group mind as a repository of those associations of ideas which are responsible for the instinctive behavior patterns peculiar to the species.* However, by not postulating an all-embracing group mind, Carington deprived himself of the only method by which his theory could have been stretched to cover the facts normally classified as clairvoyance. (See below.)

The other line of reasoning which may underlie an appeal to a collective unconscious was made explicit in a paper given to this Society in 1937 by Professor C.A. Mace.[29] This involves extending to ESP the kind of explanation which is most commonly given of memory, namely that a person's earlier experiences leave engrams or traces in his brain, and that these engrams can later be excited by appropriate stimuli, thereby giving rise to recollections (or to learned behavior patterns). Mace suggests that the conception of the collective unconscious may be interpreted as implying that each person's experiences leave engrams, not only in his brain, but also in some inter-personal stuff, and that, in special circumstances, such an engram may affect the experience or behavior of people other than the person whose experience was the source of the engram. This would be a way of explaining telepathy. Notice, however, that it does not imply that the hypothetical stuff which bears engrams is mental rather physical. Mace makes this point by acknowledging that, although 'untutored opinion' would think of it as 'psychic ether', it should be described, non-committally, as 'our Tertium Quid'. (He might have used John Locke's phrase: 'something I know not what'.) Now if this sort of theory is to be stretched to cover clairvoyance, then, as Mace says, we should have to adopt the extravagant hypothesis that 'anything that happens anywhere is duly recorded', i.e. in the Tertium Quid. Though Mace did not

*Compare this with Sir Alister Hardy's views in ch. IX of *The Living Stream, op. cit.*
[29]"Supernormal Faculty and the Structure of the Mind," *Proceedings,* XLIV, esp. pp. 300-301.

say so, it would then be but a short step to identify the Tertium Quid with the Divine Mind. What else, one might ask, *could* record everything that happens everywhere? In that case clairvoyance would be reduced to telepathy, telepathy in which God is function- ing as the agent. (And this is how Carington's theory could be stretched to accommodate clairvoyance.) I doubt, however, whether many theologians will wish to embrace this explanation of ESP. It would be different if the information conveyed by ESP were reliable and beneficial to the recipient or others like Rosalind Heywood's 'Orders'. (And if any of you do not know about Mrs. Heywood's Orders, I urge you to read her admirable book *The Infinite Hive.*) But why should the Deity vouchsafe useless information about card-symbols but only to a select few and only a little more fre- quently than the chance-level?

I shall now consider another type of mentalistic theory, one which has been commended as the most hopeful by Professors Price[30] and Broad.[31] This is the theory of perception adumbrated by Henri Bergson in *Matter and Memory* and applied to ESP in his presidential address to our Society in 1913.[32] Broad once said about this theory: "I find it impossible to precipitate anything definite from the cloud of metaphors in which it hovers in Bergson's works," and what I shall say about Bergson's thought is subject to the qualification "if I understand him correctly." His theory of perception grew out of his theory of memory. He held that a person retains memories of *all* of his past experiences and previously acquired knowledge; that remembering must be a function of an immaterial mind, on the ground that memories cannot be stored in the brain, which is designed as a switching centre and not as a storehouse; that memories are retained as mental images; and that the relevant function of the brain is not positive, not to *produce* memory-images or awareness of them, but negative, i.e. to *exclude* from consciousness all memory-images apart from those few which are relevant in choosing one's present action (though he qualified this by saying that when we are idle, e.g. daydreaming, we may

---

[30]*Aristotelian Society,* Supp. Vol. XVI, (1937), pp. 227-228.
[31]His paper in *Philosophy, op. cit.,* p. 306.
[32]*Proceedings,* XXVI.

become aware of memory-images which are not relevant to present actions). Note that the fact that special techniques, like hypnosis, enable people to dredge unexpected details from the past gives plausibility to Bergson's assumption that all of our past experiences are retained, but it does nothing to support his view that the role of the brain-processes is negative. Bergson went on to sketch a similar theory of perception; according to which the function of the relevant processes in the sense-organs and brain is not positive, not to *produce* either sense-data or an awareness of the external objects which are consciously perceived, but is negative, i.e. to *exclude* from consciousness the perception of everything except those physical things which are relevant to one's present actions. Bergson assumed that the central nervous system has evolved as an instrument to serve our *practical* needs, to facilitate our acting in ways which have survival-value; and that unless our brains suppressed from consciousness almost all of the available data of memory and perception, we should be bewildered by a mass of useless information. According to this theory, it is not the existence of clairvoyant perception which needs to be explained, but the fact that so much of it is suppressed. Bergson simply assumed that a person is clairvoyantly acquainted with all* contemporary physical objects and events. Combining this with his account of memory, it seems to be implied that a person is capable of recollecting not only everything which he has ever *consciously* perceived, but every physical event which has happened anywhere since he was born!

What are we to say about this bold theory? I suggest that this way of making sense of the occasional occurrence of clairvoyance exacts too high a price, notably that it makes nonsense of nearly everything that the sciences have established about sense-perception. Admittedly there is one respect in which our perceptual apparatus may be said to exclude information. Our sense-organs are insensitive to many forms of physical energy, e.g. magnetic forces, and our eyes are unresponsive to light-waves whose wave-lengths fall outside a narrow range of less than one octave. But there are hosts of familiar facts which indicate that the function of physical stimu-

---

*In his presidential address, Bergson expressed qualms about saying 'all.' But if not all, *which?* He offered no answer.

lation of our sense-organs is positive, i.e. to convey information about the sources of the stimuli. The contents of one's sense-experience can be systematically altered in so many detailed ways by changes in the stimuli. Changes in the wavelength or the strength of the light alter the sense-given colors or brightness of the things seen, changes in the frequency of the sound-waves alter the pitch of the sound heard, and so on. In view of such facts, what could scientists make of the suggestion that the function of such stimuli is to make the brain suppress our knowledge of everything other than the sources of the stimuli? And if, as Bergson held, the sense-organs and brain have evolved this role because of its survival-value, why has natural selection been so uncharacteristically inefficient? If a rabbit's brain did not suppress its clairvoyant perception of the fox hidden in the bracken, if our brains did not suppress our clairvoyant vision of things behind our backs, this would have had considerable survival value, much more than, e.g. our ability to see rainbows. Bergson's theory makes it an incredible coincidence that sense-perception informs us only of things which are transmitting energy to our sense-organs, and only of features of these things which are (or have been)* represented by features of the stimuli. Yet despite its extravagance, his theory does not accommodate telepathy. The clairvoyant perception of all the people in China which I now have, according to Bergson, is presumably of the same kind as my present perception of you (my audience). This informs me about some of your visible features, of the noises you may emit, but *not* of your concealed thoughts or feelings or corresponding processes in your brains. There is a hint in Bergson's presidential address that he recognised this point and that, to explain telepathy, he would have wished to adopt also a theory of a common unconscious.†

I have postponed discussion of what strikes me as the strangest class of the strange facts, if it is taken at its face value. I refer to precognition conceived as non-inferential knowledge about future events. Some people regard precognition as non-puzzling on the

---

*I add 'or have been' to take account of the role played in perception by memory.
†"Mais si elles [nos consciences] ne tiennent au corps que par une partie d'elles-mêmes, on peut conjecturer que, pour le reste, elles ne sont pas aussi nettement séparées" (*op. cit.*, p. 475).

ground that a theory which makes sense of it is already available, a theory popularised by recent physics, namely that the physical universe is a 4-dimensional manifold, time being conceived as a fourth dimension of space, at right angles to each of the other three dimensions. This conceptual scheme could render intelligible precognition and also paranormal retrocognition, provided that it is itself intelligible. But is it? There may seem to be no difficulty in supposing that the whole history of the universe timelessly coexists, that the past and the future are spread out in a fourth dimension along which we observers move. We are invited to picture a point moving along a line, and the point is to represent one's consciousness conceived as a searchlight which illuminates a changing 3-D slice of the 4-D manifold. But consider the implications.

I think that we should have to reject this theory as intolerably extravagant if it implied, as J.W. Dunne believed, that there is an infinite number of time dimensions and that each of us is a sort of Chinese box—a 3-D observer within a 4-D observer within a 5-D observer and so on *ad infinitum*.[33] Actually Dunne did not need to draw these conclusions. He did so because his premises were inconsistent. One of his inconsistencies was in assuming that each of us is a *3-D observer* moving through a 4-D world. But if the physical universe is a 4-D manifold, each of the physical objects which it contains must be a 4-D solid, and this must apply to human bodies as well as inanimate objects. If one spatialises time and supposes that past and future coexist, one is logically obliged to exclude motion from the physical universe. (Unless you suppose that the physical universe *as a whole* moves in some time-dimension other than the one which has been spatialised, but this would not explain precognition.) What would correspond, in the new conceptual scheme, to what we now think of as the movement of a 3-D body, would be purely *geometrical* relationships between different parts of a 4-D body. It is, however, an empirical fact that we are conscious of things moving and otherwise changing. Since, in the new conceptual scheme, movement and change cannot be ascribed to physical things, including human bodies, our consciousness of change must be ascribed to something nonphysical. Presumably it

---

[33]*An Experiment with Time,* (1928), and *The Serial Universe,* (1934).

must be an immaterial mind which is successively conscious of adjacent cross-sections of the 4-D manifold. That the 4-D world theory commits them to dualism is not usually recognised by the physicists who accept this theory.

I am not committed to any specific theory about the relationship between mind and matter. I think that epiphenomenalism and orthodox dualism are both intelligible and that either of them *may* be true. My main objection to the 4-D world theory is that it commits one to a form of dualism which seems incredible. According to orthodox versions of dualism, there is *two*-way interaction between a person's mind and his body, and some of a person's bodily movements are his actions by virtue of their being initiated by his states or acts of mind, e.g. wishes or choices. But the theory which I am considering requires that what you now conceive of as your bodily actions should not be so conceived, since they are not really movements at all, but rather bends or twists in the *shape* of a 4-D solid all of which existed before you became conscious of anything. It is a corollary of the 4-D world theory that the role of the mind is confined to being a passive spectator of what is there waiting to be perceived. The feature of epiphenomenalism which makes it most repugnant to orthodox dualists is shared by this strange form of dualism, namely that states of consciousness have no causal efficacy—they are determined by the structure of the physical world but they cannot affect or alter that structure. Dunne tried to avoid the fatalistic implications of this sort of theory. He claimed that a person may have a precognition of an undesirable event and, as a result of this, may prevent the fulfilment of the precognition. Just as you can alter the shape of a piece of cardboard along its whole length by bending it at one point, so according to Dunne, you can instantaneously alter future stretches of the 4-D world by your present action. Well, suppose it is written in the book of history that John Brown is to die in an air-crash on his twentieth birthday, but a few days earlier he has a precognitive dream and this leads him to cancel his passage on the aircraft which crashes. He then lives to a ripe old age and begets children, who beget children, who beget children. He founds a dynasty of Browns. Dunne's would-be solution implies that Brown's descision to cancel the air-passage *instantaneously* created, and is *inserted* into the

4-D world, many 4-D bodies, the bodies of all his descendants. Is this intelligible?

I know of no theory capable of accommodating precognition which does not have implications as paradoxical as those of the type of theory I have discussed. I am therefore inclined to think that we should explain precognition *away*. In principle, it is always possible to do this in one or other of two ways: (i) by supposing that an apparently precognitive experience is due to unconscious inference from facts acquired by non-precognitive ESP, or (ii) by supposing that the event which fulfils an apparent precognition is caused by the wishes or fears which caused the owner of the pre-cognitive experience to have that experience. We should then have to suppose that, by telepathy or psychokinesis, one person can cause *other* people to act out his own wishes or fears. But in some cases we should have to suppose, what is much harder to believe, that the subject in a card-guessing experiment can influence by psychokinesis the mechanical devices which are later used to ran-domise the target-cards.

Before closing I shall say a few words about some of the recent experiments with animals which are described in the current num-ber of our *Journal*.[34] Experiments have been designed to test whether animals can exercise psychokinesis. By a method which seems impeccable, Dr. Helmut Schmidt and others have apparently shown that cats, lizards, chickens and even chicken embryos in unhatched eggs have mysteriously influenced a randomising ma-chine which switched a heater on or off, and that they did this in such a way as to raise, or lower, the temperature of their environ-ment to suit their own needs. Cockroaches, however, were set a different task, and they apparently influenced the randomising machine in such a way as to increase above the chance-level the frequency with which they received *electric shocks*. Schmidt tells us that the cockroaches' 'dislike' of electric shocks was 'obvious'.[35] Schmidt assimilated his results to cases where human subjects, who are (consciously at least) trying to score high, obtain scores signifi-cantly below the chance-level; and accordingly he interpreted this

---

[34]"*Recent Experiments in Animal Parapsychology*," *Journal*, (No. 753, Sept. 1972). References to the experimental reports will be found in this article.

[35]*Journal of Parapsychology*, Vol. 34 (Dec. 1970), p. 259.

experiment as evidence of 'PK-missing' on the part of the cock-roaches. In other words, the cockroaches unintentionally used their psychokinetic powers to masochistic effect!

This might appear to be a *reductio ad absurdum* of the experi-mental method involved. But before jumping to this conclusion we should recall a point which I made earlier. If people can exercise psychokinesis, then, when an experimenter seeks to verify a hy-pothesis, his own wishes may influence his results in the desired direction. The mysterious control of the randomising machine may have been due to psychokinesis exercised by the experimenters rather than by their animal subjects. Notice that this interpretation makes sense of the negative results with the unfortunate cock-roaches, if we assume that the experimenters in question dislike cockroaches as most of us do, and that they like (or do not dislike) cats, chickens and lizards. If, however, we interpret these experi-ments as their authors have done, as evidence of psychokinesis exercised by animals, we have what seems to be a *reductio ad absurdum* of the theory which inspired psychical research: the theory according to which its subject-matter is 'the action of mind [soul or spirit] apart from the body'. There seems little doubt that Sidgwick and Myers would not have wished to ascribe immortal souls to insects or unhatched eggs.

It is not obvious to me that the strange facts do, as the founders of our Society hoped, provide evidence for dualism. When we con-sider the theories so far formulated, it is not obvious that the ma-terialistic theories are both less intelligible and less comprehensive in their application than the 'psychic' theories, i.e. theories which involve dualism of mind and matter. And I doubt whether we shall presuade many scientists to pay heed to the facts by explaining them in terms of theories which are themselves so hard to believe. What scientists want are not metaphysical theories but verifiable hypotheses. This may not be true of those physicists who construct novel metaphysical systems at the drop of a new particle. But it is, I think, true of the scientists who ought to be continuing our ex-periments—the psychologists and biologists. To avoid scaring them off, it might be best to follow, even more strictly than Sidgwick did, his maxim that we should 'ascertain the facts . . . without any foregone conclusions as to their nature'. One application of this is that we should not talk as if "ESP" is the name of a positive and explanatory hypothesis. "ESP" should be defined, negatively, as meaning 'the acquiring of information without any *known* sensory mechanism', in other words '. . . by means which are not yet understood.' It may seem desperately dull and deflationary to end by implying that all that psychical research has established is the occurrence of various phenomena which cannot yet be understood. But let's not alarm the psychologists. Let's just challenge them to confirm the facts and try to explain them. Such fascinating facts may, perhaps, be allowed to speak for themselves.

SECTION II
PSI AND COGNITION

CHAPTER 6

INTRODUCTION

HOYT L. EDGE

A BASIC PHILOSOPHICAL QUESTION for parapsychology is whether psi gives us knowledge or not. Many philosophers would argue that it does. Indeed, we see that Broad defines ESP partially in terms of the means by which one acquires knowledge (Basic Limiting Principle 4). Wheatley, in "Knowledge, Empiricism, and ESP," assumes that we can gain knowledge (and can even verify sensory knowledge) through ESP. On the other hand, two philosophers in this section, Price and Thalberg, argue that ESP does not give us knowledge, at least not knowledge by acquaintance.

Traditionally, philosophers have distinguished between two kinds of knowledge. The first kind can be called "propositional knowledge," in which one is said to "know" that a particular thing is the case (that grass is green, that Tom is coming). Usually, philosophers have argued that there are three elements involved in this knowing process. 1) proposition P is true (usually in corresponding with the facts), 2) the subject S believes P is true, and 3) S has reason for believing P. The second kind of knowledge is knowledge by acquaintance, in the sense in which I know directly and immediately the contents of my own consciousness (pain, for instance). Traditionally, it has been argued that one has access only to the contents of his own mind in this direct and immediate way. Perhaps, though, it is possible to argue that through telepathy, we have direct acquaintance with the contents of another's mind. This would be particularly helpful in the question of how I know that other minds exist. If I could have knowledge by acquaintance of another's mind, I could be just as sure that he existed as I am that I exist (because I directly experience my own mind-contents, I know that I exist. I think, therefore, I am. Could we say, "I think, therefore, he is"?). The answer to this epistemological question might solve a problem in the philosophy of mind, i.e. is there knowledge by direct acquaintance of another's mind?

Price and Thalberg contend that such knowledge gained through telepathy does not exist. Price points out that knowledge by acquaintance has an "all or none character," and that information received from ESP, especially in tasks like calling ESP cards, has only statistical support for its correctness. Indeed, most of the calls are incorrect! Since there is no experienced difference in consciousness on the part of the subject between correct and incorrect calls, we can say only that certain calls correspond to or correlate with the facts rather than say that the subject has knowledge in those cases where his answers are correct. "Thus Telepathy is a form of 'cognition,' if you like, but it is not a *knowledge* of other minds."

Thalberg argues that we cannot have acquaintance with another's sensations without being in the same physical condition as the other person. Say, for example, that Tom has a bad cold. The only way Bill's telepathic awareness of Tom's cold could be called acquaintance would be for Bill to suffer all of the physical symptoms that Tom feels, such that if Bill went to the doctor, the doctor would have to say that Bill had a cold. Since this is not the case, Thalberg maintains, there is no knowledge by acquaintance.*

At this point, a further question arises: Does telepathy bring us propositional knowledge about another's mind? In cases where mediums claim to have telepathic awareness of the sensations of another, the usual claim of the medium is not that she has direct acquaintance with the sensations of another. Rather, the sensation that the medium feels is taken to be a sign that another is having a particular sensation. This may be Swiggart's point when he says that "Bill can obtain some knowledge of Tom's state of mind— knowledge unobtainable in any other way." If a medium has propositional knowledge of another's state of mind, the three criteria must be met. Let us say that the medium is correct in her statement. Criterion 1) would be met. Can the second two be met? Wheatley argues that sometimes number 2) does not hold, but let

---

*The Thalberg article we have published is actually a revision of the article Swiggart was criticizing. Swiggart's quotes are from Thalberg's original article.

us say that the medium believes in her prediction. Does the medium also have sufficient grounds for her belief? The situation becomes difficult here because the medium is not always correct in her predictions. In one sense, she has grounds for believing Tom has a cold because the tickle in her throat usually symbolizes that the subject has a cold. On the other hand, if she has been wrong in the past and she cannot subjectively distinguish between predictions that are correct and those that are incorrect, does she really have reason for believing that Tom has a cold? The question here is whether propositional knowledge, in opposition to knowledge by acquaintance, can be of a statistical sort.* If a medium is correct *most* of the time (or at least to a statistically significant degree), could we not say that she has reason for believing her prediction? In such a case, she would possess, in a propositional form, knowledge of another's mind in a way that it might be impossible to gain through normal means.

The relationship between ESP and sense-experience is one of the basic concerns of the articles by Wheatley and Roll. Roll argues the psychological aspect of the traditional empiricist *Weltanschauung* by saying that ESP simply supplies a stimulus that activates memory traces and that the content of the ESP message consists of activated memory traces (perhaps affected by imagination). To Wheatley's question of whether there could be knowledge of the world derived merely from clairvoyance with no traces of sense-experience in the content, Roll would answer negatively. All knowledge begins temporally with sense experience. It is indeed an interesting problem of research to discover whether or not such a conclusion could be experimentally tested.

Wheatley is concerned, however, with the logical question of whether one could validate a proposition through means, i.e. through ESP, other than though sense-experience. He affirms that it is logically consistent with empiricism (although empiricists have not admitted so in the past) to use ESP as a basis of knowledge. Empiricism says that all knowledge is based on experience, but this experience logically need not be sense-experience. Thus, he argues

---

*Price is unclear as to whether he would accept this. He seems to want to generalize his argument about knowledge by acquaintance to propositional knowledge.

that ESP could be used as a basis for knowledge of empirical matters.

If Wheatley is correct, can the process of gaining this empirical information through extra-sensory perception be rightly called "perception"? Price introduces this question, and he asserts that the process of gaining information through ESP is not analogous to normal perception and thus should not be referred to as "perception." He goes on to conclude his article by saying that the attempt to explain ESP leads to nonsense since "our present linguistic conventions were mainly designed for talking about the physical world." Perhaps, as Price suggests, we must at this time be satisfied with a bit of "nonsense" as a step to a more accurate description of the world. At the very least, we must consider bold new models of reality.

CHAPTER 7

SOME PHILOSOPHICAL QUESTIONS ABOUT TELEPATHY AND CLAIRVOYANCE*

H. H. PRICE

THE FOUNDER OF PSYCHICAL RESEARCH, though he has not yet received the honor due to him, seems to have been King Croesus of Lydia, who reigned from 560 to 546 B.C. He carried out an interesting experiment, recorded in detail by Herodotus,[1] to test the clairvoyant powers of a number of oracles. He sent embassies to seven oracles, six Greek and one Egyptian. They all started on the same day. On the hundredth day each embassy was instructed to ask its oracle, "What is King Croesus, the son of Alyattes, now doing?" The answer was to be written down and brought back. The oracle of Delphi replied as follows, in hexameters, as its custom was: "I know the number of the sands and the measures of the sea. I understand the dumb, and I hear him who does not speak." Then it went on: "There comes to my mind the smell of a strong-shelled tortoise, which is being cooked along with lamb's flesh in a brazen vessel; brass is spread beneath it, and with brass it is covered." As a matter of fact, this answer was perfectly correct. Herodotus tells us that "having considered what would be the most difficult thing to discover and to imagine," Croesus "cut up a tortoise and a lamb, and himself boiled them together in a brazen pot." What happened afterwards illustrates the difficulties of this sort of investigation, difficulties which still perplex us to this day. Croesus argued, reasonably enough, that if the Delphic priestess had clairvoyant powers, she probably also had

---

*Reprinted from *Philosophy*, 1940, by permission of the author and the Royal Institute of Philosophy. A paper read to the Jowett Society, Oxford, May 15, 1940.
[1]Herodotus, *Histories*, Book I, chs. 46-49.

the precognitive powers which she claimed to have. But when he consulted the oracle later about his forthcoming expedition against the Persians, he received two answers, one of which was ambiguous—"When Croesus crosses the Halys he shall destory a great empire"—and the other correct, but too obscure to be easily interpreted.[2]

After this promising beginning, Psychical Research languished for some twenty-four centuries. It is true that the early history of Christianity, as of other great religions, abounds in stories of supernormal phenomena, including telepathy, clairvoyance, and precognition. But, unfortunately, they were treated as topics of edification, not as materials for scientific inquiry. It is true, too, that in the course of those twenty-four centuries there was a great deal of Occultistic theorizing, and a good deal of Spiritualistic practice—notably among the Neo-platonists of the later Roman Empire, during the Renaissance period, and again towards the end of the eighteenth century. It is probable, too, that the witches of the Middle Ages and the early modern period possessed what we should now call mediumistic powers, and even cultivated them in a crude and haphazard manner. But neither Hagiography, nor Occultist theory, nor Spiritualistic practice, nor witchcraft can be regarded as a form of scientific investigation. Psychical Research proper—the systematic attempt to investigate supernormal phenomena by scientific methods—only began in earnest in the year 1882, when the English Society for Psychical Research was founded. (It is interesting to remember that one of its founders was the Cambridge philosopher Henry Sidgwick.) One of its first acts was to carry out a Census of Hallucinations; the results were embodied in a work called *Phantasms of the Living,* by Gurney, Myers, and Podmore, which is still a classic in this field. For some fifty years now the published *Proceedings* of the Society have contained a mass of very carefully sifted evidence concerning supernormal phenomena of all sorts. There are similar societies in other countries. The most celebrated, though not the oldest, is perhaps the French Institut Métapsychique. It publishes an excellent periodical,

---

[2]*Ibid.,* ch. 55. "When mule shall become king of the Medes," etc. The "mule" was afterwards supposed to have been Cyrus, whose father was a Persian while his mother was a Mede. *Ibid.,* chs. 107-108.

the *Revue Métapsychique,* to which I shall refer more than once in the course of this paper.

For many years the devoted labors of these bodies made little impression. Official science, with a few illustrious exceptions, was frankly hostile; the educated public was for the most part contemptuous; and philosophers went on writing their books about mind and matter exactly as if supernormal phenomena had never been heard of. But in the last thirty years or so there has been a gradual change of opinion, partly because the mass of good evidence has now become so great, and partly because our prejudices have altered, and we are now willing to believe that even the physical world is a much stranger place than our grandfathers supposed. Most educated people are now prepared to admit the occurrence of super-normal *cognitive* phenomena at least. At any rate they are prepared to admit the reality of Telepathy and Clairvoyance, and even to give a fair hearing to the case for Precognition. Here I think that the educated public is quite right. The evidence for Telepathy and Clairvoyance is both abundant and good; and the evidence for Precognition—the most paradoxical, perhaps, of all supernormal phenomena—is very considerable.

I say that the educated public is now prepared to accept these things. But the philosophers, for the most part, have lagged behind.* They do not so much reject them as ignore them. Now this attitude seems to me indefensible. If Telepathy and Clairvoyance do occur—and I see no way of denying it—then surely they *must* be extremely important. For it will follow that the human mind has powers entirely different from sense-perception, introspection, memory, and inference. If Precognition occurs, we shall probably have to revise our theories of Time and Causation in the most drastic manner. Even Haunting raises some problems for the student of Perception. I am afraid there is some truth in the taunt of Professor von Mises. Philosophers, he says, are always on the side of the big battalions; they erect the scientific conclusions of the last generation into *a priori* truths.

---

*There are, of course, notable exceptions: in this country, Professor C.D. Broad; in France, Professor Bergson; in Germany, Professor Driesch. As I have already mentioned, Henry Sidgwick was one of the founders of the S.P.R., and William James took a great interest in its work.

I may be told, perhaps, that Psychical Research is an empirical science, and that Philosophy has no concern with empirical facts; they should be left to the experts, whose business they are. It is not the philosopher's job to "give us news about the Universe." Now I confess that I am very suspicious about all these attempts to draw a sharp line between philosophy and other subjects. Certainly it is not the philosopher's business to *establish* the facts; but it may, nevertheless, be his business to discuss them. And if they appear *prima facie* to conflict with the conclusions established by other methods, say those of Physics or Physiology or Orthodox Psychology—and these supernormal facts certainly do appear to conflict with them—it is his business to bring about a reconciliation which will do justice to all sides. Perhaps some of you will object that Philosophy is entirely concerned with language, with systems of notation, and not with the facts or experiences which we describe by means of them. If this be said, I will reformulate my contention as follows. It is part of the philosopher's business—and an important and urgent part of it—to devise a terminology which will enable us to do two things, neither of which can be done at present: (1) It must enable us to classify supernormal phenomena themselves and to talk about them unambiguously and self-consistently; (2) it must enable us to talk self-consistently *both* about supernormal phenomena *and* about normal ones. In other words, we need a unified system of notation which can be applied to *all* departments of Nature, including the strange and disconcerting department which Psychical Researchers have disclosed to us.†

One further remark: Those who say that the study of supernormal phenomena may safely be left to the experts, and is none of the philosopher's business, seem to be deceived by a false analogy. For in this field there *are* as yet no experts in the sense intended, the sense in which we speak of experts in Physics or Chemistry or Physiology. All we can say is that some people are more familiar with the facts and others less. When once a science has established itself, by devising some comprehensive hypothesis which will unify all the phenomena within its field, even though in a provisional manner; and when, consequently, it has been able

---

†Perhaps this suggestion has some bearing upon Professor Lévy Bruhl's theory concerning the "pre-logical" thinking of savages.

to formulate with tolerable clearness the questions it wishes to ask, and has devised a reliable experimental technique which can be trusted to provide the answers—once all this has been accomplished, we *can* draw a sharp distinction between the people who are experts in that science, who understand and practice the technique of it, and the philosophers who are not. But Psychical Research is not yet in this happy position. What is more, it never will be in it, unless philosophers lend a hand, or—what comes to the same thing—unless Psychical Researchers do some philosophizing for themselves. If we want a parallel, let us consider the position of Physics in the early seventeenth century. An entirely new way of looking at the material world had first to be devised before Physics could establish itself as a science. And the people who devised that new outlook were the philosophers of that century, from Bacon to Leibniz, and chiefly Descartes. They succeeded so well that we almost forget how indispensable and how revolutionary their work was. For despite much clever sniping both from the Right and from the Left, that way of looking at Nature has been taken for granted by scientists from that day to this. The whole of modern European civilization—its defects no less than its virtues—is based on nothing else.

But now suppose that the seventeenth-century philosophers had said, "We are not concerned with empirical facts; we leave them to the experts; these alleged discoveries of Galileo are no business of ours." If they had said this, where would Physics be now? It would never have outgrown its infancy. I will not press the parallel further, though I think it is somewhat disquieting. The moral I wish to draw is only this: In the early stages of any inquiry it is a mistake to lay down a hard-and-fast distinction between a scientific investigation of the facts and philosophical reflection about them (or, if you like, about the terminology in which they are formulated). At the later stages the distinction is right and proper. But if it is drawn too soon and to rigorously those later stages will never be reached.

So far I have been trying to convince you that philosophers ought to take an interest in Psychical Research, and that if they do not they are not doing their job. But exhortation is uphill work, and may even bring a good cause into odium. It is better to show by

examples that Psychical Research does raise philosophical problems: problems, moreover, which are so curious and so interesting
that, once we see what they are, we shall *want* to discuss them,
whether we feel it is our duty or not.

The examples I am going to take are Telepathy and Clairvoyance. I choose them because the evidence for them is so good and
so abundant. I am going to assume that the processes called by
those names certainly do occur, whatever the right analysis of them
may be. If anyone doubts whether I am justified in assuming this,
I can only beg him to look at the evidence for himself.*

The classical definition of *Telepathy* is "the communication of
impressions of any kind from one mind to another independent of
the recognized channels of sense." The person *from* whom the
communication comes is commonly called "the agent," and the
person *to* whom it comes "the percipient." I shall use these expressions, because they are the current ones. But it must be understood
that the "agency" of the agent is commonly, though not always,
unconscious, and that the "perception" of the percipient is not very
like what is ordinarily called by that name.

In the *spontaneous* cases, which first draw attention to the phenomenon, the agent is usually undergoing some crisis or other;
for example, he is involved in an accident of some kind, such as a
shipwreck or a railway accident, or he is seriously ill, or at the point
of death. He usually, but not always, has some emotional linkage
with the percipient; for example, he is a near relative of an intimate
friend. The percipient's experience varies extremely. Sometimes it is
no more than the emergence of an unaccountable conviction about
the present situation of the agent, accompanied by a feeling of
distress or anxiety. (Of course this is only of evidential value if the
conviction is pretty detailed, and provided, further, that the fact
which it corresponds to was antecedently improbable upon the
information the percipient had at the time.) Sometimes the experience takes the form of a vivid and detailed visual hallucination—
the seeing of a "telepathic phantasm" or "apparition." In the best
cases the hallucination is found to correspond in detail with the

---

*I would refer him in the first place to Mr. G.N.M. Tyrrell's admirable book, *Science
and Psychical Phenomena* (Methuen, 1938), then to the *Proceedings* of the S.P.R.,
and to the *Revue Métapsychique*, mentioned above.

agent's situation at the time. Sometimes, again, there is no hallucination, but there is a vivid "sense of presence." The percipient "feels," and feels intensely, that the agent is there in the room, though he *sees* nothing. At other times the hallucination is auditory, or, again, it may be both visual and auditory. In one interesting case, the percipient wakes up in the morning and has a visual hallucination of a half-sheet of notepaper lying on the pillow; the paper contains the written words "Elsie was dying last night." The one person whom the percipient knew with that name did in fact die on the night in question.[3] Sometimes, again, the "message" is conveyed in the form of a vivid and detailed dream. In view of these great variations, it is natural to suppose that the original telepathic "impact"—whatever its nature may be—is always received unconsciously, and that the precise form in which it reaches consciousness depends upon the permanent idiosyncrasy or temporary state of the percipient. Sometimes, perhaps, the impact, or rather the effect of it upon the percipient's unconscious, is "repressed" during waking hours, and only emerges in sleep, in the form of a dream-image.

But we are not confined to the evidence of spontaneous cases, numerous and striking though these are. Telepathy has also been investigated experimentally. When we consider the experimental cases, it becomes obvious that strong emotion is not essential, either on the agent's side or the percipient's. Nor need there be any emotional linkage between the two, or at any rate it need not be at all intimate. Again, intense concentration does not seem to be a necessary condition in either party; on the contrary, it seems sometimes to have an inhibiting effect (but perhaps there is more than one sort of concentration). It also becomes clear that the "message" may be *distorted* in various ways. If A thinks of a picture or diagram, B may get an image of a rather different picture; for instance, it may be turned the wrong way round. Unimportant details in the agent's original may become central in the percipient's reproduction. For example, the agent looks at a picture of a face with wavy lines in the background. The percipient has a visual image of a wire grill (the same shape as the wavy lines) together with the idea

---

[3]Tyrrell, *op. cit.*, p. 24. "Elsie" is a pseudonym.

of a prison. Another percipient at the same time has a visual image of a grill with rectangular lines instead of wavy ones. Neither has an image of the face, which was what the agent concentrated on.[4] The reception seems to be, so to speak, "totalistic" rather than bit by bit (contrast the process of transmitting a picture telegraphically, where the reproduction *is* built up bit by bit, out of spots). Yet it is also often inaccurate. Sometimes no more than the "general idea" get across to the percipient.

In more recent experiments, what are called Zener cards have been used, and it is possible to apply statistical methods to the results. The Zener cards are a simplified form of playing cards; the pack contains five suits of five cards each. If I am asked to guess the suit of the card you are looking at, one would expect on the hypothesis of chance coincidence that I should be right one time in five, i.e. in 20 percent of the total number of trials. If we find in a long series of trials that I guess right in say 25 percent of the cases, we have evidence of a mild telepathic effect, and we have a measure of its magnitude. A similar technique can be used for investigating Clairvoyance, Precognition, and Retrocognition. If the card is not looked at, but is merely taken from the pack and laid face downwards on the table, Telepathy can be excluded. And if we compare the percipient's guesses not with the card simultaneously drawn, but with those drawn before or after, we have a measure of his Retrocognitive and Precognitive powers. It appears from some recent work by Mr. Whately Carington and Mr. Soal[5] that a certain amount of Retrocognition and Precognition *is* often mixed up with Clairvoyance and likewise with Telepathy: It is found that the percipient's guess, when it does not correspond to the card which *is* being drawn, nevertheless does correspond in a significantly great proportion of cases with the one which is *going to be* drawn a little later, or *has been* drawn a little time before. Another noteworthy result of these card experiments—a result which one would never have anticipated from a study of the spontaneous cases—is that very frequently there appears to be nothing *cognitive* about the phenomenon at all, in any ordinary sense of

---

[4]R. Warcollier, *Revue Métapsychique,* (July-October 1938), pp. 247-248.
[5]Cf. *Proceedings* of the S.P.R., (June 1940).

the word "cognitive"; it seems to be purely *motor*. The percipient just calls out the suit of the card, and in a long series of trials he gives the right answer in a proportion of cases which exceeds the chance expectation. He does not see or feel anything in particular. He just utters words, and in such and such a proportion of cases they are found to be the right ones. The drawback of this experimental method is the necessarily uninteresting character of the material; neither Zener cards nor ordinary playing cards are likely to arouse the faintest emotion in anyone's breast. From this point of view the older experimental method, which used pictures, seems to be better; on the other hand, it is then more difficult to give a precise figure to the chance expectation, so that statistical technique cannot be applied so readily to the results. How important these respective drawbacks and advantages are we cannot at present say.

I have now described some of the ascertained facts about Telepathy. But the question which interests a philosopher is, how are we to explain them? The most natural hypothesis at first sight is the *Radiation Hypothesis,* suggested by the analogy of wireless telegraphy. May we not suppose that some form of physical radiation is emitted by the brain of the agent, and "picked up" by the brain of the percipient? But when we consider the empirical facts more closely, we find that this hypothesis is beset with all sorts of difficulties.[6] (1) Telepathy seems to be independent of distance in space. It often occurs between people whose bodies are separated by many hundreds of miles; and it often fails to occur between people whose bodies are only a few feet apart. Moreover, when it does occur, the intensity of the telepathic effect does not seem to vary with the distance. (2) How could a complex proposition or even a complex picture be transmitted by radiation, even if an emotion like fear or anger might be? In the transmission of a message by ordinary telegraphy or wireless, the thought-content of the sender must first be translated into a *code* of some kind, e.g. dots and dashes, or spots arranged in a spatial pattern. Then there must be a series of waves corresponding to these. Then the receiving station reacts to these waves, and translates them back into dots and dashes, or spots; and that again must be translated into words,

---

[6]Cf. Tyrrell, *op. cit.,* p. 119.

and finally the words must be understood. Is there any conceivable analogue to all this in the case of Telepathy, especially when we remember that the code of dots and dashes (or whatever it may be) has first to be established by *convention*? (3) Is there any independent evidence for the existence of telepathic radiations or for the hypothesis that the human brain can either emit or receive them?

Such are the arguments which have convinced most investigators that the Radiation Hypothesis is false. Is there any evidence on the other side? It is sometimes claimed that there is. It is alleged that the electrical state of the human brain varies concomitantly with variations in the emotions; and further, that these electrical changes in a human brain can be detected by physical instruments some feet away. If so, physical radiations of some sort are presumably being emitted. Finally, it is alleged that in some cases *another* human organism is found to respond to these radiations, the response taking the form of muscular reactions. But if radiations of this sort can be both emitted and received by human organisms, does not this provide a physical basis for Telepathy? Now this evidence, or alleged evidence, about "brain-radiations"—radiations in the literal, physical sense—should no doubt be treated with the utmost caution. Nevertheless, we shall do well to consider it hypothetically, and ask ourselves how far it would take us, *if* it were securely established.

I think it would not take us all the way by any means. (1) These "brain-radiations"—assuming they do really occur—are admittedly of very faint intensity, and do not penetrate more than a few feet; whereas telepathic communications can be transmitted over much greater distances than this (if "transmitted" is the word), even over hundreds of miles. (2) You remember the "Code" difficulty mentioned above. How is this to be dealt with? The transmission of "brain-radiations"—assuming again that the facts really are as reported—only seems to occur in cases of *undifferentiated emotional* Telepathy, where this difficulty does not arise. There is no question of transmitting a *proposition* (a piece of information) nor even a picture. What is transmitted is just an emotion. And on the side of the recipient there is hardly any discrimination as between one emotion and another. It is indeed alleged that the recipient is not absolutely undiscriminating, and that he reacts differently according as the transmitter is in a "Yes" state or a "No" state. But still I think it would be admitted that the response is *relatively* undiscriminating. Moreover, the process, as described, seems to be purely behavioristic. The recipient does not feel the emotion himself, nor does he know or believe or take for granted that the transmitter is feeling one. All that happens on his side is a muscular reaction.

It would appear then—assuming for argument's sake that the facts are correctly reported—that the Radiation Hypothesis will only explain, at most, certain elementary forms of Telepathy, viz. *short-range, undifferentiated, emotional* Telepathy. If the evidence about "brain radiations" were to be securely established, we should have to conclude, I think, that the word "Telepathy" was ambiguous and covered two entirely different processes: (*a*) A short-range process, concerned only with the transmission of emotions—a process having a physical basis, and analogous in some respects to wireless transmission. (*b*) A quite different process—Telepathy proper—which is not so much long-range but rather independent of spatial conditions altogether—a process which is to all appearance purely mental, which is not limited to the transmissions of emotions, and displays in favorable cases a high degree of discrimination.

So let us now turn once more to Telepathy proper, and consider again what explanation could conceivably be given of it. Should we say, perhaps, that it is a hitherto unrecognized form of *direct acquaintance,* in which one mind has immediate knowledge of another mind, or of some state of another mind: an *extrospective* acquaintance parallel to the introspective acquaintance which each of us has with states of his own mind? I do not think we can accept this suggestion, though it was natural to make it in the days when the only known examples of Telepathy were certain very striking spontaneous cases, in which the percipient's "impression" turned out to be correct in every detail. The difficulty is that knowing has, so to speak, an *all or none* character. There is no half-way house between knowing and not knowing. It is true that knowing admits of various degrees of definiteness. If *x* is in fact scarlet, I may know only that it is red; I may even know no more than that it has some shade of color or other. But it is self-contradictory to say that an act of knowing is partly correct and partly incorrect, or that it is nearly right but not quite. Now this is just what we do have to say of much telepathy, as the experimental cases show. The percipient's "impression" *is* often partly right and partly wrong, and the extent of the rightness or wrongness varies very much from one telepathic experience to another. Again, in a long series of trials the percipient may be right in a proportion of cases which significantly exceeds the chance expectation (say in 25 percent, when by chance alone he should only be right in 20 percent); and yet the experience on his side seems to be exactly the same both when he is right and when he is wrong. If he were knowing in the correct cases and only guessing in the incorrect ones, there ought to be an experienced difference between the two.

It seems then that we have to do with a process of *reproduction* or *representation* rather than with knowledge in any strict sense. The bare empirical facts come to this: with certain pairs of persons there is a surprisingly large degree of *correlation,* greater than the chance expectation, between A's images, dreams, hallucinations, or utterances on the one hand, and certain approximately contemporary experiences of B on the other. In some instances the correlation is substantially perfect in every detail; in others it is only partial. Thus Telepathy is a form of "cognition," if you like, but it is not a *knoweldge* of other minds. All that the so-called percipient *knows,* or is directly aware of, is an image or hallucinatory sense-datum of his own, or sometimes only an utterance which he finds himself making; and this *corresponds* more closely or less closely, and sometimes exactly, with something which is happening in another mind. If I may use a crude analogy which I have already used elsewhere, Telepathy is more like infection than like knowledge. When A catches influenza from B, his disease corresponds more or less closely with B's, though his own physiological idiosyncracies will generally make some difference. But A's influenza is not a *knowing* of B's—merely an effect of it, which reproduces its cause more or less exactly.

If Telepathy, then, is not a form of knowing, but rather an experience which is *caused by* and more or less closely *corresponds with* an experience of someone else, how are we to conceive the causal process involved? As we have seen, it seems to be of a purely mental sort. Now I think this has an important philosophical consequence. The plain man, and even the plain philosopher, assumes with Descartes that the world of minds is divided up into a number of separate and isolated mental substances. No mind, it is supposed, has direct causal relations with any other mind, nor indeed with anything at all except its own brain. But it now appears that this view is true only of the conscious part of our mental life. When we consider unconscious mental processes—those which their owner is not, or perhaps cannot be, aware of by introspection—there seems to be no such isolation. It appears that my unconscious may on occasion stand in direct causal relations with yours. (I do not like this language much, but it is the only one available at present, so I must use it.) The facts of Dual and Alternating Personality have already made us doubt whether the *unity* of any one mind is quite so absolute and unconditional as our predecessors supposed; it now appears that the *diversity* of different minds is not absolute and unconditional either. It begins to look as if both the unity and the isolatedness of a single mind were the result of certain special restrictive conditions, which are generally but not always fulfilled; or perhaps not even that, but rather a mere appearance arising from the extremely limited and superficial character of ordinary self-consciousness. The hypothesis of a "Collective Unconscious," common to all human minds, which certain speculative writers have suggested, begins to look more plausible. Let us consider for a moment what this hypothesis would amount to. What sort of unity would this Collective Unconscious have, if it existed? So far as I can see, its unity would be purely causal. The causal relations *between* Smith's mind and Brown's would be the same in kind as the causal relations *within* either of them, and equally direct. The Collective Unconscious would not be a "thing," but rather a "field" of (purely mental) interaction. In fact, the phrase "Collective Unconscious" would just be a way of saying that unconscious events in one mind can directly produce unconscious events in any other; from which it would follow that the distinction between unconscious mental events "in me" and unconscious mental events "in you" is no longer a hard-and-fast one. Now this hypothesis may seem altogether too speculative, and it would certainly need a good deal of clarification before we could accept it; nevertheless, the existence of Telepathy does suggest that some hypothesis on these lines is true, or at any rate nearer the truth than the common-sense view, which regards the mental world as a mere collection of causally isolated mental substances.

I admit, of course, that the whole terminology of "unconscious mental events" is far from satisfactory. They were originally called "mental" because the effects which they produce (or rather which they are postulated to explain) are exceedingly similar to those produced by events which *are* indubitably mental; but what their intrinsic nature is we cannot at present say. On the one hand, it is natural to suggest that in their intrinsic nature they are physical, or rather physiological. As Spinoza remarked, no one can yet lay down limits to what the human body can do; it might be able to produce effects which are indistinguishable from the effects of conscious forethought and conscious wishing. On the other hand, the hypothesis of "unconscious" events which are mental in their intrinsic nature is perfectly conceivable. It amounts only to saying that there are mental events which are not introspected by anyone, and this involves no contradiction whatever; just as there are unperceived physical events, so there *may* perfectly well be unintrospected mental ones. Moreover, there may be some which it is *causally impossible* for human minds to introspect, just as there are physical events (e.g. in the center of the Earth) which it is causally impossible for human minds to perceive. So far, then, there seems to be nothing much to choose between these two opposed theories about the intrinsic nature of "unconscious" events. It is sometimes maintained that the evidence of Abnormal Psychology and Psycho-therapy supports the theory that they are mental. On this I cannot offer an opinion. But the theory that they are purely physiological would certainly get into difficulty over Telepathy. It would commit us to a physical explanation of Telepathy, that is, to the Radiative Theory; for what other physical explanation could there be? And as I have tried to show, the Radiative Theory covers only a small part of the facts at the best, and not the most important part. Finally, we have to remember that this disjunction—either the Unconscious is mental in its intrinsic nature, or it is physiological— is not necessarily exhaustive. The Cartesian division of Nature into two parts, a mental part and a physical part, may not cover all the facts. There may be a third realm which is neither mental in the ordinary sense nor physical in the ordinary sense, but possesses some of the properties of both. If so, evidence against the physiological theory of the Unconscious would not by itself suffice to establish the mental theory of it, for there would be a third alternative. I know this sounds like nonsense to the modern educated European, whose whole outlook on the world, whether he knows it or not, has been powerfully influenced by the genius of Descartes. Nevertheless, this hypothesis of a third something, intermediate between what we ordinarily call "mind" and what we ordinarily call "matter," has long been familiar in the philosophy and cosmology of the Far East; and something not unlike it is found in Neo-platonism. Perhaps it is not nonsense after all. Perhaps if we reject it out of hand, as most of us would do, we are merely being parochial.

Before leaving the subject of Telepathy, I have one further suggestion to make. Is it possible that when we discuss causal hypotheses about Telepathy we are asking the wrong question? Perhaps the right question to ask, anyhow at the beginning, is not "Why does Telepathy occur sometimes?" but rather "Why doesn't it occur all the time?" (Compare M. Bergson's discussion of Memory. According to him, it is forgetting, rather than remembering, which needs a causal explanation; and the problem is "Why do we remember so little?" rather than "Why do we remember at all?") If we approach the matter in this way, there is one biological point which strikes us at once. *Too much* Telepathy would be paralysing to action. It would distract us from the immediate practical problems which we have to solve if we are to survive in this world. It might even lead to the utter disintegration of our personality, if the content of our consciousness varied from moment to moment under the influence of a perpetual and continually varying telepathic bombardment. One would therefore suppose, on general biological grounds, that any species of organisms which has managed to survive has developed some "repressive" mechanism (on the lines of those which Freud has described) whereby the majority of telepathic "impacts" are prevented from reaching consciousness. On the other hand, it is possible that no *special* repressive mechanism is needed. The repression may come about automatically and of itself. It may be that we all receive a vast multitude of telepathic "impacts" all the time, and that their very number and variety causes them to inhibit *one another*: so that either they do not influence consciousness at all, or else their influence is in the nature of a "mass-effect," a modification of our general emotional tone. If there is a special repressive mechanism, the good telepathic subject will be the person who can suspend its operations, either voluntarily or involuntarily, and so let through into consciousness the telepathic "impressions" which are reaching him all the time. Certainly it does appear that telepathic experiences occur more readily in states of relaxed attention. As we have seen, they often take the form of dreams; and when we dream, the ordinary repressive mechanisms of waking life are to a large extent suspended. The most striking example of all is the mediumistic trance, which is a particularly fertile source of telepathic phenomena; for it seems clear that at least a good many alleged "spirit-messages" are due to telepathy from the living. What exactly the mediumistic trance is, no one can yet say. But it certainly seems to involve a greater or lesser degree of dissociation of personality, and in such dissociated states normal inhibitive mechanisms are presumably suspended.

Suppose, on the other hand, that there is no special repressive mechanism, and that what happens in normal life is merely that many different telepathic impacts inhibit one another. In that case, the good telepathic subject will be the person who can single out some one of these impacts from the total mass. He will not be more *receptive* to telepathy than other people, but only more *selective*. And this selectiveness might even be a deficiency, rather than an extra endowment. He might be *less* receptive than the normal man: all but a few telepathic impulses might fail to reach him. Whereas normal men would receive a vast and indiscriminate multitude of impulses, which would have at most a confused mass-effect upon their consciousness, this abnormal man would receive only one or two, and so he might be aware of a tolerably distinct image, or hallucination. We might then suppose that some normal men at some times get into this state of *reduced* telepathic receptivity, which enables some one telepathic impulse to push through into consciousness in a distinct and definite form.

Of these two hypotheses—the hypothesis of a special repressive mechanism and the hypothesis of mutual inhibition—I am disposed to prefer the first, on grounds of analogy. For we know, or have good reasons for thinking, that there *are* repressive mechanisms in the human mind; and, thanks to Freud and others, we can form some plausible conjectures about the way in which they work, and about the psychological and psycho-physical conditions upon which their effectiveness depends. Or could we say that the two hypotheses are not mutually exclusive? There might be some cases where a telepathic impulse fails to reach consciousness because it is repressed by a special repressive mechanism; and there might also be some in which a number of telepathic impulses inhibit one another, so that either nothing at all "gets through," or only a general mass-effect upon our emotional tone. However, I do not propose to discuss these two hypotheses any further. I only mentioned them to illustrate the kind of considerations we are led to if we start by asking "Why doesn't telepathy occur more frequently?" —instead of asking the more usual question "Why does it occur at all?"

I now turn from Telepathy to Clairvoyance, which is in some ways an even more puzzling phenomenon. I am afraid I do not have time to treat it as fully as it deserves; but fortunately some of the things I have said about Telepathy, especially about attempts to give a physical explanation of it, will apply to Clairvoyance too, and there will be no need to repeat them. Clairvoyance is usually defined as the awareness of some approximately contemporary* object or process in the material world without the use of the sense-organs or of rational inference. (The word "awareness" must not be taken too strictly, as we shall see. But let it stand for the moment.) The first problem we come upon is, that it is not at all easy in practice to distinguish Clairvoyance from Telepathy. (I am afraid that Croesus was not aware of this difficulty when he carried out his experiment with the oracles.) Let us consider a fairly frequent and well-established type of case. Suppose that the percipient tells me the contents of a letter sealed up in an envelope. He has no normal means of discovering what the letter contains, either by

---

*I put in this qualifying phrase to exclude Precognition and Retrocognition. But one may say, if one likes, that these are special forms of Clairvoyance.

observation or by inference; yet his description of it turns out to be correct. Are we to say that he had clairvoyantly "perceived" the letter, whatever we may mean by "perceive"? Or is it that he has gotten in touch, not with the letter itself, but with the mind of the writer, who presumably still retains a memory of what he wrote? If so, the process is telepathic. It is true that in such cases the percipient often does not know the writer personally and does not even know that he exists. But this is no obstacle to the telepathic explanation. As we saw earlier, telepathy can still occur even where there is no emotional linkage between the two parties. Now consider another type of case, where the percipient is able to give directions for finding a lost object—an object which was lost in a place many miles away, a place which the percipient has never seen, and lost by a person whom he does not know. Even this might be explained telepathically. It is true that the owner of the object does not consciously remember where the object is: otherwise he could not be said to have "lost" it. Nevertheless, the experience of putting the object down somewhere, say in a drawer, may well have left some "trace," some persistent modification, in his unconscious (it may indeed be that he *wanted* to lose the object, and that his forgetting is what Freud calls "active forgetting"; such things can happen). Now perhaps this trace has affected the percipient telepathically. We cannot absolutely exclude this explanation.

Nevertheless, I think there are some cases where telepathy *can* be excluded. A celebrated one is that of Mme. Morel,[7] which occurred in March 1914. An old man had disappeared from the village of Cour-les-Barres (in the Department of Cher, in Central France). He was repeatedly and carefully searched for, but could not be found. Mme. Morel, who was in Paris and had never been in the Department of Cher, was given a scarf belonging to the old man, and told to "look for" its owner. She said she saw him lying dead on the ground, in a place which she described in detail. She also gave a detailed description of the appearance and posture of the body. Asked to say how he had got there, she gave a detailed account of the route he had followed, and of his feelings on the way.

---

[7] I quote this from Mr. G.N.M. Tyrrell's *Science and Psychical Phenomena*, pp. 34-35. It was originally reported by Dr. Osty.

People on the spot then followed the route Mme. Morel had described, arrived at the place she had described, and found the body lying there. The details she had given about the posture of the body and the clothes were verified exactly. The place also corresponded exactly to her description, with one instructive exception. She said that the body was lying near a rock. Actually it was a piece of a fallen tree which did look like a rock.

Now when she described the route the old man had taken, and the feelings he had had, you may say that this might have been Telepathy. If so, it was *retrocognitive* Telepathy, since the events had happened three weeks earlier. But when she described the situation and the posture of the dead body, this can hardly have been anything but pure Clairvoyance—the awareness of a material object at a distance without any use of the normal sense-organs, and of determinate facts about it which were not known to any living person. (Incidentally, the mistake about the rock and the tree trunk suggests that the experience was in some sense *visual,* and conformed to the etymological meaning of the word "clairvoyance" more closely than some experiences of this sort.)

This was a spontaneous case. But in recent years Clairvoyance has been investigated experimentally, both with pictures and with playing-cards, and special precautions have been taken to exclude Telepathy. For example, a pack of cards is shuffled, and a card is drawn by the experimenter. He sees only its back and at once lays it face downwards on the table. The percipient is placed at the other end of the table, and there is a screen in the middle, which prevents him from seeing what is going on. As soon as the card is drawn, he has to say what card he thinks it is, and his answer is written down. The same procedure is followed for all the cards in the pack. Then, and only then, they are turned face upwards, and their denominations, and the order in which they were drawn, are recorded. Then the pack is shuffled again and the whole procedure is repeated. Now if we find that in a long series of trials the proportion of correct guesses is significantly greater than the chance expectation, we have to conclude that the percipient is using the power of pure Clairvoyance. Telepathy is excluded, since no one sees the faces of the cards till afterwards. A good many experiments have now been carried out on these lines, though sometimes the procedure is more complicated. (Mr. Tyrrell, for example, has devised an elaborate electrical apparatus, in which electric light bulbs concealed inside boxes are substituted for the cards.) Several of these experiments have yielded positive results. We very seldom find a percipient who guesses right every time, even in a comparatively short series of trials. But there seem to be quite a number whose proportion of correct guesses is strikingly greater than the chance expectation.

When we set about giving a *theory* of Clairvoyance, or rather trying to give one, we are confronted with much the same difficulties as we found before in discussing Telepathy. No radiation hypothesis seems at all plausible, since Clairvoyance, like Telepathy, seems not to be affected by spatial distance nor yet by physical obstacles. Again, it cannot be a form of direct acquaintance, an immediate knowledge of a spatially distant object or event, since it is liable to mistakes. Moreover, despite the etymological meaning of the word "clairvoyance" ("clear seeing"; cf. "second sight"), the phenomenon does not necessarily involve visual images or visual hallucinations; sometimes these are present—for example, hallucinatory scenes appear in a crystal, or as if projected on a cinematograph screen—but often they are not. Further, the vision, when it *is* a vision, may be partly symbolic, as in an allegory or a dream—a feature which is found in precognitive visions too. Sometimes the percipient says not "I see so-and-so," but "They tell me so-and-so," as if the data presented to him were *auditory* images, or hallucinations, rather then visual ones. You remember that in Croesus' experiment the Delphic priestess professed to *smell* the tortoise being cooked in the brazen pot. If the story is true, she must have had an olfactory image or hallucination, presumably accompanied by a visual one. There is some modern evidence for the occurrence of olfactory images in Telepathy. I do not know whether there is any modern evidence for their occurrence in Pure Clairvoyance; but on analogical grounds one would expect that they ought sometimes to be present, just as they sometimes are in ordinary memory. Finally, in some cases of Clairvoyance, and notably in some of the card-guessing experiments, the phenomenon seems to be almost wholly motor. The percipient just utters the *words* "five of spades," or whatever it may be, without any relevant form of cognition at all, and it is found afterwards that his words correspond to the facts in a significantly large proportion of instances. Here, too, the parallel between Clairvoyance and Telepathy is a close one. For sometimes, and especially in the experimental cases, Telepathy too seems to be a purely motor phenomenon.

Thus, whatever the underlying causal process may be, Clairvoyance, like Telepathy, can manifest itself in consciousness in a great variety of ways, differing from one percipient to another. Like Telepathy, again, it is often partly erroneous, so that it cannot be a form of direct knowledge in any strict sense of the word "knowledge." If we consider it from an epistemological point of view, the theory we hold about it must be a "representative" theory, not a "prehensive" theory. As with Telepathy, so with Clairvoyance, the bare empirical facts are *correlations*: between the percipient's images or hallucinations or utterances on the one hand, and certain facts about material objects on the other—facts not accessible to him by any form of normal sense-perception nor by inference. The correlation is not always perfect, though sometimes it approximates to begin so; often it is partial; and sometimes it is only just greater than chance-coincidence would account for. Evidently, then, it is a matter of "reproduction" or "representation," not of knowledge proper.

If these are the facts, what explanation are we to suggest? In the case of Telepathy, we could at least produce a *causal* hypothesis, vague as it might be. We said that an event in one mind could directly produce an event in another. The causal laws involved might still be ordinary psychological causal laws, or something sufficiently like them, with the proviso that their field of application is extended, so that they would link together events in *different* minds instead of being confined, as in Orthodox Psychology they are, to events within the *same* mind. But when we consider Clairvoyance, it is difficult to suggest any cause for it at all, still more to see how such a cause could work. When we are looking for the causal explanation of an unfamiliar phenomenon, we have to begin by relying upon analogies drawn from more familiar spheres. What else can we do, unless we are favored with a special revelation? With the help of these analogies, we formulate a working hypothesis. It will almost certainly be a crude one, burdened with inessential details, and it may be completely mistaken. But it does at least enable us to get started. Further study of the empirical facts will show us how to correct it and refine it, until at last, perhaps centuries later, we arrive at a tolerably satisfactory theory. But Clairvoyance seems utterly unlike any other phenomenon we know of, unless it be Precognition; and Precognition is if possible even more difficult to understand than Clairvoyance itself. There is no occurrence within the field of *normal* experience which is at all like either of them. How can someone perceive a material object, if "perceive" is the word, without the use of any sense-organ, and without any train of physical events (radiations or anything else) intervening between the object and his own body? You may call it "perceiving" if you like, but the causal process underlying it must be something utterly different from anything which occurs in normal perception. We cannot hope to find any helpful analogy in that quarter. And if not there, where *can* we hope to find it?

But it will never do to give up the struggle in despair; still less to pretend that the facts do not exist, because they will not fit into our traditional scientific schemes. On the contrary, the very difficulties of the subject testify to its extreme importance. If Clairvoyance does occur, as I am persuaded it does, our ordinary theories of the human mind, or of physical nature, or perhaps of both, are badly wrong somewhere. For if those theories were wholly right, it would not occur at all. The world must be a much stranger place than we have supposed. Thus, just because Clairvoyance is so unlike every other phenomenon we are familiar with, it is specially incumbent on us to try to understand it. It is quite certain that, if only it could be understood, we should get altogether new light upon the nature of the human mind, and perhaps upon the nature of the physical world as well.

Now I myself have got no theory of Clairvoyance to offer. I only want to make certain tentative suggestions as to the directions in which we might look for one. First, I want to suggest, as I did before in discussing Telepathy, that perhaps we are asking the wrong question. Perhaps what we should seek a causal explanation of is the absence of Clairvoyance rather than its presence. In that case the proper question to ask, anyhow in the first place, would be this: Why is our ordinary perceptual experience limited in the way it is? Why is it confined to those material objects which happen to exercise a physical effect upon our sense-organs? Ought we perhaps to assume that Clairvoyance is our normal state, and that ordinary perception is something subnormal, a kind of myopia? The question you ask depends on the expectation with which you begin. Ought we to have expected that by rights, so to speak, every mind would be aware of everything, or, at any rate, of an indefinitely wide range of things? The puzzle would then be to explain why the ordinary human mind is in fact aware of so little. We might then conjecture that our sense-organs and afferent nerves (which, of course, are physiologically connected with our organs of action, i.e. with the muscular system) are arranged to *prevent us from attending* to more than a small bit of the material world— that bit which is biologically relevant to us as animal organisms. We might still have an unconscious "contact"—I can think of no adequate phrase—with all sorts of other things, but the effects of it would be shut out from consciousness except on rare occasions, when the physiological mechanism of stimulus and response is somewhat deranged. In that case, what prevents us from being clairvoyant all the time is—in M. Bergson's phrase—*l'attention à la vie.* If so, we should expect that habitual clairvoyants would be physiologically or psycho-physically "abnormal" or "unbalanced"; or at any rate that their "balance"—I have to speak in metaphors again—would be more easily upset than other people's.

My second suggestion is already prefigured in my first; but as it will shock some of you, I had better state it quite openly. If we are to give an explanation of Clairvoyance, I am afraid we may have to look for light in works of Speculative Metaphysics. I myself should be disposed to look for it in the *Monadology* of Leibniz and in the more speculative parts of Lord Russell's book *Our Knowledge of the External World,* which admittedly starts from a somewhat Leibnizian point of view. But these are not the only metaphysicians who might be useful. For instance, we might find some help in Berkeley too.

Having administered the shock, I hasten to mitigate its effects. The more Positivistically minded members of my audience may tell me that whatever we may think of the *epistemological* doctrines of metaphysicians, their *speculative* doctrines were certainly nonsensical; the propositions of speculative metaphysics, they may say, are mere pseudo-propositions, not even false. To this I reply, first, that perhaps the great speculative metaphysicians of the past did not quite know what they were doing (men of genius often do not). They may have *thought* they were using *a priori* propositions to demonstrate matters of fact, or sometimes to demonstrate that matters of fact are not matters of fact at all, but only appearances or illusions. But perhaps they were really doing something else. And secondly, I will try to placate my critics with an analogy. Consider the history of non-euclidean geometry. During the nineteenth century a number of non-euclidean geometries were worked out by pure mathematicians. They were worked out as mere speculations in a purely deductive manner. No student of physics supposed that they had any application to the physical world. But in the last thirty years it has turned out that non-euclidean geometry does have the most important applications to the physical world. New physical facts have turned up, facts which were unknown and unsuspected at the time when non-euclidean geometry was first developed; and either they cannot be fitted into a Euclidean framework at all, or they can only be fitted into it with the aid of unplausible *ad hoc* hypotheses. Now I suggest that the theories of some speculative metaphysicians may turn out to be useful in a similar way. At the time when they were first invented they may have been purely deductive systems; whether their inventors realized it or not, these systems may have had no relevance one way or the other to the empirical facts known at the time, so that they were incapable of being either confirmed or refuted by experiential evidence, and the Positivists of the day could plausibly regard them as nonsensical. But when we consider the new facts which Psychical Research has brought to light, some of these metaphysical speculations begin to wear a different look. We find that some of them do at least provide a conceptual framework into which supernormal cognition can be fitted, whereas it appears to be an inexplicable oddity so long as we stick to our ordinary (ultimately Cartesian) views of mind and of Nature. For example, in the *Monadology* of Leibniz every monad has clairvoyant and telepathic powers, not occasionally and exceptionally, but always, as part of its essential nature. Every monad represents the entire Universe from its own point of view (Clairvoyance) and the perceptions of each are correlated with the perceptions of all the rest (Telepathy). In fact, what Leibniz calls "perception" is always both clairvoyant and telepathic. Moreover, he tells us that this perception is to a greater or lesser degree unconscious. I do not say that the system of Leibniz is workable as it stands. But I do suggest that we may gather useful hints from it. One of Leibniz' contemporaries described the *Monadology* as "a philosophical romance." So it was, at the time when it was written. But like some systems of non-euclidean geometry, it may have been a kind of unconscious anticipation of the science of the future. Indeed, we do not have to go outside the history of Metaphysics itself to find hopeful and suggestive parallels. At the time when it was first put forward, the atomistic philosophy of Leucippus and Democritus was a piece of pure metaphysical speculation. But it turns out to have been a crude anticipation of some of the most important conclusions of modern science. Another instance, perhaps, is Schopenhauer's metaphysics of "the Will," which anticipates some of the discoveries of Psycho-analysis.* We must not be too proud, then, to take what hints we can from the theories of speculative metaphysicians. They may turn out to have some empirical application after all, especially when we consider that seamier side of Nature of which Psychical Research gives us a glimpse.

With these somewhat disturbing thoughts in mind, let us turn back to Clairvoyance. If we determine not to be frightened of Metaphysics, three hypotheses suggest themselves. First, we might suppose that there is an *omnisentient consciousness* which is aware of everything that is going on in the material world, and possibly of some future events as well. If you like, it would be a kind of God; but the present argument does not oblige us to attribute intelligence to it—whatever other arguments might do—still less moral predicates of any sort. It will be safest just to call it a "World-Soul," if you want some old-established name for it. This omni-sentient consciousness would enjoy unlimited clairvoyance; and human clairvoyance would be due to a telepathic relation between ourselves and it.

---

*I owe this suggestion to Dr. F. Waismann.

Secondly, we could suppose with Leibniz that every mind clair-voyantly perceives or represents the world from its own proper point of view, and that each is telepathically correlated with all other minds. We should then have to explain why there *seems* to be so little clairvoyance, and why the vast bulk of our perceptions or representations remain unconscious.

Thirdly, we might start from the modified form of Leibnizian metaphysics suggested by Lord Russell in his book *Our Knowledge of the External World*. According to this, the physical world itself consists of a multitude of "perspectives." Each of these perspectives exists from a certain place; it exists from that place whether it is sensed or not; and a particular material object, a poker for example, is a complicated system of such perspectives, each existing from its proper place. When a suitably arranged sense-organ and nervous system occupies one of these places, the perspective is sensed, and the sensibilia of which it is made up turn into sense-data. If we now wish to fit Clairvoyance into this scheme, we may take one of two courses. On the one hand, we could suppose that a human mind is capable of being at one of those places (using it as a "point of view") otherwise than by putting its sense-organs there. If my body is in Oxford at twelve o'clock, and I have a clairvoyant vision of an event occurring at twelve o'clock in Piccadilly Circus, we then say that my "point of view" is for the moment in or near Piccadilly Circus, though my sense-organs remain in Oxford. Or, secondly, we could take a more extravagant line, which incidentally might come in useful when we considered other sorts of supernormal phenomena not dealt with in this paper, such as Haunting and Psychometry. Instead of stretching our ordinary notions of sense-perception, we could stretch our ordinary notions of *memory*. We could say that memory is not just a property of living organisms, as we ordinarily think; but that it, or something essentially like it, is a property of every point in physical space, or at any rate that it is a property of all those places from which "perspec-tives" exist. We could then suggest that these rudimentary "place-memories" can on occasion affect human minds telepathically, and this would be the explanation of Clairvoyance. This amounts to saying that every point in physical space, or at least every point from which perspectives exist, is the "point of view of" a rudimentary mind, and that there is a telepathic linkage between these rudimentary minds or sub-minds and ourselves. And you will notice that this brings us back to something very like the full-blooded Leibnizian cosmology which Lord Russell started out from.

Few of you perhaps will want to go as far as this. But if anyone does, I am afraid he may have to go further still. For we saw before that once Telepathy is admitted, the sharp distinction between one mind and another breaks down.[8] Suppose that a sub-mind, or place-memory, or sub-human Leibnizian monad, whose point of view is at P_1, telepathically affects me, whose body is at P_2; and suppose that as a result I have a clairvoyant vision of the sensibilia existing from P_1. Then you can equally well say, if you like, that I or "me" is at both places, although my body is only at one of them. Or again, if you prefer the "World-Soul" hypothesis, the hypothesis of an omnisentient consciousness, and explain Clairvoyance by saying that we are sometimes in telepathic communication with it, then again there will be no sharp line between us and the "World-Soul." We might have to say that we individual minds are, as it were, dissociated personalities of it, and that there are occasions when this dissociation is temporarily suspended.

Whatever we may think about these very strange speculations, there is one point which they have in common, and I think we must hold fast to it, extraordinary though it is: namely, that sense-experience, or something not wholly unlike it, is not necessarily connected with an organism or nervous systems. There can be sense-experiences, or something like them, from places *not* at the moment occupied by sense-organs and brains. You may say that the owner of these "extra-somatic" sense-experiences is an omnipresent and omnisentient being, or a Leibnizian monad; or you may say that its owner is the clairvoyant human being himself, whose body and sense-organs are somewhere else. But, whoever and whatever owns them, they do seem to occur. Nor are they prevented from occurring by the fact that we have at present no language for describing them intelligibly. If we are to talk about these subjects at all, we can hardly avoid talking a certain amount of nonsense. Indeed, how could we expect to avoid it? Our present linguistic

---

[8]Cf. pp. 117-118 above.

conventions were mainly designed for talking about the physical world. Even the data of Normal Psychology (to say nothing of Abnormal) already subject them to a considerable strain. It would not be surprising if supernormal phenomena, such as I have discussed in this paper, sometimes strained them to breaking point or beyond it. Nevertheless, we must take the risk. The facts are too important to be ignored. We must be content to talk a certain amount of nonsense for the present. Otherwise we cannot get on at all, and must simply ignore a group of phenomena which of all others it most concerns us to understand. Our better-instructed successors can be trusted to put matters straight. Philosophy, and science too, begins in nonsense; but it does not end there.

CHAPTER 8

TELEPATHIC AWARENESS OF ANOTHER'S FEELINGS*

I. THALBERG

WRITERS ON THE PROBLEMS of other selves frequently wonder if telepathy might enable us to scale the battlements surrounding another person's mind, and to become directly acquainted with sensations, aches, twinges, itches, and the swells of terror and rage which occur within him. John Wisdom, for instance, examines cases where Jones receives images in a blue frame, or with the label 'Smith', and knows "that such and such an image signifies that Smith is seeing such and such a thing."[1] After due consideration, Wisdom decides that these telepathic feats will not qualify as acquaintance with another person's feelings or sense-impressions. He declares: "Telepathy's not . . . what is wanted by the real metaphysician when he asks for real knowledge of the mind of another."[2] When Arabella judges that Bill is angry, not from attending to Bill's demeanor, but from the telepathically induced choking in her own throat, Wisdom thinks she only has access to her own experience.

I want to investigate briefly what we mean when we envisage one person taking telepathic possession of the contents of another's mind. I shall not discuss the questions (1) whether telepathic experience constitutes real knowledge, (2) whether both parties have a single item before their consciousness, and (3) how we

---

*Author's revision of "Telepathy," *Analysis,* 1960-61. We thank the editor of *Analysis* and the author for permission to reprint.
[1]*Other Minds* (Oxford, 1956), p. 95.
[2]*Ibid.,* p. 98.

could prove that telepathy has occurred, and that a single item, or an original and its duplicate, must be on view.

We should observe, initially, that the traditional notion of telepathy is too elastic to satisfy a philosopher's standards for acquaintance with the contents of another's awareness. Even a sophisticated writer like Mrs. Sidgwick, in her article "Telepathy,"[3] extends the notion to cover such phenomena as one person receiving a vision of a distant friend at the moment when the friend is dying. I gather that the popular conception is that telepathy consists, for the most part, in transference of *thoughts* from one individual to another without overt methods of communication. The model is a long-distance conversation with no telephone, wireless, or smoke signals.

A philosopher would not be interested because this account fails to imply that the telepathic observer gets at something which is ordinarily hidden from him. Must there be any particular item in a man's stream of consciousness while he thinks—as there is when he smells an acrid odor, experiences a stab of pain, or boils with indignation? It seems a contingent matter, and not universally the case, that things pass before our consciousness as we engage in various forms of thought. There may be nothing to transmit telepathically.

But when you communicate a thought—make your listener understand your words—must you not produce a feeling, or a click of understanding, in his mind? Not in any obvious way. An electrician's apprentice can follow the instructions of the master electrician, repeat or paraphrase them for a fellow worker, and decide they are inappropriate under some unexpected circumstance; nevertheless he may deny having any current inner feelings. Still it is clear that he understood what the master electrician wanted him to do. Perhaps this sort of transaction should not be called 'communicating a thought.' But if not, what kinds of occurrences merit that title?

Whatever we are supposed to mean by 'transferring' and 'communicating' thoughts, it should be plain that these broad analyses of telepathy are not germane to the philosophical question, "Are

---

[3]J.M. Baldwin, "Telepathy," *Dictionary of Philosophy,* London (1901-1905).

the contents of another's mind necessarily inaccessible to me?" So instead of dealing generally with telepathy, we ought to discuss it in connection with mental states for which there is a fairly definite range of associated inner sensations. An example would be the way Tom feels when he is suffering from a head cold. An observer, his friend Bill, can see Tom's inflamed nose, his rheumy, bloodshot eyes, his grimaces. He can hear Tom's sneezes and expectorations, and feel the heat of his brow. When we come to bodily sensations, however, we notice many that Tom alone has: tickling in his nose, dryness of his throat, smarting eyes, a cottony feeling in his cerebrum, an overall sense of aching lethargy. Therefore when Bill says, consolingly, "I know just how you feel," he cannot possibly mean that he is acquainted with Tom's feelings. Regardless how many colds Bill has endured, no matter how minutely he has recorded his bodily sensations when he displayed the same symptoms as Tom exhibits now, Bill cannot ever be sure that Tom now has sensations like those he had.

How about telepathic remedies for the *lacunae* in Bill's observations? Bill might seek access to Tom's somatic feelings in at least two relevant senses of 'feelings'; (i) the short-range sense, in which a particular jab of pain would be the object of acquaintance; (ii) the long-range sense, in which the object would be an enduring sensation, a series of sensations, or one evolving sensation.

Take short-range feelings. If Bill felt a tickle as Tom wrinkled his nose, would we say that he is acquainted with one of the feelings of Tom's cold? I would reject such a conclusion. Suppose Bill undergoes no other discomforts. Unlike Tom, who is overwhelmed by his cold, Bill feels quite fit—except for the tickle in his nose. Then isn't there a crucial difference between Tom and Bill *vis à vis* their tickling? Their reactions might diverge widely. Tom might groan, "Lord, here goes another sneezing fit!" Bill would be surprised, but hardly distressed, to have a tickle in his nose when he is generally at ease. Because of this disparity in practical significance which the tickling possesses for each man, we have two alternatives.

Instead of saying that Bill is telepathically acquainted with his friend's sensation, we can argue either: (a) that both feel the same tickle, but it feels differently to each man; or (b) that Tom feels one tickle which is very unsettling to him, while his friend feels another which is not at all disturbing. If we were concerned with material objects like stones, we would have no difficulty deciding, for example, whether two children who are digging at the beach together feel the same rock, or whether each is pressing against a separate rock. Evidently a single rock can feel differently to each child—warm to one whose fingers were immersed in the chilly ocean, cool to the one who has stayed away from the ocean. With sensations, however, we lack methods of counting in the situation we imagined. But luckily this does not affect our philosophical inquiry about telepathic acquaintance. Whether we espouse conclusion (a) or conclusion (b), we have to admit that telepathy does not provide Bill with direct awareness of how Tom feels. At best, (a) Bill has access to the same sensation, but it does not feel to him as it does to Tom. So he can still wish he knew how it felt to Tom. Alternatively, (b) he only has access to a partly similar sensation of his own—not much of a telepathic leap into another's mind![4]

This philosophical shortcoming of telepathy becomes more evident if we turn to long-range feelings. To vary the illustration for a moment: It would be odd for a man to claim that he was acquainted, telepathically, with the feelings of his cousin who is presently trying to swim the English Channel, if he nevertheless feels dry and warm. Although we still have options like (a) and (b), we could not make a very strong case for holding that this telepathic observer experiences the agony of his water-logged cousin.

Similarly if we turn to the long-range case where Bill claims acquaintance with Tom's sensations during a week's bout of the flu. Telepathic transference of Tom's feelings of congestion, shortness of breath, and so on, would hardly count as 'feeling the way Tom did.' For we must suppose that generally Bill's experiences are attuned to his own untroubled activities during the week of Tom's illness: He goes to the office, dressed in a business suit, instead of being clad in pyjamas and confined to his room. He attends movies and parties in the evening, while Tom attempts

---

[4]I have added the clarifications in this paragraph in respense to Peter Swiggart, "A Note on Telepathy," *Analysis,* Vol. 22 (December 1961), pp. 42-43.

fitfully to sleep. Bill's eyes appear clear, not bloodshot and watery, when he looks in the mirror; his cheeks are rosy, not frighteningly pale. Again we can hold to a conclusion like (a), rather than (b); however, we cannot plausibly maintain that telepathy gave Bill much insight into Tom's feelings of discomfort during the week. Tom felt as if he had a cold; Bill did not, although he was afflicted with incongruous feelings from time to time over an otherwise agreeable period.

Telepathic transference should include more context, before Bill can appreciate how Tom feels. So imagine that Bill notices streaming eyes whenever he looks at himself in the mirror. Besides the tickle in his nose, he is afflicted with paroxysms of sneezing. He feels too weak to continue working. We might go overboard and say that telepathic acquaintance with Tom's cold-feelings must comprise all Tom's sensations, thoughts, abilities, and memories. If Bill must psychologically resemble Tom in every respect, then he will be unable to distinguish Tom as another person with whose cold-feelings he has telepathic contact. Bill would see Tom's suffering face in the mirror. He would not remember, longingly, his own days of robust health, but he would recall Tom's fishing trips and hiking expeditions.

This is too fanciful and self-defeating a requirement. Perhaps we ought to say that telepathic awareness of Tom's cold-feelings must comprise only Tom's sensations of discomfort, and certain aspects of his mental outlook, which are pertinent to his suffering from a cold here and now. This is vague, but we mean to show that Bill feels as if he had a cold himself. Since Bill can observe his own behavior, or at least seek information from observers, any behavioral clue that Bill is not afflicted with a cold might come to Bill's attention, with the result that he feels less ill than Tom. For example, if his physician told Bill that his respiration is perfectly normal, his overall discomfort might diminish, so that he no longer feels the way Tom does. Thus Bill has to feel like Tom in all relevant respects, and resemble him in symptoms. It would be unreasonable to give a different medical diagnosis of Tom and Bill. I would be baffled if someone added, "But only Tom really has a cold; Bill merely has Tom's feelings of a cold." What lack in Bill's sensations and comportment would justify us in saying that he only has access to Tom's cold-feeling, or its replica, but has nothing physically wrong with him? If this case is typical of those forms of telepathy which concern 'other minds' philosophers, then to be telepathically aware of another's feeling is to be in the same general condition as him. Therefore even if telepathy were possible, it would not be an easy method of access to the contents of our fellow men's consciousness.

CHAPTER 9

A NOTE ON TELEPATHY*

PETER SWIGGART

RECENT DISCUSSION OF THE PROBLEM of other selves has tended to discredit the view that knowledge of another's mental state through telepathy is theoretically possible. John Wisdom argues that telepathic experiences are not what the philosopher desires "when he asks for real knowledge of the mind of another."[1] And in a comment on Wisdom's statement, I. Thalberg explains why in his opinion telepathy cannot give us such knowledge. "Being acquainted, telepathically, with another's feelings," he writes, is nothing less than "being in the same condition as the other person."[2] Thalberg suggests that unless Bill has a cold he cannot sense what Tom senses in having a cold. If Bill feels only a nose tickle, whereas Tom has a nose tickle plus other cold symptoms, we cannot say that Bill and Tom feel the same way or that Bill can have telepathic acquaintance with Tom's sensation. "I would say that Bill is not acquainted with Tom's tickle, because there is a crucial difference between Tom's tickle and Bill's tickle."

Certainly the popular conception of telepathy as telephone communcation *sans* telephone is not relevant to the philosopher's quest. But Thalberg's description of what telepathy must mean for the philosopher investigating the problem of knowing other minds is unsatisfactory for two reasons. First, it is evident that if Tom's nose tickle is characterized as distinct, it can be isolated from the complex of sensations with which it might be associated. And if a distinct sensation can be communicated by telepathy there is no

---

*Reprinted from *Analysis,* 1961-62, by permission of the author.
[1]*Other Minds,* p. 95.
[2]*Analysis* (January, 1961).

special reason why Tom's tickle cannot be communicated to Bill. Thalberg is perhaps confusing the sense in which the quality of a sensation is conditioned by accompanying sensations with the notion of a sensation's distinct quality. His objection that a difference must exist between Tom's tickle and Bill's tickle is only the objection that a nose tickle accompanied by say a headache and a runny nose is a different sensation from a nose tickle independent of other cold symptoms. But such a difference could not prevent Bill who doesn't have a cold, but who might feel as if he did, from having a nose tickle exactly like Tom's. One might arbitrarily state, by way of defining 'sensation,' that the quality of a person's sensation is uniquely influenced by his thoughts, his personality, or the state of his health. But this would be to raise the question of whether or not one person's sensation can be exactly communicated to another. If Tom's distinct nose tickle can be exactly given to Bill, it is irrelevant whether Tom's sensation belongs to a cold or not.

Second, even if we assume that a person's sensation cannot be identical with another's, the philosopher's question is not solved. For the possibility of telepathic acquaintance need not be restricted to instances of identical sensations. Let us suppose that Bill is healthy and in good spirits, but has a tickle in his nose. Let us further assume that Bill's tickle is by no means identical with the nose tickle of Tom, who has a nasty cold. These assumptions do not preclude the possibility that Bill's tickle is similar to Tom's and is telepathically derived from Tom. Nor does the assumption that Bill and Tom cannot have the same nose tickle prevent us from saying that through his awareness of the telepathic origin of his own nose tickle, Bill can obtain some knowledge of Tom's state of mind—knowledge unobtainable in any other way. Customary accounts of the possibility of obtaining knowledge through telepathic communication have assumed, rather strangely, I think, that such knowledge would involve identity and not mere similarity of sensation. This restriction has led to the obvious objection that it does not make sense to speak of a person's *having* another person's sensation. The recognition that telepathic communication need not involve identical sensations removes this objection. But the admission that an individual sensation might be telepathically derived does not automatically justify the claim that knowledge obtained by telepathy is in principle more reliable than knowledge obtained by conventional means. Even if Bill knew positively that his nose tickle was derived telepathically from Tom's, he would not necessarily know how similar the two nose tickles were. And if he knew that his tickle was almost identical to Tom's, he might still be in doubt as to whether Tom had a bad cold or just an allergic condition.

Perhaps the only way to solve the dispute over telepathy is to explore the difference between having a means of obtaining knowledge and actually obtaining knowledge. Knowledge obtained by telepathy might be more reliable than knowledge received through ordinary sense-experience, but the fact of its reliability would lack positive verification. Moreover, the knowledge thus obtained would tend to be trivial and unsatisfactory. Bill's nose tickle, regardless of its source, is not his best way of finding out if Tom has a cold.

CHAPTER 10

KNOWLEDGE, EMPIRICISM AND ESP*

JAMES M. O. WHEATLEY

EPISTEMOLOGY IS THE BRANCH OF PHILOSOPHY concerned with the scope and structure of knowledge—its foundations, ingredients, and validity. In an exploratory spirit I wish to set out certain questions which arise when extrasensory perception is approached from an epistemological viewpoint and which I believe require more discussion than they have received. In particular, the concepts I shall consider are chiefly knowledge, evidence, and verifiability. While the material on evidence and verification with reference to ESP is already voluminous, it is some specific and not so familiar questions about nonsensory bases of knowledge and evidence that I intend to discuss. I shall first consider the concept of knowledge and then refer to that of verifiability.

We may lead into the first question by referring to the classical debate between rationalism and empiricism. According to empiricism, all knowledge (except, perhaps, in logic and mathematics) is *a posteriori,* that is, depends on experience. According to rationalism, some knowledge of the nature and character of reality is extrasensory and *a priori.*† Do the findings of psychical research

---

*Reprinted from *International Journal of Parapsychology,* 1961, by permission of the Parapsychology Foundation, Inc. This reprinting incorporates minor stylistic revisions and omits some of the original footnotes.

†For rationalists, *a priori* knowledge may take numerous forms. Sometimes they speak of knowledge that is *chronologically a priori,* and this relates to doctrines of innate ideas. Kant, concerned with *logical* apriority, defines "*a priori* knowledge . . . [as] knowledge absolutely independent of all experience [and even of all impressions of the senses]. Opposed to it is empirical knowledge, which is knowledge possible only *a posteriori,* that is, through experience." (*Critique of Pure Reason,* transl. by Norman Kemp Smith (London, Macmillan and Co., 1933), pp. 42-43.) By some, *a priori* knowledge is held to be based on "rational intuition." Descartes, for example, thought

or parapsychology bear on this doctrinal question about the foundations of knowledge? Do they, for example, lend support to the rationalist's claim that some facts are knowable *a priori?* As a science, one might suppose, parapsychology is disposed to accept empiricism as a theory of knowledge. If, then, its findings show that it is possible to know extrasensorially, does this point to an inconsistency between its results and its presuppositions?

To use no stronger word, parapsychology at least *suggests* that it is possible to have extrasensory knowledge, and if any science proceeds on the assumption that all genuine knowledge of the world must be directly or indirectly grounded in sensory experience, then parapsychology is unique among the sciences in reaching conclusions which place in doubt this very assumption. But knowledge need not be *a priori* for being extrasensory, and so I believe that no science really is committed to that assumption. If it is a fact that all actual knowledge is based on *sense*-experience, I think it is a contingent fact, not a necessary one. And to say this is not to repudiate empiricism.

In the debate between rationalism and empiricism the psychological and the philosophical elements have not always been clearly distinguished. Let us note the distinction between: (1) knowledge as psychologically based on sensation and *temporally* posterior to it, and (2) knowledge as epistemologically based on sensation and *logically* posterior to it. (1) pertains to learning, to an individual's acquisition of knowledge, (2) to the logical validation of claims to knowledge. Expressing this distinction, Kant held that all knowledge "begins with" sense-experience but denied that all knowledge "arises out of" experience. (Jung, on the contrary, when he states that in the unconscious there is evidently *a priori* knowledge of some situations, appears to be thinking of chronological, rather than logical, apriority.)

---

that the highest avenue to knowledge is intuition, by which he meant the clear and undoubting conception of an attentive mind that is detached from the senses. But unlike ESP, intuitive knowledge in the rationalist sense may be held to differ from sense-belief both with respect to its intrinsic character and with respect to its *objects,* which in the former case—at least for such a rationalist as Plato—are eternal, unchanging, and necessary. ESP, on the contrary, is often concerned with the same subject matter as is ordinary perception, e.g. that Jones is involved in a car accident or that there is a cross on the card which Jones is holding.

Whether Kant was right in saying that all knowledge begins with sense-experience is a psychological question and one with which I am concerned only in this paragraph. Partially, it would seem to turn on whether it is possible to acquire concepts without having sensory acquaintance with instantiating particulars, e.g. clairvoyantly. (A case where one acquired them telepathically from someone who had himself obtained them sensorially might be considered intermediate.) Conceivably, this could form a subject for future research: To what extent does extrasensory perception presuppose sensory perception? Might the understanding of color concepts possessed by a man lacking sight since birth be affected by telepathy? A distinction is necessary between paranormal knowledge of a situation prior to sensory experience of that situation and knowledge of certain situations prior to all sensory experience. The question may be put in an extreme form: Could a being devoid of sensation and memories derived from sensation learn truths about the world clairvoyantly? And here is meant the sensible world of ordinary experience; if there is a world of, for example, psychic objects that cannot be perceived through normal sensory channels at all, this raises further questions, which I must ignore.[1]

Whatever the psychological relations between sensation and extrasensory impressions may be, I am more concerned with whether all knowledge of the world necessarily depends on sense-experience with regard to *validity*. I think the answer is no, and the following may serve to show why. It is subject, however, to far-reaching qualification, in that it rests on the realist assumption of a valid, though perhaps an indefinite, distinction between a knowing subject and the world whose form and nature he knows. If, as some idealists contend, the distinction between knower and known is ultimately untenable (as on their view, indeed, would be the distinction between one knower and another), then the following ac-

---

[1]Cf. P.D. Payne and L.J. Bendit, *The Psychic Sense*, rev. ed. (London, Faber and Faber, 1958). *Passim*. As my colleague Dr C.W. Webb has pointed out to me, I am overlooking also the intermediate possibility of nonsensible qualities being possessed by the material objects and situations which *we* apprehend through sensation, and the question of becoming aware of such qualities extrasensorially. I am referring now, of course, not to what some would regard as the "nonsensible qualities" that we already contrive to perceive by "normal" means (qualities like goodness, beauty, and humor), but to unsuspected nonsensible (occult?) qualities that could be perceived only by clairvoyance or other "supernormal" means.

count is not pertinent. For present purposes, I adopt a realist framework, in which there are objects of knowledge (i.e. things *about* which something is or can be known) that normally and to a large extent are distinct from and independent of the mind, and in which one mind normally is distinct from another.

By knowledge is meant belief that is not only true but also well-founded. But to be well-founded it does not have to be based, either sooner or later, on sensory perception. What *is* required is a trustworthy channel of some kind between knower and known. In fact, the most trustworthy we have is sense-perception. It may be the only medium we possess which is sufficiently reliable for knowledge; in any case, it is perfectly consistent to acknowledge the existence of ESP and still deny that as a matter of fact anyone ever *knows* anything through it. Yet knowledge through extra-sensory perception is logically possible. Circumstances are conceivable in which we might allow that someone knew such and such to be the case even though his belief that it is the case could be validated only by reference to, say, telepathy. In particular, all our knowledge *of* ESP presumably is derived from observations and experiments in which sensory perception plays a prominent part, but if I am right, one person might even come to know by telepathy that a second person were telepathizing with a third. Science, I submit, does not necessarily require sensation. I have in fact read science fiction in which it is hinted that science is being carried on without any recourse to sense-experience, and this suggestion, however unrealistic, does not seem to be self-contradictory.

What I am suggesting is that the empiricist thesis that (apart from logic and mathematics) all knowledge is based on experience, as opposed to being *a priori,* need not mean that the experience involved has to be sensory (even though empiricists traditionally have supposed that it always is sensory). Somewhat comparably, by using the term "sensory experience" we need not imply that in experience which *is* sensory the *humanly familiar* senses are necessarily involved. We may leave open the possibility of there being involved other senses or unfamiliar sense organs (a magnetic sense, for instance, or a sense organ directly responsive to changes in altitude or humidity, eyes sensitive to ultraviolet light, or even sense organs reacting to stimuli of sorts of which we are now totally unaware). The view that extrasensory perception may serve as a basis for knowledge seems to be consistent with empiricism.

Subjectively or introspectively, indeed, extrasensory experience may be indistinguishable from ordinary experience of one sort or another, except to the extent, perhaps, that sensations are distinguishable from memory images. The introspectable vehicles or units of ESP may always be images, feelings, or impressions that are intrinsically the same as those we experience through the functioning of our senses. Certainly this seems *often* to be the case, which is to say that to a very considerable extent extrasensory experience is, so to speak, colored by the body in or through which perception is typically sensory. To this extent, it is quasi-sensory. On the other hand, if there are incorporeal beings that are capable of extrasensory awareness, *their* experience, may, from a subjective point of view, be unimaginably different from our own ESP, somewhat as the visual experience of bees, if they can see ultraviolet light, must be unimaginably different from our own visual experience. Also, there may be incarnate persons whose extrasensory perceptions are free of the sensory accompaniments with which ESP is normally present to introspection, perhaps because they can be aware of purely psychic objects, whereas in most known cases ESP seems occupied with the physical world or with the sense-linked contents of other minds.

Hypothetical circumstances in which we might say that someone had knowledge not logically dependent on sense-experience but still *a posteriori* can be illustrated roughly by means of the following example. Suppose someone living in America finds himself believing on numerous occasions that it is raining in Timbuktu, without on any of these occasions having ordinary evidence, of a sensory or rational nature, for this belief. Always, however, the belief is accompanied by a characteristic feeling or image, which he comes to identify as his rain-in-Timbuktu indicator. If we find that over a long period of time (this, of course, is vague, but so is the concept of knowledge itself), the person's belief is always or perhaps even nearly always true, and we are satisfied on adequate grounds that he has not discovered that it is raining in Timbuktu by any normal means and that the introspectum I have referred to as his indicator is not of sensory origin, then we may decide that he has extrasensory knowledge of the weather there.[2]

Against this, if it turned out that his information came telepathically from someone who had good sensory evidence for believing that it was raining in Timbuktu, we should be able to object that the knowledge attributed to the recipient of the information were still itself sensorial. (In practice, this interpretation could scarcely be excluded as long as there is no sure way of distinguishing cases of clairvoyance from cases of telepathy, and of being able to rule out telepathy in a given situation.) Moreover, it might be argued that the basis of even telepathic or clairvoyant knowledge is after all sensory, on the grounds that telepathy and clairvoyance can plausibly be construed as unusual types of sensation.

The question whether "extrasensory perception" is really sensory, or the "sixth sense" really extrasensory, has sometimes been debated.[3] Without entering into the pros and cons, I suggest that the intended force of describing telepathy and clairvoyance as non-sensory is not actually as much to deny that they are *sensory* as to deny that they are *physical*. If, accordingly, when we have learned a good deal more about the *modus operandi* of "ESP" than we have so far, we are able to explain it physically (say in terms of the "muscle rustle" recently reported on or as a function of the brain),[4] we might then be inclined to regard it as sensory. At present, how-

---

[2]Partly comparable examples are given by Professor A. J. Ayer in *The Problem of Knowledge* (Harmondsworth, Middlesex, Penguin Books, 1956): "Suppose that someone were consistently successful in predicting events of a certain kind . . . like the results of a lottery. If his run of successes were sufficiently impressive, we might very well come to say that he knew which number would win, even though he did not reach this conclusion by any rational method, or indeed by any method at all . . . In the same way, if someone were consistently successful in reading the minds of others without having any of the usual sort of evidence, we might say that he knew these things telepathically. But in default of any further explanation this would come down to saying merely that he did know them, but not by any ordinary means. Words like . . . 'telepathy' are brought in just to disguise the fact that no explanation has been found" (pp. 32-33).

[3]See, for example, J.B. Rhine, *New Frontiers of the Mind* (New York, Farrar and Rinehart, 1937), pp. 128-131, and L. Warner, "Is 'extra-sensory perception' extra-sensory?", *Journal of Psychology*, Vol. 7 (1939), pp. 71-77.

[4]See, for example, the report entitled "Body's electromagnetic signals may hold clues to telepathy" in *Newsletter of the Parapsychology Foundation, Inc.*, Vol. 7 (March-April, 1960), p. 1, and N. Marshall, "ESP and memory: a physical theory," *The British Journal for the Philosophy of Science*, Vol. 10 (1960), pp. 265-286. Dr. Marshall advances an interesting theory which is "physical" without being cast in terms of space, time, and energy transmission.

ever, the prevalent view is that it is nonphysical (though it is not easy to discover precisely what is meant by calling it this), and if eventually it were accounted for in extraphysical, extrasomatic terms, that might well confirm the suitability of the expression "extrasensory," whatever misgivings we retained about the word "perception." Yet not to mention the Eastern conception of the *mind* as a nonphysical *sense organ,* it is surely good English to use the word "sense" to mean—here I paraphrase my dictionary—a faculty or function *of the mind or soul* analogous to perception through the bodily senses. And no one denies that many persons have a sense of humor as well as a sense of smell. Anyhow, for the present discussion I assume that telepathy and clairvoyance *are* extrasensory.

I have been speaking of the logical possibility of extrasensory knowledge and I need not try to decide here whether any such knowledge actually exists. But the following points may be noted. It is not uncommon in the literature of psychical research for writers to attribute "supernormal" or "paranormal" knowledge to mediums or other sensitives, and I am inclined to agree that the attributions are sometimes justified. Nevertheless, knowing, in Ayer's felicitous phrase, requires having the right to be sure, and it is doubtful that in these cases of alleged knowledge such right is *usually* present. In any event, even if some persons possess or have possessed extrasensory knowledge, cases of telepathic or clairvoyant *knowledge* must be far fewer than cases of telepathy or clairvoyance. For one thing, much ESP occurs, it would seem, in the absence of belief and therefore could not constitute knowledge as understood in this paper. Although the relationship between belief and the introspectable mental processes to which he refers must here be left unexplored, I take Professor Broad to be making essentially the same point when he observes that "in much of the experimental work the word 'cognition' must be interpreted behavioristically, at least as regards the subject's introspectable mental processes."[5]

---

[5]C.D. Broad, *Religion, Philosophy and Physical Research* (London, Routledge and Kegan Paul Limited, 1953), pp. 16-17. It is worth noting that Broad's term "cognition" embraces much besides knowledge, including as well belief, doubt, direct apprehension, etc.

Also, while the cases just referred to are those in which the subject, though not *believing* that what he says is true, nevertheless guesses, with a significant degree of accuracy, *that such and such is the case* (e.g. that the target is a star), there are other situations in which the "object" of ESP (the "extrasensory perceptum") is not a proposition at all, but merely an image or a series of images (as in a dream), a feeling (e.g. a pain in the chest), a mood, or an apparition. It seems likely that such cases would be instances of what Broad calls *telepathic interaction,* which he distinguishes from *telepathic cognition.* Telepathic interaction, he says, is "supernormal causal influence of one embodied mind on another," telepathic cognition "supernormal cognition of one embodied mind by another."[6] In his view, the latter probably presupposes the former, while telepathic interaction can take place without telepathic cognition. It occurs, for instance, when "the occurrence of a certain sensation or imagination or bodily feeling in M's mind causally determines [supernormally] in N's mind the occurrence of a sensation with a similar sensum, or of an imagination with a similar image, or of a bodily feeling with a similar quality and feeling-tone."[7] At such times N may or may not believe that M is trying to convey an impression to him. It is true that if one person, as a result of telepathy, were to feel pain *other than his own,* this *would* be a case of telepathic cognition, according to Broad; but he believes there is no reason to think that such direct apprehension of others' experiences ever happens. Even if it sometimes does happen, it still would not constitute knowledge in the sense with which I am concerned, any more than seeing a red surface or hearing a loud noise constitutes knowledge in that sense, although it is sometimes called knowledge in another sense.

To assert that all knowledge is experiential, i.e. derived from experience, is not to assert that it is all empirical. This is relevant to the submission made above that scientific endeavor, as evidence-gathering and problem-solving activity, does not logically require sensation. Certain distinctions are now called for. Without supposing that these could be sharply or precisely upheld, I propose to

---

[6]*Ibid.,* p. 48.
[7]*Ibid.,* pp. 53-54.

mark off (1) some experiential knowledge as *empirical* and (2) some empirical knowledge as *scientific,* and to admit corresponding distinctions with regard to evidence. I assume that in any factual issue only empirical evidence can be decisive or *intersubjectively* convincing, and I suggest that by "scientific evidence" is meant the most exact and systematic, the most carefully and critically obtained empirical evidence; being reached experimentally whenever possible. The following examples may help to clarify these distinctions.

There is *scientific* evidence for the generalization known as Boyle's Law. But suppose, taking a different subject matter, that I phone the railroad station to find out when the next train for Ottawa leaves, and am told, 4:15 P.M. Then I have *empirical* grounds for believing that the next train for Ottawa leaves at that time, but hardly scientific grounds. Nevertheless, both scientific and other (sub-scientific?) empirical evidence is *deliberately* obtained, in attempting to find out something. So much may be suggested by the etymology of "empirical." Much knowledge, on the other hand, comes to us without our intending or trying to acquire it; we get evidence for countless truths—and falsehoods—without deliberate inquiry. Various examples could be cited. For one, I don't, and indeed couldn't, have empirical evidence for the proposition that I have a toothache, though if I do have a toothache, I *ipso facto* have *experiential* evidence for that proposition. An observation of Bacon's is pertinent. "Simple experience," he asserted, ". . . if taken as it comes, is called accident; if sought for, experiment."

In view of the above, it would seem that the question whether empirical science, which has provided the most decisive evidence for the existence of extrasensory perception, can itself be extrasensory, turns partly on whether ESP-potential, like ordinary sight, can be deliberately employed, or exercised at will, whether one can *try* to perceive extrasensorially, and so on. But what such trying would or does amount to is very obscure. We have some idea about what it is to "perceive" extrasensorially, but scarcely any about what it is to try to do so. In the proportion *seeing:looking for =* *ESP:x,* we are much in the dark about the final term. Extrasensory perception is one thing, "extrasensory watching" another.

This leads to the final question, which refers to the *principle of verifiability*. The latter has sparked much discussion in recent philosophy and has been closely associated with contemporary empiricism. Earlier empiricists held that knowledge is limited to experience. Later, this claim was enlarged, becoming the thesis that not only knowledge but cognitively meaningful discourse cannot transcend possible experience. In considering the logical positivists' theory of meaning, epitomized by the principle of verifiability, we may justifiably view it first, I think, as an antithesis of such a text as the following, found in Tyrrell's *The Personality of Man:* "Nature does not come to an end where our senses cease to register it and our minds become incapable of dealing with it."[8]

In one of its many formulations the verifiability principle said that "To state the meaning of a sentence is to state the way in which it can be verified (or falsified)" (Schlick). Very roughly, the idea was that any proposition, to be cognitively meaningful (i.e. true or false), must be either analytic—true or false *ex vi terminorum*—or capable, in principle, of being verified (where "verified" should be understood to mean verified or falsified); and that we exhibit what a synthetic proposition means by explaining what situation *would* verify it. But successive attempts to formulate a statement of this principle that would serve to delimit the meaningful proved abortive. Though trying to define "cognitively meaningful" in such a fashion is evidently vain, however, it has seemed to some that the verifiability principle might fruitfully be used to specify the notion of "empirical proposition."

Thus, instead of saying that a (synthetic) proposition is *cognitively meaningful* if, and only if, it is in principle verifiable, perhaps we can say that a proposition is *empirical* if, and only if, it is in principle verifiable. It has remained difficult to state exactly what is meant in this context by "verifiable": distinctions have been drawn between direct and indirect verifiability and strong and weak verifiability. Sooner or later, though, reference is made to *experience,* and the essential point is that a verifiable proposition is in principle both testable and logically grounded in experience. If it is true, the experience of a properly placed observer will be differ-

---

[8]G.N.M. Tyrrell, *The Personality of Man* (Harmondsworth, Middlesex, Penguin Books, 1947), p. 263.

ent from what it would be if it were false. All empirical propositions, therefore, whether true or false, are in this sense experiential.
The value of the verifiability principle, then, when it is conceived
as a definition of "empirical proposition," will lie in making precise
the relationship between an empirical proposition of whatever logical level and the experiential content which gives it its "cash value."

Now, need the experience involved be sensory? The answer, I
think, is that despite what the positivists may have intended, it
need not be. Two things can be said here. First, that what was
stated earlier regarding the experiential basis of knowledge could
be repeated, *mutatis mutandis,* about the experiential basis of empirical meaningfulness or verifiability. It is true that in actually
testing an empirical proposition we shall in all likelihood have to
apply for and rely on *sensory* experience. To check on the truth of
a proposition about the time of a train's departure it is easier to
pick up the telephone than to telepathize with the ticket agent. But
this appeal to sensory perception is demanded by our evident
factual inability to have extrasensory perception at will, not by the
verifiability principle itself.

The principle's independence of sensory perception was already
called for by Professor Broad in 1949. He noted: "Many contemporary philosophers are sympathetic to some form of the . . .
'verification principle', i.e. roughly that a synthetic proposition is
significant if and only if we can indicate what kind of experience
in assignable circumstances would tend to support or to weaken it.
But this is generally combined with the tacit assumption that the
only kinds of experience which could tend to support or weaken
such a proposition are sense-perceptions, introspections, and memories. If we have to accept the occurrence of various kinds of paranormal cognition, we ought to extend the verification principle to
cover the possibility of propositions which are validated or invalidated by other kinds of cognitive experience beside those which
have hitherto been generally admitted."[9]

Second, although I agree substantially with what Professor Broad
says here, I wonder if he has not overestimated the extension that
may be required. The "other kinds of cognitive experience" to

---

[9]C.D. Broad, *op. cit.,* p. 23.

which he refers will admittedly be other than normal in their *genesis,* but so far as we know, are they not the same with respect to *intrinsic nature* as some of the usual kinds of experiences which he describes as "sense-perceptions, introspections, and memories"? I suggested earlier that extrasensory experiences, being as it were qualified by the body which normally affords us experience of a sensory origin, are themselves quasi-sensory and introspectively may not be distinguishable from ordinary experiences of one kind or another. Thus suppose we did commonly verify a proposition by, say, voluntary clairvoyance. The resulting experiences which we would take as tending "to support or to weaken it" might be just such images as would ordinarily result from acts of recollecting sense-perceptions.

On the other hand, if in connection with ESP there do occur experience-contents which are roughly analogous to, but yet intrinsically quite different from, the sense-data, images, and feelings that occur in connection with sensory perception, then a radical reformulation of the verifiability principle would seem to be indicated. But the existence of such strange data of consciousness (or data of strange consciousness) does not necessarily follow from that of ESP and must, indeed, be regarded as very dubious.

To sum up briefly, my conclusion is that even if it constitutes a ground of knowing, ESP seems basically consistent with an empiricist theory of knowledge and science, even one which includes the principle of verifiability. From this standpoint, at least, parapsychology, to be scientific, need not embrace principles concerning the foundations of knowledge that are incompatible with the findings of its own research. What I have said does not mean that either empiricism or the verifiability principle is tenable; but neither, I believe, is invalidated by the existence of extrasensory perception.

CHAPTER 11

ESP AND MEMORY*

W. G. ROLL

INTRODUCTION

THE RELATIONSHIP BETWEEN EXTRASENSORY PERCEPTION (ESP) and familiar biological and psychological processes has been the subject matter of several parapsychological investigations. A particularly fertile area of research has been the study of the connection between ESP and motivational factors as explored, for instance, by G. R. Schmeidler[1] and M. Anderson and R. White.[2] Perhaps the most convincing argument for the reality of ESP is that it is affected by psychological needs in much the same way as better understood perceptual and cognitive functions are affected.

Aside from that, we know very little. We do not even know whether extrasensory perception can rightly be called a form of perception. There seems to be no sense organ for ESP and the process appears to leave no characteristic experience in consciousness in the manner say, of vision and hearing. The only obvious similarity between sensory and extrasensory perception is that both are usually responses to external events. Also, both are at least to some extent influenced by motivational factors.

In addition to being influenced by external stimuli and psychological needs, sense perception is influenced by a person's memory record. Without memories of previous experiences, we could not

---

*Reprinted from *International Journal of Neuropsychiatry*, 1966, by permission of the editor of *Behavioral Neuropsychiatry*.

[1]G.R. Schmeidler and R.A. McConnell, *ESP and Personality Patterns* (New Haven, Yale University Press, 1959).

[2]M. Anderson and R. White, "A Survey of Work on ESP and Teacher-Pupil Attitudes," *Journal Parapsychology*, Vol. 22 (1958), pp. 246-268.

interpret our sense-data. A man who has been blind from birth and who recovers his eyesight, does not know what he sees till he can interpret his visual sense-data, say, by touch. He learns to identify the new sensations by means of the old, remembered, ones. This paper will be concerned with the question whether memory also plays a role in ESP.

For the purposes of this discussion, we may distinguish four memory functions: learning, retention, remembering, and forgetting. Learning is the process of acquiring information; retention is the process by means of which this information persists through time; remembering is the process whereby the information is manifested in the present; and forgetting is the process whereby it is temporarily or permanently lost.

The term "memory trace" is used for the hypothetical change in the cortex or elsewhere by which information is stored.

The ESP process has been pictured as consisting of three aspects: source, channel, and receiver. In an experiment, the source is the ESP target, for instance, a series of ESP card symbols (star, circle, square, cross, waves). If the target is not known to anybody at the time of testing, this is an experiment in "clairvoyance," or ESP of objective physical events. If the target is in the mind of some person, we are dealing with "telepathy," with ESP of mental events. If the card order will be determined only *after* the subject has made his responses, this is a test in "precognition." These differences do not necessarily reflect differences in the ESP process. For instance, it is possible that telepathy is in fact clairvoyance of brain events in the person who thinks of the target and that "precognition" scores are produced by clairvoyance and psychokinesis. However, these possibilities need not concern us here. We shall also not discuss the ESP channel, the means whereby ESP information reaches the receiver from the source. It is a matter for lively debate in parapsychology whether or not ESP stimuli are comparable to known physical stimuli, such as electromagnetic radiation. I believe they are,[3] but this problem is outside our present scope. We shall consider mainly the ESP receiver, more particularly we shall ask, what are the characteristics of the ESP response?

[3]W.G. Roll, *The Psi Field*. Presidential Address. Seventh Annual Convention of the Parapsychological Association (Oxford University, September 3-6, 1964).

MEMORY TRACES AS ESP RESPONSES

An ESP card test is in certain obvious respects a memory test. It is part of the experimental procedure to familiarize the subject with the five ESP cards or whatever the targets will be, so that he can remember them during the test itself. If he forgets any of the symbols, he is not likely to do as well as if he remembered them all. (If he is such a poor learner that he can only remember one card and always responds with it, he will score at chance, assuming that the target series is random and does not contain an excess of the favored symbol.) If it is essential that the subject should remember the five ESP symbols, it is just as essential that in the test itself, he must *forget* or ignore the order in which they were initially shown to him as well as the order of his previous guesses. This applies to any learning situation. To learn something new, the old often must be forgotten: "learning involves forgetting."

It appears that in the common card tests and in other experiments where a limited range of targets is used, the responses are, in a sense, memory responses. Before the ESP guessing begins, certain memory traces are laid down which are then aroused during the test itself. However, though the acquisition of the memory trace is established by sensory perception, its arousal is caused by external ESP stimuli—at least if a significant score is obtained in the test. It appears as if the effect of ESP stimuli is to revive memory traces, much as do other external stimuli in sense perception.

In the search for clues about the nature of ESP, the investigator may get important insights by looking beyond controlled scientific research. A study of the more informal material, however, gives essentially the same picture as the ESP card tests. F.W.H. Myers,[4] the English pioneer in parapsychology, was one of the first to notice that in ESP hallucinations ("apparitions") "mind has been at work upon the picture—that the scene has not been presented, so to say, in crude objectivity." Another English investigator, G.N.M. Tyrrell,[5] thought that "the apparitional drama" is worked

---

[4]F.W.H. Myers, *Human Personality and Its Survival of Bodily Death* (London, Longmans, Green and Co., 1903).
[5]G.N.M. Tyrrell, *Science and Psychical Phenomena. Apparitions* (New York, University Books, 1961).

out on unconscious regions of the personalities of the agent and the percipient. These regions, it appears, may be the memory records of the persons involved. H.F. Saltmarsh,[6] another English researcher, concluded from his study of Mrs. Warren Elliott, that "the contents of the subliminal memory" were used for her ESP responses. The late French parapsychologist, René Warcollier,[7] described the process this way: "the images which appear to the mind of the percipient under the form of hallucinations, dreams, or more or less well-formed images, spring exclusively from *his own mind,* from his own conscious or subconscious memory. *There is no carrying of the visual impression from the agent to the percipient,* any more than there is actual carrying of a letter of the alphabet from the sending apparatus of a telegraph office to the receiving office. The transmission of the message consists in making the same letter *appear,* but it already *exists* at the receiving apparatus, along with all the others, before the transmission took place." The Polish investigator, Eduoard Abramowski,[8] gave a succinct description of ESP when he said that "the telepathic process, in its psychological essence, is . . . only a process of cryptomnesia."

More recently, W.H.C. Tenhaeff,[9] the Dutch parapsychologist, commenting on the behavior of his "paragnosts" in free response tests, was reminded "of persons thinking intently of a word or a name which they have learned or heard before, or of an event they have witnessed in the past." L.E. Rhine,[10] in her study of spontaneous cases of precognition, noted that many of the people who had such experiences "marvelled at the fact that the precognitive experience was just like 'remembering' the future."

It appears not only that a person's memory traces influence his ESP responses, but, more fundamentally, that his ESP responses

[6]H.F. Saltmarsh, "A Report on the Investigation of Some Sittings with Mrs. Warren Elliott," *Proceedings Society Psychical Research,* Vol. 39 (1929), pp. 47-184.

[7]R. Warcollier, *Experimental Telepathy,* trans. by J.B. Gridley (Boston, Soc. for Psychical Rsch., 1938).

[8]E. Abramowski, *Le Subsconscient Normal* (Paris, Librarie Felix Alcan, 1914).

[9]W.H.C. Tenhaeff, Proceedings of the Parapsychological Institute of the State University of Utrecht (No. 3, January, 1965).

[10]L.E. Rhine, "Conviction and Associated Conditions in Spontaneous Cases," *Journal Parapsychology,* Vol. 15 (1951), pp. 164-191.

consist of revived memory traces. This is not to say that ESP is
only remembering. There is an external stimulus but the way this
affects a person's awareness or behavior in ESP is by first affecting
his memory traces. What is experienced or expressed in ESP is not
something "new" but rather memories of past events. The mechanism whereby the appropriate memory traces are revived in ESP
is, we may assume, the same that is used in normal perceptual and
cognitive functions. However, ESP appears to rely even more
strongly on memory than, say, visual perception, for in ESP there
are no sense-data at all, but only revived memory traces. In a way,
memory images are the "sense-data" of ESP. If we wanted another
term for ESP, we might call it "extrasensory remembering."

The theory that ESP responses consist of memory traces we
might call the "memory theory of ESP." H.H. Price,[11] the English
philosopher, refers to it as the "ecphorising theory of psi cognition"
(ecphorise: to revive or rouse from latency) and contrasts it with
the "sixth-sense theory" according to which ESP is an original
source of ideas. Price notes that the ecphorising theory conforms
to David Hume's view that all ideas have been acquired either
from normal perception or from normal introspection. He finds it
more economical and plausible than the sixth-sense theory.

In the next few pages, I shall discuss some of the findings in
parapsychology in the light of this theory. It will be seen that a
number of apparently unconnected discoveries about ESP fall into
place and that some facts which hitherto have resisted interpretation
now make sense.

THE LAWS OF LEARNING AND ESP

It has long been known that certain conditions facilitate learning.
These are described in the "laws of learning." The best known are
the laws of recency, frequency, and vividness (or intensity). In
other words, recent events, all other conditions being equal, are
more likely to be remembered than events in the more remote
past; frequent events are more likely to be remembered than infre-
quent ones; and vivid or emotionally intense events have an ad-

---

[11]H.H. Price, *Memory and Paranormal Cognition.* Convention Paper. Seventh Annual
Convention of Parapsychological Association (Oxford University, September 3-6,
1964).

vantage over bland and emotionally neutral ones. If the memory theory of ESP is correct , we expect ESP responses to be expressed in terms of memory traces that are recent, frequent, and vivid. In other words, ESP stimuli are likely to trigger memory traces that are already prepared to "fire." (We are not here concerned with the question which *target events* have the greatest stimulating power, but only with the question which of the perceiver's memory traces are likely to be activated in an instance of ESP.)

In some of the material reported by the Dutch parapsychologist, W.H.C. Tenhaeff,[12] the memory basis of ESP comes out clearly and illustrates some of the laws of learning. For instance, his subject, "Beta," stated correctly that a visitor came from the Dutch town of Wageningen. Beta's reason for making this statement was that he received a mental image of the agricultural college at Wageningen, a building he had often seen in the past, a good illustration of the law of frequency. The law of vividness is also represented in this material. For instance, the image of a German Weinstube where Beta and his father had an argument with the owner came to mind and suggested, correctly, that the name of another visitor was "Wijntje" ("wijn," Dutch for "wine"). Childhood events are often more intense than later ones and may be recalled more easily, though many years remote. The introspections of Beta and of Gerard Croiset,[13] the most famous of Tenhaeff's subjects, provide many examples where ESP responses consisted of memories of childhood events. Similar observations have been made by E.D. Dean[14] in his ESP experiments with the plethysmograph. The scoring was best when the names Dean used as targets belonged to people whom the subject had seen recently and who were emotionally important to him.

ASSOCIATIVE HABITS AND ESP

If a memory trace is aroused in the course of normal perceptual or introspective activities, it may, in turn, arouse other memory

---

[12]Tenhaeff, *op. cit.*

[13]W.H.C. Tenhaeff, *Psychoscopic Experiments on Behalf of the Police.* Conference Report No. 41, First Int. Conference of Parapsychological Studies (Utrecht, Holland, 1953).

[14]E.D. Dean, see paper in this symposium.

traces which are associated with it but unrelated to the situation at hand. For instance, the perception or idea of a table may make us think of a chair and this, in turn, of a particular person seated on a chair. Such associations are one of the main characteristics of mental life, though we are often unaware of their existence. The conditions which facilitate the formation of these connections are described in the "laws of association." Some of these are similar to the "laws of learning" (the laws of recency, frequency, and vividness).

If the effect of an ESP stimulus is to arouse a memory trace, then we should expect that other memory traces associated with the former will also be evoked, not because of their relationship to the ESP stimulus but because of their relationship to the first memory trace. Such associative effects emerge strongly in ESP card tests. For instance, J.G. Pratt and S.G. Soal[15] found striking evidence for guessing habits when they analyzed the responses of Mrs. Gloria Stewart, a highly successful ESP subject. Soal[16] elsewhere suggested that the reason the five ESP symbols (star, circle, square, cross, and waves) have been so successful in ESP tests is that there are fewer preestablished associations between them in the minds of most subjects than between, say, playing cards or numbers. For the same reason, nonsense syllables are used in learning tests. However, with repeated usage, associations are likely to be formed and it is possible that this is related to the decline to chance observed in so many high-scoring subjects after extended testing, including those of Soal.

The suggestion has been made by C.T. Tart[17] that such extinctions of ESP capacity are due to the parapsychologist's failure to follow basic procedures for teaching skilled behavior, in particular to his failure to give immediate rewards for correct responses or punishments for incorrect ones. Tart notes that in ordinary learning situations if reward and punishment cannot be clearly associated with correct and incorrect responses by the organism, the desired

[15]J.G. Pratt and S.G. Soal, "Some Relations Between Call Sequences and ESP Performance," *Journal Parapsychology*, Vol. 16 (1952), pp. 165-186.

[16]S.G. Soal and F. Bateman, *Modern Experiments in Telepathy* (London, Faber and Faber, 1954).

[17]C.T. Tart, "Card Guessing Tests: Learning Paradigm or Extinction Paradigm?" *Journal of American Society Psychical Research*, Vol. 60 (1966), pp. 46-55.

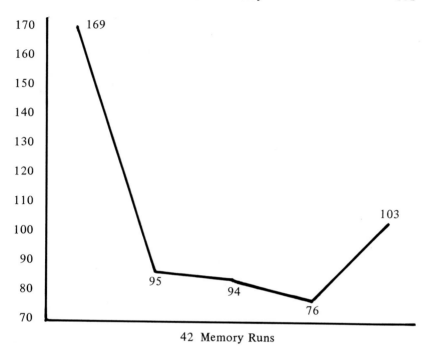

42 Memory Runs

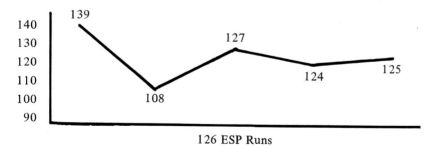

126 ESP Runs

FIGURE 1. Distribution of Scores in Memory and ESP Tests.
The decline between the first and second segment in the memory tests represents odds of several thousands to one against chance. In the ESP tests the odds are fifty to one (CR diff. = 2.19).

behavior is not learned, or if already present, is extinguished.

In addition to this gradual extinction of ESP in the course of time, declines are often observed during individual tests, sometimes with an upswing toward the end resulting in a "U-curve." These resemble the learning curves found in serial learning trials. In ESP card tests such curves have been found, for instance, by R. Cadoret,[18] W.A. McElroy and R.K. Brown,[19] K. Osis,[20] J.B. Rhine,[21] and S.G. Soal.[22] J.G. Pratt[23] and J.B. Rhine[24] attribute the tendency to score best in the first and last segments of the experimental series to less interference from guessing habits in these parts of the run. In a series of forty-two tests I did in England, a subject took a memory test, using an exposed sequence of twenty-five ESP cards and then did three ESP runs. There was a sharp initial decline in the memory curve with the typical upswing toward the end. The ESP scoring was also highest in the beginning of the run but there was no final salience[25] (see Figure 1).

At the same time as memory traces are the means for expressing ESP, they may also be a factor in suppressing it. The ESP response contains the seed of its own destruction. If it is true that guessing habits block ESP, we should expect that conditions which disrupt guessing habits would improve ESP. We should also expect that persons who are less prone to such habits than others are better ESP subjects. There are several studies which seem to bear this out. In the course of ESP experiments with cats, K. Osis and E.B. Foster[26] obtained the best scores shortly after a habit response was

---

[18]R.J. Cadoret, "Effect of Novelty in Test Conditions on ESP Performance," *J Parapsychol,* Vol. 16 (1952), pp. 192-203.

[19]W.A. McElroy and R.K. Brown, "Electric Shocks for Errors in ESP Card Tests," *J Parapschol,* Vol. 14 (1950), pp. 257-266.

[20]K. Osis, "A Test of the Occurrences of a Psi Effect Between Man and the Cat," *J Parapsychol,* Vol. 16 (1952), pp. 233-256.

[21]J.B. Rhine, *Extra-Sensory Perception* (Boston, Bruce Humphries, 1935).

[22]G.R. Schmeidler, "ESP and Tests of Perception," *J Am Soc Psychical Rsch, Vol. 56* (1962), pp. 48-51.

[23]J.G. Pratt and S.G. Soal, "Some Relations Between Call Sequences and ESP Performance," *J Parapsychol,* Vol. 16 (1952), pp. 165-186.

[24]J.B. Rhine, *New World of the Mind* (New York, William Sloane, 1953).

[25]W.G. Roll, *op. cit.*

[26]K. Osis, and E. Foster, "A Test of ESP in Cats," *J Parapsychol,* Vol. 17 (1953), pp. 167-186.

broken. In a previous test with cats, Osis[27] found that "novelty in the situation helped prevent habit formation and thus offered more opportunity for a psi (i.e. parapsychological) effect." R. Cadoret's[28] scores were higher when he read or sang to himself between guesses, and R.L. Van de Castle's[29] subject scored best when the responses were interrupted by long intervals during which she could smoke, talk, read, or listen to the radio. She also did better with ESP cards and colors as targets than with drawings, letters, and numbers. The author suggested that "the associative value of a stimulus may be inversely related to its effectiveness as an ESP target." Similarly, in J.G. van Busschbach's[30] experiments with school children, the rate of success with arithmetical symbols and colors as the targets was higher than with words.

In my experiments in England referred to earlier,[31] a study was also made of the relationship between ESP scores and the tendency repeatedly to call certain sequences of ESP symbols or to call certain symbols especially often. Indications were found of an inverse relationship between ESP and these habits.

Response bias is a function not only of the material to be learned but also of the learner's mentality. People who are rigid or compulsive in their behavior and thinking are not as good learners as those who are capable of a more flexible approach. Consequently, we should expect that good ESP subjects are those whose memory traces have less rigid internal relations. J.G. van Busschbach[32] thought that young children gave better results than older ones because they were more capable of "spontaneous giving-way to intuition." A.O. Ross, G. Murphy, and G.R. Schmeidler[33] found

---

[27]K. Osis, *op. cit.*

[28]R.J. Cadoret, *op. cit.*

[29]R.L. Van de Castle, "An Exploratory Study of Some Variables Relating to Individual ESP Performance," *J Parapsychol,* Vol. 17 (1953), pp. 61-72.

[30]J.G. van Busschbach, "An Investigation of Extra-sensory Perception in School Children," *J Parapsychol,* Vol. 17 (1953), pp. 210-222; "A Further Report on an Investigation of ESP in School Children," *J Parapsychol,* Vol. 19 (1955), pp. 73-81; "An Investigation of ESP Between Teacher and Pupils in American Schools," *J Parapsychol,* Vol. 20 (1956), pp. 71-80.

[31]W.G. Roll, *op. cit.*

[32]J.G. van Busschbach, *op. cit.*

[33]A.O. Ross, G. Murphy, and G.R. Schmeidler, "The Spontaneity Factor in Extrasensory Perception," *J Am Soc Psychical Rsch,* Vol. 46 (1952), pp. 14-16.

that children with an "unreflective originality" scored better than those who were constrained. In experiments with an intelligence test which measured the "mental alertness of a student," B.M. Humphrey[34] got a positive correlation with ESP scores. W.A. McElroy and R.K. Brown[35] found that the ESP scoring was best in runs where the subjects received electric shocks for errors (although the shocks did not result in a reduction of ESP errors) and suggested that the shocks had an "excitement value," favorable for ESP. Improved scores after electroshock have been claimed by H.F. Urban[36] and in tests by Schmeidler,[37] cerebral concussion patients appeared to be superior ESP subjects. By disrupting habit responses the cortical disturbances may have created openings for ESP.

In a study where children were instructed to look for "hidden" figures in drawings, G.R. Schmeidler[38] found that the best subjects also were the highest ESP scorers. She suggests that "there is a common factor between ESP ability and the ability, while taking a new look at some situation . . . to shift one's way of looking so as to notice obscure cues not previously observed." Perhaps the common factor is lack of constraint in the association that a subject superimposes on his perceptions.

LEARNING PERFORMANCE AND ESP

If memory traces are vehicles for ESP impressions, we expect a person with good recall ability to perform well in ESP and, conversely, a good ESP subject to perform well in memory tasks. Some observations reported in the literature bear this out. E. Osty,[39] the French physician and parapsychologist, thought good ESP subjects have exceptional memories. One of his subjects could

---

[34]B.M. Humphrey, "ESP and Intelligence," *J Parapsychol*, Vol. 9 (1945), pp. 7-16.

[35]W.A. McElroy, *op. cit.*

[36]H. Urban, *Parapsychological Research at a Psychiatric Clinic*. Conference Report No. 18, First International Conference of Parapsychological Studies (Utrecht, Holland, 1953).

[37]G.R. Schmeidler, "Rorschachs and ESP Scores of Patients Suffering from Cerebral Concussion," *J Parapsychol*, Vol. 16 (1952), pp. 80-89.

[38]G.R. Schmeidler, "ESP and Tests of Perception," *J Am Soc Psychical Rsch,* Vol. 56 (1962), pp. 48-51.

[39]E. Osty, *Supernormal Faculties in Man*, trans. by S. de Brath (London, Methuen, 1923).

recall verbatim the statements he had made in a previous session. The Russian physiologist, V.M. Bekhterev[40] obtained high ESP scores with an eighteen-year-old girl who had good visual and kinetic memory and Eduoard Abramowski and Jeanne Hirschberg[41] reported that among their (Polish) subjects those who were best at recalling "forgotten" material also were the best telepathic subjects. Similar observations were made about some of the English "mediums." William James[42] and Sir Oliver Lodge[43] noticed that Mrs. Piper had a good memory in her trance state. C.D. Thomas[44] and Mrs. W. H. Salter[45] commented similarly about Mrs. Leonard. J.G. Piddington,[46] in a discussion of automatic writing, was struck by "the remarkable tenacity of the script memory, for it often involves the repetition of little catchwords from a script written, it may be, many years earlier and perhaps never seen again by the automatist." W.H.C. Tenhaeff[47] has found that his subjects "show a most remarkable hypermnesia with respect to all sorts of data given at earlier sessions."

Young people seem to do best in learning tests and the same may be true of ESP, as noted by J.B. Rhine,[48] and R. White and J. Angstadt.[49] Fatigue, whether induced naturally or by drugs,

[40]V.M. Bekhterev, *Further Observations of "Mental" Influence of Man on Behavior of Animals.* Conference of the Inst. of Study of Brain and Psychic Activities, Feb. 2, 1920 (Private translation from the Russian at the Foundation for Research on the Nature of Man, Durham).

[41]E. Abramowski, *op. cit.*

[42]W. James, "A Record of Observations of Certain Phenomena of Trance," *Proc Soc Psychical Rsch,* Vol. 6 (1889-1890), pp. 443-557.

[43]O. Lodge, "Report on Some Trance Communications Received Chiefly through Mrs. Piper," *Proc Soc Psychical Rsch,* Vol. 23 (1909), pp. 127-285.

[44]C.D. Thomas, "The Modus Operandi of Trance Communication According to Descriptions Received Through Mrs. Osborne Leonard," *Proc Soc Psychical Rsch,* Vol. 38 (1928-1929), pp. 49-100.

[45]Mrs. W.H. Salter, "Some Incidents Occurring at Sittings with Mrs. Leonard Which May Throw Light upon Their Modus Operandi," *Proc Soc Psychical Rsch,* Vol. 39 (1930-1931), pp. 306-332.

[46]J.G. Piddington, "Forecasts in Scripts Concerning the War," *Proc Soc Psychical Rsch,* Vol. 33 (1923), pp. 439-605.

[47]W.H.C. Tenhaeff, *op. cit.*

[48]J.B. Rhine, *op. cit.*

[49]R. White, and J. Angstadt, "Student Preferences in a Two-Classroom GESP Experiment with Two Student-Agents Acting Simultaneously," *J Am Soc Psychical Rsch,* Vol. 57 (1963), pp. 32-42.

tends to depress scores in serial learning tasks and in ESP card tests.[50] Rhine[51] observed that the ESP scores of Zirkle dropped markedly when he was given sodium amytal. It was also noted that his recall of recent events was impaired. S.R. Feather[52] found that subjects who did well in memory trials also scored well in ESP and those who did poorly in memory had low ESP scores.

PARAPRAXES AND PSI-MISSING

One of the peculiarities of ESP is the tendency of some subjects consistently to go below chance expectancy. Instead of positive deviations, fewer scores are produced than chance allows. In some experiments the subjects have been instructed to avoid the target and consciously to aim for negative scores. More often this avoidance tendency appears to be unconscious: the subject, though consciously trying to score positively, nevertheless produces negative deviations, or what is called "psi-missing." Needless to say, it is inadmissible to use negative scores, or positive ones for that matter, as evidence for anything unless the experimenter has predicted such scores beforehand for the experiment in question. Many tests have been conducted with the purpose of analysing the results for negative scores. I shall refer to some of these shortly.

If the theory about the memory basis for ESP responses is correct, we may gain insight into the nature of psi-missing by regarding it as a memory phenomenon. The errors of memory, known as "parapraxes," such as slips of the tongue and pen, resemble psi-missing. Parapraxes generally seem to be due, not simply to chance actions, but to needs which are unknown to the persons in question. David Rapaport[53] calls parapraxes *"unsuccessful* attempts at forgetting." They result from "prohibited strivings" which, unable to enter consciousness, distort ideas or actions. "Parapraxes are memory phenomena embedded in thought processes: instead of the

---

[50]J.B. Rhine, *op. cit.,* J.B. Rhine, B.M. Humphrey, and R.B. Averill, "An Exploratory Experiment on the Effect of Caffeine upon Performance in PK Tests," *J Parapsychol,* Vol. 9 (1945), pp. 80-91.

[51]J.B. Rhine, *Ibid.*

[52]S.R. Feather ,*A Comparison of Performance in Memory and ESP Tests,* in *Parapsycology from Duke to FRNM* by J.B. Rhine and Associates (Durham, Parapsychology Press, 1965).

[53]D. Rapaport, *Emotions and Memory* (New York, Science Editions, Inc., 1961).

emergence of a memory fitting the chain of thoughts, either the memory fails to emerge or one not fitting the chain of conscious thoughts emerges, or the relevant memory forms a compromise with a seemingly irrelevant memory. This compromise results from the interplay of the prohibited but upsurging strivings and others which strive to prevent it from entering consciousness.[54] Parapraxes have been experimentally produced. For instance, a subject was given a post-hypnotic suggestion to the effect that he would be bored by a conversation but would attempt to conceal his boredom. At one stage he closed the door to the room and when asked what he was doing, replied, "Why, I just shut the bore."[55]

If negative ESP scores are to be regarded as parapraxes, they are instances where the relevant memory trace, say, of the symbol "star" which corresponds with the ESP target "forms a compromise with a seemingly irrelevant memory," say, with "circle," thus making for an incorrect response.

The parapraxes of memory occur when there is a conflict between the demands of an actual situation and a psychological need. If negative ESP responses are parapraxes, we expect they, too, will be found in conflict situations. This appears to be the case. For instance, G.R. Schmeidler[56] found that subjects who said they did not believe there could be evidence for ESP in a given experiment tended to score negatively while the believers scored positively. Here, we have a clear conflict between a person's belief and the actual situation in which he finds himself: the subject has agreed to undertake a task which he believes to be impossible. In tests with school children by M. Anderson and R. White,[57] the conflict is of a different nature. The teachers who administered the ESP tests were rated by the children into liked and disliked categories. It was found that while the children scored positively with liked teachers, the tests with the disliked teachers gave negative deviations. Again, there is a conflict between the task at hand, namely, to respond correctly to the ESP symbols, and the psychological situation, namely, the negative relationship to the person in charge

[54]D. Rapaport, *Ibid.*
[55]*Ibid.*
[56]G.R. Schmeidler, *op. cit.*
[57]M. Anderson, and R. White, *op. cit.*

of the tests. Other examples where a conflict between the demands of the ESP test and its psychological setting was associated with psi-missing are reviewed by K.R. Rao.[58]

SYMBOLISM

A symbol is an object or activity which represents something else. Symbols play an important part in our mental life. Sometimes we are consciously aware of the connections between a thing and its symbol; other times, we are not. "Symbolization," D. Rapaport[59] says, "is a representation, or in other words reproduction, of an idea in visual images using the available memory-traces for this purpose."

Most parapsychologists who have studied cases of ostensible ESP outside the laboratory, such as ESP dreams or tests using free re-sponse methods, have observed that ESP is often symbolic. Among those who have paid special attention to this are E. Osty,[60] L.E. Rhine,[61] and W.H.C. Tenhaeff.[62] There are several examples in the excerpt from Tenhaeff referred to earlier.[63] For instance, mental images or fjords were a symbol of Norway for Beta and an image of a bottle of wine was a symbol for a name, the first bottle of wine was a symbol for a name, the first part of which means "wine" in Dutch. The latter example illustrates that a person does not always know what a symbol represents. The association that first came to mind was wine drinking, which led to an ESP error; only afterwards was the "correct" association seen. One thought or image may be represented by several symbols. Symbolic representations have also been found in card tests. R. Cadoret and J.G. Pratt[64] found evi-dence in what they called "the consistent missing effect" that the subject substituted another of the five ESP card designs for the one that was target. For instance, if the card was "circle," the sub-ject might say "cross" or "square" instead.

---

[58]K.R. Rao, "The Bidirectionality of Psi," *J Parapsychol,* Vol. 29 (1965), pp. 230-250.

[59]D.Rapaport, *op. cit.*

[60]E. Osty, *op. cit.*

[61]L.E.Rhine, *op. cit.*

[62]W.H.C. Tenhaeff, *op. cit.*

[63]*Ibid.*

[64]R.J. Cadoret, "Effect of Novelty in Test Conditions on ESP Performance," *J Para-psychol,* Vol. 14 (1950), pp. 244-256.

There appear to be several reasons for symbolism in familiar mental processes. For instance, prohibited strivings may be represented in consciousness by images whose meaning the person is hiding from himself. This type of substitution is similar to those that are found in parapraxes and are likely, in ESP tests, to lead to psi-missing. Another reason for symbolic ESP responses may be, simply, a deficiency in the percipient of available memory traces corresponding with the target. If the target idea can be represented by a symbol, then at least the general meaning may be conveyed.

THE UNCONSCIOUSNESS OF ESP

One of the features of ESP which sets it off from such sensory modalities as vision and hearing is the absence of any introspective characteristics whereby ESP responses can be identified for what they are. There appears to be no way in which we can recognize an ESP impression before it is compared with some actual state of affairs, such as the series of cards used as targets. ESP is sometimes "conscious" insofar as it may be associated with an experience in awareness, such as a mental image, but it is "unconscious" insofar as the person who experiences the image apparently cannot, at the time, be certain that it is due to ESP. The absence of an introspective guide is one of the greatest impediments to the practical use of ESP. If we could know when an impression was due to ESP, this would greatly improve the prospects for practical application, even if such impressions were rare and erratic. However, the images and other forms of expression that ESP assumes do not, by themselves, give any clues about their parapsychological origin. This, of course, is to be expected if ESP responses consist of memory traces. Since memory traces are the products of sensory perceptions and other familiar psychological processes, introspectively, they reflect these rather than the ESP stimulus that evokes them.

W. Carington,[65] the English parapsychologist, in tests with drawings as ESP targets, found that his subjects could not distinguish their correct responses from incorrect ones. Similarly,

---

[65]W. Carington, "Experiments on the Paranormal Cognition of Drawings," *Proc Soc Psychical Rsch,* Vol. 46 (1941), pp. 277-344.

B. Shackleton, the highly successful subject of S.G. Soal,[66] failed to distinguish card hits from misses. My experience with English college students was the same.[67] Also in card experiments in the United States, for instance by B.A. McMahan and E.K. Bates,[68] C.E. Stuart,[69] and by J.L. Woodruff and R.W. George,[70] the subjects were unable to identify their hits.

So-called mediums and sensitives are often thought to produce more striking evidence of ESP than card-calling subjects. However, they do not seem to be better at distinguishing right responses from wrong ones. E. Osty[71] observed some forty-five years ago that "it is impossible to judge of the origin and the quality of . . . information at the time of a seance." As J.B. Rhine[72] says, "the psi process itself leaves no identifying trace in the subject's mind to make it known as a psi experience."

There are a few experiments which seem to contradict this observation. In ESP card tests by B.M. Humphrey and F. Nicol[73] and by L. Eilbert and G.R. Schmeidler,[74] the subjects appeared to succeed when asked to identify which of their previous responses were ESP responses. In these experiments, however, there was actually no evidence for ESP in the guesses the subjects estimated. The only paranormal material were the estimates themselves. The hypothesis advanced by Schmeidler, that her subjects did not show awareness of ESP but simply made a second ESP guess as to which earlier (chance) guesses matched their targets, seems to be the most economical explanation for both experiments. The same ap-

---

[66]S.G. Soal, *op. cit.*

[67]W.G. Roll, *op. cit.*

[68]E.A. McMahan, and E.K. Bates, "Report on Further Marchesi Experiments," *J Parapsychol,* Vol. 18 (1954), pp. 82-92.

[69]C.E. Stuart, "An Analysis to Determine a Test Predictive of Extra-Chance Scoring in Card-Calling Tests," *J Parapsychol,* Vol. 5 (1941), pp. 99-137.

[70]J.L. Woodruff, and R.W. George, "Experiments in Extra-Sensory Perception," *J Parapsychol,* Vol. 1 (1937), pp. 18-30.

[71]E. Osty, *op. cit.*

[72]J.B. Rhine, *op. cit.*

[73]B.M. Humphrey and F. Nicol, "The Feeling of Success in ESP," *J Am Soc Psychical Rsch,* Vol. 49 (1955), pp. 3-37.

[74]L. Eilbert and G.R. Schmeidler, "A Study of Certain Psychological Factors in Relation to ESP Performance," *J Parapsychol,* Vol. 14 (1959), pp. 53-74.

plies to the studies by C.B. Nash and C.S. Nash,[75] C.B. Nash,[76] and G.R. Schmeidler[77] where there was evidence of ESP in the calls which the subject afterwards identified as ESP responses. Unless it can be determined whether the correct guesses which the subjects identify are *only* their ESP hits, and not also their chance hits, we cannot know whether a subject is introspectively aware of the occurrence of ESP or is only making another ESP response when he correctly says that a previous guess matched its target.

This, however, is not to say there are no ways to identify ESP responses at the time they are made. If a subject's guessing habits are known, it may be possible to identify ESP responses when these interrupt the guessing habits. For instance, in the cat experiments by Osis and Foster,[78] ESP scores were found when a guessing response had terminated. When a sequence of responses is interrupted which is known to be due to subjective associative factors, this may be the place to look for psi. The psychoanalysts, J. Ehrenwald[79] and J. Eisenbud[80] report that in this way they have distinguished ESP images from subjective ones in their patients' dreams.

In her studies of "conviction of ESP," L.E. Rhine[81] noted that the percipient sometimes seemed to know when his experience had a psi origin. Since there is nothing to suggest that this awareness stems from a peculiar quality inherent in the ESP impression, I suggest it is due to the observation by the percipient of a contrast between the ESP experience and its context. A psi basis is inferred when the experience is inconsistent with previous mental or overt activities. That this is the correct interpretation is suggested by the

---

[75]C.B. Nash and C.S. Nash, "Checking Success and the Relationship of Personality Traits to ESP," *J Am Soc Psychical Rsch*, Vol. 52 (1958), pp. 98-107.

[76]C.B. Nash, "Can Precognition Occur Diametrically?," *J Parapsychol*, Vol. 24 (1960), pp. 26-32.

[77]G.R. Schmeidler, "An Experiment on Precognitive Clairvoyance, Part V. Precognition Scores Related to Feelings of Success," *J Parapsychol*, Vol. 28 (1964), pp. 109-125.

[78]K. Osis, *op. cit.*

[79]J. Ehrenwald, *New Dimensions of Deep Analysis: A Study of Telepathy in Interpersonal Relationships* (London, Allen and Unwin, 1954).

[80]J. Eisenbud, "Analysis of a Presumptively Telepathic Dream," *Psychiatric Quarterly*, Vol. 22 (1948), pp. 103-135.

[81]L.E. Rhine, "Frequency of Types of Experiences in Spontaneous Precognition," *J Parapsychol*, Vol. 18 (1954), pp. 93-123.

fact that ESP experiences in the waking state are more likely to carry conviction than ESP impressions in dreams. If a person suddenly receives an "irrational" impression, for instance, that "something is wrong at home," he is more likely to take notice than if this occurred in a dream where it is not unusual to experience (apparently) unconnected or irrational thoughts and images. In other words, when memory traces which are aroused by ESP are identified, this is because the person was aware that no familiar external or internal stimulus was present which could have aroused them. ESP responses may be identified, not because they possess something which ordinary memory traces lack, but on the contrary, because they lack something which ordinary memory traces often possess, namely, an obvious stimulus.

HYPNOSIS, MEMORY, AND ESP

In the effort to control ESP or to increase the yield, several experimenters have used hypnosis. There are two schools of thought in parapsychology regarding the efficacy of hypnosis and allied states. Some investigators believe that hypnosis and dissociated states facilitate the emergence of ESP; others find them ineffective. G. Pagenstecher,[82] a German physician practicing in Mexico, discovered the ESP abilities of his patient, Mrs. Maria Zierold, only after he had hypnotised her (to cure her insomnia). Similarly the Swedish psychiatrist, J. Björkhem,[83] found marked ESP abilities in hypnotised subjects who showed none in their waking state. Again, most of the mediums studied by members of the Society for Psychical Research in England[84] worked in more or less pronounced trance states, usually self-induced. L.E. Rhine,[85] in her analyses of non-experimental instances of ESP, found that "realistic" cases, that is, cases where there was the closest correspondence with the

---

[82]G. Pagenstecher, "Past Events Seership: A Study in Psychometry," *Proc Am Soc Psychical Rsch,* Vol. 16 (1922), pp. 1-136.

[83]J. Björkhem, *Det Ockulta Problemet* (Uppsala, Lindblads Forlag, 1951).

[84]R. Hodgson, "A Further Record of Observations of Certain Phenomena of Trance," *Proc Soc Psychical Rsch,* Vol. 13 (1897-1898), pp. 284-584; H.F. Saltmarsh, *op. cit.;* S.G. Soal, "A Report on Some Communications Received through Mrs. Blanche Cooper," *Proc Soc Psychical Rsch,* Vol. 35 (1925), pp. 471-594; C.D. Thomas, *op. cit.;* Mrs. A.W. Verrall, "Notes on the Trance Phenomena of Mrs. Thompson," *Proc Soc Psychical Rsch,* Vol. 17 (1901-1903), pp. 164-244.

[85]L.E. Rhine, *op. cit.*

events, usually occurred in dreams rather than waking states (but she did not find a greater number of ESP cases in the dreaming state than the waking). In recent experiments by M. Ullman, S. Krippner, and S. Feldstein[86] with drawings as targets and free verbal responses, the subjects were asleep at the time of testing. Gardner Murphy[87] concluded that dissociated states are helpful to ESP because they entail "freedom from inhibitory conscious factors" and "removal from contact with the conscious system of ideas." A similar view has been expressed by M.P. Reeves,[88] and R. White[89] concluded from her survey of the older experimental material that the "first general requirement is to achieve a state of complete relaxation."

However, when we turn to the tests with ESP cards and similar materials, we do not find the same emphasis on dissociated states. J.J. Grela[90] and J. Beloff and I. Mandleberg did not find that hypnosis was an aid to ESP. J.B. Rhine,[91] in a summary of the experimental material on this subject, concluded that there is no indication that hypnosis improves ESP. Add to this that high-scoring subjects such as Soal's[92] were not in any kind of trance. A study of the experimental literature, on the contrary, indicates that wakefulness and alertness, sometimes approaching a high pitch of excitement, supported with rewards and other forms of reinforcement, are associated with success. It would be going too far to say that the issue is clear cut. Thus, J. Fahler,[93] J. Fahler and R. Cadoret,[94]

---

[86]M. Ullman, S. Krippner, and S. Feldstein, see paper on this symposium.

[87]G. Murphy, "Psychical Research and Personality," *Proc Soc Psychical Rsch,* Vol. 49 (1949), pp. 1-15.

[88]M.P. Reeves, "A Topological Approach to Parapsychology," *J Am Soc Psychical Rsch,* Vol. 38 (1944), pp. 72-82.

[89]R. White, "A Comparison of Old and New Methods of Response to Targets in ESP Experiments," *J Am Soc Psychical Rsch,* Vol. 58 (1964), pp. 21-56.

[90]J.J. Grela, "Effect on ESP Scoring of Hypnotically Induced Attitudes," *J Parapsychol,* Vol. 9 (1945), pp. 194-202.

[91]J.B. Rhine, Extrasensory Perception and Hypnosis, L.M. Lecron, ed. *Experimental Hypnosis* (New York, Macmillan, 1952), pp. 359-375.

[92]S.G. Soal, *op. cit.*

[93]J. Fahler, "ESP Card Tests with and without Hypnosis," *J Parapsychol,* Vol. 21 (1957), pp. 179-185.

[94]J. Fahler and R.J. Cadoret, "ESP Card Tests of College Students with and without Hypnosis," *J Parapsychol,* Vol. 22 (1958), pp. 125-136.

and L. Casler[95] report that hypnosis increased their subjects' card-hitting output. The work of M. Ryzl[96] falls into a different category. His hypnotic training procedure is used only with subjects who show evidence of ESP in initial tests. These subjects then participate in a lengthy training program in which Ryzl attempts to promote their experiences of mental images in ESP test situations. Once their ESP performance has been stabilized, however, hypnosis need no longer be used. Thus his remarkable subject, P. Stepanek, is not hypnotised during card testing.

There are many kinds of hypnotic procedures and suggestions and perhaps some of these can affect ESP card-calling tests. At the present, however, we are concerned only with the limited question whether the hypnotic state as such facilitates scoring. Ryzl's work with Stepanek and most of the other card tests do not suggest that hypnosis is likely to increase the output of serial ESP tests but that it may help in the free impression kind of ESP experiment.

We can summarize these contrasting findings by saying that in situations where the subject describes his mental images and impressions in free verbal statements, hypnosis and other dissociated states appear to facilitate ESP. On the other hand, in serial ESP tests, where there is a restricted choice of responses such as the five ESP symbols, it is doubtful whether hypnosis or other states of dissociation improves the scores.

This apparent inconsistency is resolved if we regard the ESP response as a memory response. If we ask what effect hypnosis has on memory, we find it does not improve scores in the type of serial learning tests that resemble card calling but that it does improve recall of memories of meaningful past events such as those that make up the memory traces used for ESP responses of the free impression type.

R.W. White, G.F. Fox, and W.W. Harris[97] found that there was

[95]L. Casler, "The Improvement of Clairvoyance Scores by Means of Hypnotic Suggestion," *J Parapsychol*, Vol. 26 (1962), pp. 77-87; L. Casler, "Self-Generated Suggestions and Clairvoyance." Convention Paper. Eighth Annual Convention of the Parapsychological Association (New York, September 9-11, 1965).

[96]M. Ryzl and J.G. Pratt, "The Focusing of ESP upon Particular Targets," *J Parapsychol*, Vol. 27 (1963), pp. 227-241.

[97]R.W. White, G.F. Fox, and W.W. Harris, "Hypnotic Hypermnesia for Recently Learned Material," *Journal Abnormal and Social Psychology*, Vol. 35 (1940), pp. 88-103.

no improvement under hypnosis of the recall of the nonsense syllables used in serial learning tasks but there was a significant gain for meaningful verbal material. This finding was confirmed by B.G. Rosenthal.[98] The observation that hypnosis helps recall of material of this nature agrees with the commonly known fact that childhood and other early memories are more likely to return during sleep and other periods of dissociation than during periods of heightened consciousness. There is no conflict then between the adherents of ESP tests under hypnosis or other dissociated states and those who prefer waking state tests *as long as the target material is adapted to the subject's state.* The difficulties only arise if we expect good results from a card-calling subject merely by hypnotizing him or if we expect that a subject in tests with free verbal material will do better if we keep him wakeful and alert. It does not take much reflection to see that on the one hand, the five ESP symbols can easily be remembered under most conditions, while the memory traces that may be required to convey an unlimited target range must themselves cover a wide variety of events, and that the emergence of such a wide selection of memory traces usually only occurs in dissociated states where we are removed from the demands of everyday life.

MEMORY TRACES AS ESP STIMULI

There are strong indications that the ESP response is formed by the percipient's own memory traces. There is also some indication that in telepathy, where the source of information is another brain or mind, memory traces play a role in the transmission of information. Parapsychologists have not in recent years been as interested in the nature of ESP transmission as in the reception end of the process. The findings that suggest a relationship between memory and ESP transmission are mostly of older date.

René Warcollier,[99] who also mentioned the importance of memory traces for the ESP response, found that material in the unconscious of the telepathic agent is transmitted better than ma-

---

[98]B.G. Rosenthal, "Hypnotic Recall of Material Learned under Anxiety and Non-anxiety Producing Conditions," *Journal Experimental Psychology,* Vol. 34 (1944), pp. 369-389.

[99]R. Warcollier, *op. cit.*

terial on which he concentrates his attention. E. Osty[100] concluded that the further removed from the agent's attention the item is, the more likely it is to serve as a telepathic stimulus. Transmission of something on which attention is focused is, he said, "very rare indeed." More frequent is the communication of material which is within the range of consciousness but not actually thought of at the time. Most common is the communication of material which "lies, as if statically, in the reservoirs of memory." A report by the Russian Committee for the Study of Mental Suggestion, headed by V.M. Bekhterev[101] stated that an image "to which the voluntary and deliberate attention of the sender was *not* directed was more easily transmitted to the percipient."

In England, S. Soal[102] reported that the medium, Mrs. Blanche Cooper, produced the best results when Soal was not thinking about the target. Similarly, Mrs. A.W. Verrall,[103] discovered only a few cases where the medium's correct statements corresponded with what the agent was thinking about at the time, more often they corresponded with ideas that were at the back of his mind. In an experiment with Mrs. Piper, R. Hodgson[104] instructed her to report on the activities of a third party at that moment. Instead, she described in great detail that person's activities on the previous day. E.R. Dodds[105] and C.D. Broad[106] also have commented on the greater incidence of the transmission of material that is not in the foreground of consciousness.*

---

[100]E. Osty, *op. cit.*

[101]L.L. Vasiliev, *Experiments in Mental Suggestion,* Institute for the Study of Mental Images, Church Crookham (Hampshire, England, 1963).

[102]S.G. Soal, *op. cit.*

[103]A.W. Verrall, *op. cit.*

[104]R. Hodgson, *op. cit.*

[105]E.R. Dodds, "Why I Do Not Believe in Survival," *Proc Soc Psychical Rsch,* Vol. 42 (1933-1934), pp. 147-172.

[106]C.D. Broad, *Religion, Philosophy and Psychical Research* (London, Routledge and Kegan Paul, 1953).

*It is not certain that these investigators always took account of the fact that on any one occasion there will be a great number of items in the memory record of a person and only a few at the center of attention. If the probability of responding to all items is the same, on the basis of chance expectancy we anticipate more hits on material in the memory record than on material in consciousness. The observations by these authors are not offered as proven facts but as suggestions that should be tested in properly designed experiments.

If the memory traces of the telepathic agent are used in ESP transmission, we expect that the "laws of learning" and the other characteristics of the memory process affect the transmission process in the same way we found that they affected the reception. W. Carington[107] discovered that drawings which had been frequently shown to the agent seemed to make better targets than others. G. Pagenstecher[108] and J. Björkhem[109] found that events which were accompanied by strong emotions tended to be transmitted more easily than emotionally neutral events. R. Heywood[110] also noted that the medium responded to her "emotional memories" and mentioned the problem facing a medium of "being swept down the stream of a sitter's associated thoughts or memories." Telepathy, it appears, is an interaction between the memory records of both agent and percipient.

THE BRAIN, RNA, AND ESP

The existence of a relationship between memory and ESP makes discoveries about memory of possible interest to the parapsychologist. Two recent discoveries may have implications for our understanding of ESP, namely the findings that certain brain areas and certain chemicals play a role in memory processes. W. Penfield[111] has shown that memories of past events can be elicited in human subjects by electrical stimulation of the temporal lobes when these are exposed during brain operations. On the other hand, when the electrodes are applied, say to the visual cortex, the patient only experiences meaningless sounds or sights. Penfield calls the area of the brain connected with memory the "interpretive cortex."

If memory traces are part of the ESP reception system and if the interpretive cortex specializes in the retrieval of memory traces, it is possible that it also plays a part in the ESP process. The interpretive cortex in that case would function as an "ESP cortex,"

---

[107]W. Carington, *Telepathy; An Outline of Its Facts, Theory and Implications* (London, Methuen, 1945).

[108]G. Pagenstecher, *op. cit.*

[109]J. Björkhem, *op. cit.*

[110]R. Heywood, "The Labyrinth of Association," *J Soc Psychical Rsch*, Vol. 42 (1964), pp. 227-229.

[111]W. Penfield, "The Interpretive Cortex," *Science*, Vol. 129 (1959), pp. 1719-1725.

having a similar relation to ESP stimuli as the visual cortex and optic nerve have to light rays.

Memories of the past are not necessarily destroyed by destroying even large parts of the interpretive cortex; however, injury or diseases that affect the interpretive cortex as a rule also affect recall ability. For instance, epileptic fits which are due to discharges in the interpretive cortex are often preceded by compulsive recall, say, of a childhood event. The normal behavior of epileptics also often shows persevering and compulsive features characteristic of impaired learning ability.[112] It would be interesting to know how such persons perform in ESP tests.

In addition to the relationship between memory and macroscopic brain structure, there is evidence that molecular brain patterns affect learning and remembering. For instance, the long-term administration of yeast ribonucleic acid (RNA) is said to improve impaired ability to remember in humans and to increase the rate of learning in animals.[113]

If the amount of RNA or other molecules in the brain facilitates learning and recall, we expect it may also facilitate ESP. However, as in any other attempt to influence ESP performance, the conditions we introduce must be adjusted to the test. RNA could only be expected to aid ESP in the case of a subject who is attempting to respond to targets which correspond to temporarily forgotten memory traces, the recall of which may be restored by ingestion of RNA. RNA is not likely to be of use in tests, say, with the five ESP symbols, unless the memory of the subject is so poor that without it, he cannot recall even these.

THE NATURE OF MEMORY TRACES

It has been shown that the ESP response can be understood in terms of the familiar processes of memory. These, however, are not themselves fully understood. In particular, we do not know what a memory trace is nor where it is stored. The discovery that RNA facilitates learning and remembering has stimulated the hope that the RNA molecule is itself the long-sought-after memory trace.

---

[112]*Ibid.*

[113]W. Dingman, and M.B. Sporn, "Molecular Theories of Memory," *Science,* Vol. 144 (1964), pp. 26-29.

W. Dingman and M.B. Sporn[114] have cautioned, however, that we still lack grounds for identifying memory traces with RNA molecules. Before this step can be taken, it must be shown that changes in RNA metabolism caused by learning last as long as the memory in question can be demonstrated and that the destruction of the altered RNA state results in permanent loss of the memory. K.S. Lashley[115] found that large parts of the cortex of rats can be destroyed without impairing the animals' recognition of shapes. Similarly, in man, large parts of the cortex can be destroyed, including the interpretive cortex,[116] without permanently abolishing memories of past events. These facts appear to argue against the hypothesis that memory traces consist of localized structures in the brain such as specific RNA molecules.

Some findings in parapsychology suggest that the capacity to store information exists also in inanimate physical systems. If this is true, an examination of these findings may give us some insight into the retention aspect of memory.

The parapsychological phenomenon that may be relevant to this question is "psychometry," or as research on this form of ESP is also known, "object association" or "token object" tests. In such an experiment the subject seems to obtain information about events in the past by holding, or being in the physical proximity of, an object which has been in the neighborhood of these events. The tests are usually in the form of free association experiments in ESP in which the subject says anything that comes to his mind in connection with the past history of the object. The method has been widely used by the mediums studied by members of the English Society for Psychical Research,[117] by the "paragnosts" of W.H.C. Tenhaeff[118] and others.[119] F.W.H. Myers[120] said that "objects which have been in contact with organisms preserve their trace;

---

[114]*Ibid.*

[115]K.S. Lashley, *Brain Mechanisms and Intelligence* (Chicago, Chicago University Press, 1929).

[116]W. Penfield, *op. cit.*

[117]R. Hodgson, *op. cit.;* H.F. Saltmarsh, *op. cit.;* S.G. Soal, *op. cit.;* C.D. Thomas, *op. cit.;* A.W. Verrall, *op. cit.*

[118]W.H.C. Tenhaeff, *op. cit.*

[119]J. Björkhem, *op. cit.;* G. Pagenstecher, *op. cit.*

[120]F.W.H. Myers, *op. cit.*

and it sometimes seems as though even inorganic nature could still be made, so to say, luminescent with the age-old history of its past." Sir Oliver Lodge,[121] the English physicist who was one of the pioneers in the development of wireless telegraphy, remarked that "it appears as if we left traces of ourselves, not only on our bodies, but on many other things with which we have been subordinately associated, and that these traces can thereafter be detected by a sufficiently sensitive person." N. Kotik,[122] an early Russian investigator, found he could transfer the "psychic energy" from a person's brain to a piece of paper and use this paper to develop corresponding ideas in another person. G. Pagenstecher,[123] who found a remarkable psychometry subject among his patients, used pumice stones and other objects for his studies of their "stored vibrations."

The idea that there can be a close causal relationship between ESP and material objects is foreign to the thinking of many present day parapsychologists. Nevertheless, the effect appears to have turned up in card testing experiments. For instance, in the tests by G.W. Fisk and D.J. West[124] where packs of sealed cards were sent to the subjects, the subjects tended to avoid scoring on the cards West had handled though they were unaware of his participation in the experiments and though West did not know when his packs were being used. This avoidance tendency was similar to one West often had observed when he personally directed the testing. But here he seemed to inhibit the subjects' ESP by means of the cards themselves. Conversely, it appears that cards which have been endowed by the experimenters with favorable psi traces make better ESP targets. M. Ryzl and J.G. Pratt[125] discovered that P. Stepanek scored particularly high on two cards which seemed to differ from the rest only in that they were the cards that corresponded to the

---

[121]O. Lodge, "Report on Some Trance Communications Received Chiefly through Mrs. Piper," *Proc Soc Psychical Rsch,* Vol. 23 (1909), pp. 127-285.

[122]V.M. Bekhterev, "Further Observations of 'Mental' Influence of Man on Behavior of Animals," Conference of the Institute of Study of Brain and Psychic Activities (February 2, 1920). Private translation from the Russian at the Foundation for Research on the Nature of Man, Durham.

[123]G. Pagenstecher, *op. cit.*

[124]D.J. West, and G.W. Fisk, "A Dual ESP Experiment with Clock Cards," *J Soc Psychical Rsch,* Vol. 37 (1953), pp. 185-189.

[125]M. Ryzl, *op. cit.*

first two numbers on the experimenters' code sheet and might therefore have stood out more strongly in their minds. However, Ryzl and Pratt had no way of knowing during the experiment which particular cards the subject was guessing. Evidently, Stepanek responded directly to the cards' psi traces. The authors noted the similarity between this effect and those found in psychometry testing.

Findings such as these open up the possibility that in other card experiments the subjects also responded to such traces rather than to the familiar physical properties of the cards. Card experiments directed at this problem by M. Johnson[126] and myself[127] have shown that some subjects respond to blank cards whose only differences appear to be their different past histories. The hypothetical change caused by an event in an object or in some medium or "field"[128] surrounding it, whereby information about this event is stored, has been termed a "psi trace."

The similarity between psi traces and memory traces has been noted by the Australian physicist, Raynor Johnson:[129] "Rocks cannot remember—but they may hold a memory (in their associated psychic ether), which the mind of a man in favorable circumstances can cognize." The German embryologist, Hans Driesch,[130] suggests that in remembering, the brain has the same function as the object used in object association experiments. Similarly, C.B. Nash,[131] in his Presidential Address to the Parapsychological Association, suggested that the same process is involved in remembering as in ESP of past events ("retrocognition").

The theory that memory traces are a special form of psi traces, we may call the "psi trace theory of memory." Such a theory would explain the apparent lack of cortical localization of memory traces. Once a memory trace has been formed by physical events in a brain

---

[126]W.G. Roll, *op. cit.*

[127]W.G. Roll, "Token Object Matching Tests: Third Series," *J Am Soc Psychical Rsch,* Vol. 60 (1966), pp. 363-379.

[128]W.G. Roll, *op. cit.*

[129]R.C. Johnson, *The Imprisoned Splendour* (London, Hodder and Stoughton, 1953).

[130]H. Driesch, *Psychical Research,* trans. by T. Besterman (London, G. Bell and Sons, 1933).

[131]C.B. Nash, "Physical and Metaphysical Parapsychology," *J Parapsychol,* Vol. 27 (1963), pp. 283-300.

(e.g. by a special RNA configuration) it can be communicated to another part of that brain (and there evoke corresponding RNA configurations) as in remembering, or to other brains, as in ESP. H.H. Price[132] theorizes along such lines when he suggests that ESP hallucinations ("apparitions") of the kind which are said to recur in special places may be due to mental images which have lost their connection with the mind in which they originated and have become attached to a region of physical space. Here they create a "psychic atmosphere" which, when it overlaps with the psychic atmosphere of a person sensitive to it, may cause him to see an "apparition."

The proposal that information about past events can actually be stored in physical objects is likely to strike one as highly implausible. What, after all, could be the physical structure which could contain such information? If we address ourselves to this question, we discover that physicists have in fact postulated structures in the universe which could do exactly this, that is, could contain information about past events. The "world-line" of relativity theory is such a structure. A world-line can be described, simply, as the spatial path of an object over a period of time. However, world-lines are not only a means of representing the location of an object in space and time, they are held to have real existence. If this is indeed the case, then the concept of world-lines may help to provide an explanation of the retention capacity of inanimate matter and perhaps also of animate matter. C.B. Nash[133] suggests that "Memory . . . is autoscopic retrocognition by means of the world-lines of particles in the brain." We might similarly say that in object association, the subject follows the world-lines of the object into its past and in this way obtains information about events that happened in its neighborhood. The test of a concept lies in its predictive powers. It might be worth the effort to explore with physicists what the empirical consequences would be of regarding psi traces and memory traces as world-lines. At the present, however, it will be enough to indicate this as a possible area of exploration. Whether or not this approach is fruitful, it is consistent with the general

---

[132]H.H. Price, "Haunting and the 'Psychic Ether' Hypothesis," *Proc Soc Psychical Rsch*, Vol. 45 (1939), pp. 307-343.

[133]C.B. Nash, *op. cit.*

rapprochement between the physical and life sciences. For instance, A.A. Cochran[134] has found that the wave properties of inanimate matter are highly predominant in protein, the most important substance of living matter, and that the most abundant chemical elements in protein, carbon and hydrogen, are also the elements with the highest degree of wave predominance. Perhaps we shall similarly find that what we might call the "trace properties" of living matter are also found in inanimate matter and perhaps even predominate in these substances.

EPICRISIS

If we distinguish between the learning, retention, remembering, and forgetting aspects of memory, the ESP response can be described as an instance of remembering something that the organism learnt in the course of its past sensory experiences or other familiar activities. This part of the ESP process is an ordinary psychological or biological one. It is only because there is evidence that the evoked memories are relevant to some actual event which the person could not have known about by sensory or rational means that we are dealing with a parapsychological phenomenon. A survey of ESP investigations conducted at different times and in different parts of the world supports the theory that the ESP response consists of the percipient's own memory traces and is, therefore, subject to the same "laws" and conditions that affect learning and remembering. As other cognitive and perceptual functions, ESP involves forgetting. In order to respond to something new, the organism must be able to "forget" the old, either permanently or temporarily.

Except in the limited case of telepathy, I have not discussed the nature of psi stimuli. In telepathy, it appears these are often the memory traces of the telepathic agent. In other forms of ESP, the subject may respond to traces associated with inanimate systems. The apparent existence of psi traces suggests that retention is a property of inanimate as well as of animate matter.

The mechanism whereby ESP stimuli reach the percipient may be similar to those that govern known physical processes.

---

[134]A.A. Cochran, "Mind, Matter, and Quanta," *Main Currents,* Vol. 22 (1966), pp. 79-88.

The evidence suggests that ESP, as sense perception, is the result of an interaction between a biological organism and its physical environment.

SECTION III
PSI AND PRECOGNITION

CHAPTER 12

INTRODUCTION

HOYT L. EDGE

OF ALL OF THE PHENOMENA STUDIED in parapsychology, pre-cognition is perhaps the strangest, although its history goes back at least to the Delphic Oracles. Precognition has not been studied as much as clairvoyance and telepathy, but the amount of evidence for it is substantial. Its existence reintroduces philosophical problems of long standing, most notably the important medieval problem of foreknowledge. At that time the question was how one could maintain that God is omniscient—and thus has complete knowledge about the world, both past and future—and still argue that man is free; for if God knows what one is going to choose at a future time, then that decision cannot be free. The same problem is presented by precognition, except that God's foreknowledge is replaced by that of a medium, or any person having a precognitive experience. Perhaps this unexplained problem of foreknowledge and personal freedom would explain why so many people have feared mediums through the ages and refused to accept the possibility of precognition. In addition to the logical problems one must face in accepting precognition, the concept also assumes that man has abilities once ascribed only to God, and for any person to say that he has precognition would be, in that he would be attributing God-like characteristics to himself, the highest form of blasphemy.

Leaving this basically psychological argument against precognition and getting into some of the logical problems, we see that it is often possible to explain precognition by using other forms of psi. Some instances of ostensible precognition could be, for example, the result of a person's receiving from another telepathically what

187

is merely the conclusion of the other's correct inference about the future. In such a case, the knowledge of the future would not be paranormal, only the telepathic reception could be considered paranormal. Although this is logically possible in many instances, especially in everyday-life situations, such an explanation does not seem adequate in a statistically-oriented test of precognition in which the subject precognizes the order of a deck of cards that will be mechanically shuffled or precognizes a series of numbers that will be produced by a randomizing device. In such cases, however, one might argue that the subject uses a combination of clairvoyance and psychokinesis to affect the mechanical device to produce the desired order of cards or numbers that the subject has written down. Although this explanation is logically possible (and would rid us of many of the problems we have to face in accepting precognition), it forces us to accept an explanation that, intuitively, is just as abstruse as precognition.

Let me mention one more general point before I move to a more specific discussion of the articles that appear in this section. In the attempt to prove precognition experimentally, parapsychologists face the same problem as in other areas of psi research—experiments conducted with mechanical instruments which allow us to compile rigid statistical results seem often to be too sterile and inhuman to motivate the subjects to do their best. But the question remains, of course, as to how one could control the many variables in a normal life situation so that one could be sure the results are due to precognition. There is a special problem in precognition, though. This is illustrated by an example reported to me by a medium shortly after the event. She said that two women came to her for a reading and that after the reading she warned them not to drive back home by a certain route. The women, however, were in a rush, and nevertheless chose to drive back by this shorter, more accustomed route, and were subsequently hit by an oncoming car which crossed over the median and killed one of the women. This is a typical case of spontaneous precognition. The question, of course, arises—what if the women had heeded the advice of the medium, had driven back another way, and, thus, avoided the accident? Could we still call this a case of precognition? How could we possibly know what would have happened on the return journey if the women had taken the recommended route? How could we then know if the prediction would have been fulfilled? Were the women free, really, to choose which route they would take, or was their action already determined?

This fundamental question as to whether or not precognition undercuts personal freedom is considered by Ducasse in the first article of this section. The basic argument for the position that precognition does negate one's freedom is as follows: if future events can be precognized, then the future event must be determined. If the future is determined, one cannot have freedom of choice. Without freedom of choice, there is no individual freedom of the will, and without freedom of the will, there is no moral responsibility. For how can we say that someone is morally responsible for a deplorable act and thus call him "evil" when he could not help but make the "evil" decision; much as we cannot say that a falling meteorite is morally responsible for any persons it may kill in colliding with the earth. Ducasse's solution to this problem is to use the traditional soft-determinist argument, which says that free-will, rightly defined, and determinism are compatible. Free-will means the freedom from compulsion—the freedom to do what one wants to do, and the fact that one's desires may be determined by past events does not mean that one is forced to make a decision. Moreover, determinism does not mean compulsion, and thus a decision can be determined and free at the same time. Indeed, Ducasse goes on to argue that freedom of the will actually requires determinism, and that a person could not rightly be considered free unless he were at the same time determined. We will return to Ducasse's argument a bit later for further clarification of it.

In discussing the possibility of foreknowledge *per se,* C.D. Broad discusses three kinds of objections that can be made against its acceptance. The first is the epistemological objection, which says, in effect, that one cannot know a future event, since that which is known (the object of knowledge) is always immediately presented to consciousness (prehended), whereas a future event, because it does not yet exist, cannot be immediately presented. To overcome this objection, Broad distinguishes between the event and the image of the event. Using the analogy of memory, he argues that it is the *image* which is prehended and not the future event itself. Thus, according to Broad, one is incorrect if he describes precognition as having a non-existent (or not yet existent) object as the object of knowledge. The image of the future event is presented, not the future event itself.

The second objection is the causal one. This objection, also discussed by Brier as an *a priori* objection, questions whether the very possibility of backward causation is possible. In the memory process, it is the past event (the event to be remembered) along with a present stimulus that causes a remembrance to occur. The causal sequence is clearly understandable in that it goes from a past event to a present one. If one has a precognition of a future event, however, it seems that the possibility of a past event causing the present image is by definition unacceptable. What is the cause? It must be the future event, but how can a future event cause a present image? This is perhaps the most difficult objection to overcome and to do so, one is led inevitably to radical revisions of basic conceptual schemes. Broad suggests that we can better understand backward causation by postulating a five-dimensional space (i.e. three-dimensional space with two time dimensions). In such a world, what would be considered future in one time dimension may not be future in the other.

Finally, Broad discusses the fatalistic objection, which is very similar to the argument with which Ducasse dealt. Broad's solution is a bit different from Ducasse's in that he distinguishes between an event being "predetermined" (which is a causal relation) and an event being "predeterminate" (which is a logical relation). The fatalistic objection arises then from a failure to make this distinction. Thus, the future event may be predeterminate without being predetermined, and if the future event is not predetermined, this leaves open the possibility for a voluntary (and free) decision affecting the future event after that event has been precognized. One wonders whether Ducasse would accept this solution. It is not probable. Although he might accept the conceptual distinction between "predeterminate" and "predetermined," he would most likely argue that, in a causal world, this distinction makes sense only when an observer lacks the knowledge which forms the basis of giving a causal explanation. The situation is much like the one in which Leibniz's monads find themselves. If one had enough knowledge (which, for Leibniz, only God does) one would know exactly what the causal and logical relations of a monad are, for each monad is completely determined (in Ducasse's sense) from the first moment of its existence. In other words, the causal and logical relations turn out, in fact, to be one. In such a case, only Ducasse's soft determinism would leave room for freedom of the will. An interesting point to ponder is whether once we accept a complete determinism in the world, it would not be easier to explain precognition by saying that the individual, in some hyper-normal (but not necessarily paranormal) way, has viewed his past and present and has then merely inferred his future. An analogous situation would be for one of Leibniz's monads to be self-conscious enough to see an event in its future.

In an attempt to solve what Broad calls the causal objection, Ducasse presents in the next article his "Theory Theta." Here, essentially, Ducasse distinguishes between what he calls the psychological event, which has intrinsic time as measured by its "liveness," and the physical event, to which one can predicate time only conditionally in a triadic relationship. (For instance, an event E is temporally after an event D from a third event C.) The causal objection arises, then, because we confuse the temporal attributes of the physical and the psychological events. Thus, in a case of precognition, the physical event is presented twice: at time t^1, when it is precognized, and at time t^2, at which time it actually occurs. If one makes this distinction, one does not have to say that there is backward causation, for it is not the future physical event that is causing the present psychological event. Ducasse concludes:

> That it [the physical event] can be present several times [as perceived through psychological times] without itself occurring several times is an automatic consequence of the cardinal fact that, *in itself,* it is neither present nor past nor future but acquires presentness by being perceived and as often as it is perceived.

Even if we admit Ducasse's conclusion, one is still left, however, with the main question unanswered: What caused the present psychological event, i.e. the perception of the future physical event? Ducasse's theory does not tell us this, and it is this question that leads one to assume (as Broad points out) that, in precognition, it can only be the future event which is the cause.

Finally, Brier argues that backward causation is not impossible. He discusses Dummett's point that understanding backward causation is possible only through changing our conception of cause, and Flew's assertion that backward causation is logically impossible, and after finding both these objections inadequate, Brier goes on to make some interesting distinctions, such as the difference between "changing" and "affecting" the past.*

---

*Although not included in this article, Brier has elsewhere pointed out that current physics appears to be making some observations that would seem to involve a cause coming after the effect. If so, it is possible for science, including parapsychology, to experimentally alter our notion of causation very radically (much as some say that through quantum mechanics it has undercut the law of excluded middle).

CHAPTER 13

KNOWING THE FUTURE*

C. J. DUCASSE

NORMALLY, the events we perceive are simultaneous with, or slightly anterior but never posterior to, our perception of them: One cannot normally *perceive* what has not yet occurred, but only sometimes *predict* it on the basis of past experience of the regular modes of behavior of things animate or inanimate, and of perception of their present state. The prediction of eclipses, of tides, of the migrations of birds and of salmon, would be examples of this.

But there is another equally normal way in which some future events can be known, namely, by present resolution on our part so to act as to cause them to occur. This particular manner of knowing the future we may call *predetermination,* as distinguished from prediction. An example would be my resolution now to mow the grass later today. On the basis of it, I know now, in a normal manner, that this afternoon the grass will be shorter than it is at this very moment.

Of course, neither our predictions nor our predeterminations of future events give us infallible knowledge that they will occur, but only more or less probable knowledge of it. The probability, however, is often so high as to amount virtually to certainty: that a man who has been shot through the heart will die is theoretically not quite certain, but in practice is usually taken as certain.

Now, what is called *precognition* is neither prediction nor predetermination, but, paradoxically, is *pre-perception* of an as yet

---

*Reprinted from *Tomorrow,* 1955, by permission of Garrett Publications and Mrs. C. J. Ducasse.

future event—ostensible *perception* of it at a time when it has not yet occurred. Precognition takes a variety of forms, but the form consisting of a dream or a waking vision is especially suitable to illustrate the points to be discussed in the present article.

The following instance of a precognitive dream has been mentioned before in the pages of *Tomorrow* and often elsewhere; for, besides being quaint, it is also clear-cut and well attested. But its authenticity is not important for the present purpose, which is only to remove some of the confusions widely prevalent as to what precognition does or does not imply regarding determinism, free will, and moral responsibility. The instance in view is that of a dream which Mrs. Atlay, wife of the bishop of Hereford, had while her husband was away. She dreamt that, he being absent, she was reading morning prayers to her children, their governess, and the servants in the hall of the episcopal residence; that, prayers being ended, she stepped into the dining room adjoining; and that she saw there, between the table and sideboard, a large pig![1]

When she awoke, she remembered the dream and, having come downstairs, related it to the governess and children while waiting for the servants to assemble in the hall. After the prayers, she opened the dining room door, and there, in the same place as in her dream, saw the pig! Later, it was ascertained that it had escaped while the household was at prayers—the gardener, who was cleaning the sty at the time, not having fastened the gate.

Now the train of thought, to which this or any of the numerous similar precognitive episodes on record commonly gives rise, is something like this: If the future can thus be precognized, this can be only because future events are now already determined; but if even the future experiences and actions of human beings are thus already determined, then human free will is only an illusion, and there is really no such thing as moral responsibility.

Some of the fallacies which vitiate this popular piece of reasoning may be made patent by the following comments:

That future events are now "already determined" means only that they will be the eventual effects of the effects of the effects of certain present causes. It does *not* mean that a future event—

---

[1]*Proceedings*, S.P.R. Vol. XI, pp. 487-488.

for instance, the pig's presence in the dining room—was predetermined in the sense that some person, whether human, devilish or divine, had *resolved* that it should eventually occur and then so *acted* as to cause it to occur irrespective of anybody else's possibly opposing actions.

Hence "determinism," that is, the contention that *every* event, including human volitions and experiences, not only causes certain succeeding events, but itself is caused by certain preceding ones, does not entail at all that every event is "predetermined." For only some are so; for example, that later today the lawn grass will be shorter than now is "predetermined" by my desire that it shall be shorter and by my ensuing present resolution so to act as to cause it to become shorter. This future state of the grass is thus "predetermined" not in spite of, or irrespective of, my will in the matter, but by my very volition now to cut the grass later today.

Moreover, the fact that this volition of mine was itself caused by some preceding events—among them, my *having noticed* that the grass is now too long—does *not* mean that that volition was not free but "compelled." The popular prejudice against determinism is based on the tacit but false assumption that causation of a volition automatically constitutes compulsion. The truth, however, is that it constitutes compulsion only when what one is caused to will to do is something one *dislikes*—for instance, handing one's money to a hold-up man who threatens to shoot. But on the contrary when keen appetite, for example, causes one to eat and one *likes* what he eats, he is properly said to be eating not under compulsion but *freely;* and this notwithstanding that his volition—in one case to eat, and in the other to yield his purse—is, equally in both cases, determined by, i.e. is the effect of, certain causes.

That determinism is not inherently incompatible with freedom to do what one wills becomes evident as soon as one notices three things. The first is that to say, for example, that I now *"can"* or "am *free* to" raise my arm if I will means simply that *volition by me now to raise it would cause it to rise.* The second is that, since my arm is not now paralyzed or tied down, I *am now free* to raise it if I will. And the third is that my having now this freedom does not in the least presuppose that the volition, which at this moment is causing my arm to rise, had itself no cause—that is, was a matter of pure chance; for, obviously, it was caused by the desire—itself caused by this very discussion—to test my possession of that freedom.

But although I am now free to raise my arm if I will, I am not similarly free to fly through the air like a bird if I will. That is, man's freedom always has limits: Some things he can do if he but wills to do them, and others he cannot do even if he wills to do them. That he has "free will"—freedom *to do, or not do,* such things as he can do if he but wills, does not mean that he is omnipotent.

Lastly, it is often alleged that determinism is incompatible with moral responsibility. But the truth is, on the contrary, that to say of a person that he is "morally responsible" for what he does means that, in a situation involving moral issues, what he does *is determined* by such factors as memories of praise or blame or of reward or punishment for behavior of a certain kind in similar situations in the past; by anticipation of the probable consequences of so behaving again in the present situation; and by desire for, or aversion to, those consequences. When on the contrary the voluntary behavior of a person—for example of an infant or of an insane man—is *not* shaped by such factors, then he is commonly and quite properly said to have been, not morally "free," but morally *irresponsible* as "not having known what he was doing," or "not having known right from wrong." But of course, that he *did not then* know it, or know it well enough, is no reason why he should not now be taught it; for example, by praise or blame or by reward or punishment for what he did, or by exhibition to him of the good or evil caused by what he did. This is how young children are gradually caused to become morally responsible. On the other hand, persons who cannot thus be taught moral responsibility are termed in so far morally "insane" and are locked up for the protection of society.

Keeping in mind the preceding remarks on determinism, predetermination, freedom, and precognition, we may now return to Mrs. Atlay's precognitive dream of the pig in her dining room.

The pig's eventual presence there was of course determined, i.e. caused, by a complex train of antecedent events. Some of these—for instance, the gardener's insecure closing of the sty gate, and the servants' leaving open the doors of the house—were human actions. But another contributing and indeed decisive human factor was Mrs. Atlay's *not* having regarded her dream as precognitive, for had she *regarded* it as precognitive, she would have made certain that the gate and doors would be well closed, and the dream would then have been *not in fact* precognitive. That she did not take her dream seriously was itself determined, of course, by the extreme improbability, according to past experience, of the outlandish situation the dream depicted.

The determinism which obtained through every stage of the affair thus does not mean that some "fate" enforced the pig's presence against opposition to it by Mrs. Atlay's will, for there was no such opposition. On the contrary, the fact that she did not in fact do what would have prevented it—as she could have done, had she so willed—was itself one of the factors which determined its occurrence.

CHAPTER 14

THE PHILOSOPHICAL IMPLICATIONS
OF FOREKNOWLEDGE*

C. D. BROAD

WHEN THE SECRETARY ASKED ME TO INTRODUCE a philosophical discussion on a subject connected with psychical research, I felt that I had a plain duty to consent, although I would much rather have declined. As readers of my books are aware, it has always seemed to me most strange and most deplorable that the vast majority of philosophers and psychologists should utterly ignore the strong *prima facie* case that exists for the occurrence of many supernormal phenomena which, if genuine, must profoundly affect our theories of the human mind, its cognitive powers, and its relation to the human body. I could say a good deal, which might be interesting but would certainly be painful, about some of the psychological causes of this attitude; but I prefer to welcome the very evident signs of a change in it, and to congratulate 'the Aristotelian Society and the Mind Association on their courage in treating with the contempt that it deserves the accusation of "having gone spooky" which they will certainly incur in some circles.

I do not myself think that the evidence for alleged supernormal *physical* phenomena is good enough to make them at present worth the serious attention of philosophers. I have no doubt that at least 99 percent of them either never happened as   orted or are capable of a normal explanation, which, in a great many cases, is simply that of deliberate fraud. We may, therefore, confine our attention to alleged cases of supernormal cognition. These may be

*Reprinted from *Proceedings of the Aristotelian Society,* 1937, by courtesy of the Editor of the Aristotelian Society. Copyright 1937 The Aristotelian Society.

198

roughly classified as follows. We may divide them first into super-normal cognitions of contemporary events or of the contemporary states of things or persons, and supernormal cognitions of past or future events or the past or future states of things or persons. Under the first heading would come Clairvoyance and Telepathy. In my opinion the evidence, both experimental and nonexperi-mental, for the occurrence of these kinds of supernormal cognition is adequate to establish a strong *prima facie* case, which philoso-phers and psychologists cannot ignore without challenging in-vidious comparisons to the ostrich. I have dealt with the philosophi-cal implications of clairvoyance and telepathy to the best of my ability in my presidential address on *Normal Cognition, Clairvoy-ance, and Telepathy* to the Society for Psychical Research in May, 1935. It will be found, by anyone whom it may interest, in Vol. XLIII of the S.P.R. *Proceedings*.

Under the second heading would come such knowledge of the past as was claimed by Miss Jourdain and Miss Moberley in their book *An Adventure,* and such foreknowledge as is claimed by Mr. J.W. Dunne in his book *An Experiment with Time.* We will call these "Supernormal Postcognition" and "Supernormal Precog-nition," respectively. In the present paper I shall be concerned primarily with supernormal precognition, but I shall have to refer occasionally to supernormal postcognition by way of comparison.

I will begin by stating what parts of the subject I do, and what parts I do not, intend to discuss. (1) I am not going to put forward or to criticize any theory about the *modus operandi* of veridical supernormal precognition, supposing it to be possible and suppos-ing that there is satisfactory evidence that it actually occurs. I have no theory of my own to suggest. The only theory known to me which seems worth consideration is that proposed by Mr. Dunne in his *Experiment with Time.* I have tried to restate and to criticize it in an article entitled *Mr. Dunne's Theory of Time* in *Philosophy* for April, 1935. As anyone who cares to consult that article will see, I cannot accept the theory as it stands, though I think it reflects very great credit on Mr. Dunne's originality and ingenuity. (2) I am not going to state or appraise the evidence which has been produced for the occurrence of supernormal foreknowledge. So far as concerns the English evidence, this has been admirably done by

Mr. H.F. Saltmarsh in his *Report on Cases of Apparent Precognition,* which will be found in Vol. XLII of the S.P.R. *Proceedings.* There is also a great deal of very impressive evidence from French sources in Dr. Osty's *La Connaissance Supranormale* and Richet's *L'Avenir et la Précognition.* I shall assume that the quantity and quality of the evidence are such as would make the hypothesis that veridical supernormal precognition occurs worth serious consideration *unless* there be some logical or metaphysical impossibility in it. No amount of empirical evidence would give the slightest probability to the hypothesis that there are squares whose diagonals are commensurate with their sides, because this supposition is known to be logically impossible. Now a great many people feel that the hypothesis of veridical supernormal precognition is in this position. (3) It is therefore very important to discover why this *a priori* objection is felt, and whether it is valid or not. This is a question for professional philosophers, like ourselves, and it is this question which I shall make the central topic of my paper.

I think that the *a priori* objection which many people feel against the very notion of veridical supernormal precognition can be dissected into at least three parts. No doubt they are closely interconnected, and no doubt the plain man does not very clearly distinguish them; but it is our business to do so. I propose to call them the "Epistemological," the "Causal" and the "Fatalistic" objections, and I will now treat them in turn.

(1) *The Epistemological Objection.*—We must begin by noticing that veridical precognition would not raise any special *a priori* difficulties if it consisted in inferring propositions about the future from general laws and from singular facts about the present or the past. It might still be supernormal in some cases. But, if so, this would only be because in some cases it might require a supernormal knowledge of general laws or of singular facts about the present or the past or because it might require supernormal powers of calculation and inference. The epistemological objection with which we are going to deal is concerned only with veridical precognition which is assumed to be non-inferential.

This being understood, the objection may be put as follows. To say that a person P had a non-inferential veridical cognition of an object O at a moment *t* is to say that the object O stood at the moment t in a certain relation to the person P, viz. in the relation of being cognized by P. Now an object cannot stand in any relations to anything unless and until it exists. But to say that P had a non-inferential veridical *pre*cognition of O at the moment t implies that O did not exist at t, but only began to exist at some later moment t_1. So the phrase "non-inferential veridical precognition by P of O at t" involves a plain contradiction. It implies that O stood in a certain relation to P at a time when O did not exist, and therefore could not stand in any relation to anything.

Is there anything in this objection? The first point to notice is that, if it were valid at all, it would be just as fatal to memory of events in the past as to veridical non-inferential cognition of events in the future. If it is obvious that a term which does not yet exist cannot yet stand in any relation to anything, it is equally obvious that a term which no longer exists can no longer stand in any relation to anything. But to say that I remember at t_2 an event which happened at t_1 is to say that at t_2 this event has the relational property of being cognized by me. On the other hand, since the event no longer exists at t_2, it can have no relations to anything at that time. The argument is precisely parallel in the two cases. Since memory is certainly non-inferential postcognition, and since we are not prepared to reject the possibility of veridical memory, there must be something wrong somewhere in the epistemological objection to the possibility of non-inferential veridical precognition. What is it? I will first give the solution for memory; it will then be easy to apply it to non-inferential precognition.

It is worth while to remark at the outset that non-inferential precognition, if it happens at all, must on any view be more like memory than like perception of contemporary events. For such precognition would agree with memory and differ from sense-perception in that the cognized object is cognized as occurring at a different date from the act of cognizing. Let us then begin by considering the nature of memory. Here, of course, we shall be confining our attention to memory in the sense of a present non-inferential cognition of certain events as having happened in the past. The word "memory" is also used to mean an acquired power to repeat or to utilize in the present something that was learned in the past, as when I say that I remember the opening lines of *Para-*

dise Lost or the first proposition of Euclid. Memory, in this latter sense, has obviously no close likeness to precognition.

I must begin by pointing out and removing certain tiresome verbal ambiguities. In ordinary language to say that X is remembering such and such an event implies that the event actually happened. If we believe that it did not happen, we say that X does not really remember it, but only thinks he remembers it. Yet, from a purely psychological and epistemological point of view, the experience may be exactly alike whether it be veridical or delusive. Now we want to analyse such experiences psychologically and epistemologically, without implying by the words which we use anything whatever as to whether they are veridical or delusive; for we know that some are delusive and we believe that others are veridical. Therefore we want a purely psychological term with no implications about truth or falsity. I propose to use the terms "ostensible memory" and "ostensible remembering" in this purely psychological sense. We can then distinguish two sub-classes of ostensible rememberings, viz. "veridical" and "delusive" ones. What is expressed in ordinary speech by saying that X is remembering so-and-so would therefore be expressed by us in the phrase "X is ostensibly remembering so-and-so, and this ostensible remembering is veridical." What is expressed in ordinary speech by saying that X only thinks he is remembering so-and-so would be expressed by us in the phrase "X is ostensibly remembering so-and-so, but this ostensible remembering is delusive." We must now try to analyse the experience of ostensibly remembering an event.

Such an experience contains two utterly different but intimately connected factors. In the first place, the person concerned is imaging a certain image, visual or auditory or otherwise. This image is a *contemporary* existent; and, if the person who is imaging it attends to the question of its date, he has no hesitation in saying that it is present and not past. The second factor is that the experient uncritically and automatically takes for granted that there was a certain one event in his own *past* life, of which this image is the present representative; and he automatically bases on certain qualities of his present image certain beliefs about the character and the recency of this assumed past event. These two factors may be called respectively "imaging" and "retrospectively referring."

Imaging can occur without the image being retrospectively referred. I may image a certain image, and it may be uniquely related to a certain one event in my past life in such a way that it is *in fact* the present representative of that past event; and yet I may not base upon it a belief that there was such an event. In that case I am not ostensibly remembering that past event. On the other hand, the second factor cannot occur without the first. One must be imaging an image in order to have something as a basis for retrospective reference. I propose to call any image which is *in fact* the present representative of a certain past event in the history of the person who images it a "retro-presentative" image, regardless of whether the experient does or does not retrospectively refer it.

Now the retrospective beliefs which a person bases on his awareness of a present image may, like any other beliefs, be true or false. There may or there may not have been one particular event in his past life of which this image is the present representative. And, if there was such an event, it may or may not have had the characteristics which this retro-presentative image causes him to believe that it had. If the retrospective beliefs are true, the ostensible memory is veridical; if they are false, it is delusive.

I have said that in ostensible memory we have certain retrospective beliefs "based upon" awareness of a present image and its qualities. I must now say something about this vague phrase "based upon." In the first place it does *not* mean "inferred from." Of course we have plenty of inferential beliefs about the past, and many of them are about events in our own past lives. But the very essence of ostensible memory is that it is not inferential. In any inference there must be at least one general premise and there must be a process of reasoning. Plainly there is nothing of the kind in ostensible remembering. Moreover, we could not have any inferential beliefs about the past unless we already had some non-inferential beliefs about it. For the general laws or the statistical generalizations which are used as premises in such inferences are believed only because of observations which we ostensibly remember to have made in the past. What is meant by saying that the retrospective beliefs are "based upon" awareness of a present image and its qualities is roughly as follows. These beliefs would not have occurred when and where they did if the experient had not then and there been aware of an image; and the propositions believed by him would have been different in detail if the image had been different in certain respects.

It is useful to compare the part played in ostensible memory by awareness of an image with the part played in ostensible sense-perception by awareness of a sensum, i.e. by sensation. In ostensible sense-perception, whether veridical or delusive, I sense a certain sensum, visual, auditory, tactual or what not; and I automatically and uncritically base on this experience a belief that there is a certain one physical thing or event, outside me in space, which is existing or happening *now* and is manifesting itself to me by this sensation. In ostensible memory I image a certain image, and I automatically and uncritically base on this experience a belief that there *was* a certain one event in my own past life, of which this image is the present representative. The three vitally important points for us to notice are the following:—(i) Both ostensible sense-perception and ostensible memory are "immediate" experiences, in the sense that they do not involve inference. In this respect they can be contrasted respectively with my present belief that there are chairs in the next room and my present belief that England was formerly connected by land with the Continent. (ii) Both of them *seem* to the uncritical experient to be "immediate" in the further sense of being acts of *prehension* or *acquaintance,* in the one case with contemporary physical things or events, and in the other with past events in one's own life. (iii) In both cases a little philosophical reflexion on the facts of delusive ostensible sense-perception and delusive ostensible memory shows that they are not "immediate" in this sense. They do indeed involve acts of pre-hension as essential constituents. In ostensible sense-perception, whether veridical or delusive, the experient really is acquainted with *something,* viz. a sensum; and in ostensible memory, whether veridical or delusive, he really is acquainted with *something,* viz. an image. But what he claims to be perceiving, in the one case, is not a sensum, but a contemporary physical thing or event outside him in space; and what he claims to be remembering in the other case is not a present image, but a past event in his own life.

We are now in a position to remove the epistemological objection to memory, and to see how it arises. And, when we have done this, we shall be able to see how non-inferential precognition must be analysed if it is to escape this kind of objection. The epistemological objection to the possibility of veridical memory rests entirely on the tacit assumption that to remember an event is to have a present prehension of an event which is past. This would entail that the event, which *no longer* exists, nevertheless stands to the act of remembering, which is *now* occurring, in the direct two-term relation of prehended object to act of prehending. And this is condemned as absurd.

The answer to this objection is simply to give the right analysis and to point out how the wrong one came to seem plausible. On the right analysis *something* is prehended, viz. an image. But this is contemporary, and it is not the remembered event. Again, something is judged or believed on the basis of this prehended image. This something is a *proposition,* to the effect that there was an event of such and such a kind in the experient's past life and that the prehended image is its present representative. This proposition, like all propositions, has no date; it is not an event or a thing or a person, though it is about a person and about a past event. There is, therefore, no difficulty in the fact that it can be the object of a present act of believing. Lastly, if, and only if, the ostensible remembering is veridical, there actually *was* such an event in the experient's past life as he believes there to have been on the basis of the present image which he is now prehending. In that case, and only in that case, there *is* a relation, though a very indirect one, between this past event and the present experience of ostensibly remembering. It is this. The past event then corresponds to or accords with the present belief about his own past which the experient automatically and uncritically bases on his present image.

No doubt, the causes of the wrong analysis of ostensible memory being so prevalent are the following. In the first place, people are inclined to confine their attention to ostensible memories which are veridical, and to forget that there are plenty which are delusive and that the latter are *psychologically* indistinguishable from the former. Now the purely prehensive analysis of ostensible memory has no plausibility whatever when applied to ostensible memories which are delusive, but it seems quite plausible if one forgets about them and thinks only of those which are veridical.

Secondly, the fact that ostensible memory, like ostensible sense-perception, is "immediate," in the sense of being non-inferential, may lead people to think that it is "immediate" in the sense of being purely prehensive. And they may be confirmed in this mistake by the fact that ostensible memory really does contain a prehension as an essential factor, and that it is rather easy to overlook the other factor which is equally essential. This other factor is not a prehension of a particular existent, but is the uncritical acceptance of a proposition (true or false) about one's own past life.

Lastly, it must be noted that everyone who is not a professional philosopher tends to regard sense-perception as purely prehensive, viz. as consisting in a prehension by the percipient of some contemporary physical thing or event. It is only reflective analysis which shows that this account is much too simple to fit the facts as a whole. Now there are likenesses between ostensible memory and ostensible sense-perception, and there are striking differences between both of them and discursive or inferential cognition. Therefore there will be a strong tendency to think that memory is prehensive of past events, since sense-perception is mistakenly believed to be prehensive of contemporary physical things and events.

It remains to apply these remarks to precognition, and to remove the epistemological objection to the possibility of veridical non-inferential precognition. I shall begin, as before, by stating how I propose to use my terms. I am going to use the term "ostensible foreseeing" as equivalent to "ostensible non-inferential precognition." And I am going to use both these equivalent phrases in a purely psychological sense, just as I used the terms "ostensible memory" and "ostensible sense-perception." Then I shall distinguish between ostensible foreseeings which are veridical and those which are delusive. There is no doubt that there are ostensible foreseeings; the only question is whether any of them are veridical and whether these are too numerous and too detailed to be attributable to chance.

Now, in order to avoid the epistemological objection, we have simply to analyse ostensible foreseeing in the way in which we analysed ostensible remembering. When a person has an ostensible foreseeing the experience involves two factors. He images a certain image, which is, of course, contemporary with his act of imaging. And he automatically, uncritically, and non-inferentially bases upon his prehension of this image a belief that there *will be* an event of a certain kind, of which this image is the present representative. If his ostensible precognition is veridical, this present belief will eventually be verified by the occurrence of such an event as he believes to be going to happen. If it is delusive, the belief will be falsified by the non-occurrence of any such event in the context in which it was expected to happen. Even if the ostensible foreseeing should be veridical, there is no question of its being a present prehension of the future event which later on happens and verifies it. *Something* is prehended, but it is the present image and not the foreseen future event. Something is judged or believed, viz. a timeless proposition to the effect that there will be an event of a certain kind in a certain context and that the prehended image is its present representative.

So the purely epistemological objection to the possibility of veridical non-inferential precongition vanishes in smoke. The fact is that most people who have tried to theorize about non-inferential precognition have made needless difficulties for themselves by making two mistakes. In the first place, they have tried to assimilate it to sense-perception, when they ought to have assimilated it to memory. And, secondly, they have tacitly assumed an extremely naive prehensive anlysis, which is plausible, though mistaken, when applied to ostensible sense-perception, and is simply nonsensical when applied to ostensible remembering or ostensible foreseeing.

Before leaving this topic I must mention the following possibility. In talking of memory I said that a person may be aware of an image, which is *in fact* retro-presentative, without at the time basing any retrospective belief on it, and therefore without ostensibly remembering the past event which it in fact represents. Suppose that this person keeps a diary, and that at some later date he is reading through one of his old diaries. Then a certain passage in the diary which he is now reading may both make him remember having had this image and give him reason to believe that it was a representative of a certain earlier event which is recorded in this passage. Now suppose that veridical foreseeing occurs, and suppose that our analysis of ostensible foreseeing is correct. Then it is likely that there would be "pro-presentative" images on which the person who has them bases *no* prospective belief at the time, just as there are retro-presentative images on which the person who has them bases no retrospective belief at the time. Let us suppose that this happens to a person in a dream, for instance. Then at the time he does not have any experience which can properly be called "ostensibly foreseeing" a certain future event, any more than the person in my previous example had any experience which could properly be called "ostensibly remembering" a certain past event. But suppose that the dream was, for some reason, recorded or told to another person at breakfast. Later on, events may happen which give the dreamer or the friend to whom he related his dream good reason to believe that the dream was *in fact* pro-presentative of those events. Much of the evidence adduced for super-normal precognition is really evidence for the occurrence of images which were *not* prospectively referred by the experient at the time when he had them, but were shown by subsequent events to have been *in fact* pro-presentative.

It remains to notice an intermediate case which is fairly common. A person may dream that he is witnessing or taking part in certain events at a certain familiar place, and in the dream he may take those events to be present. For example, he may dream that he is watching a race at a well-known racecourse, that he is seeing a certain horse coming in first, and that he is hearing the crowd shouting a certain name. On waking he, of course, recognizes that the incidents which he has been ostensibly previewing are not contemporary, and he may recognize that the dream refers to a race in which he is interested and which he has arranged to attend next week. He therefore now refers the image of the winning horse and the shouted name to that future race-meeting. If that horse should win in that race, this will *pro tanto* be evidence in favor of the view that his dream contained images which were *in fact* pro-presentative. But it cannot be said that the *dream itself* was an instance of veridical foreseeing; for it was not an instance of ostensible *precognition* at all. It was an instance of ostensible sense-perception; and, in that respect, it was delusive, though subsequent reflexion on it enabled the experient to precognize a certain event correctly.

(2) *The Causal Objection.*—Suppose that, at a certain moment t_2, I remember a certain event e which happened at an earlier moment t_1 in my life. If we ask for a causal explanation of the occurrence of a memory of this particular event at this particular moment, we are given the following answer, which we find fairly satisfactory in principle. We are told that the original experience e at t_1 set up a characteristic kind of process or a characteristic structural modification in my mind or my brain or in both; that this process has been going on, or that this structural modification has persisted, during the interval between t_1 and t_2; that at t_2 a certain other experience (which we may call a "reminder") occurred in me; that, for certain reasons which could often be assigned, this reminder linked up in a specially intimate way with this structural modification or with the contemporary phase of this continuous process; and that the cause of my remembering e at t_2 is the conjunction of the reminder at t_2 with the simultaneous phase of this continuous process or with the persistent structural modification initiated by my experience at t_1. There may be a good deal of mythology in this causal explanation; but it is acceptable mythology, bearing a close analogy to certain observable facts in other departments of phenomena.

But suppose that, instead of remembering at t_2 an event which happened at an earlier moment t_1, I veridically foresaw at t_2 an event which did not happen until a later moment t_3. Or suppose that, even if I did not have at t_2 an experience of ostensible foreseeing, I had then an image which subsequent experience shows to have been in fact pro-presentative of a certain event at t_3. How can we account for the occurrence of a pro-presentative image of this particular moment? Since the event which it pro-presents had not yet happened when the pro-presentative image occurred, it cannot yet have had any effects. It cannot yet have initiated any characteristic kind of process or structural modification in my brain or my mind. Any *past* experience of mine may have causal *descendants* in all the later stages of my history. But an experience which has not yet happened can have no causal descendants until it has happened. It may, of course, have causal *ancestors* in the earlier stages of my history. It will do so, e.g. if it is the fulfilment of an intention which I had formed earlier and gradually carried out. But in most cases of veridical foreseeing, or of images which turn out to have been pro-presentative though they were not prospectively referred at the time, there is no question of the pro-presented event being brought about by a process which was already going on in the experient at the time when he had the image. No doubt the pro-presented event had then a causal ancestor *somewhere* in the universe, if the Law of Universal Causation be true. But, as a rule, this causal ancestor was completely outside the mind and the body of the experient.

So the causal objection comes to this. At the time when a certain person had an image which was pro-presentative of a certain event, that event cannot have had any causal descendants. And, in many cases, its causal ancestors lay wholly outside the experient's body and mind. How, then, could we possibly account for the occurrence in this person at this particular moment of an image which is pro-presentative of this particular future event? The pro-presented event had no causal representative, either ancestor or descendant, in the experient at the time when his pro-presentative image of it occurred.

Before considering the causal objection it is desirable to consider a little more fully the analogy between ostensible remembering and ostensible foreseeing. In my definition and analysis of "ostensible remembering" I said that the experient judges that there was a certain event *in his own past life,* of which the image which he is now having is the present representative. Now it might justly be objected that this is too narrow. We claim to remember events which are not our own experiences; thus, e.g. a person who had been to King George VI's coronation would claim to remember the coronation. On the other hand, it would be contrary to English usage to claim to remember an event which was neither a past experience of one's own, e.g. an attack of toothache, nor the object of a past perception of one's own. Nobody now alive could properly say that he remembers George III's coronation, because no one who is now alive witnessed that event.

Consider now the case of Miss Moberley and Miss Jourdain, the experients who wrote the book *An Adventure.* They claimed to have non-inferential veridical postcognition of certain events which happened at Versailles during the French Revolution. But they did not claim to *remember* those events; and, if they had done so, they would have been understood to be claiming to have pre-existed their present bodies, to have animated other bodies at the time of the French Revolution, and to have witnessed these events when they were happening.

I shall express this limitation, which is part of the definition of "memory," by saying that memory is veridical non-inferential post-cognition which is "intra-subjectively circumscribed."

Now this is, so far, merely a question of the meanings and usages of words. But we now come to a point which is not verbal. It is this. We always assume that every normal veridical postcognition is *either* intra-subjectively circumscribed *or* is due to inference from observed present facts and general laws *or* is due to hearing reports or reading records made by other human beings. When our attention is called to an alleged case of veridical postcognition which is apparently not intra-subjectively circumscribed and yet apparently does not rest either on inference or on testimony, such as the case presented by Miss Moberley and Miss Jourdain, we feel extremely puzzled. If we accept it as veridical and as too detailed to be due to chance coincidence, we have to regard it as supernormal, and we try to bring it under our general rule in one way or another. Thus, e.g. some people would try to assimilate it to memory by suggesting that the minds of these two ladies had pre-existed their present bodies, and that they had been witnesses (in bodies, which they had previously animated) of the events which they post-cognized in a subsequent incarnation. Others would try to assimilate it to knowledge based on testimony by suggesting that the souls of the persons concerned in these incidents at Versailles in the eighteenth century survived and communicated telepathically with these ladies in the twentieth century. Others again would try to assimilate it to looking at an old photograph, depicting a past scene, which was taken when the scene was still present and has been preserved.

Plainly the difficulty which makes people fly to these rather far-fetched suggestions is a *causal* difficulty. If we adopt any of these suggestions, we can see, at least in outline, a continuous causal chain connecting the original events with the occurrence of the postcognition of them. On either of these theories the original events would be factors in a certain total state of affairs in the eighteenth century which is a causal ancestor of the subsequent postcognitive experience in the twentieth century. But, unless we accept one or other of these suggestions, there seems to be no continuous causal connexion between the occurrence of the post-cognitive experiences and the events which are postcognized. In that case why should the images which occurred in the minds of Miss Moberley and Miss Jourdain at a certain moment have corresponded to *any* actual past event? And why should they have corresponded to the particular past event to which they did correspond, rather than to any other of the infinitely numerous events in the past history of the world which these ladies had never witnessed?

Now it is evident that we must draw a distinction among ostensible precognitions like that which I have just been drawing among ostensible postcognitions. In the first place, there will be intra-subjectively circumscribed ostensible precognitions. Here the events which are ostensibly precognized are either future experiences of the subject or are events which he will himself perceive. Secondly, there may be ostensible precognitions which are not intra-subjectively circumscribed. Here the events which are ostensibly pre-cognized are neither future experiences of the subject nor events which he will perceive.

Among events of the latter kind three sub-classes must be distinguished:—(i) Those whose occurrence will be reported to the subject or verified by his own observations and inferences *after* they have happened. (ii) Those which the subject will be able, at some *intermediate* date to anticipate with reasonable confidence by normal means from information which will by then be available to him. (iii) Those which fall under neither of these headings. Now the first and the second of these sub-classes could easily be assimilated to the class of intra-subjectively circumscribed veridical pre-cognitions. For it might be suggested that, in these cases, what the subject primarily precognizes is the report which he will in future hear or read, or the anticipation which he will later make on the basis of data which will then be available to him.

Now only intra-subjectively circumscribed veridical precognitions, in the strictest sense, would be analogous to memories. The

first sub-class of precognitions which are not intra-subjectively circumscribed would be analogous to remembering a report which
one had heard or read, of an event which one had not personally
witnessed. The second sub-class would be analogous to remembering an inference which one had made, to the effect that a certain
event had probably happened at some earlier date. It is only the
third sub-class which would be analogous to the completely anomalous kind of veridical postcognition which is alleged to have happened to Miss Moberley and Miss Jourdain. From the nature of
the case most ostensible precognitions which have been shown to
be veridical are either intra-subjectively circumscribed or fall into
the first or the second of our two sub-classes. The following would
be an instance of our third sub-class. Suppose that I have an ostensible precognition of a certain event, that I write it down without
mentioning it to anyone, and that I die before it is due for fulfilment. Suppose that my executors find the prediction among my
papers, and that it is subsequently fulfilled. This would fall into our
third sub-class, and would be analogous to the veridical postcognition claimed by Miss Moberley and Miss Jourdain.

So far I have been pointing out analogies between ostensible
postcognition and ostensible precognition. But now we must note
the difference in our attitude towards the two. We have not the
least *a priori* objection to the possibility of veridical memory. But
our *a priori* objection to the possibility of that kind of veridical
precognition which would most closely resemble memory is almost
as strong as our *a priori* objection to the possibility of that kind of
veridical precognition which would resemble the anomalous post-
cognitive experiences of Miss Moberley and Miss Jourdain. This
difference in our attitude is bound up with the causal objection,
as I will now show.

Even if what I veridically precognize is an experience which *I*
am going to have or is an event which *I* am going to witness, there
seems to be no possible causal explanation of why a certain image
which I now have should correspond to *any* future event or to *this*
rather than to any other of the infinitely numerous events which
will happen from now onwards. The complete cause of the occurrence of a present image in my mind must be in the *past*. If this
image is pro-presentative of a certain event, the event which it pro-

presents is in the *future*. In the case of memory the causal explanation is in terms of a "trace," left in the subject by a past experience, and a present "reminder." The trace is the present causal
descendant in him of a certain past experience of his; and the reminder is some present experience of his which stirs up this particular trace. The immediate causal condition of the ostensible
memory-experience is the present excitement of *this* trace. It therefore seems intelligible that the present ostensible memory should
correspond to a certain past event, viz. to that particular experience which was the causal progenitor of this particular trace. But
there cannot now be in a person a "trace" of an experience which
he has not yet had. And, unless there is now in him something
analogous to a "trace" of a future experience, how can anything
that happens to him here and now play the part which is played by
a "reminder" in memory? What conceivable causal account, then,
can be given of veridical non-inferential precognition, even when
it is confined to the subject's own future experiences or to events
which he will personally witness?

In face of this causal difficulty, which attaches equally to *all*
ostensibly non-inferential veridical precognition, we tend to act as
many people have acted in face of the anomalous kind of ostensibly
non-inferential veridical postcognition claimed by Miss Moberley
and Miss Jourdain. We tend to fall back upon one or other of the
following five theories:—(i) That the subject has himself subconsciously inferred, from data which he has subconsciously noted,
that a certain event will probably happen in a certain context; and
that the results of this inference have emerged into consciousness
in the form of an ostensibly non-inferential veridical precognition.
(ii) That the subject himself has subconsciously formed an intention to bring about a certain event, and has initiated a course of
action which is likely to fulfil this intention; and that the veridical
precognition is a by-product in consciousness of this subconscious
intention. (iii) That the occurrence of the ostensible precognition,
however it may have been caused, sets up a desire for its fulfilment;
and that this sets up processes, of which the subject remains unaware, which tend to bring about the ostensibly precognized event
and thus to verify the precognition. (iv) That some other human
being, now living on earth, has consciously or unconsciously in-

ferred that a certain event will probably happen in a certain context, or has formed a conscious or unconscious intention of bringing it about; that knowledge of his inference or of his intention has been conveyed telepathically to the subconscious part of the subject's mind; that the information, thus subconsciously received, emerges into the subject's consciousness in the form of an ostensible non-inferential precognition that this event will happen; and that this is correct, either because the other man's inference was sound or because the other man's intention is eventually carried out. (v) This theory is the same as the fourth, except that we now substitute the phrase "some non-human person or the surviving soul of some dead man" for the phrase "some other human being, now living on earth." We may, if we like, ascribe to such minds a much greater knowledge of past and present facts and general laws and much greater powers of inference than those possessed by any human being now living on earth.

important

These five alternative theories are not, of course, mutually exclusive. The first three of them do not *explicitly* involve any supernormal factor. But I think it is certain that a great deal of the alleged evidence for veridical foreseeing could not be fitted into them except on the assumption that human beings have supernormal powers of perception, of inference, and of action on the external world. The fourth involves no supernormal *agents* but it does presuppose the supernormal *process* of telepathic conveyance of information from one embodied human mind to another which may be in no obviously close relationship with it at the time. It would seem, however, that some such process as this has to be postulated in order to account for many well-attested facts of mediumship which have nothing ostensibly precognitive about them. The fifth theory involves both supernormal processes and supernormal agents, for the existence of which we have little, if any, independent evidence. It is, therefore, to be avoided if possible. Yet, if there were many well-attested cases of veridical ostensibly non-inferential precognition which could not be brought under any of the first four heads, we might be forced to accept the fifth theory as a *pis aller* in view of the causal difficulties.

All these rather fantastic theories are proposed in order to avoid the causal difficulty about veridical foreseeing. Is that difficulty genuine and insuperable? Let us consider what a person means when he says that the available evidence suffices to show that there is veridical foreseeing. Plainly he does not mean simply that in many cases a later event, which a person had no rational ground for expecting, *happens* to accord to a very high degree with an earlier experience in this person of ostensible foreseeing. He means that there is an amount of accordance between such subsequent events and ostensible foreseeings which is too great to be ascribed to "chance coincidence." He may admit that, if each case stood alone, it might be reasonable to count it as a chance coincidence. But he asserts that, when the reported cases are taken together, this view of the accordance between ostensible foreseeings and subsequent events cannot reasonably be held.

Now we are not concerned here with the truth or falsity of this opinion, but with its implications. What is implied by saying that a certain correlation between the intrinsic characteristics of x and those of y is not a "chance coincidence"? It is equivalent to saying that this correlation is due either (a) to x being a cause-factor in a causal ancestor of y, or (b) to y being a cause-factor in a causal ancestor of x, or (c) to x and y being effect-factors in causal descendants of a common causal ancestor z. Suppose now that x is an ostensible foreseeing or an image which turns out to have been pro-presentative, and suppose that y is a subsequent event whose concordance with x is said to be "something more than a chance coincidence." Alternative (b) is ruled out by the self-evident general principle that an event cannot be a cause-factor until it has happened, and that it can then be a factor only in determining *later* events. We are thus left with alternatives (a) and (c). The first of these alternatives is equivalent to saying that the ostensible foreseeing or the pro-presentative image was a cause-factor in a causal ancestor of the event which subsequently verified it. The theory (iii) in our enumeration of five theories above is an instance of this alternative. The other alternative is equivalent to saying that there is a certain causal ancestor which has a series of successive causal descendants, that the ostensible foreseeing or the pro-presentative image is an effect-factor in one of the earlier of these causal descendants, and that the event which verifies it is an effect-factor in one of the later of them. Theory (ii) in our enumeration above is an instance of this alternative.

Since we are tied down to alternatives (*a*) (*b*), and (*c*) by the definition of "not being a chance coincidence," and since (*b*) is excluded by a principle about causation which appears to be self-evident, it would seem to be legitimate to infer that all possible theories about veridical ostensible foreseeing must be variations on the following four themes:—(i) That the concordance between an ostensible foreseeing or a pro-presentative image and a certain subsequent event, however detailed it may be and however numerous may be the instances of it, is merely a chance coincidence. (ii) That the precognitive experience is only ostensibly non-inferential, but really depends on inference either in the subject himself or in some other mind; and that the pro-presentative image is just a by-product which arises in the subject's mind as a result of inferring a certain conclusion about the future. (iii) That the ostensible foreseeing or the pro-presentative image is a cause-factor in a causal ancestor of the event which subsequently fulfils it. (iv) That there is a certain causal ancestor which has a series of successive causal descendants, that the ostensible foreseeing or the pro-presentative image is an effect-factor in one of the earlier of these, and that the event which subsequently verifies it is an effect-factor in one of the later of them. If this be granted, the fundamental difficulty of the subject is this. It is alleged that ostensible foreseeings have been verified by subsequent events too often and too accurately to allow us to accept the first alternative. On the other hand, many of the best cases are such that it is impossible to bring them under any of the remaining three alternatives unless we postulate additional dimensions of space or agents and causal laws which are quite unfamiliar and for which we have no independent evidence.

If I were faced with a choice between these evils, I should consider that the least of them is to postulate additional dimensions of space, provided that this will account for the facts. If I thought, as Mr. Dunne seems to do, that I should have to postulate an unending series of dimensions and then an "observer at infinity" (who would plainly have to be the last term of a series which, by hypothesis, could have no last term), I should, of course, reject this alternative as nonsensical. But it is certain that these extravagances are not needed in order to account for the possibility of veridical ostensible foreseeing on the lines of Mr. Dunne's theory. For this purpose five, and only five, spatial dimensions are needed. The fallacy which caused Mr. Dunne to embark on his wild-goose chase after the "observer at infinity" can easily be detected and avoided. Therefore there is no *prima facie* objection to a theory which tries to explain veridical ostensible foreseeing in the way in which Mr. Dunne tries to do so. And, although I am wholly dissatisfied with Mr. Dunne's detailed explanation, as it stands, because I cannot see what would correspond in the physical and mental world to the various geometrically defined entities involved in the theory, I do think that there is at least a chance of working out a satisfactory theory on his general lines.

If this much be granted, I think it is obviously preferable to postulate a five-dimensional space rather than to pursue the other alternatives that I have enumerated. After all, nothing could be more completely contingent than the apparent fact that the space of nature has just three dimensions. As Hinton showed, there are some physical facts which would be rather neatly explained by the assumption that it has four dimensions. The assumption of a fifth dimension, in order to explain certain very odd cognitive phenomena, is internally consistent and intelligible, and we have no ground for holding it to be antecedently improbable. I do not think that this can be said of any of the other alternatives open to us.

If I were wise, I should leave the matter at this point. But I propose to "go in off the deep end" while I am about it, and to make a perfectly fantastic suggestion. I believe that this suggestion is of some interest on two grounds: (i) So far as I can see, it is the one and only way in which the prehensive analysis of ostensible foreseeing, which we rejected long ago, could possibly be made intelligible and rehabilitated. And (ii) even if we continue to reject the prehensive analysis, the suggestion would enable us to deal with the causal difficulty in a way which we have hitherto shunned as impossible.

It will be remembered that we rejected the prehensive analysis of ostensible foreseeing because it entails that an event which has not yet happened "co-exists with" the foreseeing of it, and therefore in some sense "already exists." Let us ask ourselves now whether there is any possible way of giving a meaning to such apparently nonsensical statements.

So far as I can see, the only way in which a sense could be given to such statements would be to ascribe a second dimension to time. A point which is *east* of another point may be either *north* of, or *south* of, or in the *same latitude* as the latter. Suppose that "east of" corresponds to "later than" in the only temporal dimension that we ordinarily recognize. And suppose that there were a second temporal dimension, and that "later than" in this dimension corresponds to "north of" in the case of points on the earth's surface. Then an event which is "after" a certain other event, in the only temporal dimension which we ordinarily recognize, might be either "after" or "before" or "simultaneous with" this other event in the second temporal dimension which persons who accept a prehensive analysis of foreseeing would have to postulate.

Now, if we had to postulate a hitherto unsuspected second dimension of time, we should have to revise all our "axioms" about the connexion between time and causation. We might have to say that x cannot be a causal ancestor of y unless x is before y in *at least one* temporal dimension; but that x can be a causal ancestor of y, provided it is before y in *one* temporal dimension even if it be after y, in the other temporal dimension. Nothing could seem more self-evident to most people than the proposition that a material object could not get into or out of a continuous spherical shell unless a hole were made in the latter. Yet it is easy to show that this proposition is not *intrinsically* necessary, but is only a necessary consequence of the quite contingent proposition that the space of nature has but three dimensions.

It may be worth while to develop this very wild suggestion a little further. Consider any two points x and y on the earth's surface. Let us represent the proposition "x is due north of y" by the symbol xNNy; and let us use similar symbols, *mutatis mutandis*, for the other possibilities. Then there are eight possible spatial relations in which x may stand to y, viz. (1) xNNy, (2) xNEy, (3) xEEy, (4) xESy, (5) xSSy, (6) xSWy, (7) xWWy, and (8) xWNy. The corresponding relations in which y may stand to x are, of course, (i) ySSx, (ii) ySWx, (iii) yWWx, (iv) yWNx, (v) yNNx, (vi) yNEx, (vii) yEEx, and (viii) yESx. A person who could recognize the distinction of east and west but not that of north and south would lump together cases (1) and (5) and say that *x* and *y* "coincide in position" in each case. He would lump together cases (2), (3) and (4), and would say that *x* is "east" of *y* in each case; and he would lump together cases (6), (7) and (8), and would say that *x* is "west" of *y* in each case.

Now we supposed above that the temporal relation "after," in the one temporal dimension which is familiar to us, is analogous to the spatial relation "east of." And we supposed that "after," in the second temporal dimension with which we are not normally acquainted, is analogous to the spatial relation "north of." Let us denote "after" and "before," in the first temporal dimension, by A and B respectively; and let us denote "after" and "before," in the second temporal dimension, by α and β respectively. Then, in the spatial analogue, A corresponds to E, B to W, α to N, and β to S.

Suppose now that *x* and *y* are two events. If a person judges that *x* is *simultaneous with y,* it may be that (*a*) *x* is simultaneous with *y* in both temporal dimensions, or (*b*) *x* is simultaneous with *y* in the first and before *y* in the second, or (*c*) that *x* is simultaneous with *y* in the first and after *y* in the second. These alternatives may be symbolized respectively by $x=y$, $x\beta\beta y$, and $x\alpha\alpha y$. There is no spatial analogue to (*a*); but (*b*) is analogous to $xSSy$, and (*c*) is analogous to $xNNy$. Next let us suppose that a person judges that *x* is *before y.* Then it may be that (*a*) *x* is before *y* in both dimensions, or (*b*) that *x* is before *y* in the first dimension and simultaneous with *y* in the second, or (*c*) that *x* is before *y* in the first dimension and after *y* in the second. These alternatives may be symbolized respectively by $xB\beta y$, $xBBy$, and $xB\alpha y$; and they correspond respectively to $xWSy$, $xWWy$ and $xWNy$ in the spatial analogy. Lastly, let us suppose that a person judges that *x* is *after y.* Then it may be that (*a*) *x* is after *y* in both dimensions, or (*b*) that *x* is after *y* in the first dimension and is simultaneous with *y* in the second, or (*c*) that *x* is after *y* in the first dimension and before *y* in the second. These alternatives may be symbolized respectively as $xA\alpha y$, $xAAy$, and $xA\beta y$; and they correspond respectively to $xENy$, $xEEy$ and $xESy$ in the spatial analogy.

Now let us suppose that the true rule about the connexion between causation and temporal relations is the following:—An event

x can be a cause-factor in a causal ancestor of an event y if, and only if, x is *before* y in *at least one* of the two temporal dimensions. (The spatial analogue is that it is necessary and sufficient that x should be *either west or south* of y.) Plainly these conditions are fulfilled in the following five cases, and in them only, viz. $xA\beta y$, $x\beta\beta y$, $x\beta By$, $xBBy$ and $xB\alpha y$. (These correspond to $xESy$, $xSSy$, $xSWy$, $xWWy$ and $xWNy$, respectively, in the spatial analogy.) How would these five cases appear to a person who recognizes only the B-A dimension of time? In the first he would judge that x is *after* y; in the second he would judge that x is *simultaneous with* y; and in the remaining three he would judge that x is *before* y. Thus, other things being equal, the cases in which it would appear to him that a *later* event is a cause-factor in a causal ancestor of an *earlier* event would be only one-fourth as numerous as the cases in which it would appear to him that this causal relation relates an earlier event to a later one or relates two simultaneous events to each other. And it is easy to conceive of special conditions which would reduce this proportion enormously below one-fourth. This would be so if, for some reason, there is a very high negative correlation between standing in the A-relation to an event and standing in the β-relation to the same event.

There is one more point to be noticed before leaving this topic. The relations from y to x which are equivalent to the five relations from x to y enumerated above are, respectively, $y\alpha Bx$, $y\alpha\alpha x$, $yA\alpha x$, $yAAx$ and $y\beta Ax$. Let us now apply our rule about causation to these. We see that y could be a cause-factor in a causal ancestor of x in the *first* and the *fifth* and in them only. For these are the only two in which either B or β occurs. How would these two cases appear to an ordinary observer? It is plain that they would present a double paradox to him. In the first place, as we have already seen, it is possible that what appears to him as a later event may be a cause-factor in a causal ancestor of what appears to him as an earlier event. But, further in this case x may be a cause-factor in a causal ancestor of y, while y may *also* be a cause-factor in a causal ancestor of x. For here x is before y in one of the temporal dimensions, while y is before x in the other of them.

I will now sum up about this fantastic suggestion. (i) As I have pointed out, there is nothing in the least fantastic in the hypothesis of more than three *spatial* dimensions, as in Mr. Dunne's theory. But the suggestion that *time* may have more than one dimension may be simply nonsensical. Certainly it ought not to be lightly admitted into society merely on the dubious claim to kinship with perfectly respectable hypotheses about additional spatial dimensions. (ii) I believe that some such suggestion as this is the only way to make sense of a purely prehensive analysis of veridical foreseeing and of memory. But this does not do much to recommend it to me. For I do not hanker after such an analysis of these experiences, and I think it most unlikely that any such analysis of them is correct. (iii) The main interest of the suggestion is in reference to the Causal Objection. Although the non-prehensive analysis of ostensible foreseeing does not *require* the hypothesis of a second temporal dimension in order to make it intelligible, as the prehensive analysis appears to do, yet it *could* be combined with that hypothesis if this were found desirable. Now it will be remembered that we rejected (as contrary to a self-evident principle about causation) the suggestion that the event which subsequently verifies an ostensible foreseeing or concords with a pro-presentative image might be a cause-factor in a causal ancestor of the foreseeing or of the image. We see now that, if we are prepared to swallow the hypothesis of a two-dimensional time and to relax our causal "axiom" in a certain way, we need not necessarily reject this alternative. So we must now, very tentatively, add this alternative to the list of four which we previously stated to be exhaustive.

(3) *The Fatalistic Objection.*—In order to state this objection clearly it will be necessary to define certain terms. I will begin by defining the statement that a certain event *e* was "dependent on" a certain voluntary decision *d*. It is to have the following meaning. If the person who made the decision *d* had instead chosen a different alternative, and all the other circumstances at the time had been as they in fact were, then *e* would not have happened. There is no doubt that we all believe, with regard to many events, that they are in this sense dependent on voluntary decisions.

Next, I will define the statement that a certain event *e*, which happened at t_1 in a certain place or in a certain person's mind, was "already completely predetermined" at a certain earlier moment *t*. It has the following meaning. There is a set of facts about the dispositions, the mutual relations, and the internal state at or before the moment t of the various substances then existing, which, together with the laws of matter and of mind, *logically entails* that an event exactly like e will happen after an interval t_1—t in the place or the mind in which e did happen.

Suppose now that e depends on d, in the sense defined, and that d is not completely predetermined at any moment. Then it follows that e is not completely predetermined at any moment *before* that at which d happens. Of course, e may still be completely predetermined at moments *after* d has happened.

Finally, the following proposition seems self-evident to many people. If an ostensible precognition occurs and is subsequently fulfilled, then, unless this is a mere chance coincidence, the event which subsequently fulfilled it must have been already completely predetermined at the time when the ostensible precognition took place.

Now in many cases an ostensible precognition or a pro-presentative image has been fulfilled by a subsequent event which was, to all appearance, dependent on a voluntary decision which took place *after* the ostensibly precognitive experience. Suppose we hold that the fulfilment was not a mere chance coincidence; and suppose we accept the proposition which many people find self-evident. Then we shall have to draw the following conclusion: Either (a) the event which subsequently fulfilled the precognition did *not* really depend on the voluntary decision on which it seemed to depend; or (b) if it did, then that voluntary decision must have been *already* completely predetermined at the time when the precognition took place. On the first alternative, the voluntary decision was quite irrelevant and ineffective as regards the event which seemed to depend on it. On the second alternative, the voluntary decision was completely predetermined some time before it took place. Now many people find it highly repugnant, both intellectually and emotionally, to admit either of these alternatives about voluntary decisions and the events which apparently depend on them. Hence they feel a strong objection to admitting the possibility of veridically precognizing events which are apparently dependent on subsequent voluntary decisions. I think that this is the essence of the Fatalistic Objection.

So far as I can see, there is nothing wrong with the reasoning. It only remains, then, to examine the premise, i.e. the following proposition:—"If an ostensible precognition occurs and is subsequently fulfilled, then, unless this is a mere chance coincidence, the event which subsequently fulfilled it must have been already competely predetermined at the time when the ostensible precognition took place." Is this really self-evident?

I think that it is very important to distinguish a certain pair of statements, which are rather liable to be confused with each other, and to see logical connexion or lack of connexion between them. One is the statement that "the future is already *predeterminate*"; the other is the statement that "the future is already *predetermined.*" I have explained what the latter means. What is the meaning of the former? Let c be any characteristic that can be manifested in time. Suppose that a judgment is made at any moment t to the effect that an event manifesting the characteristic c *will* happen in a certain place or in a certain mind at a certain future moment t_1. Then this judgment is *already* true or it is *already* false, as the case may be, at the time t when it is made. The actual course of future history will *show* that it *was* true or will *show* that it *was* false, as the case may be; but the judgment will not *become* true or *become* false, from being neither the one nor the other, when the moment t_1 is reached. I do not know whether this proposition is important or is a mere triviality; but, whichever it may be, it is all that is meant by saying that "the future is already predeterminate."

Now consider an event e which actually happened at a certain moment t_1 in a certain place or in the mind of a certain person. What would be meant by saying that e "was already completely predeterminate" at a certain earlier moment t? It would have the following meaning: If c be any characteristic which e manifests, then a judgment made at t to the effect that there will be a manifestation of c at t_1 in this place or in this mind would *already* have been true at t.

It is now plain that to say that an event was already *predetermined* at a certain moment and to say that it was already *predeterminate* at that moment are two entirely different statements. The former is a proposition involving the notion of causation, while the latter involves no such notion. There is not the least inconsistency in saying that a certain event e, which happened at t_1, was already completely predeterminate at t but was not then completely predetermined.

Now, so far as I can see, the premise on which the Fatalistic Objection depends seems to be relevant only because these two notions are not clearly distinguished. I think that the following two propositions *are* self-evident: (i) The occurrence of e at t_1 could not be *inferred with certainty* at an earlier moment t from facts about what has existed or happened at or before t unless it were already completely *predetermined* at t. (ii) An event e which did not happen until t_1 could not have been *prehended* at an earlier moment t unless it were already *predeterminate* at t. The first of these is an immediate consequence of the definitions of the terms which occur in it. The second of them is a consequence of the nature of prehension and the definition of being "predeterminate." If an event can be pre-prehended, it must in some sense co-exist with the pre-prehension of it; and the precognition must consist in knowing by acquaintance that it has such and such characteristics. This would be impossible unless it is in some sense *already* true that it has these characteristics, i.e. unless it is in some sense already predeterminate. Supposing that a meaning can be given to the notion pre-prehension, it is quite clear than an event need not be completely *predetermined* at the time when it is pre-prehended. All that is necessary is that it should then be *predeterminate*.

I suspect that the premise of the Fatalistic Objection is a confused mixture of the two propositions which I have distinguished above. Now no one supposes that veridical ostensible foreseeing consists in inferring from facts about the past and the present with complete certainty that certain events will happen in the future. Hence the first of these propositions is irrelevant to the whole subject of this paper. On the other hand, the second of these propositions has nothing to do with *predetermination*, and is therefore irrelevant to the question of the determination and the causal efficacy of voluntary decisions.

Now that this confusion has been removed we can easily settle the question for ourselves. Suppose that the occurrence of e at t_3 was foreseen by A at t_1. Suppose, further, that the occurrence of e at t_3 was in fact dependent on the occurrence of a certain voluntary decision in B at an intermediate date t_2. Does this entail that the occurrence of this decision in this person at t_2 was already predetermined at t_1?

It certainly *does* entail the following proposition. If A had recognized at t_1 (as he very well might in some cases) that the occurrence of e at t_3 would be dependent on the previous occurrence of such a decision as d in B, then he could have inferred that B would make this decision at some time between t_1 and t_3. But this is *not* equivalent to, nor does it entail, the proposition that the occurrence of d in B at t_2 was already predetermined at t_1. In order to see this it is only necessary to look back at our definition of "being completely predetermined at a certain moment." In accordance with that definition the statement that the occurrence of d in B at t_2 was already completely predetermined at t_1 would have the following meaning. It would mean that there is a set of facts about the dispositions, the mutual relations, and the internal states *at or before* t_1 of the various substances *then* existing, which, together with the laws of matter and of mind, logically entails that an event which has all the characteristics of d *will* occur in B *after* an interval t_2-t_1. The difference between the two propositions is now obvious. The first (which really is entailed by our original suppositions) is about the possibility of inference from factual data about the *remoter future* to factual conclusions about the *less remote future*. The second (which is not entailed by our suppositions) is about the possibility of inferring from factual data about the *present or the past* to factual conclusions about the future.

Finally, the following point is worth noticing. I can infer from events in the less remote past that Julius Caesar decided in the more remote past to cross the Rubicon. No one imagines for a moment that this fact shows that Caesar's decision to cross the Rubicon was completely predetermined at any previous date. Suppose now that an augur at Rome had foreseen those later events from which *we* infer that Caesar had decided at an earlier date to cross the Rubicon. Obviously, he could have drawn precisely the same conclusion about Caesar's *then future* decision as we draw about his *now past* decision. And, if the possibility of our making this inference from these data does not require Caesar's decision to be completely predetermined, why should the possibility of the augur's making the same inference from the same data require this?

CHAPTER 15

A THEORY OF THE RELATION OF CAUSALITY TO PRECOGNITION*

C. J. DUCASSE

THE THEORY ABOUT TO BE outlined, which for brevity of reference may be labelled theory Theta, does not profess to give an
account of the *modus operandi* of precognition, but only to show
that precognition does not, as it *prima facie* seems to do, require
causation of a present event by an as yet future one. That is, the
paradox in precognition arises from violation not of Basic Limiting
Principle *I*.1, but of one of the others.

Also, theory Theta concerns precognition only (a) of events
which are *physical* but which (or physical signs of which) are
eventually perceived by the precognizer or by someone else; or
(b) of psychological events which are perceivings of *physical* events
(or of physical signs of them), by the precognizer or by someone
else. That is, theory Theta does not consider and does not purport
to resolve the causal paradox in cases, if any, where the event
precognized is a psychological event *that is not a percept of a
physical event or of a physical sign of a physical event.* So far as
I know, however, there are no such cases.

The fact from which theory Theta starts is that no definition of
the adjectives "past," "present," or "future," *simpliciter,* i.e. applied
categorically, can be given in purely physical terms; and hence that
physical events, *in themselves,* i.e. apart from the psychological
events which are percepts of them, are not categorically either
past, present, or future.

*The Philosophy of C.D. Broad, Paul Arthur Schlipp, ed., pp. 387-393. Reprinted by
permission of Open Court Publishing Company.

To physical events considered independently of percepts of them, the predicates "past," "present," or "future" are therefore applicable not categorically but only conditionally. That is, one can say of a physical event E so considered, that it is future to (or temporally after or beyond) a certain other one D *from a certain third* C; but not simply that it is *future*. Similarly, one can say of D that it is past relatively to (or temporally before or cis) E *from* C; but not simply that it is *past*. And, concerning any one of them, say E, one can say that it is simultaneous with (or co-present with) a certain other one, S, *relatively to a certain third,* Q; but not simply that it is *present* or *now*.

This state of affairs entails that the serial time order of physical events in themselves *has no intrinsic direction.* For the physical event E, although future to D *from* C, is on the contrary past to D *from a fourth event* F so selected that E is temporally between D and F. This follows from the fact that the relation "temporally between," which determines the serial order of physical events, does not determine one rather than the other of the two theoretically possible directions within that order. In terms of entropy, all that could be said would be that, in one of the two directions, entropy never decreases; whereas in the other direction it never increases, and this does not, *in itself,* i.e. independently of our perceptions of physical events, specify as "real" one rather than the other direction in the series of physical events.

The three terms, "past," "present," "future," as predicated categorically instead of, as above, conditionally, are essentially psychological terms. Their meaning lies in the fact that psychological events, as experienced, have in different degrees a certain characteristic which is distinct from intensity, from clearness, and from interestingness. Nor is it, as suggested by J. D. Mabbott,[1] the characteristic which Hume has in mind when he speaks of "force of vivacity," since by this Hume means what differentiates the believing of something from the mere imagining of it.[2] I shall, more or less arbitrarily, call "liveness" the characteristic to which I refer. It cannot be described but can easily be identified introspectively in the concrete.

---

[1] "Our Direct Experience of Time," *Mind* (April 1951), p. 162.
[2] *Treatise of Human Nature,* Part III, § V, Selby-Bigge Edition, p. 86.

Consider, for example, one's auditory experience as he hears or imagines the sound of some word—say, the word "inductively." The characteristic here denominated "liveness" then is that which, as that *whole* word is heard, is possessed in its maximal degree by the syllable "ly;" in somewhat lower degree by the syllable "tive;" in still lower degree by the syllable "duc;" and so on. And possession of this characteristic in its maximal degree by a psychological event—here, by the sound "ly"—is the meaning and the whole of the meaning of the statement that the event concerned is "strictly present" in the psychological sense of this term.

On the other hand, being "speciously present" though "strictly past" is the name of the status, in the serial order of psychological events, of e.g. the other syllables of the word "inductively" when the syllable "ly" is strictly present. That they are then speciously present means that, although "strictly past," they have then not yet lapsed from consciousness in the sense of needing to be recalled if one wishes to attend to them. Each of them is termed "earlier" or "less recent" in proportion to the degree of inferiority in liveness it has when the syllable "ly" has the maximal degree of liveness. To experience a psychological event as "earlier" than another means nothing more and nothing less than that. Psychological events which, at the moment, can be attended to only if recalled are termed not then speciously present, but simply "past." And "future," *simpliciter,* is the name of the status, in the serial order of psychological events, of whatever psychological events are neither past nor speciously present nor strictly present. Broad rightly rejects William James' conception of the specious present as including a bit of the future. The fact that the specious present is thus not a "saddleback" automatically disposes of the theory of precognition suggested by Saltmarsh, according to which precognition would be made possible by a subliminal specious present, *analogous to,* but longer at the forward end than, the supraliminal specious present.[3] Psychological events that have been experienced can of course be *considered,* reflectively, in any order one pleases; but psychological events can be *actually experienced* only in the order of their respective degrees of liveness, and thus of recency, at the

---

[3]H.F. Saltmarsh, "Report on Cases of Apparent Precognition," *Proc. S.P.R.,* Vol. 42 (1934), pp. 72-93.

time of the one strictly present. This entails that *the time-series of psychological events has intrinsic direction.*

To what was said above concerning the "strictly present," it should be added that, even within the sound "ly," we could if we would distinguish the "l" sound from the "y" sound—which latter would then alone be "strictly present." But when one analyzes a given psychological event into its shorter component events, he quickly reaches components which, psychologically, are temporally atomic because no temporal parts can be distinguished within them. Moreover—and this is the essential point—application of the term "strictly present" to a psychological event is governed not by the difference of liveness we could discriminate if we specially tried, but by those which we actually do, and do not, discriminate. In introspective experience, *esse est percipi.*

At this point, I shall pause in the outlining of theory Theta in order to compare its account of the specious present with that offered by Broad.

The characteristic which, in what precedes, I have denominated "liveness" is I believe the same as that which Broad had (unknown to me until recently) earlier termed "presentedness."[4] I nevertheless retain "liveness" in my account because this term seems to me less likely to generate confusion, such, for example, as appears to underlie W. Kneale's statement in his review of Broad's book,[5] that "to say that *a* has a lower degree of presentedness than *b* is surely not the same as to say that *a* is presented earlier than *b*." What I believe Broad would hold (and I then with him) is that to say that *a* is *prehended* (not, as Kneale has it, *presented*) "earlier than" *b* means that *a* has a lower degree of presentedness (i.e. of what I call instead "liveness") than *b* has. That characteristic, under either name, is, as Broad rightly asserts, "the experiential basis of our notion of *presentness* in the strict sense." Also, Broad's diagrammatic representation of the specious present as a wedge (vs. a saddleback) is I think quite appropriate.

On the other hand, the notion of "instantaneous event-particles," which Broad introduces into his discussion, seems to me not only as he says "a rather elaborate and sophisticated product", but,

---

[4] *EMcP*, Vol. II, p. 282.
[5] *Mind* (October 1939), p. 509.

psychologically, pure myth. That notion is useful in mathematical physics, but importation of it into psychology is illegitimate and gratuitously trouble-making because no psychological events are instantaneous in the mathematico-physical sense; but only in the psychological sense already stated, that no parts actually are, or in some cases can be, empirically discriminated within them. An event is either a change, or a state's remaining unchanged, and an atomic psychological event is atomic in the empirical sense just stated, which is the only one not psychologically incongruous. Psychological time is thus "granular," not infinitely divisible as the time of mathematical physics is postulated to be. I would therefore insist that, in Broad's statement that presentedness "is the experiential basis of our notion of *presentness* in the strict sense," the relevant "strict sense" is the psychological strict sense, not the mathematico-physical one.

Again, it seems to me wrong to speak, as Broad does, of a "series of successive Specious Presents." What are many and successive are the *events,* which pop into *the* specious present at the perpendicular end of the wedge which represents it. And the arrow, pointing right, which Broad uses to represent "lapse of time," should point left instead and represent the order of decreasing "presentedness" or "liveness" within the specious present; for it is in terms of *this* that "lapse of time" gets defined. Again, Broad's assumption that "all Specious Presents of the same mind are of the same duration" is I think illegitimate because, in one mind, there are not several specious presents but only one, through which, as it were, crawls an endless variously mottled snake. It is its mottled markings, i.e. the events, which are many and successive. Moreover,

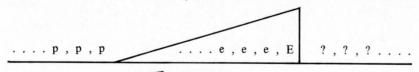

. . . . p , p , p :	Past events, some accessible to memory
. . . . e , e , e :	Events strictly past, but speciously present
E :	The event strictly present
? , ? , ? . . . . :	Events as yet future

FIGURE 2.

psychologically, "duration" is a term applicable *within* the specious present, that is, to events there, but not *to* the specious present itself, which is not an event at all. What varies is not the "duration" of the specious present—to which this term is not applicable —but the number of events it contains. When a given event E is (psychologically) strictly present, the number of events speciously present may be, say, five; and when another given event F is strictly present, the number of speciously present ones might be, say, only three—or as the case may be, seven—according, apparently, to the degree if intrinsic interest of the events concerned, or to their relevance to what happens to be our governing interest at the time. What seems to me all-important to remember in connection with statements about the specious present is that they must not be worded in temporal terms, as if we already somehow knew, independently, what such terms mean; the fact being, on the contrary, that "presentedness" or "liveness" and its degree are the experiential basis not only, as Broad says, of our notion of presentness, but of our notion of "earlier" and "later," and thus *of our notion of time.*

I return now to the exposition of theory Theta. The account of it, so far as already given, makes evident that, in any attempt to show that precognition does not involve violation of Basic Limiting Principle *I*.1, we have to take account of two different time-series. In one of them—that of physical events in themselves—no event is categorically past, present, or future; and, because the series of those events has no intrinsic direction, no event in it is categorically earlier, or categorically later, than a given other, but only earlier than it *from a certain third,* and later than it *from a certain fourth.* In the other time-series, on the contrary—that of psychological events—the serial order does have an intrinsic direction; and always, in that series, some one psychological event, simple or complex, is categorically present, and all others categorically past or categorically future. That is, in that series, "earlier" and "later" are dyadic relations, not triadic as in the other series.

The physical series, however, gets related to the psychological one by the fact that some psychological events are percepts of physical events. Then the physical event perceived, in virtue of its being object of a percept categorically present, is spoken of also categorically as present; but, let it be noted, it is categorically present, i.e. present *simpliciter,* only in the *elliptical* sense of being object of a percept itself on the contrary present categorically in the *literal* sense described above, which applies only to psychological events.

Now, we ordinarily assume naively that a physical event can be perceived only if it is present; (or more exactly, on reflection, if it is past by the amount of time—negligible in most cases for practical purposes—occupied by the causal process extending from the physical event concerned to the sense organs and from them to the brain cortex). But what on the contrary is made evident by the preceding remarks is that *present perception* of a physical event (which event *in itself* is neither present nor past nor future) *automatically confers categorical presence on that event* in the elliptical sense stated, which is the only sense in which a physical event ever is categorically present at all.

From this, however, it evidently follows that no causal paradox is really involved in so-called precognition; for what really occurs there is only that one individual physical event, although occurring of course only once, nevertheless is *present several times* because perceived at several psychological times—once, perhaps, at night in a dream; and again, perhaps the next day, in ordinary waking perception. That it can be present several times without itself occurring several times is an automatic consequence of the cardinal fact that, *in itself,* it is neither present nor past nor future but acquires presentness by being perceived and as often as it is perceived.

This account of precognition, however, still leaves to be answered the question as to what then differentiates a veridical precognitive dream-percept from an ordinary veridical waking percept. The answer, so far as it goes, is that, in the case of the dream percept, the qualitatively relevant sense organ—say, the eye—is not functioning; but on the contrary is functioning in the case of the ordinary waking percept. That a percept, i.e. an ostensible perceiving, *can* be caused somehow otherwise than through the functioning of the sense organs at the time is proved, of course, by the frequent occurrence of hallucinatory percepts, whether oneiric or waking ones. But that a hallucinatory percept should happen to be veridical—except as a pure matter of chance—*still is something para-*

normal. It is paranormal, however, *not* as violating Basic Limiting Principle *I*.1, which is analytic and therefore certain; but as violating the weaker, ultimately empirical Basic Limiting Principle *IV*.1, to wit, that physical events can be veridically perceived only by means of sensations (if, by "sensations" as distinguished from hallucinations, we mean vivid images caused at the time through the functioning of the sense organs).

CHAPTER 16

MAGICIANS, ALARM CLOCKS, AND BACKWARD CAUSATION*

BOB BRIER

O F THE THREE KINDS OF ESP, precognition raises the most fundamental philosophical questions. Clairvoyance and telepathy,
although they are unexplained by modern physics, could be explained by stretching existing physical concepts such as wave, or
force. The problem with precognition is that the physicist does not
have concepts which could be stretched to explain how we can
obtain nonsensory knowledge of a future event. Even the theoretical physicist does not speak of waves that travel into the future
and return to the present with information about an event that is
yet to occur.

Philosophers have argued that if precognition occurred, then it
would involve a cause coming after its effect. That is, if I precognize a plane crash at time t_1 and the plane crashes at t_2, then if
we ask what caused the premonition, the answer should be the
plane crash. The situation is similar to one in which a plane crashes
and I observe the crash. The crash is the cause of my observation
and in a precognitive experience we merely have a reversal of the
cause-effect sequence. Most philosophers who have dealt with
this matter have argued that this reversal of causal sequence is
logically impossible and since precognition would involve this,

---

*Reprinted from *The Southern Journal of Philosophy*, 1973, by permission of the
editors. The text of this article, which was originally written for the present volume,
differs slightly from the version to be found in *The Southern Journal of Philosophy*.
For instance, the first three paragraphs and the final paragraph of the present version
are omitted in the latter, which did not reach us in time to allow revision of our
manuscript. In the journal, the article is paired with a brief criticism by Antony Flew
(pp. 365-366).—Eds.

precognition is also logically impossible.

One is forced by the data presented by parapsychologists to make a choice. Either we must revise our conceptual schema and admit that what we thought to be logically impossible—something in the future having an effect in the present—is possible or we must assert that the evidence for precognition couldn't possibly have been obtained and error or fraud must be involved. In this paper I will argue that backward causation is logically possible and does not even involve the conceptual revision that is usually claimed of it.

When discussing the question of whether it is logically possible for an effect to precede its cause, philosophers usually take one of two positions. Either they argue that such an event is logically impossible or they argue that it is possible, but only with alterations of the notion of cause. In this paper I will try to show that reluctance to accept the possibility of an event in the future having an effect in the present is unfounded and is based either on a misunderstanding of the question at issue or on a misunderstanding of what is involved in the notion of causality. To do this I will deal with the work of two philosophers, each holding one of the two positions mentioned above.

In a paper entitled "Can an Effect Precede Its Cause?"[1] M.A.E. Dummett argues that backward causation is possible only in a context in which we alter the notion of cause. Using the notions of *remote* and *immediate cause,* Dummett presents a very forceful argument against backward causation. Any cause is either remote or immediate. Since they are simultaneous with their effects, immediate causes present no case for backward causation. Only remote causes remain. For a cause to be remote, it must be the immediate cause of the beginning of some process which continues and eventually is the immediate cause of the effect in question. Dummett then says this shows that a remote cause cannot come after its effect. "A remote cause can be connected to its remote effect only by means of a process which it sets in motion, i.e. which begins at the moment it operates and goes on after that . . ."[2] In a sense, by definition Dummett has ruled out backward causa-

---

[1]M.A.E. Dummett, "Can an Effect Precede Its Cause?" *Aristotelian Society Proceedings* supp., Vol. 28 (1954), pp. 27-44.
[2]*Ibid.,* p. 31.

tion. This he does in the last two words of the sentence quoted ("after that"). That is, what would be required in a case of backward causation would be a remote cause which instigates a process which has gone on before that instigation—a process going backward in time rather than forward. Since this is what is at issue, Dummett should not rule it out as he does.

Since Dummett has rejected the possibility of a cause coming after its effect, it is surprising that the remainder of his article offers much support to the backward-causation thesis. This is so, however, because he next turns his attention to what he calls "quasi-causal" explanations. (It will be seen that there is little discernible difference between a cause and a quasi-cause.) In these cases it might be observed that an event is a sufficient condition for the occurrence of some earlier event. To have such a quasi-causal explanation these conditions would have to be met:

(1) The earlier event, which is to be explained by the later event, would have to be incapable (as far as can be judged) of being explained by a simultaneous or an earlier event.

(2) The earlier event must not be the remote cause of the later event.

(3) It must be possible to give a causal account of this later event which does not contain a reference to the occurrence of the earlier event.

If these three conditions were satisfied and there was evidence for the constant conjunction of the two events, this backward quasi-causal explanation would have to be accepted. Dummett offers an example which seems to satisfy the above conditions.

A man always wakes up three minutes before the alarm of his clock goes off. Frequently he does not know whether the alarm is set, and if so, for what time. An instance might even be stipulated in which the man wakes up and, for some irrelevant reason, a friend walks into his room and sets off the alarm exactly three minutes later. In such a case it might be said that the man wakes up because the alarm clock is going to go off.

Dummett points out two limitations involved in most quasi-causal explanations. First, unless one can specify the process initiated by the cause which eventually results in the effect, one will not have much of an explanation. Second, it is generally preferred that causal laws connect as wide a range of phenomena as possible. It would be desirable to say that events of the same kind as A cause events of the same kind as B. In the example, he says, neither of these two conditions is satisfied.

It might be the case that in backward causation there is difficulty in tracing the process. With the case of the alarm clock, one might try to envision an echo from the clock going backward in time. There would be difficulties however. One might trace the sound from the time the alarm goes off at t_{10} to t_9, t_8 . . . t_0. But this would involve hearing the alarm at these times as well as when the man wakes up. Thus the situation could be described as: the man hearing the alarm; the man waking up and continuing to hear the alarm up until t_{10} plus the time it takes to shut off the alarm. The question might also be asked, When does the sound stop, and if it ceases to be audible when the man wakes up, why at that time? These are merely examples of the kinds of problems which arise when one is trying to specify the process in backward causation. Here, Dummett seems to have a point when he says there will not be much of an explanation. However, there are also cases of forward causation in which one cannot specify the process initiated by the remote cause but is still willing to call the relationship causal. Thus a causal connection is not ruled out merely because there is difficulty in connecting two events.

The matter concerning the possible generality of a backward-causation law is not easy to settle. It is difficult to specify criteria for generality, but just why Dummett asserts that such laws cannot cover kinds of causes and kinds of effects is not clear. It is conceivable that under certain conditions, S, whenever A occurs B occurs, and B is prior to A. Thus events occurring under conditions S might be said to form a kind, and the backward-causal law would appear to be general. From the discussion of the two restrictions Dummett places on his quasi-causal explanation, it would seem as if they do not have to be the impoverished explanations Dummett feels they must be. Indeed, when Dummett presents his famous example of the magician who controls the weather and defends this example against *a priori* attacks on the possibility of its being a case of backward quasi-causation, he is really defending backward causation.

A magician has a spell for causing the next day's weather to be good. Whenever he recites the spell, he subsequently finds out that on the next day at the place mentioned in the spell the weather is good. There arises an occasion on which the magician wishes the weather to have been good yesterday at a certain place. Not knowing what will happen, he recites his spell, putting yesterday's date where he usually recites tomorrow's. Later he finds out that there was, in fact, good weather. Further, every time he tries his spell in this manner, he learns that there was good weather.

The *a priori* argument against this being a case of backward causation is expressed by Dummett as follows:

> . . . to suppose that the occurrence of an event could ever be explained by reference to a subsequent event involves that it might also be reasonable to bring about an event in order that a *past* event should have occurred, an event previous to the action. To attempt to do this would plainly be nonsensical, and hence the idea of explaining an event by reference to a later event is nonsensical in its turn.[3]

One way of illustrating the *a priori* error involved is utilizing the distinction between the absurdity of doing a certain kind of action and the absurdity of describing a situation in a certain way. In backward causation what is absurd is the way the situation would have to be described. With forward causation it can be said that *A* is brought about in order that *B* should occur. In backward causation it must be stated that, by seeing if *B* could be brought about, whether *A* occurred is being discovered.

Dummett is quick to point out that the magician would not say that the reciting of his spell is *finding out if the weather was fine.* One uses such a description only when there is no question of bringing about, and all that is left is discovery. This is not the case with the magician. Thus this argument is surely not sufficient to rule out backward causation *a priori.*

The second *a priori* argument against backward causation (or a quasi-causal explanation as Dummett prefers) involves the magician's not being able to recite the spell. Either the weather was fine or it was not. If it was fine (and if the weather having been fine is a necessary condition for his reciting the spell), then it fol-

---

[3]*Ibid.*, pp. 34-35.

lows that he cannot help but say the spell. But to say this is to deny that the spell is a sufficient condition of the weather's having been fine. That this argument is not compelling can be seen from the fact that an analogous attack against forward causation can be made: Either an event will take place or it will not. If it will take place, then one cannot help but perform the action in question, but this is tantamount to admitting that the action cannot be a sufficient condition for the future event.

In the volume of the *Proceedings of the Aristotelian Society* in which Dummett's paper appears, Antony Flew argues that it is logically impossible for a cause to succeed its effect.[4] Flew argues that the crucial difference between causes and effects is that causes *bring about* their effects. Given this, any attempt to discuss effects prior to their causes must "either be frustrated by contradictions; or end in a fraud. . . . the contradiction [is] that what has been done might be undone."[5] The fraud would involve calling something a cause which could scarcely be called an analogue, since it could not involve *bringing about*. Flew is correct with respect to one horn of the dilemma: It would be a fraud to call something a cause which does not bring about an effect. Flew seems mistaken, however, with regard to the other horn: with backward causation one is not committed to saying that the past can be undone. This would be nonsense. Rather, here one can readily make use of the distinction between changing the past and affecting the past. One cannot change the past or undo what has been done. Rather, what is at issue is whether one can affect the past; that is, by a present action cause something to have happened which would not have happened otherwise. This does not seem to entail a contradiction. Thus Flew's first attack on Dummett must be rejected.

In his brief analysis of Hume's pioneering work on the notion of cause, Dummett points out that, since sufficiency seems to be the Humean criterion for causality, there is nothing to rule out a cause coming after its effect. This is merely the noting of an obvious point. This observation, however, causes Flew to discuss at considerable length the deficiencies in the Humean view. Flew's main objection is that Hume's discussion of causality is from an *ob-*

---

[4]*Ibid.,* pp. 45-62.
[5]*Ibid.,* p. 48.

server's rather than a *participant's* point of view, and this leads to overlooking an important aspect of causality. Because an observer merely notes the constant conjunction of *A* and *B*, he is not confronted with the temporal aspects of causality. Were Hume dealing with the problem from a participant's point of view, he would have observed that *A* can be used to bring about *B*. This notion of use (power or effectiveness) in bringing about might have led Hume to the realization that causes must come before their effects. Thus the fact that it permits backward causation should cause one to re-examine the Humean thesis, rather than accept it.

What Flew is saying is not a very serious criticism of the backward-causation thesis. The question at issue merely re-emerges in the form of asking why someone could not perform an action to bring about an earlier effect. This would be causing something to have happened. Flew has begged the question.

Flew next turns his attention toward Dummett's example of the alarm clock and suggests alternative explanations. The first is coincidence. This is certainly a logical possibility, no matter how strong the evidence. But Flew goes on to say that one can consider the correlation between the man's waking and the alarm going off as coincidence "yet not dismiss it, but use the slug-abed's waking as a sign of the imminent sounding of the alarum."[6] When one grants that an observed connection between two events is a coincidence, one also grants that one does not expect the correlation to hold up in the future to the same degree. This is part of the meaning of "coincidence." If a person guesses cards randomly chosen from a deck of playing cards and is 100 percent accurate, it might be said that his success was due to coincidence. If this is said, however, it entails that his future guesses are not expected to be 100 percent correct. Further, it would not be expected that his guesses could be taken as signs of what the cards would be. Thus it is surprising to see Flew both advocating the coincidence hypothesis and suggesting that the man's waking be used as a sign that in three minutes the alarm will go off.

It might be asked, how, on Flew's account, does one distinguish between coincidence and constant conjunction (i.e. cause in gen-

---

[6]*Ibid.,* p. 56.

eral)? It is clear that such distinctions are made with forward causation and coincidence. Here, such distinctions are often based on the repetition of the conjunction of the events. If it happens once, it may be coincidence. If the later event always follows the earlier, the coincidence-connection hypothesis will be rejected for a stronger kind of connection. With backward causation, there is no need to postulate a different decision-making procedure.

Flew's second attack on the alarm-clock example involves Dummett's second criterion which any case of quasi-causal explanation must meet. This criterion Dummett presents in two ways which he believes are equivalent: ". . . there would have to be reason for thinking that the two events were not causally connected; i.e. there must be no discoverable way of representing the earlier event as a causal antecedent (a remote cause) of the later."[7] The first thing that comes to mind is that the two formulations of the criterion are not equivalent. The first formulation seems difficult to satisfy, since it requires evidence ("reason for thinking") for a negatively stated hypothesis ("not causally connected"). The second formulation is perhaps preferable, if for no other reason that that it avoids the problem involved in the first. Here again, however, there might be trouble, not in satisfying the criterion, but in knowing when the criterion has been satisfied. What is required is that there be no *discoverable* way of viewing the earlier event as the cause of the later. Here, even though such a relationship may not have been discovered, one might not know of a relationship which is discoverable, but as yet undiscovered. Perhaps a combination of the two formulations might better express Dummett's intention and be more reasonable in terms of being satisfied: There must be no reason (apart from temporal order) for thinking that the earlier event is the cause of the later one.

It might be argued that whenever the alarm clock and the awakening are conjoined, the situation can be viewed as the awakening causing the alarm to go off, as well as the alarm causing the awakening. To this objection it might be said that what is being argued is merely the *possibility* of backward causation, and this condition seems satisfied by the example. This, however, only

---

⁷*Ibid.*, p. 56.

postpones the philosophical showdown. It can then be said that what is meant by *logically possible* is that, in some conceivable situation, backward causation is the best explanation. Thus, although in every case of backward causation there may be alternative explanations, what is necessary for the backward-causation thesis is to present an example in which backward causation is not only a possible explanation, but the best alternative.

What is at issue here is really the explication of the notion of logical possibility. The above argument asserts that logical possibility involves the best alternative in some possible world. Against this thesis one might point out that, traditionally, logical possibility involves merely a lack of contradiction. Thus if no contradiction can be drawn by entertaining the idea of backward causation, then it is a logical possibility.

Further, even in the explication involving possible worlds, the position presented is unorthodox. Here, logical possibility has traditionally been interpreted as *true* in some possible world, while the above position interprets it as entailing *the best available evidence* in some possible world. That the two positions are not identical should be evident since false propositions are often believed on the basis of available evidence. A complete discussion of this topic would involve what is entailed by the notion of truth, and this is clearly a topic beyond the limited scope of this paper.

Flew's objection to Dummett's second condition is that it would be almost impossible to grant that it has been satisfied, since one would not know where to decide to give up the search for the forward-causal connection. The reformulation of the criterion takes care of this objection, since all that is required is that at any given time a forward-causal connection has not been found. Surely only such a tentative position can be required from science.

The third objection to the alarm-clock illustration is not a clear objection. Flew points out that the experimentalist testing the causal connection will be in a peculiar position. If he has a quasi-effect, he must try to stop the quasi-cause from occurring. If he succeeds, then it was not really a quasi-effect. Only if he observes the effects and continually fails to stop the causes will they seem genuine. Why Flew considers this description an objection is not clear. He makes no attempt to derive a contradiction, and it does not seem as if there is one to derive.

The fourth objection is a linguistic one and asserts that any explanation in terms of *causes* "in any new sense of the word" will not be precisely what is desired since it will be only "a substitute carefully wrapped in the old verbal pocket." Flew seems to be ruling out any possible solution to the problem, since he seems to be rejecting "any new sense of the word." Surely if one wishes to change a feature of a concept (but still have an analogue), one will have to consider the result, or new sense of the word. What should be the issue is not whether there is a new sense of the word, but whether there is an analogue. Flew seems to have collapsed the distinction between a new sense of the word and an analogue.

Finally, Flew's last attempt to show Dummett's example to be unsatisfactory is not an argument, but an assertion of what is to be demonstrated. One sentence is offered: ". . . any attempt to suggest that pseudo-causes *operate,* that is, are (and could be used as) levers to control the past, as real causes operate, that is do (and can be used to) bring about effects, must be radically absurd."[8]

To summarize, we have heard Dummett argue that only in a weakened sense of "cause" is backward causation possible. We have also heard Flew present five objections to the possibility of backward causation in even an impoverished sense of the word. Concerning Dummett's position, it seems as if there is no real need to alter the sense of "cause." All he has done is suggest new realms in which the old term might be applied. In the case of Flew, it seems that in rejecting the possibility of backward causation he has repeatedly begged the question. If one is to reject the possibility of a cause coming after its effect, it will have to be on grounds other than have been offered.

From the above it will be seen that even if precognition does involve backward causation this is not sufficient grounds for claiming that precognition is a logical impossibility. Those who argue that the evidence claimed for the existence of precognition could not possibly have been obtained have not supported that assertion adequately.

---

[8] *Ibid.*, p. 57.

SECTION IV

PSI AND SURVIVAL

CHAPTER 17

INTRODUCTION

HOYT L. EDGE

IS THERE SURVIVAL OF human personality after bodily death? This is the central question to be dealt with in this section. Surveying the literature of parapsychology on this point, Wheatley cites five representative positions, spanning the extremes from the view that survival is logically impossible to the position that survival has been empirically proved. One immediately finds himself in difficulties, however, if one wants to deal empirically with the question of survival. For, as Wheatley points out, the hypothesis of survival does not seem to be falsifiable and, thus, cannot be admitted as a scientific hypothesis. In discussing this problem, Wheatley proposes finally that the hypothesis of survival be *assumed* in order to allow certain kinds of research. This is not to say, however, that one must presuppose that everyone will survive bodily death. Indeed, that question itself must be fully researched as well.

Exactly what evidence then leads us to consider survival as possible? Most of our data stems from sessions with mediums, especially from seances during which a medium becomes entranced and brings accurate, detailed information said to be brought by a deceased person, often so much in the manner of the deceased individual that it seems as if the medium is "possessed" by that person. Many such sessions are so impressive that such a possession theory indeed seems *prima facie* the most suitable. But is there another way to explain the evidence? Price refers to the results of research in abnormal psychology, especially the cases of split or multiple personality. As such a phenomenon is widely accepted in current psychology, could we not view the case of the "possessed" medium as simply the manifestation of a second personality of the medium's own self? Certainly, such a view is supported by the evidence of those parapsychologists who argue that psi seems to be elicited more frequently, and perhaps manifested more clearly, in an altered state of normal consciousness—as a second personality could be classified. However, if one accepts this view of trance mediumship (the "This World-ESP Hypothesis" as Price calls it) two things follow, according to Price. The first is that one must accept psi as a fact, for one can argue against survival only by arguing for the factual existence of telepathy, clairvoyance, and precognition. The second result is that such a view of human personality means that the traditional Cartesian view of the mind (or soul) as being a unitary being, a *res cogitans,* does not seem to be adequate, for the existence of multiple personality brings into question the unity of mind and forces us to view that unity as one of degree.

Is the "This World-ESP Hypothesis" then adequate? Price questions its adequacy, concluding that we have evidence for, but not proof of, survival. Ducasse concerns himself in a more detailed manner with the adequacy of such an hypothesis. After discussing Dodds' attempt to dispose of the objections to this hypothesis, Ducasse concludes by arguing that, although the hypothesis cannot be proved to be false, it demands that we stretch our understanding of psi far beyond the limits of any independent evidence for the existence and effectiveness of psi. In other words, the accomplishments of entranced mediums and the characteristics of their information so greatly surpass any other kind of evidence we have for the existence of telepathy, clairvoyance, and precognition that it is no longer evident that it is the same kind of ability we find proved, for example, in Rhine's laboratory tests.

Ducasse next asks the question: What could be considered adequate proof of survival? He lists three criteria, which, if fulfilled, should lead us to accept information coming from another human being as evidence for the survival of that individual. It will, however, be noticed that these criteria are such that it is difficult to know when they are fulfilled, so that even if one accepts these as valid criteria for survival, there may be much disagreement as to whether and when the criteria have been met, or, indeed, can be met.

Yet, the question that Wheatley raises in his article still remains. Can we make some sense of the idea of "survival after bodily death"? Can we get a clear conception of what it means to survive in a disembodied state? Viewed from this perspective, the problem of survival is basically a problem of the individuation of human personality. Nayak, Flew, and Penelhum all address themselves to the question of whether bodily continuity is a necessary and sufficient condition of personal identity. If so, disembodied survival becomes impossible. If disembodied survival is inconceivable (because our concept of human personality demands physical predicates), then no evidence from trance mediumship can be accepted as evidence for survival (at least disembodied survival). Nayak argues that one can understand the self-identity of a person through memory, and he gives criteria, based on memory, which would have to be fulfilled in order for us to consider a person as having survived in a disembodied state or as having been reincarnated.

Penelhum also deals directly with the question of whether memory can be taken alone as proof of self-identity. He admits, as does Broad, that the problem of the characterizatoin of self is an altogether different problem from that concerning the identification of a disembodied person with a pre-mortem human being. Both Broad and Penelhum consider the former problem to be primary (in order of logical dependence, at least). Further, Penelhum accepts the possibility of a disembodied person being able to perceive and act upon the world. Essentially, Penelhum's question is whether one can make intelligible the concept of a disembodied person existing through time. Those who argue, as Nayak does, that it is possible to make this concept intelligible, usually do so depending on the concept of memory to supply the identity. But, Penelhum argues, there is no way to verify memory except by the physical presence of the person during the remembered event. Memory, then, is no independent standard of identity and therefore, no standard of identity for a disembodied person. As Penelhum puts it: "Memory is essentially a parasitic concept, and needs a body to feed on." Consequently, although memory can be considered a criterion, its being so depends on the bodily criterion of identity. Thus, in opposition to Nayak, bodily identity is for

Penelhum a necessary and sufficient condition of personal identity.

As we shall see in the Broad article, conclusions to these questions will vary depending on whether one accepts only the evidence of normal experience or whether one also includes the evidence of paranormal experience. Is Penelhum perhaps guilty of admitting normal evidence alone in his argument and would the acceptance of psi change his concluison that memory is an epistemic concept and needs to be verified by the actual physical presence of the person? Penelhum says: "When he does claim to remember his past his claim can only be true if he was physically present at the episode he seems to recall." If one accepts clairvoyance, it may well be that one could remember an event at which one's physical body was not present. Certainly, if one argues that one can only have an experience of an event that is in direct physical proximity to one's body, one is *a priori* excluding the possibility of clairvoyance over a distance. Since there is independent evidence for the existence of clairvoyance, one's view of experience, and therefore one's view of the memory of experience, would seem to be inadequate if clairvoyance is excluded as a possible source of experience.

Agreeing, in essence, with Penelhum that we cannot hope to make sense of disembodied survival (and asserting that the reconstructionist approach is "inept" and 'unfair"), Flew takes the characteristic stance of those philosophers who argue on *a priori*, i.e. linguistic, grounds that disembodied survival is impossible. For him, "personality" must be defined in corporeal terms, at least partially. "Personality is essentially some sort of function of persons; and persons are—surely equally essentially—corporeal." Even "ESP" is defined by Flew in terms of corporeal faculties and capacities, i.e. as information gained while not using sensory faculties. Furthermore, when one tries to make sense of disembodied survival, Flew asserts that two problems cannot be overcome: (1) forming a coherent notion of an incorporeal being and, (2) showing how such a surviving being could be said to be identical with a former physical entity. He concludes that all evidence for survival can be explained by the "This World-ESP Hypothesis," and that although the concept of the survival of an astral body may be made to make sense, we have no need for such an hypothesis.

In relation to survival, Broad discusses the necessity of having a dispositional basis for personality (that is, that a human personality will, generally speaking, act in a certain way in a particular circumstance. Such a basis guarantees the general continuity of human personality). He further argues that this dispositional basis must survive in order for us to be able to say that the person survives. Noting that such a dispositional basis must be based on certain persistent minute structures, Broad sees how these structures could be understood in terms of physical objects, but can one make sense of such a basis for a disembodied person? To do so, Broad suggests that we assume a dualism—but not necessarily the Cartesian variety. Indeed, we seem to have definite evidence from paranormal research for such a dualism. But even with the assumption of this kind of dualism, it is possible for there to be at least four kinds of survival, ranging from survival without any concrete experiences whatsoever to survival of a disembodied personality which, in Broad's words, "might remember experiences had by the deceased human being, just as a human being in his waking state at one time remembers experiences had by him in his earlier waking states." In effect, only this latter case could be termed survival of human personality in the full sense of the concept. In searching for evidence for some form of survival, Broad concludes that if we view only the results of non-parapsychological research, the evidence tends to support the former view of personality—which, at best, could survive but have no experiences. Only when we consider parapsychological evidence do we find any evidence for survival of human personality in its fullest sense.

As one immediately grasps from a consideration of the articles in this section, the question of survival has far-reaching implications for philosophy, and especially for philosophical psychology. The data produced by parapsychological research cannot in itself prove survival. Before one can even judge whether certain facts are valid as evidence for survival, one must answer several basic philosophical questions—such as, what is precisely human personality, and what kind of entity could survive bodily death? This section is an introduction to those questions.

CHAPTER 18

THE QUESTION OF SURVIVAL: SOME LOGICAL REFLECTIONS*

JAMES M. O. WHEATLEY

THE QUESTION OF INDIVIDUAL personal survival of bodily death†
has aroused opposing attitudes toward the *desirability* of post-
mortem existence, but it has also elicited a gamut of appraisals
of its possibility and likelihood. The following views can be
distinguished:

(a) Survival is logically impossible. (*Cadit quaestio.*) (b) Survival is logically possible, but empirically impossible, or at least
singularly improbable. (c) Survival is both logically possible and
empirically possible. (To allow less would be dogmatic; to say
more, unduly hazardous.) (d) Survival is logically possible and
empirically probable, at least more probable than not. (e) Survival
is not just logically possible but empirically assured. Among philosophers, I believe, these standpoints are exemplified, respectively,
by (a) A.J. Ayer in *Language, Truth and Logic,* (b) Bertrand
Russell (and also Ayer in later works), (c) C.D. Broad and

---

*Reprinted from *The Journal of the American Society for Psychical Research,* 1965,
by permission of the Society.

†In what follows I shall not be concerned with any views about, or possibilities of,
the survival of some *impersonal* or *non-individual* factor pertaining to the deceased;
a factor, e.g. to be identified not with the person himself but with all or part of a
cosmic mind or reason by or through which the person may somehow have been
actuated, animated, or energized during his lifetime. Aristotle, for instance, is sometimes said to have held a doctrine of impersonal or non-individual immortality. But
the present paper will not deal with any conception of this sort and when I speak
of survival, therefore, I must be understood to mean survival in an individualistic
sense.

H.H. Price, (d) C.J. Ducasse, and (e) Plato and Aquinas.‡

Curiously, all of these views, with the likely exception of the fifth, can commend themselves today to any inquirer who is rational, open-minded, and well-informed. The first can do so because of the evident strength, logically speaking, in analyzing the very meaning of personal identity by reference to bodily persistence; the second because of all that we know of the ways in which mental phenomena are dependent on and determined by events and processes in the bodily organism; the third, on the other hand, partly because of much that we do *not* know of the normal fabric of the mind and its relation with the physical body, and also because of the possibilities suggested by parapsychological research; and the fourth because of certain experimental results of parapsychology, conjoined with some outcomes of studies of mediumship and other phases of psychical research. There must be few other questions, outside of ethics, politics, and art, which are answered in such diverse ways by numerous contemporary thinkers, none of them being notably deficient in rationality, open-mindedness, or well-informedness. The question of survival is oddly provocative.

If facts of emotional involvement and religious orientation are overlooked and the survival hypothesis is contemplated from a logico-scientific standpoint, does the reason it is so controversial stem from the imposing difficulty of amassing evidence for it? This is undoubtedly an important factor. But a more basic factor, I believe, is the problem of *falsification*: the difficulties of obtaining evidence *for* the survival hypothesis are surpassed by those of obtaining evidence *against* it. Is it not apparent, indeed, that no conceivable experimental results could really be taken as discon-

‡With regard to the second paragraph of this chapter, Professor Robert Binkley (see Bibliography) has criticized my placing Plato and Aquinas in class (e), contending that for the former, at least, survival is "logically, or at any rate metaphysically, necessary." I agree there is something odd about saying that for Plato, survival is empirically assured. But in drawing up the schema, I restricted myself, at the risk of some oversimplification, to the two key categories, *logical* and *empirical*. As far as Plato is concerned, I meant to imply not that survival was for him an "empirical issue," but that he believed the world to be such that survival does occur and that we can be sure of it. It's true, though, that *if* survival is indeed a logical necessity for him (and Aquinas), then I erred in placing them in class (e). At any rate, Binkley has a point: a sixth position—survival is logically necessary—should be acknowledged. (Note added for this reprinting.)

firming the hypothesis to an extent sufficient to dispel all scientific interest in it? But hypotheses which are unfalsifiable in this sense are rightly deprecated. When an hypothesis, so-called, is visibly immune to falsification, this is usually because logical securities against disconfirmation have gradually been built into it or added, either to explain away seeming counter-evidence already recorded or else to shelter it in advance from anticipated observations which would otherwise impugn it. A classic example of such logical protectionism is provided by the ether hypothesis. Yet the "survival hypothesis" is not in the same category. There appear to be no artificial safeguards involved which serve to preclude its being falsified; rather, it is simply that in the very nature of the case we cannot, if it is false, *know* that it is false. In the circumstances, therefore, it is doubtful that anyone can properly claim to have empirical evidence that survival occurs. The situation seems partly analogous to one in which someone claims to believe on empirical grounds that God exists. If we ask him what these grounds are, he will cite certain facts about the universe which we may be fully prepared to countenance. But then if we put to him the question, what would he count as empirical evidence that God does *not* exist, it becomes apparent that he would not be willing to construe *any* facts met with as telling against God's existence. Under such conditions, where nothing can ever count as empirical evidence against a given proposition, we shall rightly dispute a person's assertion that he possesses empirical evidence for it.

The foregoing does not imply that personal continuation beyond bodily death is, scientifically, unimportant or irrelevant. Not at all. But if a conjecture is construed as a scientific hypothesis and therefore amenable to empirical test, it does prove embarrassing if no experimental result can be specified which would, if obtained, count as definitively repudiating it. Inferably, then, since the hallmark of experiments is that they serve to test hypotheses, experimental inquiries into survival are concerned with hypotheses which *are* subject to both verification and falsification, but which cannot be logically equivalent to or implicative of the idea of personal survival itself. For example, hypotheses more limited or circumscribed than the latter, and which, unlike it, lend themselves to experimental decision, have included or could include such comparatively specific statements as: hypotheses relating to the psychology of entranced mediums; hypotheses pertaining to the linkage problem in ESP or to the occurrence of deathbed apparitions; hypotheses stating (say) that certain characteristics are to be found in the trance utterances of some mediums only at certain times of the year.

If, however, the proposition that survival occurs lacks the status of an hypothesis, what is its logical role and how is it related to the results of relevant scientific inquiries? I wish to suggest that it is a sort of working assumption which we must employ in order to make such inquiries meaningful. Unless we *presuppose* that survival occurs, not only will much of the experimental and other research seem scientifically pointless, but the likelihood is nil of being able to attach cognitive significance to such ostensibly interesting and meaningful questions as the following: "What is life like after death?" "Are survivors disembodied, somehow nonphysically embodied, or do they become re-embodied in physical form?" "Who survives?" "Are women, for example, more (or less) likely to survive than men?" "What is the average length of the period of survival?" "What are the processes and mechanics of communication between survivors and 'pre-mortem' individuals?" The survival *assumption* will stand to the relevant experiments and their results somewhat as a postulate of a theoretical system in a more advanced science stands to experiments and results in that science. In fact, is it inconceivable that the survival assumption, in a refined form, will serve at a future time as an axiomatic part of some theoretical network in psychophysics and biophysics which will constitute an inclusive expression of our knowledge of human nature? Until the time that a context of this sort may be fruitfully elaborated, however, the survival assumption may play a comparatively isolated role of providing a logical foothold for mounting the kinds of research and asking the sorts of questions undertaken and posed by those parapsychologists who are concerned with a post-mortem existence.

Alternatively, it is open to us to assume that survival does not occur. After all, there has been no discovery in psychical research which definitely counters such a negative assumption. It is entirely consistent logically, and perhaps even plausible, to admit all observationally verified data obtained in this sphere and yet to deny that survival occurs. There is no factual or logical mandate to take either the positive or the negative assumption in preference to the other. It might be argued that to assume survival does occur is pragmatically better on the grounds that this may serve to stimulate interesting experiments, while by assuming the opposite experimentation would be inhibited. But critics less sympathetic would no doubt describe such inhibition as altogether desirable since investigators' time could then be saved and devoted to worthier pursuits. So it appears to come to this: if we are faced with the methodological need to assume either that survival occurs or that it does not, then if we choose the former (as I think we should), it can be only because what may be called scientific intuition leads us in this direction.

The above proposal to assume the occurrence of survival should not be taken to commend the assumption that *every* person shares in such post-mortem prolongation. On the contrary, whether or not this is the case seems clearly to be a question that calls for empirical investigation. Only a few writers on the subject, however—C.D. Broad and W.P. Montague, for example—have in effect cautioned against taking for granted that survival is an all-or-none matter where human beings are concerned. Doubtless it is common to think that either all persons survive the death of their bodies or else that none do, but this is mere supposition. It may be the case that some persons do and some do not. Possibly instructive are two situations in other areas of psychical research, using this term broadly.

(a) One of the best-confirmed general hypotheses in parapsychology is that a subject's belief or attitude toward the existence of ESP tends to affect his scoring level in ESP tests. Roughly, subjects who "believe" in ESP seem to do better in such tests than subjects who reject it. The sheep-goat distinction is widely accepted as significant.[1]

(b) Studies in psychedelics afford the second example. An impressive body of data attests the striking extent to which prior expectation determines the kind of experience which a subject will

---

[1] G.R. Schmeidler, and R.A. McConnell, *ESP and Personality Patterns* (New Haven, Yale University Press, 1958).

have under the influence of these drugs. It would seem that individuals who expect beforehand that the drug will bring on quasi-psychotic experiences of a disagreeable or terrifying character are prone to react more or less in this negative fashion, so that their expectations (and/or those of the administrant) are fulfilled. On the other hand, those who look to the drug to induce an agreeable and beneficial expansion of consciousness, perhaps even an experience of a mystical nature, tend to respond in these quite different and more positive ways. In other words, whether the drug induces ecstacy or despair in the subject seems to depend largely on his prior expectations of what will befall him through its influence. As Willis W. Harman puts it, ". . . there can be no doubt that suggestibility, in one sense, plays a major role in influencing the nature of the experience provided by the psychedelic agents." And he adds that these agents are "referred to by an extraordinary heterogeneity of terms, including, besides psychedelic, 'hallucinogenic,' . . . 'psychotomimetic,' . . . 'psychoadjuvant', . . . 'mysticomimetic' and others. Which of these effects predominate depends upon [*inter alia*] the expectations of the subject. . ."[2]

I wonder, now, if it is too far-fetched to suggest that a person's expectations, attitudes, or beliefs may likewise play a major determining role in whether or not he will survive bodily death. Perhaps the Schmeidler classification[3] will assume importance in this region too, and we shall find that there is a tendency at death for sheep to survive and goats to expire. Though this may seem a fanciful suggestion, it should not be dismissed *a priori*. It is a possible area for research. How much might be disclosed or intimated if the available literature were examined along these lines? Assuming that mediumistic or other communication has in the past been effected with some death-survivors, how many of these are known to have been strong "disbelievers"? My impression is that among putative spirit communicators, at least in the better attested cases, there is a decided preponderance of sheep or believers. And this is an impression which, I think, might well repay confirming or disconfirming on the basis of a fresh scrutiny of the extant reports.

---

[2] W.W. Harman, "The Issue of the Consciousness-Expanding Drugs," *Main Currents in Modern Thought,* Vol. 20, No. 1 (September-October, 1963), pp. 5-14.
[3] G.R. Schmeidler, *op. cit.*

We have questioned the falsifiability of the idea of survival. It must be acknowledged that there is indeed one sense in which it *is* falsifiable: it can be excluded *a priori* by so defining personal identity—e.g. in terms of bodily continuity—that on logical grounds alone personal survival of bodily death becomes impossible. Philosophers have displayed conspicuous interest recently in the problem of defining personal identity, and among the accounts given are several which do insist upon bodily continuity as a necessary condition of personal sameness. Others, more tolerantly, seek to define the latter in psychological and/or ethical terms so as to let a person's identity be logically independent of his having always the *same* body; yet they may stop short of permitting him, so to speak, to have no body whatever. This further step is actually taken by some writers, who would thus try to portray personal identity without reference to bodily concomitants at all. And only this last sort of analysis, I surmise, would consort with the idea of strictly disembodied personal existence. Some analyses, however, while not countenancing completely disembodied personality, would admit as conceivable that at times a person may possess no ordinary protoplasmic body of the sort we find familiar, but only a body of a non-physical or "etheric" (*ecto*plasmic?) constitution, a so-called astral body, which at other times may be combined or associated with a body of the—to us—normal variety. Judged from a standpoint where it is assumed, in line with the above, that survival occurs, the unfolding of these various analyses implies a logical direction or progression.

Thus, perhaps the simplest account of personal identity *is* one which makes personal continuity contingent upon that of a single physical body. But despite the simplicity of such an account, it becomes plain that it ought not to be embraced since it is too restrictive. So the logical impetus acts toward relaxation of the one person-one body principle and an account which renders logically possible the transition of a single personality from one physical organism to another appears a significant move in the right direction. Yet such a formula, defining a person in terms of the presence of *some* body or other, excludes once more the possibility of surviving death with personal identity intact. A personality might somehow be transferred from one body to another, but still a corporeal substrate is presupposed. While presumably it could be reconciled with some form of *reincarnation,* where a person may "inhabit" a succession of bodies living at several non-overlapping times, this account would entail that he would simply cease to exist during periods, if any, between successive physical embodiments. To allow for personal existence during such intervals, we next turn to an account of personal identity fashioned without implying the need of a body at all.

In turning to this type of analysis, though, we meet the idea of a purely incorporeal form of personality and may find ourselves overwhelmed by its opacity. Can we really make sense of an altogether disembodied personal existence? Anthony Quinton has recently contended, and his point is hard to gainsay, that "only in our own case does it seem that strictly disembodied existence is conceivable, in the sense that we can conceive circumstances in which there would be some good reason to claim that a soul existed in a disembodied state".[4] The implications of this must be weighed attentively.

A short resume of a difficulty that seems to cripple the notion of disembodied personal existence becomes appropriate. A plausible supposition is that a bodiless person would be something non-spatial and unextended. And were it judged conceivable that such a person be occasionally, intermittently, or amorphously spatial or extended, he would *ex hypothesi* lack the spatial continuity and identity characteristic of a material body.* In any case, surely a fundamental problem with regard to a bodiless person is that of individuation: how could such a person be identified or distinguished from another? Supposedly one could not assert that a certain bundle of mental events (images, feelings, quasi-perceptions), not now associated with any body is the survived Mr. Smith unless one could assert that it contains *memories* of experiences

---

[4]A. Quinton, "The Soul," *Journal of Philosophy,* Vol. 59 (1962), pp. 393-409.

*During his lifetime many shadows were cast by the body of Mr. Smith. Let us call all these shadows collectively "Smith's shadow-family." After his death Mr. Smith, now without a body, might occasionally, intermittently, and sometimes amorphously "show up" in space somewhat as his shadow-family occasionally, intermittently, and sometimes amorphously was visible in space during his lifetime. Neither his shadow-family nor any shadow-member of it was a "body," however, nor would occasional post-mortem "spatiality" be incompatible with Mr. Smith's status as a discarnate entity.

had by Smith when embodied. This at least seems to be a necessary condition of the bundle's being identifiable with Mr. Smith. (Yet when he did possess a body, could he not have suffered a complete loss of memory without ceasing to be Mr. Smith?) But whether it is a sufficient condition thereof remains a moot point. Even if we deem it a sufficient condition, the question arises how we could possibly *know* that a given bundle of mental events contained such memories. How, indeed, could we ever detect or verify the *existence* of such a bundle unless—harking back to Quinton's point—it was our own; i.e. unless its presence were known by immediate awareness of the images composing the bundle, in the sense in which one person alone can be immediately aware of a particular toothache?

It is arguable that even if we couldn't possibly detect, verify, or know of the existence or presence of such a bundle of mental events, that would not entail its non-existence or that it was not present. This may be true, but it becomes a highly nebulous possibility and certainly smacks, to use an expression recently proposed by Professor Feigl,[5] of the "perniciously transcendent."[6] It is arguable further, however, that criticism of this sort would merely reflect a natural tendency to look at the matter from a biased pre-mortem viewpoint. Suppose that having died I find I have survived in a disembodied state. While I shall still have no way of detecting, verifying, or knowing of the existence or presence of other disembodied survivors, I may—provided I am still able to engage in thinking of this kind—decide that it is reasonable to believe other people have also survived the death of their bodies and that I am not the first or only incorporeal being in the world. I may say: "It used to seem reasonable to me to hold that even if some people survive, it may not be the case that everyone does. Nevertheless, it scarcely seems plausible now that I am the *sole* person to have reached the 'other side' and that everyone else has expired along with his body—especially when I was all along something of a

[5]H. Feigl, "The Power of Positivistic Thinking," *Proceedings and Addresses of the American Philosophical Association,* Vol. 36 (1962-1963), pp. 21-41.

[6]". . . it will be helpful," Feigl writes, to "distinguish between three kinds of transcendence: (1) The *innocuous* transcendence involved in ordinary assumptions about the past, the future, physical reality, and other minds. (2) The *precarious* transcendence of 'far out' hypotheses in the natural and social sciences. . . . (3) The *pernicious* transcendence which results in unanswerable questions, unsolvable problems, or inscrutable mysteries." *Ibid.*

'goat' in this connection!" However, I still should find the situation bemusingly nebulous. If it is urged that I might be able to detect the presence of other disembodied bundles by telepathic communication, the difficulty is how I could possibly know whether I was receiving a telepathic impression and not just having an experience of my own creation. And even if I did know it to be a telepathic impression, how could I know its source? Perhaps it might be coming from a person not yet dead and still embodied.

Now it is true that answers to such puzzles can possibly be found and that bodiless post-mortem existence may be shown logically possible. Perhaps, in fact, more obstructions than are rationally warranted are thrown in the path of seeing its logical possibility by a mind repelled by the inherent unpleasantness of such an acutely solitary condition as a way of having to spend one's post-mortem retirement. But whether the difficulties of the concept of disembodied personality be insuperable or exaggerated, altogether logical or partly emotional, it appears to the writer to be turbid and unpromising, and to explore possibilities of other forms of survival is, I think, the better part of expediency.

Indeed, we seem led in the end to acknowledge the idea of an "astral" or non-physical body as logically inviting. This idea, to be sure, may yet prove resistant to efforts to delineate it in scientifically clear and meaningful terms. But if for an account of personal identity consistent with the assumption of survival the concept of physical body is inadequate and that of bodiless existence unintelligible, to try to fathom the sense or nonsense of a "second body" may well be worth the venture.

CHAPTER 19

MEDIUMSHIP AND HUMAN SURVIVAL*

H. H. PRICE

M Y SUBJECT IS THE PHENOMENA OF MEDIUMSHIP, and I am
going to confine myself to what is called mental mediumship
(as opposed to physical).†

A mental medium is a person who has the capacity of making
verbal communications in an apparently paranormal manner, communications which usually, though not quite always, purport to
come from discarnate personalities. Whatever the right explanation
of them may be, there can be no doubt that the phenomena of
mental mediumship are of great theoretical interest. Puzzling and
paradoxical though they are—or indeed just because they are so
puzzling and paradoxical—they show that human personality has
capacities which our ordinary everyday experiences would not lead
us to expect; and the emotional repulsion which they may arouse
in our minds should not prevent us from studying them. In short,
the phenomena of mediumship must be important to the student of
human nature whatever the correct explanation of them may turn
out to be.

Perhaps I should first mention that not all mediums are females,
though many are; and for brevity's sake I shall speak of them in

*Reprinted from *The Journal of Parapsychology*, 1960, by permission of the author
and the editors.

†This article is a slightly expanded version of a lecture delivered on May 25, 1959,
under the auspices of Trinity College, Hartford, and under the sponsorship of the
Beta Chapter of Phi Beta Kappa of Connecticut and the Colloquium on the Nature
of Man. The lecture was repeated subsequently at the Symposium on Incorporeal
Personal Agency at Duke University, June 12, 1959. The *Journals* of March and
June, 1960, have contained four of the addresses given at the I.P.A. Symposium.—
Ed. [of *The Journal of Parapsychology*]

the female gender. Nor are they all persons of very low intelligence or very unstable character, though some perhaps are both. Nor are they all professionals who are paid for their services. Some of them are amateurs; and some of these, so far from wanting to exploit their gifts for commercial purposes, find them rather a nuisance and wish they did not possess them.

More important, the medium need not be in a trance at the time; that is, unconscious of her physical surroundings, unresponsive to physical stimuli, and incapable of remembering afterwards what she said and did. Trance mediumship is not the only sort, though it is the most interesting sort from a theoretical point of view and is the one I shall chiefly talk about.

I should add that in the trance cases, where the communication is made by means of spoken words, there are two different ways in which it may be made. Sometimes the medium appears to be giving a conscious description in her own words of something that she sees or hears; and what is abnormal or supernormal (in these cases) is her perceptions rather than her utterances. Sometimes these perceptions appear to amount to full blown visual or auditory hallucinations; sometimes they appear to consist only of very vivid mental imagery.

The most interesting cases, however, are those in which automatic speech occurs (i.e. the medium herself is not consciously controlling her vocal organs); and these are the ones I shall mainly consider. The phenomena are certainly very extraordinary, whatever the right explanation of them may be. The medium, when in a trance, speaks in a different voice from her usual one, with different mannerisms and vocabulary, and even occasionally in a foreign language which in waking life she does not understand. In her ordinary life she may be a naïve and uneducated person; but in her trance we may find her delivering complicated philosophical or theological discourses. This same abnormal voice, manner, and vocabulary may occur repeatedly with the same medium at different sittings. On the other hand, in the same sitting many distinct voices, manners, and vocabularies may also occur, quite different from each other, and all different from the normal voice, manner, and vocabulary of the medium herself. To anyone who has witnessed such occurrences, they almost irresistibly suggest, at the time, that some extraneous personality has got control of the medium's body or at least of her vocal organs. That is the immediate impression they make, whatever second thoughts one may have later. If you did not know you were at a seance—or if you heard the words from outside the door or over the telephone—you would conclude without hesitation that some intelligent being other than the medium herself was uttering them. It is not at all surprising that spiritualists accept this Possession Theory of trance mediumship at its face value. The appearances do strongly suggest it. Appearances may be deceptive, of course (we shall consider an alternative explanation presently); but in this case they can certainly be very impressive to anyone who actually witnesses them. Indeed, to form a fair judgment on this difficult matter, I think it is almost essential that one should have oneself attended some sitting with a "good" medium. The oddity and the impressiveness of the phenomena are not easily conveyed second hand.

Usually, though not quite always, a trance medium has what is called a "control" or "controlling spirit" corresponding more or less to the "familiar spirits" spoken of by our ancestors. (Some mediums have more than one "control," but this, I think, is unusual.) Still sticking to the *prima facie* appearances and using the language of the Possession Theory which they suggest, it seems as if there were some one extraneous personality who controls a given medium's body most easily and has made himself an expert at the job of taking possession of it. At the beginning of the trance, and sometimes again at the end, this personality takes over, often announcing himself by name. After talking for a while, he introduces other "spirits" whom he alleges to be present. Then the voice, manner, and vocabulary change abruptly; and it is as if some other extraneous personality, different from this first one but equally separate from the medium herself, had now assumed control of the medium's body, and often he announces that he is some deceased relative or some friend of one of the sitters. Sometimes the air of verisimilitude is increased, rather than diminished, by the fact that this new intruder seems to be having difficulties. He talks in a whisper, perhaps. He seems to find it hard to make himself understood, speaks in broken words, becomes confused and forgets what he wanted to say, much like an inexpert and rather flustered person who is using a telephone for the first time. (Sometimes the "control" has predicted this beforehand. He has said, "Mr. So-and-So is here, but he is not very expert. He will try to talk but he may not be very successful in getting through.")

This kind of thing may go on for quite a long time, even for several hours. It is as if a whole series of personalities, different from each other and from the medium, took possession of the medium's body one after another. Each of them, usually, though not invariably, makes an attempt to identify himself with a deceased person known to one or another of the sitters. Sometimes he does it by recalling a place, person, or incident familiar to the sitter; sometimes by making predictions which that particular person should be able to verify or by giving him advice about some problem which is worrying him; and not infrequently these predictions turn out later to be true, and the advice turns out to be good.

In other cases (still using the terminology of the Possession Theory) a single extraneous personality appears to hold the field for most of the time and utters a long philosophical or theological discourse, or again an account of the kind of life which he and others live in the next world. I myself at a seance a few years ago listened to an almost unbearably tedious exposition of a watered-down Adoptionist Christology, delivered with incredible rapidity and at enormous length by a personality who purported to have been a London street-urchin in this life. (He explained that he had learned his theology since he passed over.) Communications of this kind are often "a blend of twaddle and uplift"—as Professor Broad puts it—and are sometimes excessively boring to hear or to read. It would seem that the art of saying very little in a very large number of words is as well understood "on the other side" as it is here. There are, however, exceptions. Some of the theological and philosophical discourses are coherent and well presented, and the same is true of some of the descriptions of life "in the other world." The matter may or may not be acceptable, but the manner suggests an intelligent and thoughtful person who knows what he is about. (There are some excellent examples in an article called "A Study of the Psychological Aspects of Mrs. Willett's Mediumship and of the Statements of the Communicators Concerning Process" by Gerald Balfour.[1]) The same is true of some of the descriptions of life "on the other side," of the difficulties which a newly-dead person has in adapting himself to them, and of the various sorts of "other worlds" which there are. Such descriptions are sometimes detailed and intelligent, and are formulated in a matter-of-fact way, without any uplift at all. Of course, we have no means of verifying them, but the manner in which they are presented inspires some respect; and they are interesting to hear and to read in the way that a good book of travel is.

What are we to make of these strange happenings? We must try to make *something* of them. The evidence is too abundant to be ignored. There is no question at all that automatic speech and writing do occur. There is no question at all that the utterances of entranced mediums do strongly suggest that the medium's body is being controlled by a personality other than the medium's own. There is no doubt that the information given is often outside the medium's knowledge when she is in her normal waking state; and often it turns out to be true and sometimes, as far as we can tell, it is outside the knowledge of any living human being at the time when the communication is made. Moreover, this information is sometimes about the future and is later verified to a degree which is not easily explained by chance-coincidence. Lastly, when unverifiable things are said (as in the theological discourses or the descriptions of the other world) they are sometimes coherently and intelligently said; and the medium in her normal waking state is quite incapable of inventing them.

If we are not going to explain the phenomena by the hypothesis of discarnate agency—by the Possession Theory of the spiritualists—how are we going to explain them?

Perhaps we may get some help from abnormal psychology. The phenomena of abnormal psychology are almost as strange as those of mediumship, and some of them are stranger in an analogous way. I think that the spiritualists have not paid enough attention to them, a defect which they share with some theologians and (I am afraid) with not a few philosophers. There is the very odd phenomenon of multiple personality, for instance. It would appear that

---

[1] *Proc. Soc. Psychical Rsch.*, Vol. 43 (1935), pp. 41-318.

the human mind is by no means the "simple substance," the indivisible *res cogitans* or "conscious entity," which philosophers have imagined it to be. On the contrary, it seems to be highly complex and most of its constituents at any given time seem to be unconscious. The unity which a human mind possesses seems to be a matter of degree, not a matter of all or none. Its degree of integration varies in different conditions. Even in the most sane and normal human mind (I nearly said "the most repulsively sane and normal") there is probably some degree of dissociation, or at least some tendency to it—the faint beginnings, at any rate, of a split personality. Within each of us there are subsystems of thoughts, memories, and wishes which function with some degree of autonomy. Philip drunk and Philip sober are not quite two different personalities, but they are somewhere near it. The same could be said of Philip waking and Philip dreaming.

Now psychopathologists tell us that a severe emotional shock, or even a prolonged condition of emotional strain, may produce a complete mutation of personality, where the patient loses his memories of a long period of his life, treats his friends and relatives as complete strangers, and displays a different character from the one he had before. The organism is the same, but its behavior—its utterances and its acts—manifests another set of thoughts, emotions, and desires dissimilar to and disconnected with those we were accustomed to expect of it. A secondary personality, different from the normal one—a personality previously repressed or unconscious—is manifesting itself.

Ordinarily such a secondary personality is repressed, though it may give occasional evidence of its presence by means of dreams, or by means of isolated and apparently accidental actions, such as slips of the tongue or of the pen. But if some unusual physical or physiological condition gives it the opportunity of manifesting itself continuously for some time, by means of utterances and other forms of bodily behavior, what will happen? To the outside observer, it will be as if Mr. Smith's body was possessed by some extraneous mind, quite different from the ordinary Smith-mind to which we are accustomed. If our outside observer had been an inhabitant of the later Roman empire, he would have said that Smith's body is possessed by a *daimon,* whether benevolent or malevolent. If on the other hand he is a modern spiritualist, he will say that Smith's body is being controlled by a discarnate human mind.

Now are not these occurrences very like what happens in trance mediumship? In trance mediumship, as I have said already, the prima facie appearances do very strongly suggest that the medium's body is possessed by an extraneous personality. But the investigations of the psychopathologists suggest something different. They suggest that what is manifesting itself through the medium's vocal organs is a secondary personality of the medium herself, a relatively coherent and organized system of thoughts, memories, and desires which is part of the medium's own mind, though in normal waking life it is repressed into the unconscious.

It may be significant in this connection that the "controls" of trance mediums quite often purport to be deceased children. It is notorious that childish thoughts, desires, and memories are very liable to be repressed in adult life. The mediumistic trance (whatever its nature is) may give them their opportunity. It may also be significant that in the performances of some mediums—not the best ones—the discarnate spirits of very illustrious persons, such as the Emperor Augustus, purport to be communicating. May not this be a way in which repressed childish wishes for fame or power contrive to find an outlet?

Moreover, the phenomena of psychopathology also suggest that such secondary personalities may possess very remarkable powers of imaginative invention and dramatization. It would not be beyond them to produce plausible and coherent impersonations of other people. And as a matter of fact the dreaming mind can do this in all of us, however sane and sensible we are when awake.

What force is there in this alternative explanation of mediumistic communications—the skeptical explanation, as we might call it? Clearly there is a great deal. There is a striking analogy between the phenomena of mediumship and the mutations of personality described by psychopathologists. But, as it stands, this hypothesis is too narrow to cover all the facts. To make it cover them we shall have to add to it and stretch it in a way which may be rather impalatable to tough-minded naturalistic persons. And when we have done so, we shall perhaps find that it is not so utterly different from the survivalist explanation as it looks.

The trouble is that, as it stands, this skeptical explanation in terms of secondary personalities leaves out the paranormal aspect of mediumistic communications altogether. And the paranormal aspect is there, whatever the right explanation of it may be.

You remember I spoke earlier about the so-called controls or controlling spirits which most trance mediums purport to have. The control is a kind of master of ceremonies at the seance, and a given medium usually has the same control at different seances (or the same small group of them). Now it is a very plausible hypothesis that a mediumistic control—for example, Mrs. Leonard's celebrated control, Feda—is just a secondary personality of the medium herself. But what about the other personalities which purport to manifest themselves at the seance; for example, deceased relatives or friends of the sitters? These vary from one seance to another. Indeed that is the whole point of the performance. Mr. Jones' deceased father manifests himself at one seance, Mr. Brown's deceased business partner at another. I must add—just to make things more difficult—that sometimes they are not deceased relatives or friends of anyone who is actually present, but of some absent person, unknown to the medium even by name, for whom one of the sitters is acting as a proxy. And these "proxy sittings," as they are called, are sometimes as successful as the ordinary kind.

Granting that the "control" is just a secondary personality of the medium herself, what are we to say about those other personalities? We have to remember that these allegedly discarnate personalities sometimes give verifiable information which is quite unknown to the medium in her normal state, equally unknown to the sitters, or even unknown at the time to any living person; and that they sometimes use a vocabulary which is beyond the medium's normal understanding, or even occasionally a foreign language which she does not know. And how is it, moreover, that the characteristic mannerisms of deceased persons, known to the sitter but unknown to the medium, are sometimes reproduced so accurately that the sitter claims to recognize them at once? The same difficulty arises at least in some degree when the deceased relatives do not purport to speak in their own person, but are merely described as if the medium were seeing them and reporting what they say.

It seems perfectly clear that if the medium's unconscious is responsible for all this, her unconscious must be supposed to have paranormal cognitive powers, and pretty extensive ones too.

We shall have to suppose, first, that there is telepathy between the medium and the sitters (or the absent people for whom they are "proxies"). Some unconscious stratum in the medium's mind must somehow have access to the memories of the sitters—and not only the memories they are conscious of at the moment, but others too which are subconscious or even at the time forgotten. Out of those memories, like a very skillful actor, it presumably improvises a lifelike impersonation of some deceased person, so lifelike that the sitter cannot distinguish it from the real thing. Such a remarkable feat of dramatization probably *is* within the power of the unconscious mind; at any rate, the phenomena of psychopathology suggest so. But the materials, the information, which are used for this purpose must be obtained telepathically. There is therefore still something paranormal about the performance, even if the medium herself is wholly responsible for it.

Nor is this all. The telepathy which occurs must be selective and directed. An indiscriminate telepathic leakage from the minds of the sitters to the mind of the medium would not be enough to account for all the facts. There may be several sitters present, and one or more of them may be "proxies" for people who are absent. If memories telepathically drawn from Mr. A's mind were combined with the memories drawn from Mr. B's, the resulting impersonation would not be very convincing to either of them. Memories referring to Mr. A's late Aunt Martha must not be mixed up with memories referring to Mr. B's late cousin Agatha. If they are, the result will not be a very lifelike impersonation of either lady. Again, each individual sitter, Mr. A for instance, is sure to have memories (conscious or subconscious) of many different deceased relatives or acquaintances; and these must not be mixed up either, if a convincing impersonation is to be produced.

The telepathy, then, must be selective and discriminating, in some way purposively controlled, unlike the telepathy which we know of from other (non-mediumistic) evidence. For this other evidence suggests that the telepathic recipient receives his telepathic data in an automatic and passive manner. It suggests that telepathy, on the recipient's side, is rather like catching a disease by infection and is a process over which one has very little voluntary control, if any; whereas the telepathy which is supposed to occur in the medium according to the present hypothesis is more like a conscious and discriminating investigation of the contents of other people's minds.

We notice, further, that verifiable information is sometimes given about facts which at the moment are not known to the sitters at all, facts which the medium cannot have found out in any normal manner. Directions are sometimes given for finding lost objects, for instance, and sometimes they turn out to be correct. This information may of course be contained in the mind of some living human being or other and therefore may be obtained telepathically. But if so, how has the medium managed to direct her telepathic powers to the right person? Does she "telepathically fish" in dozens or hundreds of people's memories until she finds the information which is asked for? If so, her telepathic powers must not only be very extensive and very discriminating; she must also be able to control and direct them with a very surprising degree of accuracy.

It would be simpler, I believe, to suppose that in these last cases the information is obtained not by telepathy but by clairvoyance, which may be defined as the acquiring of true information about physical objects without the use of the sense organs or of memory or of rational inference. We have evidence from other sources that clairvoyance does occur, though we have not the remotest idea of how it works; and the name "clairvoyance" (literally "clear seeing") is not a very good one because the process, whatever it is, must be something very different from normal sense perception. But if that is the explanation we offer, we have now committed ourselves to attributing two paranormal cognitive powers to the medium (or to a secondary personality of hers); not telepathy only, but clairvoyance as well.

And we cannot stop at that, for sometimes information about the future is given and its verification by subsequently observed facts cannot be reasonably explained by chance-coincidence.

To explain such predictions, we shall have to attribute still another supernormal cognitive power to the medium, namely precognition. Of all the phenomena investigated by parapsychologists,

272 Philosophical Dimensions of Parapsychology

precognition is the most puzzling and paradoxical. But there is other evidence that it does occur quite apart from mediumistic communications. (The evidence comes partly from card-guessing experiments, and partly from precognitive dreams and visions.)

To sum up the results of the discussion so far, we can now see that this "skeptical" explanation of mediumistic communications has become much less skeptical than it looked at first. Its intention was to explain the phenomena in terms of abnormal psychology. But to make the explanation at all complete, a good deal of supernormal or paranormal psychology has to be introduced as well.

It comes to this: If you want to be skeptical about survival, you have to be *un*skeptical about paranormal cognition, or ESP. Indeed, at least as far as telepathy is concerned, you have to be more than unskeptical. You have to be almost credulous. You have to suppose that the ESP powers of the medium—at any rate of good mediums—are far more extensive and far more accurate than our other evidence about telepathy would suggest. You have to suppose, moreover, that the ESP powers of the medium, though exercised unconsciously, are under some degree of intelligent and purposive control, as if she could telepathically rummage about among the contents of other people's minds till she finds the piece of information which is wanted, and could discriminate accurately between the contents of one person's mind and the contents of another person's.

It must not be supposed, then, that this anti-survivalist theory of mediumship is a timid or unconstructive one. On the contrary, it might be criticized for being too speculative and audacious. It presents us with a bold synthesis of conceptions drawn from two different though related fields, parapsychology and psychopathology, and it uses them to provide a comprehensive explanation of all the phenomena of mediumship or at least of mental mediumship. Professor Hornell Hart has called it the "Super-ESP Hypothesis."[2] Perhaps the prefix "super" has a slightly depreciatory flavor, and suggests that too great a weight is being laid on the ESP powers of the medium. It would be better to find a quite neutral name for this hypothesis, if we could. So I am going to call it the "This-

---

[2]*The Enigma of Survival* (Springfield, Thomas), Chap. 9.

World-ESP" hypothesis.* This brings out the essential point, that the ESP powers of the medium, however extensive, are supposed to be restricted to persons and things in this world. Her telepathic powers, great as they may be, are supposed to give her access only to the minds of living and embodied human beings; her clairvoyant powers are supposed to give her access only to events and situations in the observable physical world.

It cannot be doubted, I think, that this theory of mediumship does give a very plausible explanation of some of the phenomena, indeed of many of them. There must surely be a close connection between the phenomena of mediumship and the mutations of personality investigated by psychopathologists. There would also seem to be a close connection between mediumistic phenomena and dreaming. The utterances of an entranced medium may be regarded as a kind of "dreaming aloud." (The same could be said *mutatis mutandis* of at least some forms of automatic writing.) Or, to put it more cautiously, mediumistic communications seem to originate in the same stratum of human personality as dreams do; and here, of course, we must remember that there are telepathic and clairvoyant dreams and sometimes precognitive ones.

Again, there can be very little doubt that some mediumistic communications can be completely accounted for by telepathy between the living. The first thing which strikes anyone who has personal acquaintance with mediumship is the way in which his own thoughts, memories, and wishes (including subconscious ones) are "given back" to him by the medium in the form of ostensible communications from the next world. Yet these thoughts, memories, and wishes of his are not known to the medium in any normal manner. She may never have seen him before and may not even know his name. The almost irresistible inference is that there has been some kind of "telepathic leakage" from the sitter's mind to the mind of the medium; that the mind of the sitter, including thoughts or memories or wishes of his which are not in his consciousness at the moment, is somehow accessible to the ESP powers of the medium; and that the information thus acquired is then

---

*On the continent of Europe it is sometimes called the animistic hypothesis (as contrasted with the spiritualistic hypothesis), but this rather odd use of the term "animistic" has not so far found favor in the English-speaking countries.

"dressed up," more plausibly or less, in the guise of a communication from the spirit world.

I am not convinced myself that the This-World-ESP hypothesis is a completely satisfactory explanation of all mediumistic communications, though it does give a very satisfactory explanation of some of them. Perhaps it does not tell us the whole truth about mediumship; for it might be that discarnate minds, as well as embodied ones, are accessible to the ESP powers of the medium, or of some mediums, at least sometimes. But if the This-World-ESP hypothesis tells us at any rate a part of the truth about the phenomena of mediumship—as I think we must admit that it does—then these phenomena do at least show that human personality is something much more complex and also (if I may say so) much less neat and tidy than we usually take it to be. In this respect, they provide us with further evidence for the conclusions already suggested by the phenomena of abnormal psychology. It appears that the unity of the human mind is a matter of degree and not a matter of all or none. And such unity as it has at any time is less stable than we ordinarily think. It has subconscious and unconscious strata as well as conscious ones. Portions of it which are repressed in normal waking life may emerge from time to time and take control of the body, returning later to their ordinary repressed condition. A book has been written called *The Three Faces of Eve.*[3] I think we all of us have many faces; and the thoughts, feelings, wishes, and memories which we display to the world in our normal waking state are by no means the only ones that we have. In all of us, I suggest, there is some degree of dissociation, the beginnings at least of a divided personality. In mediumship we see writ large, displayed in glaring colors, the disunity, the instability, the many-levelled character which is present in some degree in the minds of all of us.

To some this may appear a disconcerting suggestion. Is it not equivalent to saying that we are all a little mad? Yes, it does come to that. But there is such a thing as being too sane. The ideal which some preachers and even some psychologists put before us of a completely integrated personality seems to me to be an exceedingly

---

[3]Corbett M. Thigpen and Hervey M. Cleckley, *The Three Faces of Eve* (New York, McGraw-Hill, 1957).

repellent one. It has the same kind of repulsiveness as the idea of a completely integrated or totalitarian society. If all of us were what these people want us to be, everything that we call originality and inspiration (whether intellectual or artistic) would vanish from the world; and certainly genius would vanish. For all these things suggest some degree of dissociation, some abdication of the control which our normal waking self exercises over the course of our thoughts, imaginations, and feelings. They depend upon what have been called "subliminal uprushes." I think we should be thankful that the human mind is not the indivisible conscious entity which some philosophers say it is, and some preachers and educators say it ought to be.

So much for some of the implications of what I have called the This-World-ESP hypothesis and of the explanation of mediumistic phenomena which it offers us. This explanation, or something like it, is what we are driven to if we reject the survival hypothesis.

We must now ask whether we are in a position to decide between these two hypotheses. But first let us be quite clear what the two alternatives are between which we should have to choose. We have to admit, I think, that the This-World-ESP hypothesis is almost certainly the correct explanation of some mediumistic communications. Consequently, it is not open to us to reject the This-World-ESP hypothesis altogether. The only question is whether it is the correct explanation of *all* mediumistic communications. The situation is, I think, that we are confronted with a scale or series of different cases. (This may remind you of the scale or series of cases discussed by Dr. Louisa Rhine in her lecture on non-recurrent spontaneous experiences.[4]) There are some which the This-World-ESP hypothesis fits perfectly and the survival hypothesis does not fit at all. There are many where the This-World-ESP hypothesis fits the facts pretty well, and the survival hypothesis also fits them pretty well. And there are still others where the This-World-ESP hypothesis cannot absolutely be excluded, but becomes exceedingly complicated, because we should have to suppose that the medium uses her ESP powers to collect information (unconsciously of

---

[4]The Evaluation of Non-Recurrent Psi Experiences Bearing on Post-Mortem Survival, *J. Parapsychol.*, Vol. 24 (1960), pp. 8-25.

course) from the minds of many different living persons, one bit from one mind, another bit from another; that she then combines all these different bits of information (again unconsciously), excluding any irrelevant bits which she might have picked up by the way; and finally produces a lifelike impersonation of the deceased person to whom all these different bits of information refer. In these cases, assuming that the information is accurate, or accurate for the most part—as it sometimes is—and that the medium cannot have obtained it in any normal manner (and sometimes we can be pretty certain of this too), the survival hypothesis gives a much simpler explanation of the facts. If the late Mr. Jones has survived death, all this information could be obtained quite easily from one single mind, namely the mind (or memories) of Mr. Jones himself, presumably in a telepathic manner. It would not have to be collected by an elaborate process of extrasensory biographical research into the contents of many different minds; and no question would arise about how the medium knew (in an unconscious and paranormal manner) which are the appropriate minds to research into. Here the simplest explanation is to suppose that the medium's ESP powers are not confined to this world but extend to another world as well.

Nevertheless, I doubt very much whether we can find any case at present where the This-World-ESP explanation is absolutely impossible. The difficulty is obvious, and many students of the subject have already drawn attention to it. We do not know what the limits of this-worldly ESP are, or even whether it has any. Are there events in this world, whether mental ones or physical ones, which are so distant in space and time or both that they would be beyond the range of the ESP powers of even the most gifted mediums? We do not know.

We do, however, know that mediums differ a good deal from one another. At any rate, we can say, in a rough way, that some are "more gifted" than others. Rather naturally, we are inclined to restrict our investigations to the most gifted mediums that we can find. But perhaps this is a mistaken policy, at any rate if our aim is to decide between the This-World-ESP hypothesis and the survival hypothesis. It might be that in the most gifted mediums the capacities I have mentioned really do have no limits, or none that we can hope to discover; just as it is virtually impossible for us to assign limits to the imaginative powers of Shakespeare or to his powers of poetical expression or dramatic presentation. But perhaps the situation could be more hopeful if we turned our attention to persons who have some mediumistic gifts, but less distinguished ones.

Let us again consider the capacity for paranormal and unconsciously conducted biographical research, the most puzzling, perhaps, of the paranormal capacities which the This-World-ESP hypothesis has to postulate. Conceivably this capacity may be present in some degree in anyone who has mediumistic gifts at all. But surely it must have some limits in the less gifted mediums, even if it has no limits, or none that we can detect, in the very gifted ones such as Mrs. Piper or Mrs. Leonard. After all, the question we have to consider is whether a particular communication received through a particular medium can be wholly explained by the This-World powers of that particular medium. We are not asking whether someone else could consciously have collected the information by directing his or her ESP powers upon the minds of various living human beings, but whether this particular medium could have done it, being the sort of person she is. And some day we might be in a position to say that at any rate *she* could not have done it, even though some much more gifted medium such as Mrs. Piper or Mrs. Leonard conceivably could have.

I think, then, that the problem of assigning limits to this-worldly ESP powers is not necessarily insoluble. But certainly we have not solved this problem yet, and there does not seem to be any immediate prospect of doing so. What, then, is our present position? It is this. We cannot at present reach a decision between the This-World-ESP hypothesis and the survival hypothesis; or rather between the hypothesis that This-World-ESP accounts for all the phenomena and the hypothesis that it accounts for some of them but not all, and that the remainder can only be accounted for by supposing that there are discarnate personalities.

If we are looking for a proof of survival, then, we certainly have not got it. What we have got is evidence for survival. The evidence is not conclusive, because there is an alternative explanation which we are not in a position to eliminate—the explanation offered by what I have called the "This-World-ESP" hypothesis. This alternative explanation covers some of the facts very well. But there are others where it becomes too complicated to be easily credible, and we have to postulate a kind and degree of ESP power which is not easily credible either. In these cases it is simpler and easier to suppose that the information given by the medium comes from a surviving personality or, if you like, that the ESP powers of the medium are not confined to this world but extend to another world as well. These are the cases which give us evidence in favor of the survival hypothesis, though the evidence is not conclusive.

This is a disappointing result, no doubt. The investigation of the problem of survival by empirical methods, pursued in a more or less scientific spirit, has been going on for more than seventy years now, ever since the foundation of the London Society for Psychical Research in the eigthteen eighties. And we are still nowhere near a solution of it, though the investigation has certainly revealed some strange and unexpected facts about the human mind and has also provided us with some evidence which is not very easily explained unless the survival hypothesis be true.

But though, as far as I can see, it would be unreasonable to be convinced of survival on the empirical evidence we now have, it does seem to me that the evidence is sufficient to give the survival hypothesis an appreciable probability. The reasonable attitude about it could perhaps be expressed in this way: It is by no means out of the question that the survival hypothesis might be true. Or, if you like, we may say that in the light of the empirical evidence, it would not be so very surprising if the survival hypothesis should be true. There is a chance that we may find ourselves surviving after death; a chance which is not small enough to be negligible. In the light of the empirical evidence, it is a possibility which has to be reckoned with.

Or, if you prefer to look at it that way, it is a risk which a reasonable man must take into account. One would describe it as a risk (that is, a chance but an unwelcome one) if one regarded survival as an evil rather than a good, and it seems to me that quite a number of people do regard it as an evil rather than a good. I suspect that there are quite strong motives, conscious in some persons, unconscious in others, which tend to make the idea of survival repellent to many. To such people (I think I am one of

them myself, as least sometimes) I should say: "Do not be absolutely sure that your personal existence will come to an end when
you die. There is an appreciable risk that it may continue, and it
will be reasonable for you to pay some attention to that risk, much
as you may dislike doing so."

If I am right in summing the matter up in this way, the consequences are quite important. Let me give some examples. If the
chance that all or most human beings survive after death is even
as high as 1 to 50 (I use this ratio just for the sake of illustration,
to make the notion of a small but appreciable chance more concrete), our moral obligations are in some degree affected. It is a
mistake to suppose that our moral obligations are concerned only
with our outward actions. What we think privately in our hearts is
just as important as what we do publicly in the market place, or perhaps more so; and the directions which our thoughts take is in some
degree under our voluntary control, just as our outward actions
are. Now let us consider the obligations of charity or benevolence.
Suppose that someone well-known to us has recently died. If there
is a chance (or, if you prefer, a risk) of even 1 to 50 that he survives, we cannot neglect the possibility that the thoughts and feelings we have about him may make a considerable difference to his
condition. They may well affect him telepathically. If so, charity
requires us to take at least a little trouble to think kindly of him
and wish him well. We ought to spend at least a little time and
energy in thinking kind thoughts about him and in cultivating a
well-wishing attitude towards him. And it will be specially incumbent on us to do this shortly after he has died—and all the more
so if he is someone who disbelieved in survival (as the majority of
educated Western people nowadays probably do), for that is the
time when he may have special difficulty in adapting himself to his
new and probably unexpected situation and will need all the help
he can get.

True, we do not know that he survives at all; and if he does,
we do not know that our thoughts and feelings about him will have
any effect on him. But similarly, when we are driving round a
blind corner in the road, we do not know that there is a pedestrian
or a bicyclist on the far side of the corner; nor do we know (supposing that there is one) that we shall run into him if we drive

round the corner at forty-five miles an hour. Nevertheless, we have a moral obligation to slow down "just in case."

But I am most concerned to point out that questions of prudence (of enlightened self-interest) will arise, as well as of moral obligation, because this, perhaps, is less obvious. If there is a chance—let us again put it as low as 1 to 50 for the sake of illustration—that one will oneself survive death and will continue to be conscious, to have thoughts and feelings, one will be wise to spend a little time and energy in considering what kind of an existence one might have after death, supposing one does survive, and in preparing oneself for that possibility (or that danger if you prefer to look at it so). It has been said that "we brought nothing into this world, and it is certain that we can carry nothing out." With all respect, I venture to disagree with this statement, or at least with the second part of it. It seems to me that if there is personal survival, we shall take a good deal with us when we pass out of this world into the next: namely, our memories, our desires, our character (that is, our acquired conative and emotional dispositions), and any ESP powers we may have. And the memories and desires will presumably include those unpleasant or guilty ones which we have "repressed" in this present life. Indeed, I am afraid that we shall have a very considerable amount of psychological luggage to take with us if we do survive; and we shall be wise to take a little trouble, while we still can, to insure that it is of a desirable kind, just in case the survival hypothesis should be true.

I want to say again that as a student of paranormal phenomena, I am not concerned with the man who is 100 percent convinced of survival. I think rather of the man who is satisfied that there is some evidence of survival but does not regard the evidence as conclusive. And I am saying that it will be prudent for him, and in certain circumstances morally obligatory, to arrange his life rather differently from the way most people in our society arrange their lives now. The most important difference, I suggest, will concern the way he directs his thoughts, and the kind of emotional attitudes he cultivates.

Let us not say, then—as perhaps we may be inclined to—that long inquiry into the problem of survival has "got us nowhere" and shows no likelihood of getting us anywhere. It has got us somewhere, and somewhere quite important, even now. For one thing, it has thrown unexpected light on human nature. It has shown us that the human mind is at once more complex and less stably unified than we suspected. Something very strange and very interesting is certainly occurring when mediumistic communications are made, whatever the right explanation may turn out to be. But more than that, the investigation of mediumship has shown, I suggest, that the chance of survival, in the light of empirical evidence, is not so negligibly small as most educated people are accustomed to suppose. In the light of the evidence of mediumistic phenomena the probability of survival is far indeed from amounting to a certainty. But it is large enough to make a considerable difference to a reasonable man's attitude to the world and to himself.

CHAPTER 20

HOW STANDS THE CASE FOR THE REALITY OF SURVIVAL*

C. J. DUCASSE

THE POINT HAS NOW been reached where we must attempt to say, in the light of the evidence and of the criticisms to which it may be open, how stands today the question whether the human personality survives the death of its body.

1. **What, if not survival, the facts might signify.** Only two hypotheses have yet been advanced that seem at all capable of accounting for the *prima facie* evidences of personal survival reviewed. One is that the identifying items do indeed proceed from the surviving spirits of the deceased persons concerned. The other is that the medium obtains by extrasensory perception the facts she communicates; that is, more specifically, obtains them: (a) telepathically from the minds of living persons who know them or have known them; or (b) by retrocognitive clairvoyant observation of the past facts themselves; or (c) by clairvoyant observation of existing records, or of existing circumstantial evidence, of the past facts.

To the second of these two hypotheses would have to be added in some cases the hypothesis that the medium's subconscious mind has and exercises a remarkable capacity for verisimilar impersonation of a deceased individual whom the medium has never known but concerning whom she is getting information at the time in the telepathic or/and clairvoyant manner just referred to.

In cases where the information is communicated by paranormal

---

*Reprinted from C.J. Ducasse, *A Critical Examination of the Belief in a Life after Death*, Ch. XIX, by permission of Charles C Thomas, Publisher.

raps or by other paranormal physical phenomena, the hypothesis that the capacity to produce such physical phenomena is being exercised by the medium's unconscious but still incarnate mind would be more economical than ascription of that capacity to discarnate minds; for these—unlike the medium and her mind— are not independently known to exist.

It must be emphasized that no responsible person who is fully acquainted with the evidence for the occurrences to be explained and with their circumstances has yet offered any explanatory hypothesis distinct from the two stated above. As of today, the choice therefore lies between them. The hypothesis of fraud, which would by-pass them, is wholly untenable in at least some of the cases; notably, for the reasons mentioned earlier, in the case of the communications received through Mrs. Piper. And, in the case of the cross-correspondences, the hypothesis that the whole series was but an elaborate hoax collusively perpetrated out of sheer mischief for over ten years by the more than half-dozen automatists concerned—and this without its ever being detected by the alert investigators who were in constant contact with the automatists— is preposterous even if the high personal character of the ladies through whom the scripts came is left out of account.

Still more so, of course, would be the suggestion that the investigators too participated in the hoax. In this connection the following words of Professor Sidgwick are worth remembering. They occur in his presidential address at the first general meeting of the Society for Psychical Research in London, July 17, 1882:

> The highest degree of demonstrative force that we can obtain out of any single record of the investigation is, of course, limited by the trustworthiness of the investigator. We have done all that we can when the critic has nothing left to allege except that the investigator is in the trick. But when he has nothing else left to allege he will allege that . . . . We must drive the objector into the position of being forced either to admit the phenomena as inexplicable, at least by him, or to accuse the investigators either of lying or cheating or of a blindness or foregetfulness incompatible with any intellectual condition except absolute idiocy.[1]

---

[1]*Proc. S.P.R.,* Vol. 1 (1882-1883), p. 12. Cf. in this connection an article, "Science and the Supernatural," by G.R. Price, Research Associate in the Dept. of Medicine, Univ. of Minnesota. *Science,* Vol. 122, No. 3165 (August 26, 1955) and the comments on it by S.G. Soal, J.B. Rhine, P.E. Meehl, M. Scriven, P.W. Bridgman, Vol. 123, No. 3184 (January 6, 1956).

2. **The allegation that survival is antecedently improbable.** The attempt to decide rationally between the two hypotheses mentioned above must in any case take into consideration at the very start the allegation that survival is antecedently known to be improbable or even impossible; or on the contrary is known to be necessary. In a paper to which we shall be referring in the next two sections,[2] Professor E.R. Dodds first considers the grounds that have been advanced from various quarters for such improbability, impossibility, or necessity. In view, however, of our own more extensive discussion of those grounds in Parts I and III of the present work, we need say nothing here concerning Professor Dodds' brief remarks on the subject. Nothing in them seems to call for any revision of the conclusion to which we came that there is not really any antecedent improbability of survival (nor any antecedent probability of it). For when the denotation of the terms "material" and "mental" is made fully explicit instead of, as commonly, assumed to be known well enough; and when the nature of the existents or occurrents respectively termed "material" and "mental" is correctly analyzed; then no internal inconsistency, nor any inconsistency with any definitely known empirical fact, is found in the supposition that a mind, such as it had become up to the time of death, continues to exist after death and to exercise some of its capacities. Nor is there any antecedent reason to assume that, if a mind does so continue to exist, manifestations of this fact to persons still living would be common rather than, as actually seems to be the case, exceptional.

3. **What telepathy or clairvoyance would suffice to account for.** Professor Dodds considers and attempts to dispose of ten objections which have been advanced against the adequacy of the telepathy-clairvoyance explanation of the facts. The objections in the case of which his attempt seems definitely successful are the following.

(a) The first is that telepathy does not account for the claim made in the mediumistic communications, that they emanate from the spirits of deceased persons.

Professor Dodds replies that some of the communications have in fact claimed a different origin; and that anyway the claim is

---

[2]"Why I Do Not Believe in Survival," *Proc. S.P.R.*, Vol. XLII (1934), pp. 147-172.

explicable as due to the fact that communication with the deceased is usually what is desired from mediums, and that the medium's own desire to satisfy the sitter's desire for such communications operates on the medium's subconscious—from which they directly proceed—as desire commonly operates in the production of dreams and in the determination of their content.

(b) A second objection is that no independent evidence exists that mediums belong to the very small group of persons who have detectable telepathic powers.

In reply, Professor Dodds points to the fact that Dr. Soal had in his own mind formed a number of hypotheses about the life and circumstances of the—as it eventually turned out— wholly fictitious John Ferguson (mentioned in Sec. 2 of Chapt. XVIII), and that in the communications those very hypotheses then cropped up as assertions of fact. Professor Dodds mentions various other instances where things actually false, but believed true by the sitter, have similarly been asserted in the medium's communications and thus have provided additional evidence that she possessed and was exercising telepathic powers.

To this we may add that there is some evidence that the trance condition—at least the hypnotic trance—is favorable to the exercise of ordinary latent capacities for extrasensory perception.[3]

(c) Another objection is that telepathy does not account for "object reading" where the object is a relic of a person unknown both to the sitter and to the medium, but where the medium nevertheless gives correct detailed information about the object's former or present owner.

Professor Dodds' reply is in substance that these occurrences are no less puzzling on the spiritistic than on the telepathic hypothesis. Since much of the information obtained in such cases concerns occurrences in which the object itself had no part, the object can hardly be itself a record of it; rather, it must be a means of establishing telepathic rapport between the mind of the sensitive and that of the person who has the information.

And of course the correctness of the information could not be

---

[3]See for example, J. Fahler and R.J. Cadoret, "ESP Card Tests of College Students with and without Hypnosis," *J. Parapsychol.*, Vol. 22, No. 2 (June, 1958), pp. 125-136.

verified unless some person has it, or unless the facts testified to are objective and thus accessible to clairvoyant observation by the sensitive.

(d) To the objection that no correlation is found between the success or failure of a sitting and the conditions respectively favorable or unfavorable to telepathy, Professor Dodds replies that, actually, we know almost nothing as to what these are.

(e) Another objection which has been advanced against the telepathy explanation of the communications is that the quantity and quality of the communications varies with changes of purported communicator, but not of sitter as one would expect if telepathy were what provides the information communicated.

The reply here is, for one thing, that, as we have seen in Sec. 3 of Ch. XVIII, the allegation is not invariably true; but that anyway changes of purported communicator imply corresponding changes as to the minds that are possible telepathic sources of the information communicated.

(f) Again, it is often asserted that the telepathy explanation of the facts is very complicated, whereas the spiritistic explanation is simple. Professor Dodds' reply here is that the sense in which greater simplicity entails greater probability is that in which being "simpler" means "making fewer and narrower unsupported assumptions;" and that the telepathy hypothesis, not the spiritistic, is the one simpler in this alone evidentially relevant sense. For the spiritistic hypothesis postulates telepathy and clairvoyance anyway but ascribes these to "spirits," which are not independently known to exist; whereas the telepathy hypothesis ascribes them to the medium, who is known to exist and for whose occasional exercise of telepathy or clairvoyance some independent evidence exists.

4. **The facts which strain the telepathy-clairvoyance explanation.** In the case of the other objections to the telepathy explanation commented upon by Professor Dodds, his replies are much less convincing than those we have just presented. Indeed, they bring to mind a remark made shortly before by W.H. Salter concerning certain features of the cross-correspondences communications: "It is possible to frame a theory which will explain each of them, more or less, by telepathy, but is it not necessary in doing so to

invent *ad hoc* a species of telepathy for which there is otherwise practically no evidence?"[4]

The essence of these more stubborn objections is the *virtually unlimited range* of the telepathy with which the automatist's or medium's subconscious mind has to be gifted. It must be such as to have access to the minds of any persons who possess the recondite items of information communicated, no matter where those persons happen to be at the time. Furthermore, the telepathy postulated must be assumed somehow capable of *selecting,* out of all the minds to which its immense range gives it access, the particular one or ones that contain the specific bits of information brought into the communications. But this is not all. The immediate understanding of, and apposite response to, allusive remarks in the course of the communicator's conversation with the sitter (or sometimes with another communicator) requires that the above selecting of the person or persons having the information, and the establishing and relinquishing of telepathic rapport with the mind of the appropriate one, be virtually *instantaneous.* And then, of course, the information thus telepathically obtained must, *instantly* again, be put into the form of a dramatic, highly verisimilar impersonation of the deceased purported communicator as he would have acted in animated conversational give-and-take. This particular feature of some of the communications, as we saw, was that on which—as the most convincing—both Hyslop and Hodgson laid great stress, as do Mr. Drayton Thomas and Mr. Salter.

Let us now see how Professor Dodds proposes to meet these difficulties, which strain the telepathy hypothesis, but of which the spiritistic hypothesis would be free.

For one thing, he points to some of Dr. Osty's cases, where "sensitives who do not profess to be assisted by 'spirits' " nevertheless give out information about absent persons as detailed as that given by the supposed spirits.

Obviously, however, there is no more reason to accept as authoritative what a sensitive "professes" or believes as to the paranormal source of her information when she denies that it is spirits than when she asserts it. Mrs. Eileen Garrett, who in addition to being

---

[4]C.S. Bechofer Roberts, "The Truth about Spiritualism," *Journal S.P.R.,* Vol. 27 (1932), p. 331. The remark occurs towards the end of the review.

one of the best known contemporary mediums, is scientifically interested in her own mediumship, freely acknowledges that she does not know, any more than do other persons, whether her controls, Abdul Latif and Uvani, are discarnate spirits, dissociated parts of her own personality, or something else.

Again, Professor Dodds argues that recognition of the personality of a deceased friend by the sitter has but slight evidential value, since there is no way of checking how far the will-to-believe may be responsible for it; but that even if the reproduction is perfect, it is anyway no evidence that the personality concerned has survived after death; for Gordon Davis was still living and yet Mrs. Blanche Cooper, who did not know him, did reproduce the tone of his voice and his peculiar articulation well enough for Dr. Soal to recognize them.

Professor Dodds' reply is predicated on the assumption that, although Dr. Soal was neither expecting nor longing for communication with Gordon Davis, nevertheless the recognition was positive and definite. This should therefore be similarly granted in cases where the person who recognizes the voice or manner of a deceased friend is, similarly, an investigator moved by scientific interest, not a grieving person moved to believe by his longing for reunion with his loved one.

Aside from this, however, the Gordon Davis case shows only that, since he was still living, the process by which the tone of his voice and his peculiar articulation were reproduced by Mrs. Cooper was not "possession" of her organism by his discarnate spirit. Telepathy from Dr. Soal, who believed Davis had died, is enough to account for the vocal peculiarities of the communication, for the memories of boyhood and of the later meeting on the railroad platform, and for the purported communicator's assumption that he had died. But this mere reproduction of voice peculiarities and of two memories, in the single brief conversation of Dr. Soal directly with the purported Gordon Davis, is a radically different thing from the lively conversational intercourse Hyslop and Hodgson refer to, with its immediate and apposite adaptation of mental or emotional attitude to changes in that of the interlocutor, and the making and understanding of apt allusions to intimate matters, back and forth between communicator and sitter. The Gordon

Davis communication is not a case of this at all; and of course the precognitive features of the communication by Nada (Mrs. Blanche Cooper's control) at the second sitting, which referred to the house Gordon Davis eventually occupied, are irrelevant equally to the telepathy and to the spiritualist hypotheses.

Professor Dodds would account for the appositeness of the facts the medium selects, which the particular deceased person concerned would remember and which identify him, by saying that, once the medium's subconscious mind is *en rapport* with that of the telepathic agent, the *selection* of items of information appropriate at a given moment to the demands of the conversation with the sitter can be supposed to take place in the same automatic manner as that in which such selection occurs in a person when the conversation requires it.

The adequacy of this reply is decreased, however, by the assumption it makes that the information given out by the medium is derived from *one* telepathic source, or at least one at a time; whereas in the case of Hyslop's communications purportedly from his father, the items of information supplied were apparently not all contained in any one person's memory, but scattered among several. Hence, if the medium's subconscious mind was *en rapport* at the same time with those of different persons, the task of selecting instantly which one of them to draw from would remain, and would be very different from the normal automatic selection within *one* mind, of items relevant at a given moment in a conversation.

But anyway the degree of telepathic rapport which Professor Dodds' reply postulates vastly exceeds any that is independently known to occur; for it would involve the medium's having for the time being all the memories and associations of ideas of the person who is the telepathic source; and this would amount to the medium's virtually borrowing that person's mind for the duration of the conversation; and notwithstanding this, responding in the conversation not as that person himself would respond, but as the ostensible communicator—constructed by the medium out of that person's memories of him—would respond.

Concerning the cross-correspondences, Professor Dodds admits that they manifest pattern, but he is not satisfied that they are the result of design. Even if they were designed, however, he agrees with the suggestion others had made that Mrs. Verrall's subconscious mind, which had all the knowledge of the Greek and Latin classics required, could well be supposed to have designed the scheme, rather than the deceased Myers and his associates; for, he asserts, "more difficult intellectual feats than the construction of these puzzles have before now been performed subconsciously." H.F. Saltmarsh, however, suggests "that it may be unreasonable to attribute to the same level of consciousness intellectual powers of a very high order and a rather stupid spirit of trickery and deception."[5]

But in any case, more than the construction of the puzzles would be involved; namely, in addition, *telepathic virtual dictation* of the appropriate script to the other automatist—whose very existence was, in the case of Mrs. Holland in India, quite unknown at the time to Mrs. Verrall in England. To ascribe the script to "telepathic leakage" will hardly do, for, as Lord Balfour remarked concerning such a proposal made by Miss F.M. Stawell in the Ear of Dionysius case, "it is not at all clear how 'telepathic leakage' could be so thoughtful as to arrange all the topics in such an ingenious way. It seems a little like 'explaining' the working of a motor car by saying that it goes because petrol leaks out of a tank into its front end!"[6]

5. **What would prove, or make positively probable, that survival is a fact.** The difficult task of deciding where the various kinds of facts now before us, the rival interpretations of them, and the criticisms of the interpretations, finally leave the case for the reality of survival requires that we first attempt to specify what evidence, if we should have it, we would accept as definitely proving survival or, short of this, as definitely establishing a positive probability that survival is a fact.

To this end, let us suppose that a friend of ours, John Doe, was a passenger on the transatlantic plane which some months ago the newspapers reported crashed shortly after leaving Shannon without having radioed that it was in trouble. Since no survivors were reported to have been found, we would naturally assume that John Doe had died with the rest.

---

[5]H.F. Saltmarsh, *op. cit.,* p. 138.
[6]*Proc. S.P.R.,* Vol. XXIX, p. 270.

Let us now, however, consider in turn each of three further suppositions.

(I) The first is that some time later we meet on the street a man we recognize as John Doe, who recognizes us too, and who has John Doe's voice and mannerisms. Also, that allusions to personal matters that were familar to both of us, made now in our conversation with him, are readily understood and suitably responded to by each. Then, even before he tells us how he chanced to survive the crash, we would of course *know* that, somehow, he has survived it.

(II) But now let us suppose instead that we do not thus meet him, but that one day our telephone rings, and over the line comes a voice which we clearly recognize as John Doe's; and that we also recognize certain turns of phrase that were peculiar to him. He tells us that he survived the disaster, and we then talk with ready mutual understanding about personal and other matters that had been familiar to the two of us. We wish, of course, that we could see him as well as thus talk with him; yet we would feel practically certain that he had survived the crash of the plane and is now living.

(III) Let us, however, now consider instead a third supposition, namely, that one day, when our telephone rings, a voice not John Doe's tells us that he did survive the accident and that he wants us to know it, but that for some reason he cannot come to the phone. He is, however, in need of money and wants us to deposit some to his account in the bank.

Then of course—especially since the person who transmits the request over the telephone sounds at times a bit incoherent—we would want to make very sure that the person from whom the request ultimately emanates is really John Doe. To this end, we ask him through the intermediary to name some mutual friends; and he names several, giving some particular facts about each. We refer, allusively, to various personal matters he would be familiar with; and it turns out that he understands the allusions and responds to them appropriately. Also, the intermediary quotes him as uttering various statements, in which we recognize peculiarities of his thought and phraseology; and the peculiar nasal tone of his voice is imitated by the intermediary well enough for us to recognize it.

Would all this convince us that the request for money really emanates from John Doe and therefore that he did survive the accident and is still living? If we should react rationally rather than impulsively, our getting convinced or remaining unconvinced would depend on the following considerations.

First, *is it possible at all* that our friend somehow did survive the crash? If, for example, his dead body had been subsequently found and identified beyond question, then obviously the person whose request for money is being transmitted to us *could not possibly be* John Doe not yet deceased; and hence the identifying evidence conveyed to us over the phone would necessarily be worthless, no matter how strongly it would otherwise testify to his being still alive.

But if we have no such antecedent conclusive proof that he did perish, then the degree of our confidence that the telephoned request ultimately does emanate from him, and hence that he is still living, will depend for us on the following three factors.

(a) One will be the *abundance,* or *scantiness,* of such evidence of his identity as comes to us over the phone.

(b) A second factor will be the *quality* of the evidence. That is, does it correspond *minutely* and in *peculiar* details to what we know of the facts or incidents to which it refers; or on the contrary does it correspond to them merely in that it gives, correctly indeed, the *broad features* of the events concerned, but *does not include much detail?*

(c) The third factor will be that of *diversity of the kinds of evidence* the telephone messages supply. Does all the evidence, for example, consist *only of correct memories* of personal matters and of matters typical of John Doe's range of information? Or does the evidence include also *dramatic faithfulness* of the communications to the manner, the attitudes, the tacit assumptions, and the idiosyncracies of John Doe as we remember him? And again, do the communications manifest in addition something which H.F. Saltmarsh has held to be "as clear an indication of psychical individuality as finger prints are of physical,"[7] namely *associations of ideas that were peculiar to John Doe* as of the age he had reached at the time of the crash?

If these same associations are still manifest, then persistence of them will signify one thing if the communication in which they appear is made not too long after the accident, but a different thing if instead it is made, say, twenty-five years after. For a person's associations of ideas alter more or less as a result of new experiences, of changes of environment, of acquisition of new ranges of information, and of development of new interests. Hence, if the associations of ideas are the same a few months or a year or two after the crash as they were before, this *would* testify to John Doe's identity. But if they are the same a quarter of a century later, then this would testify rather that although some of the capacities he had have apparently persisted, yet he has in the meantime *not continued really to live;* for to live in the full sense of the word entails becoming gradually different—indeed, markedly different in many ways over such a long term of years.

Now, the point of our introducing the hypothetical case of John Doe, and of the three suppositions we made in succession as to occurrences that convinced us, or that inclined us in various degrees to believe, that he had not after all died in the plane accident is that the second and especially the third of those suppositions duplicate in all essentials the evidences of survival of the human mind which the best of the mediumistic communications supply. For the medium or automatist is the analogue of the telephone and, in cases of apparent possession of the medium's organism by the purported communicator, the latter is the analogue of John Doe when himself telephoning. The medium's "control," on the other hand, is the analogue of the intermediary who at other times transmits John Doe's statements over the telephone. And the fact recalled in the second section of this chapter—that survival has not been proved to be either empirically or logically impossible— is the analogue of the supposition that John Doe's body was never found and hence that his having survived the crash is not known to be impossible.

This parallelism between the two situations entails that if reason rather than either religious or materialistic faith is to decide, then our answer to the question whether the evidence we have does or does not establish survival (or at least a positive probability of it)

---

[7]*Evidence of Personal Survival from Cross Correspondences,* London, G. Bell & Sons (1938), p. 34.

must, in the matter of survival after death, be based on the very
same considerations as in the matter of survival after the crash of
the plane. That is, our answer will have to be based similarly on
the *quantity* of evidence we get over the mediumistic "telephone;"
on the *quality* of that evidence; and on the *diversity* of kinds of it
we get.

6. **The conclusion about survival which at present appears
warranted.** To what conclusion, then, do these three considerations
point when brought to bear on the evidence referred to in Chapters
XVII and XVIII?

The conclusion they dictate is, I believe, the same as that which
at the end of Chapter XVIII we cited as finally reached by Mrs.
Sidgwick and by Lord Balfour — a conclusion which also was
reached in time by Sir Oliver Lodge, by Professor Hyslop, by
Dr. Hodgson, and by a number of other persons who like them
were thoroughly familiar with the evidence on record; who were
gifted with keenly critical minds; who had originally been skeptical
of the reality or even possibility of survival; and who were also
fully acquainted with the evidence for the reality of telepathy and
of clairvoyance, and with the claims that had been made for the
telepathy-clairvoyance interpretation of the evidence, as against
the survival interpretation of it.

Their conclusion was essentially that the balance of the evidence so far obtained is on the side of the reality of survival and,
in the best cases, of survival not merely of memories of the life
on earth, but of the most significant capacities of the human mind,
and of continuing exercise of these.

CHAPTER 21

SURVIVAL, REINCARNATION, AND THE PROBLEM OF PERSONAL IDENTITY*

G. C. NAYAK

THE DOCTRINE OF *Karma* pervades almost the entire realm of Indian Philosophy as one of its most important and influential doctrines. It involves the notion of an individual surviving death and being reincarnated after a temporary stay as a disembodied spirit. Moral values on this view are not destroyed with the destruction of the body but are conserved and give rise to consequences in the forms of happiness and misery in future lives. The happiness and misery of our present life also are viewed as rewards and punishment for our past conduct. In this way the responsibility is laid on our own shoulders, and perfect justice is shown as being meted out to every individual.

It seems to have been assumed all along in Indian Philosophy that the notion of survival and rebirth at least makes sense and is not altogether unintelligible. To a number of contemporary philosophers, however, such a notion makes no sense at all. How, it is asked, can one talk intelligibly of his continuing to exist in future after his death? My mother is dead, but still I believe that she exists in a disembodied state. But if *she* is dead, what sense can it make to say that *she* still survives? Does it not involve self-contradiction? If it is replied that the body of the person in question has been destroyed, not the person herself, then what, it may be asked, may possibly serve as the criterion of personal identity when bodily identity is no longer available? Similar problems seem to arise in

*Reprinted from *Journal of the Philosophical Association,* 1968, by permission of the Indian Philosophical Association.

the case of the belief in reincarnation. What sense can be attached to the statement that John has been reborn as Jones? How can we possibly distinguish between rebirth on the one hand, and the death of an individual followed by the birth of another individual on the other? The theory of transmigration or metempsychosis, it is alleged, "secures a continuity of environment that satisfies the imagination of survivors, but at the sacrifice more or less complete of that personal continuity which we must regard as essential."[1] Here again the problem is to specify a criterion of personal identity in the absence of bodily continuity. Retributive justice cannot make sense unless the sinner and the sufferer are numerically identical, unless the person who reaps the fruit is numerically the same as the person who sowed the seeds. A sinner dies in prosperity and another person, it seems, is born blind afterwards and suffers. What does it mean to say that perhaps they are really identical?

The point on which a lot of things seem to turn is whether bodily continuity is a necessary and sufficient criterion of personal identity. That this is so is the contention of a number of contemporary philosophers, and it is natural for them to think that to talk of someone's survival or reincarnation after the destruction of his body should be nonsensical. According to Ayer, for example, personal identity is to be defined "in terms of bodily identity, and bodily identity is to be defined in terms of the resemblance and continuity of sense-contents."[2] Although Ayer has subsequently modified his earlier view by admitting further criteria of memory and continuity of character, he still considers bodily identity to be at least a necessary and primary criterion upon which the subsidiary criteria of memory and continuity of character depend. In *The Concept of a Person and Other Essays,* for example, Ayer contends that "personal identity depends upon the identity of the body, and that a person's ownership of states of consciousness consists in their standing in a special causal relation to the body by which he is identified."[3] "Even if the subsidiary criteria of personal identity

[1] J. Ward, *The Realm of Ends or Pluralism and Theism* (Cambridge University Press, 1911), p. 401.

[2] A.J. Ayer, *Language, Truth and Logic,* second ed. (London, 1946), p. 127.

[3] A.J. Ayer, *The Concept of a Person and Other Essays* (London, 1963), p. 116.

[4] *Ibid.,* p. 128.

could in 'certain' strange cases be allowed to override the primary physical criterion, they are still," according to him, "parasitical upon it."[4] A similar approach to the problem is evident in B.A.O. Williams' claim that "the omission of the body takes away all content from the idea of personal *identity*."[5]

Is bodily identity a sufficient criterion of personal identity? I think not. Let us imagine the following case. I go to meet my English friend, John, and recognize him to be the same person whom I met yesterday. But to my utter astonishment, my friend begins to display the characteristics of my deceased father, and seems to remember doing everything that my father did. He claims that he was born in a particular village where my father was born, and narrates the life-history of my father as if it was his own. On the other hand, he seems to remember nothing of his English parents, home and friends, and rather feels bewildered to find himself in what he thinks to be strange surroundings. He talks in the Indian language in which my father used to talk, and which he could not possibly have learnt through normal means. Now if this queer state of affairs continues to persist, what shall I say? Shall I say that he is the same English friend of mine? It seems not, for although his body continues to be that of my friend, his character, memory and behavior are altogether different. Whether or not I accept the possible explanation that my friend's body is at present controlled by the spirit of my deceased father, it should at least be evident to me that it is not the same person, not my friend, wih whom I am dealing at present. Supposing that my friend committtd some wrong before the occurrence of this incident, shall we be justified in punishing the person with whom we are confronted at present on that account? I think not, for it seems unlikely that the person with whom we are confronted in the present circumstances should be thought to be the same person as John. Here we seem to have a case, albeit imaginary, where psychological criteria are likely to be allowed by us to override the physiological criterion of personal identity. Bodily identity in that case cannot, I submit, be regarded as a sufficient criterion of personal identity.

---

[5]B.A.O. Williams, "Personal Identity and Individuation," *Proceedings of the Aristotelian Society*, New Series, Vol. LVII (1956-1957), p. 241.

But is it a necessary criterion? That it is not even necessary should be evident from the following imaginary example. Supposing that John vanishes into the air without a trace before my very eyes, as if by magic, and after some time reappears before me, shall we call him an exactly similar but not the same person, only because there is lack of spatio-temporal continuity and consequently of bodily identity? I think not. Will John himself appreciate my taking this course or even understand why I behave like this? The person who returns after the interval behaves exactly as my friend John used to behave, he seems to remember doing everything that John did, he seems to know those very facts about me that John knew, and his body is exactly as my friend's used to be. Now are these not sufficient to let me speak of him as being identical with John? I felt sorry when I saw John vanish without a trace, and this surely should be the occasion for me to rejoice at his return. It is not that I have got somebody exactly like him before me after the interval, for this is not how we are likely to assess an event like this if it occurred. Everyone, it seems, will under such circumstances be inclined to say that John had vanished miraculously, but has come back unharmed. Here at least is a case, again imaginary of course, where it seems that we shall be inclined to base our judgment of personal identity only on memory, or continuity of character, not on bodily identity. What if the person reappearing is not at all like John in his physical appearance? Shall we be inclined to accept him as the same person if he displays a continuity of character and an ostensibly veridical memory of John's past? No doubt it would be much more difficult for us to get used to the idea that the person in question is John; we may find ourselves completely bewildered for a while; but if the person in question (let us call him J_1) continues to display the psychological characteristics of John without fail, we shall, it seems, be ultimately persuaded to accept him as the same person, though with a different body. We may say that John is back in a different body. Now this example is significant in pointing out that neither bodily identity nor similarity is necessary for personal identity in as much as it is not inconceivable that we may identify persons on the basis of veridical memory and continuity of character only.

But the above example may be made more complicated by

imagining the possibility of the disappearance of John being followed by the simultaneous appearance of two persons, J_1 and J_2, displaying the psychological characteristics of John in an exactly similar manner. John vanishes at time t_1, and at time t_2 both J_1 and J_2 appear and claim to remember doing everything that John did and display the characteristics peculiar to John. What shall we say under such circumstances? We cannot say that John has returned to us in two different bodies, nor is there any criterion available to us by means of which we may decide that one of the persons appearing before us is identical with John and the other is not. It is certain that we should not know at first what to say, for the phenomenon in question is unusually bewildering. But if the phenomenon persists, then we shall have to adopt some linguistic convention which may appear convenient under the circumstances. We may perhaps find it convenient to say that J_1 and J_2 are exactly similar to John but that neither of them is numerically identical with him. Under the present circumstances, personal identity cannot, it seems, be based on memory and continuity of character — alone.

Does the above example invalidate our claim that in certain cases, at least, memory (and continuity of character) may be sufficient without bodily identity for the purpose of personal identity? I think not. For it seems that there are very good reasons to think that memory and continuity of character would suffice to identify a person without bodily identity in cases like the less complicated one where the disappearance of a person is followed by the appearance of a *single* individual claiming to remember doing the past acts of the person who has disappeared. I do not think that we can be *logically* coerced to admit that if we cannot speak of numerical identity in terms of memory alone in one case, then we cannot speak of identity in terms of memory in some other case. The two imaginary cases mentioned above are different at least to the extent that whereas the disappearance of John is followed in one case by a reduplication of his personality, there occurs no such reduplication in the other. It is no wonder, then, that this important difference between the two cases should make our approach to them regarding personal identity quite different too. And if we can point to a single case, imaginary or otherwise, where we are likely to talk

of identity in terms of memory (or continuity of character) alone
in the absence of bodily continuity, then there should be no reason
why we may not speak of identity in cases of reincarnation and
disembodied existence after the destruction of the body. But how,
it may be asked, does the construction of an imaginary case as
mentioned above help us at all? May it not be contended that in
ordinary circumstances we usually depend on bodily continuity as
the criterion of personal identity and that in extraordinary circumstances as stated above we just don't know what to say? And as
we don't know what to say in those extraordinary circumstances,
so also we don't know what to say in cases of disembodied existence
and reincarnation where memory alone may serve as the possible
criterion of personal identity. It is a matter of forming new rules
and of making new decisions, if and when such circumstances do
in fact arise. Now I am inclined to agree with the above contention
on the whole, but I think that certain further points should be
made in this connection. Although the above contention of the
opponent may be valid, this should not be taken to have provided
him with any *a priori* ground for claiming that personal identity
just cannot make any sense without bodily identity in cases of
disembodied survival and reincarnation, for what is contended by
him is not that personal identity makes no sense without bodily
identity but that we do not know what to say in such cases. There
is a further point to be noted in this connection. We are, it is urged,
to take decisions and to make new rules if and when such occasions
do in fact arise. But even if this may be true, can we not possibly
imagine what decisions we are likely to take if such occasions arise?
If we can imagine these decisions, and if some of the decisions
imagined happen to be favorable to making memory without bodily identity the criterion of personal identity, then may we not feel
justified in asserting that bodily identity is not a necessary criterion
after all? The imaginary case constructed by us serves us well in
being less complicated than the cases of disembodied existence and
reincarnation and in making us visualize the circumstances in
which we are very likely to admit personal identity on the basis of
memory. Once it becomes clear to us that there may be circumstances when we are very unlikely to feel awkward in basing our
judgment of identity on memory alone, the case for doing the same

in connection with reincarnation and disembodied existence may not appear so preposterous after all. And this is why I think that the imaginary case constructed by me is not altogether pointless.

I must next consider the criteria which we may possibly adopt for the identification of the *same* person in cases of survival and rebirth. In the case of survival, the disembodied mind in question may be regarded as the *same* individual if (i) there is veridical memory of many of his past events and if there is capacity under certain circumstances to recollect those he is not actually recollecting at present, and also if (ii) the dispositions and character of the disembodied mind are continuous with those of the embodied one. The point concerning the continuity of dispositions and character is no doubt an important one, for if the disembodied life is altogether discontinuous with the embodied one, there could be a strong inclination to say that the disembodied mind in question is not the same as the embodied one. But it should be noted at the same time that if the memory-claims in the disembodied state should turn out to be veridical, then some degree of discontinuity may easily be allowed. The most important of all, therefore, seems to be memory, both in its dispositional as well as its occurrent sense. Let us imagine the following. In the disembodied state just after my death, i.e. the destruction of my body, I become immediately aware of a continuity of character and dispositions. This by itself should make me feel fairly certain that *I* have survived death. I look at my body lying there, and *recognize* my relatives standing beside my body although I am unable to communicate with them. Moreover, I *recollect* how much I used to love my body, how much I used to care for it, and I now feel sorry, perhaps, to see that it is going to be buried or burnt. I also *recollect* that I had made some provisions for my family before my death, and am glad to see that my family has benefited from it. Now these and similar experiences after death should give me the conviction that *I* have survived death, that I who was so and so—a teacher of philosophy, a father of three children and so on—am now experiencing such and such things after the destruction of my body. And this I am able to ascertain through the continuity of character and dispositions to an extent, but primarily through my memory. Memory may not explain or produce self-identity, but it at least discovers it.

Even my knowledge that my present character and dispositions are continuous with my past character and dispositions is dependent on my memory. Memory, therefore, seems to be the most important and the primary criterion for the discovery of self-identity.

But how can we conceive of an independent check of the memory-claim in the disembodied state? And if we cannot conceive of any such check, how can we avoid the possibility of being misled by delusive memory? It seems to me, however, that some such check is not impossible in the disembodied state. First of all, one's memory about certain things may be checked by the same person's memory about certain other things. This is not an independent check, of course, but it may not be entirely useless. If two of my memories conflict with each other, it may lead me to investigate which one of these two is veridical and which one is not. Then I may perhaps seek the help of observation; as for example, I may remember that in my embodied state I kept some valuable treasure hidden at a particular place, and I may verify this memory-claim by visiting the place in question. I don't think that there is anything intrinsically impossible about engaging oneself in some such verification-procedure in the disembodied state, and I don't think that I should be very unreasonable if I became convinced through some such verification. Moreover, if it is conceivable that the soul in the disembodied state may not be altogether solitary but may, on the contrary, be causally related to other souls, I fail to see why something like a 'public' check of one's memory-claim should be impossible in the disembodied state. One's memory may be checked through others' memory and observation. The public check and verification in the disembodied state would no doubt be very much different from what we usually understand them to be. The public as we know it consists of embodied individuals whereas the public in the disembodied state would be constituted of disembodied souls only. In the embodied state, moreover, perception is dependent on and is conducted through sense-organs, whereas in the disembodied state it has to be conducted without sense-organs. It is possible that each and every disembodied soul may be deluded both as regards his memory as well as perception, and yet he may have an elaborate system of checking the memories against each other and against perception. If this be a fact, then it is hard to see what independent means of detecting the mass-hallucination in the dis-embodied state may possibly be adopted. I must admit therefore that the verification of a memory-claim in the disembodied state through the memories and perceptions of other souls cannot have any logical certainty. Still, it seems that a disembodied mind may have some sort of practical certainty regarding his past life and personal continuity both through his memory, which has been checked by his own perception and further memories, and through the perceptions and the memories of other members of the community.

When we come to the question of the determination of personal identity in the case of reincarnation, we find that here also we have to fall back upon memory both in its occurrent and dispositional sense. Here again the question of the discrimination between the veridical and delusive memory seems to be of paramount impor-tance, and here once more the possibility of having the public check comes to our rescue. But before discussing the nature of the certainty, if any, which we may have through such checks, it may not be altogether worthless to point out that there are, it seems, good reasons for believing the memory claims that are made with sincerity and conviction to be more often veridical than not. And I fail to see why this should not be true also of those few memory-claims of earlier lives that are made with sincerity and conviction. I do not, of course, mean to say that instances of sincere and confi-dent and yet delusive memory-claims actually do not occur, for such instances can easily be cited, but what I want to say is that the memory-claims, if made with sincerity and conviction, are generally true.

But in any case, I must admit, we cannot get rid of the necessity of checking the ostensible memories of past lives. No such check, however, can give us logical certainty, even if we may at least be practically certain that the person in question is really a reincarna-tion of some other person of the past. The crucial points to be noted here are the following: (i) The person concerned should be able to give us some important information about the dead person whose reincarnation he is supposed to be. (ii) He must not have obtained this information through the normal sources. (iii) He also must not have obtained them through paranormal powers like retrocognitive clairvoyance. Now it is indeed almost impossible to distinguish between veridical memory and retrocognitive clairvoyance. It is to be noted, therefore, that even if the memory-claim is verified to be true in respect of the objective facts, this is no logical proof that the person in question is really identical with the person whose life-history he seems to remember correctly. For it may be that the person in question has got this information not through memory but through retrocognitive clairvoyance. Memory-claims, therefore, even if verified to be true in respect of the objective facts, cannot establish the personal identity of the person in question beyond doubt, i.e. cannot establish beyond doubt that the person in question is really a reincarnation of the dead person whose life-history he seems to remember correctly. But at the same time we must take into consideration the following points. It is desirable that we should eschew the irrational tendency of trying, regardless of implausibilities, to explain all the alleged cases of memories of past lives in terms of retrocognitive clairvoyance. We must not forget that the explanation in terms of paranormal retrocognition "requires us to postulate" in certain cases "a capacity for retrocognitive clairvoyance far exceeding in scope any for the reality of which experimental evidence exists."[6] Moreover, we must make it a point that any inveterate aversion that we may have against the reincarnation hypothesis, because our religion, perhaps, prohibits us to believe in some such theory, or because of some such sentimental reasons, should not be allowed to goad us to reject the reincarnation-interpretation quite regardless of its being in some cases the least implausible interpretation of all. That such irrational tendencies have gained supremacy in the interpretation of certain cases cannot be denied.[7] Secondly, we must not forget that if it is not possible for us to have logical certainty in the case of reincarnation, it is also not possible to have it in the case of the disembodied existence of the soul. We may very well interpret that the disembodied soul is merely having a paranormal retrocognition of the past. Not only that, even in the imaginary case constructed by us in the beginning of this chapter where the disappearance of John is followed by the appearance of J_1 claiming to remember

---

[6]C.J. Ducasse, *The Belief in a Life after Death* (U.S.A., 1961), p. 243.
[7]Cf. *Ibid.*, Chapter XXV, "The Case of 'The Search for Bridey Murphy'."

doing what John alone did, we may say that J_1 has a retrocognitive clairvoyance of what John did. But if we go on explaining most of the ostensible memories as cases of paranormal retrocognition whenever we feel inclined to do so, no matter how far-fetched the explanation may appear to be, then we shall be going too far towards irrationalism. It is no doubt true that we have no established linguistic convention regarding the veridical ostensible memory-claims of past lives, and that therefore it is a matter for decision whether the person making these memory-claims should be regarded as being numerically identical with another person of the past or not. But I should think of this lack of convention as being due more to the scarcity of such phenomena, i.e. phenomena of veridical ostensible memory-claims concerning past lives, rather than to any absurdity inherent in adopting such memory-claims as the criterion for the determination of the numerical identity of a living person with another person of the past. We may therefore adopt such memory-claims as the criterion for determining personal identity in the case of reincarnation, and say that a person is numerically identical with another person of the past if the following conditions are fulfilled:

(1) The person in question claims to remember doing what the dead person did and participating in the events that happened to the dead man.

(2) These memory-claims are veridical, i.e. they correspond to known facts.

(3) The ostensible memories are genuine memories, i.e. the person in question is known to have had no opportunity to acquire this information through some other source.

If the above conditions are fulfilled, we shall call the person in question a reincarnation of the dead person whose life-history he claims to remember as being his own.

In case of one who, on the other hand, does not actually recollect any such past life, the assertion that he is the same person as some dead individual can be based only on the supposition that under certain appropriate circumstances he is capable of actually remembering his past history which includes the history of the dead individual. Personal identity under such circumstances is based on memory in its dispositional sense alone. But here the most perplexing problem is the clarification of the meanings of 'capable' and 'appropriate circumstances.' What would the 'appropriate circumstances' be like so as to enable me to recollect my past life? What are we to mean by 'capacity to remember'? If under normal circumstances one does not seem to have such capacity, shall we or shall we not say that he is devoid of this capacity? Under what circumstances shall we be prepared to abandon our claim that everyone has got the capacity to recollect his past lives? If we are not prepared to give it up under any circumstance whatsoever, then our claim, it may be urged, must be vacuous. Now I must admit that this is a serious problem. But I can only point out that the claim concerning the capacity for remembering the life-history under appropriate circumstances need not be falsifiable, for an unfalsifiable statement is not necessarily vacuous or meaningless. I do not think that I am committed to set a limit at a point in time to the capacity of a human mind to remember its past life. The notion of personal identity in the case of those who do not actually remember their past is on my view based on the idea that such persons could remember the incidents of their past life under certain appropriate circumstances which may arise in the disembodied state, or after the journey towards perfection has reached its culmination, or on both these occasions. If the soul or mind, as is supposed on the present view, is mostly capable of remembering the incidents of its past lives only under certain suitable circumstances as mentioned above, it is no wonder that it does not remember the past under unsuitable circumstances during its earthly sojourn. The soul may also be supposed to recollect its past sometimes through the hypnotic trance or the *yogic* exercises, but to fix any such limit to the soul's capacity to remember the past by specifying a condition like *yoga* or hypnosis seems to me to be both arbitrary as well as unnecessary. It should, I think, be sufficient for my purpose if I am able to specify certain *possible* circumstances under which the soul may be supposed to actually recollect its past history, and in view of my ability to specify such conditions I do not think that my statement concerning the capacity of the soul to remember its past under appropriate circumstances should be condemned as vacuous. The soul may be able to remember its past life either through *yoga* or through hypnotic trance, or during the internatal stage, or at the end of its journey to the state of perfection. The actual occurrence of memory may vary from one individual to another, so that if one may be able to remember his past life through hypnotic trance another may not. But at the same time it is possible that *all* souls do actually remember their past lives in their disembodied state during the internatal period of existence. In any case, the assertion that John is a reincarnation is intelligible on the supposition that, although he has not as yet done so, he could, in some circumstances or the other, recollect as his own the history of some other past individual.

CHAPTER 22

SURVIVAL AND DISEMBODIED EXISTENCE*

TERENCE PENELHUM

THE AREA OF RELIGIOUS BELIEFS is full of doctrines to which multitudes seem able to attach sense, but which philosophers are apt to say are unintelligible. The belief in survival is one of the most notorious.

There are two main areas of difficulty which philosophers have concentrated upon. In the first place, they have wondered whether the sort of existence envisaged after death can be intelligibly described: whether, that is to say, a sufficient number of the predicates that we would feel it necessary to ascribe to a being before it could be called a person at all can in fact be ascribed to a being that no longer has a body, or who has a resurrected body. In the second place, they have wondered whether the sort of being whose existence is predicated, even if properly called a person, can be identified with any particular pre-mortem person. If the post-mortem person is not identifiable with Jones, then its future existence is merely an interesting natural or (supernatural) fact, but not of personal moment to Jones or Jones's relatives and friends. In predicting the future existence of such a being after his own death, Jones is not predicting *his own* future existence. And only if he can predict his own future existence can he be entitled to *anticipate* it, either with pleasure or with fear.

These two problems cannot be wholly separated. In particular it is not possible to enquire into the possibility of ascribing predicates to a post-mortem being without at some stage raising the issue

*Reprinted from Terence Penelhum, *Survival and Disembodied Existence.* London, Routledge & Kegan Paul, Ltd., and New York, Humanities Press, Inc., pp. 10-15, 35-36, 43-44, 54-77, 103-105. Reprinted by permission of the publishers.

of the criteria of identity of the post-mortem being through time in the post-mortem state—an issue which would clearly bear upon the possibility of such a being being identical with a pre-mortem person. For predicates are ascribed to subjects, and the self-identity of the subject is a precondition of applying to it any predicates whose ascription implies some lapse of time. But in order to avoid ignoring, or exaggerating, one set of logical difficulties because of its connection with another, I shall impose an admittedly artificial division on the discussion that follows. I shall begin by discussing the question of what predicates can be properly ascribed to post-mortem beings, without questioning whether the qualities and activities attributed to them can really be said to belong to a continuing identical subject. This will make it possible to consider what kind of life and activity we are equipped to consider post-mortem beings to enjoy, as distinct from the kind of life and activity sometimes thought to be available to them. I shall then turn to the question that has been put aside previously, and examine the problem of the identity of post-mortem beings, both with regard to their persistence as individuals through time in the post-mortem state, and with regard to the possibility of regarding them as identical with pre-mortem beings like ourselves.

It is obviously necessary, while discussing the identity of post-mortem and pre-mortem persons, to lean on recent arguments of a more general kind concerning the criteria of personal identity. While I shall make use of these only in so far as our central theme requires this, the fact that it has always been a matter of philo-sophical controversy what the criteria of pre-mortem personal identity are shows that it will be impossible to consider the possibility of post-mortem persons being identical with former pre-mortem ones without taking sides in this controversy. There have been two main competing views. One is that the criterion for the re-identification of a person through time is the identity of the body which he has, i.e. that it is a necessary or a sufficient condition of saying that a person now before us is Jones that the body of this person is the body that Jones had. The other is that the criterion for the re-identification of a person through time is the set of memories he has, i.e. that it is a necessary or a sufficient condition of saying that the person now before us is Jones that he should have memories of doing actions that Jones did or of thinking thoughts that Jones thought, or of undergoing experiences that Jones underwent. The literature of personal identity is very largely concerned with how far if at all each of these standards is indeed necessary or sufficient, and how they are related to each other. Clearly the doctrine of disembodied survival depends on the view that the bodily criterion of identity is not fundamental, or is at least expendable. If the identity of a person is necessarily connected with the persistence of his body through time, then it is logically impossible for a person to survive the death of his body. If, on the other hand, there is no such necessary connection, it is at least logically possible that death is not the end of a person but merely one very major event in his history. Further, if the necessary connection is not between bodily identity and personal identity but between personal identity and memory, then it might be that a disembodied person might be said to be the same as some pre-mortem person because he might remember events and actions in his previous existence.

There seems no decisive reason to insist that a disembodied person could not perceive our world, or, with the aid of inherited true beliefs about its nature, make some correct judgments about it, and be able to understand and sometimes correctly use, the fundamental distinction between how it seems and how it is. Failing the addition of special powers of control over his perceptions, however, he would not be able to attain to adequate assurance on how things actually were to anything like the extent to which an embodied person can. This would not prevent his having beliefs about what was taking place in the world, or feeling emotions or attitudes to it. Emotions and attitudes usually have objects, of course; but this requirement can be supplied in this case through the disembodied person's awareness of the things and persons of which he is still conscious.

His emotions and attitudes would run the risk of being ill-founded to the extent to which his information about the world is inadequate. Furthermore, their *expression* would be circumscribed. Although the disembodied person could imagine the object of his fear to be absent, as we all do in wishful moments, he could not run from it; though perhaps the above discussion might permit us to give some intelligible account of his *moving away* from it. (But then, what would he have to fear from it?) Although he could easily enough imagine with glee that some calamity was overtaking the object of his anger, he would not be able to strike the blow himself as you or I could. This kind of possibility, however, depends on the possibility of disembodied agency.

Just as, with many provisos, it does not seem impossible to suggest that a disembodied person could perceive the world, I have not uncovered any reasons for saying that such a person could not act in it. Our reluctance to say that it could is probably due to the fact, which I would claim to have shown, that there is something necessarily occult or magical about the idea of such disembodied agency. This conclusion is hardly surprising, but it might serve at least to give our common-sense suspicions some logical, rather than aesthetic, grounds. We can comfort ourselves with the fact that one would never *have* to say that an object moved because a spirit moved it; we could always rest on saying, if ordinary explanations failed us, that some embodied person present had psychokinetic powers—perhaps unconscious ones. This person might, of course, be the medium. But the most this shows is that we can comfortingly relegate the spirit-stories once again to the realm of fantasy. It does not show that they are unintelligible. To show this much more is needed. One possible way of doing it is to resort once again to arguments deriving from considerations about self-identity. For to talk about spirits having temporary embodiments or exercising causal powers assumes that we can think of them as persisting as single non-physical entities through time, entities that can perhaps pass out of one body into another. But on this, for the present, I have elected a self-denying ordinance. It is enough to show that any demonstration of the absurdity of the notion of disembodied agency must come, indeed, from that more general source.

We have spoken of the disembodied person performing actions and having experiences. Most of these last through short or long stretches of time. To be entitled to speak in this way we have to be able to make intelligible to ourselves the continued existence of such a disembodied being through time. We have also spoken of this disembodied being inheriting certain abilities from his pre-mortem state. To be entitled to speak of this we have to be able to make intelligible to ourselves the identity of this person with some previous embodied person. So we need some way of understanding the identity of the disembodied being through various post-mortem stages, and some way of understanding the statement that some such being is identical with one particular pre-mortem being rather than with another. We shall not be able to understand either unless we can also understand the notion of the numerical difference between one such disembodied being and another one.

A natural and tempting line of argument is the following. We obviously cannot say that Smith (disembodied) at the time T_1 and Smith (disembodied) at time T_2 are identical because of their possession of the same body, or of any physical characteristics. But it is easy to say what would make them one and the same disembodied person. It would be the fact that Smith at T_2 has memories that reach back to, and encompass, the experiences of Smith at T_1. And what makes Smith at T_2 identical with Smith at T_1 rather than with Jones at T_1 is that Smith at T_2 has memories that encompass the experiences of Smith at T_1 but not those of Jones at T_1. Further, what makes Smith at T_1 and Smith at T_2 identical with pre-mortem Smith, is the same: the memories the post-mortem Smith has encompass the doings and experiences of the pre-mortem Smith and not those of the pre-mortem Jones.

This line of argument itself invites an equally natural and tempting counter-argument. Memories are, notoriously, fallible. It is clearly not plausible to say that Smith's memories of some past event show that event to have been part of his life-history. On the contrary, we can only plausibly allege that his memory beliefs show this if we know that he has a *good* memory, not a bad one. We have to know that his memories are *real*, not merely apparent. The word 'remember' is ambiguous, and has a strong and a weak sense. In the strong sense to say that someone remembers p is to commit oneself to the truth of p, and to say that he remembers doing a or experiencing e is to say that he indeed did do a or experience e. In the weak sense, to say that someone remembers is to say merely that he claims, or believes himself, to remember in the strong sense. Someone can, then, in the weak sense, remember without its being true that p exists or that he did a, or that he experienced *e*. In the weak sense one can *mis*-remember, in the strong sense only *fail* to remember, which one can do in one way by thinking that one remembers when one does not. The talk of 'memories' in the previous account of disembodied identity is ambiguous between these two senses. For the thesis to succeed the memories referred to have to be real memories, i.e. memories in the strong sense. This requires that we should be able to distinguish between those occasions when what someone thinks he remembers actually happened to him, and those occasions when they did not. This we cannot do in terms of his recollections themselves. There has to be some independent way of determining that the person who did or experienced what Smith believes he remembers doing or experiencing was, or was not, Smith himself. And this, it seems, has to be his physical presence at the occasion in question. So memory is not an independent standard of identity. Without the possibility of recourse to the bodily presence of the person at some past time we are unable to understand what it would be like to determine that some event or action is, or is not, part of this person's past life. So we would have no standard of identity to use of a disembodied person at all.

I think this refutation is in essence correct, and does contain within it enough to put out of the question an intelligible concept of disembodied survival. But in order to show this it is necessary to deal with certain difficulties that derive from the literature on personal identity, and to refine the argument both to take account of these, and to deal with the special problems that face us when we are discussing the identity of disembodied persons, not the identity of persons in general. It is sometimes said that to put the problems of personal identity in terms of the relation between *two* standards of identity, since there are a number, is misleading. It has been said that an argument like the one outlined suggests that our reliance on people's memories in disputes about their identity is merely inductively based, when it is not. It has been said that one can construct imaginary examples (or even find real ones) which strongly tempt us to concede that someone's memory-beliefs might have priority over the continuity of his body, so that we might feel forced to admit the possibility, in logic, of bodily transfer or reincarnation. I have already listed some of these examples.

If they show what they are alleged to show, it might seem that there is no absurdity in the claim that a person's identity could depend entirely on his memories. Finally, our argument is couched in terms that suggest it is at bottom an epistemological one. It seems to amount merely to the claim that we could not *know* whether a disembodied being was or was not identical with some past disembodied or embodied being. But we have put aside parallel epistemological considerations in dealing with problems about predication, in order to avoid making conceptual decisions hinge upon issues of very high philosophical generality. Might they not be put aside here? Surely the question is whether we can *understand* the belief that disembodied persons last through time, not one about how we would *know* that one had done so? In order to deal with these difficulties I must turn first to a more general discussion of self-identity, and apply the results later to our special case.

In a general discussion of self-identity it is not possible to avoid epistemological considerations, since in outlining the rules of application for an expression like 'the same person' one is bound to ask in what circumstances users (and learners) of our language are able to tell whether to apply it or withhold it, and this is, in the broadest sense, an epistemological question. (This does not prevent our going on to ask how far a doctrine like that of disembodied survival, which postulates conditions in which our language could not be learned, and in which no one would know whether or not the conditions that justified the use of the expression actually obtained, could be intelligibly expressed in our language, if its possession is taken as given.)

Confining ourselves to the conventions we now follow in our talk of flesh and blood persons (rather than the conventions we might come to follow if certain philosophical fantasies like those of Locke came true), I would suggest that both bodily identity and memory are criteria of personal identity. By saying they are criteria of personal identity I mean the following. (i) It follows from the fact that a person, Y, now before us, has the body that a person, X, previously known, had, that Y is X. (ii) It follows from the fact that a person, Y, now before us, remembers doing actions done by X or having experiences that X had, that Y is X. (iii) It is possible to establish beyond reasonable doubt, at least on some occasions, that one of these standards is satisfied without first of all establishing in some other way (by reference to the other) that Y is X.

I think that this use of 'criterion' is different from that given the term by many philosophers in their discussions of outer criteria of inner mental states, or in discussion of so-called factual criteria for the application of evaluative predicates. The basic difference lies in the suggestion here that there is a deductive connection between the satisfaction of the criterion and the conclusion that Y is X. I incline to think, however, that something like the above is what many philosophers have had in mind when they have talked about bodily identity and memory as two criteria of personal identity. They have usually gone on to discuss whether condition (iii) is really satisfiable in the case of memory, and whether, if it is, we could without difficulty envisage a world in which *only* memory was a criterion. I would answer 'Yes' to the first of these questions and 'No' to the second. But before proceeding we must look at other details.

The restriction to two criteria of identity might seem arbitrary and unrealistic. Are there not hosts of reasons for identifying people? There are indeed very many physical characteristics which enable us to recognize our friends, and many more formal tests which can be used in special circumstances to decide who someone is. There are fingerprint tests, blood tests, distinguishing marks, and the like. It is unquestionably somewhat overschematic for philosophers to sum all these together in phrases like 'bodily identity' or 'bodily continuity,' but the tests that we use would not in fact tell us what they do tell us if we could not presume that it is a conventional truth that a person is, whatever else we hold him to be, a continuous physical organism undergoing patterns of change appropriate to the type of organism he is. It is a truism of this sort that explains why the tests of identity are not of a kind that rule out change altogether.* Circumstances might arise that made us change our concepts so that certain sorts of discontinuities, such as bodily exchanges, were allowed under the concept of a person, but we must postpone consideration of this. We must also put aside

---

*See my "Hume on Personal Identity."

the suggestion that bodily identity is not a criterion of personal identity at all because we can find human bodies that do not now belong to persons, viz. corpses and live but grossly impaired organisms. This does not show that where we are, *ex hypothesi,* speaking of a *person* and asking whether he can be identified with some *person* previously known, we cannot decide affirmatively if we know that he has the body that the former person had.

In the case of both our criteria we can use many tests to determine whether a candidate is physically continuous with someone he claims to be, or remembers his actions or experiences. This would make some philosophers inclined to call the facts that serve as such tests themselves criteria for identity in some weaker sense than the one I have used. I have suggested that their serving in this way is due to the fact that they enable us to determine the continuity of the body of the claimant and the person he claims to be, and that there is a deductive connection between this decision and that to call them the same. Among corresponding 'non-physical' facts of great significance (as Quinton's story shows), are similarities of character and skills. These often affect our decision as to who someone is. But only in the case of having X's memories and being X is the connection deductive. I can have my father's character or personality without being my father; whereas I cannot have his memories, for to do so would be to be my father. Hence similarity of character or of skill (always assuming these can realistically be thought of as non-physical)[1] without memory would be worthless, and they tend to be mere corroborative tests at times when we are unsure whether Y's apparent memories are real ones. In consequence there seems no temptation to suggest that one could give sense to the notion of non-physical continuance by reference to character similarity alone, as there is in the case of memory. Nor is it at all clear what similarity of character without appropriate memories comes to beyond coincidence of personality-traits such as jocularity or solemnity; so any closeness of character that would enter seriously into identity disputes would be of a sort that would entail some appropriate memories.

I am prepared to accept that memory is a criterion of identity in the way in which I have defined this term, but will argue that

---

[1]See B.A.O. Williams, "Personal Identity and Individuation."

its being this depends in critical ways upon the existence of the bodily criterion of identity. I draw heavily here upon the contributions of Sydney Shoemaker.[2]

It is tempting to think that accepting the memory-beliefs that others have, and especially accepting their ostensible memories of their own pasts, can only be rationally founded upon observation of the reliability of individual men's memories. If this were true, it would suggest that memory could not be, in my sense, a criterion, since it would not seem that we could be entitled to say that someone now before us remembers doing X's actions or having X's experiences without either first of all having discovered from his physical features that he is X, or having a great deal of corroboration that the candidate has a trustworthy memory—which would also, in all likelihood, entail independent knowledge of the past life to which he is laying claim. If memory is not a criterion of identity, then certainly the puzzle stories would not exert the temptations they do exert upon us. We can now examine this temptation.

To decide that someone really does remember something is usually to evaluate positively memory-*claims* that he makes. These are normally put in the form of sentences beginning with 'I remember . . .' The cases that are most pertinent to the issue of self-identity are cases where the claims so expressed are claims to remember doing or experiencing actions or events in the past history of the person in question, rather than claims to remember facts. Shoemaker has argued against the view that our reliance upon people's memory-claims in such situations is inductively based. He argues that it is a necessary truth that memory-claims are usually true. I incline to accept his arguments; though for present purposes it is enough for me only to accept them for the sake of the argument, since to reject them would be to reinforce the conclusions which I wish to establish. His arguments are as follows. (i) If someone frequently said with sincerity that he remembered events which did not occur, we would be justified in concluding that he did not know how to use the term 'remember'. (ii) If a child learning the language were to behave in this way

---

[2]Sydney Shoemaker, "Personal Identity and Memory," and *Self-Knowledge and Self-Identity*. The quotations in this chapter are from the article.

with the word 'remember' or its cognates, we would say he had not yet learned how to use it. (iii) If we were translating an unknown language and were inclined to translate certain expressions in it as memory-expressions, our decision whether to do so would have to hinge in part upon the truth or falsity of the statements beginning with those expressions: if they were generally false, we could not translate them in this way.

I incline to think that unless a sceptic is prepared to deny that our language has certain features (that its users are generally successful in communicating by means of it and that it is learned), these arguments do at least refute any generalized scepticism about memory. (I think, incidentally, that parallel arguments could be constructed in connection with other epistemologically important notions like 'see' or 'know'; that it is a logical truth that many of the things people claim to see are there, and many of the things people claim to know are true.) Shoemaker puts the conclusion in the following way: ". . . inferences of the form 'He claims to remember doing X, so he probably did X' are not simply inductive inferences, for they are warranted by a generalisation that is logically rather than empirically true."

The generalization he refers to is the generalization that 'memory beliefs, and therefore honest memory claims, are generally true'. Let us accept this generalization, not spending time over whether its clear dependence on contingent facts about the learning of language makes it inappropriate to call it a necessary truth. At any rate, it does not seem to be an inductive one. Let us also put aside the question of whether the argument justifies us in saying that memory-claims must be true usually, often, or merely some of the time. What this shows is that it at least can be, and perhaps must often be, in order to accept a man's claims to remember doing something or experiencing something without applying external checks to these claims. Since the truth of such claims entails the identity of the speaker with the person who did or experienced those things, it seems reasonable to conclude that it will often be right to identify people solely on the basis of their memory-claims, without applying other, e.g. physical, tests. And this makes memory a criterion in my sense.

But this last conclusion, if sound, has to be hedged around with qualifications: (*a*) Even though generalized scepticism about memory may be absurd, scepticism about *particular* memory-claims is not. To know that even most memory-claims are correct is not to know which ones these are. It is obvious that the argument at most shows that there may be need of some *reason* for doubt for any doubt to be reasonable; but the lamentable fact of human error is enough to show that it often is. When it is, the truth of the memory-claims before us has to be established, or at least defended. (*b*) Among the wide variety of cases that appropriately generate reasons for doubt are, of course, the cases where we are trying to establish who someone is. (*c*) We can see, further, as Shoemaker has pointed out, that the argument itself requires the existence of tests or checks on memory-claims. For we have to have a use for the distinction between true and false memory-claims; for us to have such a use we must be able to recognize instances of each, and this requires a capacity to make use of some *independent* means of determining whether the man did do or experience what he claims to remember doing or experiencing. It is hard to see what means there could be if physical means of testing this could not be used. (*d*) As Shoemaker further points out, in order to elicit and recognize people's claims to remember, we have to be able to converse with them, and this entails an ability to recognize them at least over short periods of time; so there must be some means or other of doing this other than through the acceptance of the memory-claims they are making.

These last two points can be expanded. For us to know that any memory-claim about a man's own past, which there is reason to doubt, is true, we have to be able (*a*) to recognize him throughout a contemporary period of time, (*b*) to have access to our own, or some third party's, records or recollections of the stretch of past personal history to which he lays claim, and (*c*) to identify the owners of these two with each other on the basis of considerations other than the content of the memory-claims themselves. These are in principle unavailable if the memory-criterion stands alone without the bodily criterion. Hence memory could not be the only standard of personal identity, since if it were it could not, paradoxically, be applied. It is, then, not an *independent* criterion.

The emptiness of the suggestion that memory could be the sole criterion of personal identity is due, in effect, to the incoherence of the view that memories are self-authenticating. But it also has more practical sources. People forget their pasts, or a very great part of them, and we would in daily life be in a paralysing predicament, if we had nothing to use to determine who someone was, and no basis for the recognition of our friends, save their memory-claims. The occasions of actual recall of the past, though frequent, are not frequent enough for this. Yet people are at all times physically present at some point in space where observation is possible—or at least not prevented by the absence of a physical body. So physical tests of identity have a constant availability which people's recollections do not. There are two aspects to this, both of which are properly stressed by those who have argued that bodily identity is the more fundamental criterion of the identity of persons. Since bodies are spatio-temporally continuous, it is, first, always possible to try to determine who someone is by scrutinizing his physical characteristics, even though he cannot recall some critical deed or experience in his past; and, second, when he does claim to remember his past his claim can only be true if he was physically present at the episode he seems to recall. So if the bodily tests indicated that this person was not physically present when the deed was done, or the event he claims to have witnessed happened, we would reject his memory-claims.

I have so far treated it as uncontroversial that we can, if need be, apply the bodily criterion of identity without resort to the memory-criterion. There is an apparent objection to this. In applying physical tests, especially in checking on a person's physical presence at past events, it is essential to rely on one's own memory or on that of witnesses. This might seem to show that the bodily criterion of identity is dependent on memory in a way parallel to the memory-criterion's dependence on it. In a way it does show this, but it does not affect the priority of the bodily criterion. For what is shown here is that we are dependent on our memories in not being able to carry through any cognitive procedure whatever without using them. This, however, does not show that when engaged in the cognitive procedures of determining who someone is we cannot, at least in theory, dispense with the memory-claims *of the person himself,* and it is this that we would need to prove to show that there is parity of dependence between the two standards.

These considerations suggest that while both bodily identity and real memory are sufficient conditions of personal identity, the notion that memory would be sufficient if bodily identity were not sufficient also is absurd. Bodily identity is a necessary, as well as a sufficient, condition for the identity of persons. This in turn suggests that the enterprise of attempting to give an intelligible account of the identity of a disembodied person in terms of memory alone is doomed to failure.

I have argued that the memory-criterion of identity is only available to us because there is another, viz. bodily identity, and that the memory-criterion only functions because there are physical tests that we can use to determine who someone is. The question before us is whether or not this shows it to be impossible to formulate an intelligible notion of the identity of a disembodied person. It is not yet obvious that we cannot do so if we are willing to accept that we cannot expect to be in a position to *know* whether the conditions of such a person's identity are satisfied at any time.

But the arguments that have been given do not show merely that we need physical tests in order to *know* whether men's memories can establish their identities. They also reveal that without availability of these physical tests there could *be no reason* for the application of the concept of personal identity. And the removal in the doctrine of survival of the availability of the tests entails the removal of the possibility of such a reason in the disembodied case, not merely the removal of our chances of knowing whether this or that test is satisfied.

When discussing post-mortem predication we postulated that a survivor might have, for example, certain visual or auditory imagery, and then asked whether, if he could exercise control over it, this was enough to entitle us, at least in some attenuated sense, to say that he saw, or heard, even though we could never be in a position to know that he had this imagery. If the answer was affirmative, this did not show that either the imagery or the capacity to control it were anything less than essential conditions for the use of the notions of seeing or hearing in our intellectual fantasy. To say that one could admit the coherence of a hypothesis without knowing whether the conditions provided in it actually obtain is not to say that the conditions themselves are not, *in the hypothesis,* essential for the key concepts of that hypothesis to be used. The position is similar with identity and memory. The fact that in a hypothesis of disembodied survival we might not know whether some conditions for self-identity obtained would not itself show (without independent argument) that disembodied identity could not be intelligibly predicated; but this is not to say that the conditions themselves can be dispensed with. The doctrine of disembodiment unfortunately does also dispense with them.

The concept of memory is itself an epistemic one. To say that someone remembers is to say that he has knowledge of a special sort about the past, not merely that he has some present experience or makes some present claim about the past. To say that he remembers doing a certain action, or having a certain experience, is to say that he knows that he did it or experienced it. But he and we cannot know this without understanding what it is for him to have done it or for him to have experienced it. This cannot be articulated in terms of any experience he now has, or any sentence he now utters to us or to himself. For it to be true that he really remembers and does not merely seem to do so(to us or to himself) it must be the case that he, and not another person, did the action or had the experience, and our understanding of this cannot be articulated in terms of any experience he now has, or any sentence he now utters. Memory, as Butler reminded us, presupposes personal identity and cannot serve to define it. What I have referred to as physical tests of identity are physical facts about the present and past of embodied persons which help us to understand and articulate the identity which memory presupposes. This does not mean that any particular test, especially such things as photograph or fingerprint tests, must yield a conclusive result in practice. But it does mean that when we say the memory-criterion is satisfied for an embodied person we imply that there are physical facts which, if known to us, would suffice to establish the identity of the claimant and the original person, for they would establish continuity of the body between them. The fact that, for general epistemological reasons, it must sometimes be in order to dispense with the search for these facts does not mean that this implication is not present when we state that he really does remember. (That one statement implies another does not mean that we cannot have sound reasons for accepting the one without establishing the other first.)

So there are general reasons of principle for rejecting the suggestion that we can render the identity of a disembodied person intelligible, since the subtraction of the body leaves the notion of genuine memory chronically incomplete. Let us now take a closer look at ways in which we might try to articulate disembodied identity, to see how this pessimism is borne out in detail.

I must begin by saying that I can attach no sense to the notion of 'loose' or unowned experiences (or agentless actions). When I feel partially able to grasp the sense of the notion of a sensation that no one has, or an act that no one performs, I immediately reject the notion as flagrantly self-contradictory. If this is not idiosyncratic, it would seem that we can only envisage the psychical remains of persons as belonging to continuing subjects, which we may hope to identify with pre-mortem persons. *Prima facie,* however, there is also difficulty about the notion of the ownership of experiences in a disembodied state, in view of the fact that we identify the owner of experiences in the embodied state by reference to his physical presence. I have no wish to proceed as though there is no puzzle about understanding reference to a subject that has no body, merely because I also fail to understand how there could be experiences that had no owner at all. On the other hand, I do not wish to base arguments about the coherence of the notion of disembodied existence upon any particular analysis of the present ownership of experiences in the embodied state. So I will concentrate on the *re*-identification of the owner of experiences. Let us ask, then, about the identity of a disembodied person at time T_2 with a disembodied person at time T_1, and the identity of a disembodied person at time T_2 with an embodied person at time T_1.

What makes the owner of experience E_2 at T_2 the same as the owner of experience E_1 at T_1? (Whatever ownership is to be taken to mean here. Once again there is a dilemma: It is natural to put this question in terms of two experiences and what it is that makes them part of the same life-history; but this assumes the intelligibility of independent reference to the experiences without reference to the subjects that have them, which I have to question. On the other hand, in order to talk of them as owned, it is necessary to assume the intelligibility of reference to their owners, which in the present context is doubtful also. I have no wish to minimize the seriousness of this difficulty. On the contrary, I would emphasize it. But it is possible to reveal the defects in the attempt to define disembodied identity without lingering further upon this dilemma, and hardly possible otherwise. I grasp the latter horn of the dilemma to proceed.)

The only available answer seems to be that the owner of E_2 is identical with the owner of E_1 because the owner of E_2 remembers E_1. It is clear, first, that 'remembers' here must mean 'really remembers' not merely 'seems or claims to remember,' for our recollections are often faulty. It is also clear, second, that 'remembers' must mean here 'does remember', not just 'can remember'. Attempts to define personal identity in terms of memory (such as that of Locke) have always run into this difficulty. People forget. 'This is the man who drove past the policeman' does not entail 'This man remembers driving past the policeman', even if we assume he noticed doing it at the time. It is useless to counter with the notion of potential recollection and say that it entails 'This man *could* remember driving past the policeman', for in its only harmless interpretation this claim is false. It is not a logical consequence of his having driven past the policeman that *any* practical device would enable him to recall doing it. The only interpretation of 'He could remember' which makes it true that the entailment holds is one in which it means, roughly, '*No one else* could remember', and this notion obviously depends on a prior understanding of his identity with the driver. So in our present case the concept of potential memory of E_1 cannot be used, on pain of circularity. So the only use of 'remember' that is satisfactory here is the one in which it is taken to mean actual, and true recollection of E_1 on the part of the owner of E_2. So the disembodied person having E_2 is the same as the disembodied person who had E_1 if and only if, in addition to having E_2, he remembers (in this strong sense) having E_1.

This runs into two major and connected difficulties. (i) We

have to give sense not only to 'the person having E_1' and 'the person having E_2', which we have left aside, but to the complex notion of the person who has E_2 also having a memory (in this case of E_1)—for only an actual recollection will do. If the having of E_2 and the having of this memory are *successive* experiences, this is the very notion we are trying to articulate, and the enterprise already collapses. If they are simultaneous we face the distinct but equally obscure problem of what it is for two contemporary experiences to be experiences of the same person rather than of different persons. This seems to presuppose an understanding of what individuates one person from another, which is absent in the disembodied case. Many contemporaneous experiences occur in our world, and any two of them may belong to the same person and may not, and in the embodied world we usually have no problem in determining which way it is. But in speaking of bodiless persons, there seems as much problem in knowing what is to be understood by two experiences being experienced together by the same subject and not by two distinct subjects as there is in knowing what is to be understood by two experiences being experienced successively by the same subject rather than by two. The temptation is to try to make memory do duty once again and say that two simultaneous experiences are both had by the same subject if and only if they are both remembered together. But the emptiness of this move is readily apparent. If their being remembered together means their being remembered to have occurred together, the circularity is right on the surface. If their being remembered together means their being both remembered by the same person, we merely return to our original problem. And if we tried to avoid these difficulties by making it mean their being remembered in one act of recall, then since one of the two recollected experiences is itself a recollection, we would put a strain upon the notion of recalling two or more experiences simultaneously, for the recollection of the memory would have to be an instance of recalling recalling E_1, not merely recalling *that* one recalled E_1; besides which, it would make it logically impossible for a disembodied person to have two experiences simultaneously without recalling them together.

(ii) The second difficulty is simpler and more basic. E_1 has to be really remembered, i.e. remembered correctly. This means not merely that someone had E_1 as it is recalled, but that the owner of E_2 is that person. This still presupposes some independent sense for the claim that the owner of E_1 and E_2 are the same. There is nothing new here. But it would be odd if it were expected that there could be. This difficulty is not eased by the suggestion that in weaving our fantasies we can stipulate that there are in fact no erroneous recollections in the disembodied state. This proposal itself makes use of the very notion of identity we are trying to account for. A memory of an experience, even a true one, is not just one more experience, but a manner of knowing one's own past. So we must have some way of making sense already of the claim that E_1 happened to the person owning E_2 and not to another person. For this is *part of the stipulation* that the recollections persons in the next world have are all correct. This stipulation is nothing more than the assertion that the experiences disembodied persons seem to remember having they did in fact have; and we cannot understand this stipulation unless we understand what it excludes, and unless we have some idea what sorts of facts would, if they were known (which they might not be), be sufficient to warrant us to pronounce the seeming memories to be real ones. A parallel difficulty faces the suggestion that we stipulate that only one disembodied person would think he recalled any particular action or experience. Here, too, the understanding of the stipulation presupposes the understanding of the possibility that *not only one* person would think he recalled it, which we cannot have without knowing what it would be for one to think he recalled it and be wrong—or, therefore, right. Memory is essentially a parasitic concept, and needs a body to feed on.

The venerable doctrine of spiritual substance comes to mind here. Historically this notion has served dualistically-minded philosophers as a means of providing continuous ownership for the sequences of thoughts and feelings that make up men's mental lives. The main criticism levelled against it is to be found in Locke's discussion on personal identity, though Locke fails to draw out the full implications of it. Since the concept of substances is not an empirical one, there is no publicly usable set of devices for determining the continued presence of a substance, so its presence cannot serve as a criterion for applying the expression 'the same person' in ordinary life. Locke is reduced to suggesting that the criterion he does argue for (memory) happens by the goodness of God to lead us to ascribe identity on those occasions when the metaphysical substrate does persist, and only on those occasions. It might be suggested that this epistemological difficulty is irrelevant in our present context. But the inutility of the concept of substance is a sign of something deeper. Beyond the wholly empty assurance that it is a metaphysical principle which guarantees continuing identity through time, or the argument that since we know identity persists some such principle must hold in default of others, no content seems available for the doctrine. Its irrelevance to normal occasions of identity-judgments is due to its being merely an alleged identity-guaranteeing condition of which no independent characterization is forthcoming. Failing this, the doctrine amounts to no more than a pious assurance that deep down all is well. It provides no reason for this assurance.

Thus far I have argued along the following lines. Memory could not be the sole and independent criterion of personal identity, since this would undermine the distinction between true and false memory beliefs about one's past, a distinction which can only exist if there is some further content to the notion of the identity of the rememberer and the owner of the action or experience remembered. Since this further content seems to derive from the possession of a body, or at least to be absent when this possession is excluded, the notion of a persistence through time of a disembodied being, and of its identification with a pre-mortem being, does not seem intelligible.

The answer I have offered to the problem of the intelligibility of the doctrine of survival is not a tidy one, but a tidy answer is not to be expected. I have argued that the doctrine of disembodied survival founders because no intelligible account seems possible in it of the persistence of a disembodied person through time. This is not because the doctrine postulates the future existence of beings about whom the requisite facts could not be known, but because it removes the possibility of the existence of such facts altogether, and requires us to try to make the self-identity of spirits intelligible by reference to memory alone, which is self-defeating. On the other hand, arguments against the intelligibility of disembodied existence

which depend on the claim that predicates such as those of perception or agency cannot in principle be applied to non-physical
beings seem to me inadequate. . . .

A simple negative verdict would be out of place for another
reason. There are many other possible versions of a belief in survival, which are no doubt less appealing because of their air
of tasteless fantasy, but which may be free of the difficulties ours
have encountered. A doctrine of astral or ectoplasmic bodies in
which departed persons can view our world and occasionally interfere with it is held by some, and if we held to it we might be able
to use it to deal with the more intractable phenomena of psychical
research. For some, the astral body might be in some way fused in
life with our earthly body and then separated from it at death,
or it might be the body to which the pre-mortem person's identity
is transferred in the way in which we might have said our cobbler's
identity is transferred to the body of the prince. . . . the astral
body need not have all the organs we use for perception or agency,
yet might be describable in a way which is intelligible, sufficient
to give tolerable imaginative grounds for the ascription of identity
through time, and immune to very rapid empirical refutation.
Another way of generating a survival doctrine which would, *prima
facie,* have some chance of an explanatory use, would be to opt
for a thesis of instantaneous resurrection in another space, plus the
claim that from that space the resurrectee might clairvoyantly
perceive, or even from a 'distance' act in, our world. For the only
world from which I claimed to demonstrate that it is logically
impossible for this one to be seen is a Next World that is not
spatial at all. Temporary bodily transfer from the resurrection
world into the body of a medium in this one might not be logically
impossible either, for this would not be the same as the hypothesis
of the temporary occupation of her body by a disembodied person;
this is indeed ruled out of court by our subsequent difficulties
about identity.

I do not recommend these fantasies, or suggest that they cannot
be made to yield logical difficulties. Nor do I imagine any philosophers would find them attractive. Christians are likely to find
them repellent, which is no doubt why they have shown little more
interest in Psychical Research than sceptics have shown. I point

out merely that I do not think my earlier arguments rule them out as logically possible options, though I cannot imagine any circumstances which would *require* them. We must always bear in mind the philosophical (and religious) truism that reality may not conform to our theoretical or aesthetic tastes.

CHAPTER 23

IS THERE A CASE FOR DISEMBODIED SURVIVAL?*

ANTONY FLEW

THE ENORMOUS INITIAL OBSTACLE

THERE IS AN ENORMOUS INITIAL OBSTACLE confronting any doctrine of personal survival or personal immortality. This enormous initial obstacle is perfectly obvious and perfectly familiar. Nevertheless, in order to put the whole discussion into the correct perspective, it is useful to begin by actually stating what it is. For only when this has been done shall we fully appreciate for what they are the three main sorts of ways of trying to circumvent or to overcome the obstacle; and only when this is appreciated shall we be able adequately to assess the success or failure of any such attempt.

Yet the vocabulary available for describing the obstacle may well be felt unfairly to prejudice the question against the believer in personal survival or personal immortality. To meet this difficulty I propose first to say and, hopefully, later to show that it is certainly not my intention to prejudge issues in this or any other way. Very well then, the enormous initial obstacle to any doctrine of personal survival or personal immortality is the familiar fact that— with the possible exceptions of the prophet Elisha and Mary the mother of Jesus—all men die and are in more or less short order buried, cremated, or otherwise disposed of. This universal fact of

*Reprinted from *The Journal of the American Society for Psychical Research*, 1972, by permission of the author and the Society. (This paper is based upon a lecture given by Professor Flew at a meeting of the Society held on January 14, 1971—Ed. [of *The Journal of the American Society for Psychical Research*])

death is what leads us normally to distinguish after a shipwreck or an air crash, exclusively and exhaustively, between the Dead and the Survivors, with no third category of Both or Neither. This is the fact which gave the proposition *All men are mortal* its hallowed status as the first premise of the stock traditional example of a valid syllogism; proceeding from the true premises that *All men are mortal,* and that *Socrates is a man,* to the true if unexciting conclusion that *Socrates is mortal.*

SURVIVAL AND IMMORTALITY

So we have to ask how, confronted by this obstacle, any such doctrine is to get off the ground at all. Before trying to suggest an answer I wish to make a sharp, simplifying move. I propose from now on to speak only of survival, without qualification, rather than of personal survival and personal immortality. I shall thus be taking it for granted, first, that what we are interested in is our personal post-mortem futures, if any. "Survival" through our children and our children's children after we ourselves are irrecoverably dead, "immortality" through the memories of others thanks to our great works, or even our immersion in some universal world-soul—whatever that might mean—may be as much as, or much more than, most of us will in fact be getting. And it may be lamentably self-centered, albeit humanly altogether understandable, that we should be concerned about more than these thin substitutes. But, for better or for worse, what we are discussing now is the possibility of our post-mortem survival as persons identifiable as those we are here and now.

I shall also be taking it for granted, second, that survival is the necessary though of course not the sufficient condition of immortality. We can and shall concentrate on survival because this is pre-eminently a case where "It is the first step which counts." Immortality is just more of the same—survival forever. This may seem to some to be another point just too obvious to be worth making at all. I sympathize with this impatient reaction, but I believe it to be mistaken. For the point has to some persons been so far from obvious that they have boldly denied it. Some have urged that, because the Christian faith, for instance, promises immortality, difficulties about the idea of survival must be irrelevant to it.

THREE POSSIBLE WAYS OF SURVIVAL

We shall, therefore, always have in mind personal survival; and we shall be concentrating on survival rather than on immortality inasmuch as the former is the necessary but not the sufficient first step to the latter. So, now, back to the question of how, granted the undeniable fact that we shall all die, anyone can possibly maintain that some or all of us will nevertheless survive. I suggest, as I must confess I have suggested before,[1] that we can distinguish three sorts of way in which attempts can be, and have been, made to overcome the enormous initial obstacle.

The Platonic Way

The first and the most familiar of these three ways I call the Platonic or Platonic-Cartesian way. This consists in two moves, not one. The first move is to maintain that what is ordinarily thought of as a person in fact consists of two radically disparate elements: the one, the body, earthy, corporeal, and perishable; the other, the soul, incorporeal, invisible, intangible, and perhaps imperishable. The second move in the Platonic or Platonic-Cartesian way consists in the contention that it is the second of these two elements which is the real, essential person. It is obvious that if this way will go, then what I call the enormous initial obstacle is really no obstacle at all: the death of the body is not necessarily the death of the soul, which is the true person; and such an essentially incorporeal entity cannot in principle be touched by the earthy corruptions of the graveyard or the inferno of the crematorium.

The Way of the Astral Body

The second of these three ways will be equally familiar to the present audience, but not, I fear, so much respected. It is the way of the astral body. Like the first way, it consists in two moves, not one. The first move is to claim that inside and, so to speak, shadowing what is ordinarily thought of as the person is another being of the same form. And the second move is, as before, to maintain that this shadow being is the real person. The crucial difference between the Platonic-Cartesian way and the way of the astral body is that,

---

[1] *Body, Mind, and Death,* A. Flew, ed. (New York, Macmillian, 1964), pp. 4-6.

whereas in the former the soul is supposed to be essentially incorporeal, in the latter the astral body is equally essentially in its own way corporeal—albeit, of course, necessarily constituted of a different and somehow more shadowy and etherial sort of stuff than familiar, workaday matter. Strictly speaking, it could not make sense to ask of a Platonic-Cartesion soul any such everyday and down-to-earth questions as "Where is it?" "How big is it?" "How broad and long is it?" Of the astral body, on the other hand, at least some such questions must be sensibly askable even if not in practice answerable, or what would be the point of talking of an astral body and not simply of a Platonic-Cartesian soul?

Once this crucial distinguishing point is grasped, the best method of increasing one's sympathetic understanding of the way of the astral body is to think of those stock cinematic representations—as long ago in the movie version of Noel Coward's *Blithe Spirit*—in which a shadow person, visible only sometimes and only to some of the characters, detaches itself from a person shown as dead and thereafter continues to participate in the developing action at one time discernibly and at another time not.

The second way is not, I think, nowadays given the attention and respect which it deserves. One of my aims here is to do something toward its rehabilitation. Part of the reason for this disrespect is that people familiar with psychical research have been persuaded by writers such as G.N.M. Tyrrell[2] to adopt a different interpretation of those apparitions of the living, the dying, and the dead which have to others seemed to provide the main prop for an astral body view. But partly, I suspect, the way of the astral body is simply ruled out of court as unacceptably crude or intolerably materialist; and this hasty dismissal is made all the easier by the assumption—which I shall soon be challenging—that there are no serious theoretical objections to the Platonic-Cartesian way.

The Reconstitutionist Way

The third of the three sorts of way which I want to distinguish and label finds its traditional home in religion rather than in psychical research. This is the one which I call the reconstitutionist way.

---

[2] G.N.M. Tyrrell, *Apparitions* (London, Duckworth, 1953).

The nature of this third way cannot be better or, for an American audience, more suitably explained than by quoting an epitaph composed for himself by that universal genius and Founding Father, Benjamin Franklin: "The body of B. Franklin, Printer, Like the Cover of an old Book, Its Contents torn out, And stript of its Lettering and Gilding, Lies here, Food for Worms. But the work shall not be lost; for it will, as he believ'd, appear once more in a new and more elegant Edition Corrected and improved By the Author."

THE THEORETICAL DIFFICULTIES OF THE THREE WAYS

At this point let us take stock of where we are and how far we have gone. In the first section above we saw the obvious, familiar, and enormous initial obstacle to any doctrine of personal survival or personal immortality. In the second section we emphasized our concern with our personal fates, and explained in terms of the old saw "It's the first step that counts" our concentration on survival rather than on immortality. In the third section we distinguished three sorts of way by which people have attempted to circumvent or overcome the enormous initial obstacle. In the present section I want to expound the various theoretical or—more strictly—philosophical difficulties which arise altogether independent of the progress of psychical research, although it is my strong conviction that they will be most fruitfully discussed by those who are aware of that progress.

The Reconstitutionist Way

So now to the difficulties of each way, starting with the last one first. The great, and to my mind quite decisive, difficulty here may be christened the Replica Objection. Consider a short and very significant passage from *The Koran*—a work which is now, they tell me, compulsory reading for the faithful of the Kremlin. The passage is taken from Chapter XVII, "The Night Journey." As usual, it is Allah speaking:

> Thus shall they be rewarded: because they disbelieved our revelations and said "When we are turned to bones and dust shall we be raised to life?" Do they not see that Allah, who has created the heavens and the earth, has power to create their like? Their

fate is preordained beyond all doubt. Yet the wrongdoers persist in unbelief.[3]

Certainly Allah the omnipotent must have "power to create their like." But in making Allah talk in these precise terms of what He might indeed choose to do, the Prophet was speaking truer than he himself appreciated. For thus to produce even the most indistinguishably similar object after the first one has been totally destroyed and disappeared is to produce not the same object again, but a replica. To punish or to reward a replica, reconstituted on Judgment Day, for the sins or the virtues of the old Antony Flew dead and cremated in 1984 is as inept and as unfair as it would be to reward or to punish one identical twin for what was in fact done by the other. Again and similarly, the Creator might very well choose to issue a Second Edition—"Corrected and improved by the Author"—of Benjamin Franklin. But that Second Edition, however welcome, would by the same token not be the original Signer.

It was partly, though of course only partly, because he appreciated the force of this replica objection that St. Thomas Aquinas mixed a strong Platonic element into his version of the reconstitutionist way. The soul which could, and in his view did, survive death and wait for the reconstitution of the whole person on Judgment Day was for St. Thomas only an incomplete fragment and not, as it was for Plato, the real and essential person. Yet this incomplete Thomist soul should, hopefully, be just enough to bridge the gap between now and then, and to provide sufficient necessary continuity between the Flew you see and the reconstituted Flew of Judgment Day to overcome the otherwise fatal replica objection.[4]

It will be helpful if I emphasize here that in the previous section I deliberately distinguished all my three ways in ideal purity. But when we come to real cases we often find that the protagonist of what is predominantly one has been pressed by some difficulty to admit at least some element of another. Thus the primarily reconstitutionist Thomas is driven to become in part a Platonist also. Later we shall see both how Plato himself, against all his wishes and

---

[3]The Prophet Mohammed, *The Koran,* trans. by N.J. Dawood (Baltimore, Penguin Books, 1956), p. 234.

[4]T. Aquinas, *Summa Theologiae,* trans. by T. Gilby (New York, McGraw-Hill, 1963), III Supp. Q 79 A 2.

intentions, lapses into an astral body view; and how the spokesman for an astral body in his turn may find himself so qualifying the nature of his elusive hypothesized body that it must become indistinguishable from a Platonic-Cartesian soul.

The Platonic Way

The reconstitutionist way and the replica objection have no direct interest for psychical research. It is worth mentioning them here only for the sake of completeness and in order to show that the reconstitutionist way must, apparently, depend for its ultimate viability upon the possibility of the Platonic way. What surely will be of great and direct psychical research interest is to indicate some of the really fundamental difficulties which afflict that Platonic-Cartesian way. Once these are understood, it will be time to return for a second look at the way of the astral body. The first thing with which we must try to come to terms here is that the assumptions of the Platonic-Cartesian way, which in some contexts we find it so easy to make, are nevertheless both extraordinary and extraordinarily questionable.

To appreciate how easy it is in some contexts to make these Platonic-Cartesian assumptions, consider a paper by C.J. Ducasse entitled "What Would Constitute Conclusive Evidence of Survival After Death?"[5] He supposes that our friend John Doe has been on board an aircraft which crashed in the ocean, and no survivors have been found. Our phone rings "and (*a*) a voice we recognize as John Doe's is heard and a conversation with it held which convinces us that the speaker is really John Doe . . . or (*b*) the voice heard is not John Doe's but that of some other person seemingly relaying his words to us and ours to him; and that the conversation so held does convince us that the person with whom we are conversing through that intermediary is John Doe."[6] Ducasse continues: "Obviously, the two imagined situations (*a*) and (*b*) are, in all essentials, analogues of cases where a person is conversing with the purported surviving spirit of a deceased friend who either, in case (*a*), 'possesses' for the time being parts at least of the body

---

[5]C.J. Ducasse, "What Would Constitute Conclusive Evidence of Survival after Death?" *Journal S.P.R.*, Vol. 41 (1962), pp. 401-406.
[6]*Ibid.*, p. 401.

of a medium . . . or else who, in case (*b*), employs the medium only as intermediary . . . "[7]

Now certainly this constitutes as clear and vivid a description as could be desired of the model in terms of which mediums and their sitters usually think of the proceedings of the seance room. Yet it is neither obvious nor true that "the two imagined situations . . . are, in all essentials, analogues" of the seance situation. The crucial difference lies in the fact that in the case of the imaginary plane crash we know only "that no survivors have been found," whereas in the seance case we presumably know, beyond any possibility of doubt, that our friend has indeed died, and that his remains have been duly buried, cremated, or in some other way consumed. Now Ducasse in his own way appreciated all this perfectly well. The reason why he did not see it as representing any difficulty at all for "the survival hypothesis" is that here he, like almost everyone else when considering what is in psychical research called "the survival evidence," took for granted a Platonic-Cartesian view of man.

These Platonic-Cartesian assumptions are made explicit a little later, when Ducasse continues: "Thus, because the John Doe case and the case of conversation through a medium are complete analogues, the particular kind of content of the conversation that would be adequate to prove or make positively probable that John Doe had survived the crash would likewise be adequate to prove or make positively probable that the mind of our deceased friend has survived the death of his body."[8] This possibly surviving mind of Ducasse's is—as he himself again in his own fashion emphasizes—for our purposes nothing else but the Platonic-Cartesian soul: for it is an incorporeal entity which inhabits the body; and it is the real, essential person. Ducasse goes on:

> When the question of survival is formulated thus in terms not of "spirits" but of *minds,* then the allegation that the survival explanation makes gratuitously . . . four assumptions . . . is seen to be erroneous. For (*a*) that there are minds is not an assumption but a known fact; (*b*) that minds are capable of remembering is likewise not an assumption but is known; (*c*) that minds are capable of "possessing" living human bodies is also a known fact, for "posses-

[7]*Ibid.,* p. 401-402.
[8]*Ibid.,* p. 402.

sion" is but the name of the *normal* relation of a mind to its living body. *Paranormal* "possession" would be possession in the very same sense, but only temporary, and of a living body by a mind other than its own—that other mind either being one which had been that of a body now dead; or being a mind temporarily wandering from its own living body. And (*d*) that telepathic communication between minds is possible is also a known fact.[9]

Having shown by reference to Ducasse how easy and natural it is to make Platonic-Cartesian assumptions in the context of "the survival evidence," the next thing is to try to show that these assumptions are questionable. What I shall be doing is to develop, in a philosopher's way, suggestions made some twenty-five years ago by Gardner Murphy.[10] Referring to difficulties confronting the survival hypothesis, Murphy spoke of the "fact that bodies are the vehicles of personality, and that most people have no conception of personality except in such terms . . ." He challenged "the reader to try for a few minutes to imagine what his personal existence would be like if he were deprived of every device for making contact with his environment, except through the hypothetical use of continuous telepathy to and from other invisible minds."[11]

I think that Murphy understated his case. For, surely, "personality" is a term which has to be defined in terms of persons. My personality is some sort of function of my characteristics and my dispositions; and it could make no more sense to talk of my personality surviving my dissolution—of these characteristics existing without a me for them to be the characteristics of—than it would to talk of the grin of Carroll's Cheshire cat outlasting the face of which it was one possible configuration. Nor is it just "most people," as Murphy modestly puts it, it is all of us whose conceptions of personality are grounded in the corporeal. For, as I have just said, personality is essentially some sort of function of persons; and persons are—surely equally essentially—corporeal.

Consider, for instance, how you would teach the meaning of any person word to a child. This is done, and I think could only be

[9]*Ibid.*, p. 403.

[10]G. Murphy, "Difficulties Confronting the Survival Hypothesis," *Journal A.S.P.R.*, Vol. 39 (1945), pp. 67-94.

[11]*Ibid.*, p. 71.

done, by some sort of direct or indirect pointing at members of that very special class of living physical objects to which we all belong. Or again, and slightly more subtly, consider some of the things which we easily and regularly say about people, and think how few, if any, of these things could be intelligibly said about incorporeal entities. We meet people, we shake hands with them, eat with them, see them, hear them; they get up, go to bed, sit down, smile, laugh, cry; and—if they are students in free societies, but not elsewhere—they demand, confront, demonstrate, and so on. All these activities, and many, many more, could only be predicated intelligibly of corporeal creatures.

Now look again at what Ducasse called the "known facts," and what I still want to call his Platonic-Cartesian assumptions. I agree, of course, that there are minds, provided that by this we mean only that such statements as "he has a first-rate mind," or "the child is developing a mind of his own," are often true. But these statements are, in the interpretation in which we know that they are often true, statements about the capacities and dispositions of flesh and blood people. They must not be misconstrued to imply that the people in question already possess, or are in the process of acquiring, important incorporeal components; much less that these—or any—people actually are incorporeal beings.

It is also perfectly true and much to the point to insist that all normal people are capable of a certain amount of remembering. But, as I have pointed out elsewhere, to say that "minds are the possessors of these capacities is either an oddly artificial and quite misleading way of stating a familiar fact about people, or else a very vague and highly speculative suggestion about a possible explanation of that fact."[12]

Then again, granted that ESP is a known fact, there is surely no experimental reason to describe it as communication between minds or souls rather than as communication between people. Indeed, I believe that something even stronger and much more interesting might be said—something at which Murphy was perhaps hinting when he spoke a shade disrespectfully of "the hypo-

---

[12]A. Flew, "The Platonic Presuppositions of the Survival Hypothesis," *Journal S.P.R.,* Vol. 41 (1962), p. 58.

thetical use of continuous telepathy to and from other invisible minds." For could such bodiless beings, necessarily lacking all conventional sensory equipment, properly be said to communicate with one another by ESP, or even singly to possess any ESP capacity? And, if they could, could they be said to know that they were thus communicating, or that they did possess such a capacity?

These questions arise—although I cannot recall having heard them put before—because the term "ESP" is, whether implicitly or explicitly, defined negatively by reference to the absence or neglect of all ordinary and ultimately perceptual methods of acquiring and communicating information; and because it is only by reference at some stage to the conventional sources that we become able to identify authentic ESP experiences or performances as being truly such; and thus to distinguish these both from acquisitions of information through normal channels and from such autonomous features of our own lives as our spontaneous and not significantly veridical imaginings. We never should forget, what too often is forgotten, that "ESP" is not the name of some directly identifiable means of information transfer. Indeed, despite the close resemblance between the words "telepathy" and "telephony," any performance depending on telephony or any other such known and normal means is for that very reason at once disqualified as a case of telepathy; and the same applies, with appropriate alterations, as regards clairvoyance. Nor can authentic ESP experiences be picked out as such simply by reference to the strong conviction of the subject that this is the real thing. It is, or should be, notorious that subjective conviction is not a sufficient condition of either normal or paranormal knowledge: I may with complete confidence and absolute sincerity claim either to know normally or to have exercised my supposed ESP capacity, and yet in fact be totally mistaken. We must, therefore, distinguish: between (*a*) in fact possessing or exercising some ESP capacity, whether or not you believe or know that you do or are; (*b*) believing that you possess or are exercising an ESP capacity, whether or not you in fact do or are; and (*c*) genuinely knowing—as opposed to believing with however little warrant or however mistakenly—that you do possess or perhaps actually are exercising such a capacity.

Suppose now that in the light of these reminders we try to apply

ESP concepts to these putative incorporeal subjects of experiences. Suppose further that it is a fact that there acually is some close correspondence between the mental contents of two such hypothetical bodiless beings, although such a fact would not, surely, be known by any normal means by anyone—whether bodied or bodiless. Now how could either of these bodiless beings have, how indeed could there even be, any reason for saying that this close correspondence must point to some information transfer from one to the other? How could either of these bodiless beings have, indeed how could there even be, any reason for holding that some of its mental contents must have been intruded by, or otherwise correspond with, some of those of another similarly bodiless being; and some particular one, at that? How could either have, indeed how could there be, any good reason for picking out some of its mental contents as—so to speak—messages received, for taking these but not those as the expressions of an exercise not of imagination but of ESP? Fundamentally similar difficulties arise when we attempt to apply ESP concepts to the different cases of information transfer between an ordinary person and a supposed bodiless being, and between material things and such a being (telepathy from the living "to a spirit," that is, and clairvoyance "by a spirit"). The upshot appears to be that the concepts of ESP are essentially parasitical upon everyday and this-worldly notions; that where there could not be the normal, there could not be ESP as the exception to that rule.

It is too often and too easily assumed that ESP capacities could be, or even must be, the attributes of something altogether immaterial and incorporeal; partly for no better reason than that they do indeed seem to be non-physical in the entirely different sense of being outside the range of today's physical theories. Yet the truth appears to be that the very concepts of ESP are just as much involved with the human body as are those of other human capacities. It was this point that Ludwig Wittgenstein was making, gnomically, with regard to our normal attributes and capacities when he wrote in his *Philosophical Investigations:* "The human body is the best picture of the human soul."[13]

Our interim conclusion is, therefore, that we cannot take a

[13]L. Wittgenstein, *Philosophical Investigations*, trans. by G.E.M. Anscombe (Oxford, England, Blackwell, 1953), p. 178.

Platonic-Cartesian view of man for granted and proceed forthwith to consider the to us familiar question whether what we call the survival evidence is to be taken as proving survival, or whether the material can be better interpreted in terms of complex ESP transactions between embodied people.[14] Before there can be any question of construing this material as evidence for the survival of incorporeal beings, which are the essential persons, a great deal of work will have to be done to show: (*a*) that there can be a coherent notion of an incorporeal personal being, and (*b*) that a being of this sort could significantly be said to be the same person as he was when he was a creature of flesh and blood.

My own conviction is that no amount of work can turn these two tricks. It is surely significant that Plato himself—an imaginative writer of genius as well as the Founding Father of philosophy—when he came at the end of *The Republic* to describe in his Myth of Er the life of supposedly incorporeal souls, was quite unable to say anything about them which did not presuppose that they must be, after all, in some fashion corporeal. So, against all his wishes and intentions, Plato there lapsed from his own eponymous position into what was in effect an astral body view.

But suppose we take Plato's own failure in the Myth of Er—as, surely, he would have done had it been pointed out to him—as showing only that our vocabulary and our imagination are deplorably limited by our present, but temporary, enmeshment in the body. And suppose we concede—as surely we must—that the person words of our present vocabulary do not refer to incorporeal souls, but to creatures of all too solid flesh. Can we not develop a new and coherent concept of an incorporeal being to whom at least some of the characteristics presently ascribed to people could also significantly be attributed? I do not think that we can. The basic difficulties are, first, to provide a principle of individuation by which one such being could, at least in theory, be distinguished from another such being; and, second, to provide a principle of identity to permit us to say that one such being at a later time is the same as that being at an earlier ime.

This is difficult ground, though we can get much help by con-

---

[14]E.R. Dodds, "Why I Do Not Believe in Survival," *Proceedings* S.P.R., Vol. 42 (1934), pp. 147-172; G. Murphy, *op. cit.*

sidering the unsuccessful labors of Descartes and his successors. Since they mistook it that people are incorporeal subjects of experience, our problem appeared to them not as one of developing a coherent new notion, but as that of giving an account of our present notion of a person. But this does not make their efforts any less relevant to us. The first thing which emerges is that such an incorporeal personal being will have to be conceived as consisting of a series of conscious experiences—along, no doubt, with some dispositions, inclinations, and capacities. In the light of what has been argued already, we have to add that unless we can solve the problem of attributing ESP and PK capacities to such a being, these dispositions and so on will have to refer exclusively to actual or possible members of the same series of experiences. We now have a choice between two options: either, with Descartes, we attribute these experiences to an incorporeal spiritual substance—the "I" in Descartes' claim "I am a thinking substance"; or else, with Hume, we say that we can make nothing of the idea of such a substance and then go on to say that such an incorporeal being must simply consist in a series of experiences.

Neither alternative shows promise. Take the second first. Whatever difficulties there may be about the idea of a substance characterized as incorporeal, it should be easy to see why some substance is required. The word "substance" is being used here in its main—not, alas, its only—philosophical sense. In this sense a substance is that which can significantly be said to exist separately and in its own right, so to speak. Any experience requires a substance to be the experience of in exactly the same way that a grin requires a face to be the grin of. Since it makes no sense to talk of a pain or a joy or any other sort of awareness without an owner, the Humean suggestion that a person might simply and solely consist in a collection of such "loose and separate" experiences must be rated as, strictly, nonsense.

And furthermore, as Hume himself came to realize and to confess in the Appendix to his *A Treatise of Human Nature,* there seems to be no available string, no uniting principle, to bind any such collection together and to distinguish it from any other. The obvious candidate might seem to be memory, as Locke had suggested earlier in his *Essay Concerning Human Understanding.* For surely, we are inclined to think, the person himself must always be able—if only he would tell us, and would tell us true—to say whether it was in fact he or another who had the thought or did the deed. But this congenial conviction ignores the possibilities of both amnesia (forgetting what did happen) and paramnesia (seeming to remember what did not happen). Also Bishop Butler had in his dissertation "Of Personal Identity" urged the quite decisive objection: "And one should really think it self-evident, that consciousness of personal identity presupposes, and therefore cannot constitute, personal identity; any more than knowledge, in any other case, can constitute truth, which it presupposes."[15]

Expressed in modern terms, there is no possibility of giving an account of the self-identity and individuation of incorporeal collections of experiences in terms of their memory capacities. Certainly if I truly remember, and do not merely seem to remember, doing the deed, then necessarily I must be the same person as did that deed: true memory thus presupposes true personal identity. But what I remember is that I am the same person as did the deed. That I do so remember is not what it is for me to be the same person as did it.

So what about the Cartesian alternative? Can we accept that an incorporeal person would be the incorporeal substance which enjoyed or suffered certain experiences, and was endowed with certain capacities? The principle of individuation would then be a matter of being, or belonging to, one such substance rather than to another; and the principle of self-identity would be a matter of being, or belonging to, the same such substance.

But now, before we discuss the qualifications of this candidate, can we be told who (or what) he (or it) is? For when we were dealing with "regular" or "conventional" (corporeal) persons, there was no difficulty in saying—indeed, in showing—what was the substance to which we were attributing the experiences, the dispositions. They were the experiences, the dispositions, or whatever, of a flesh and blood person. But what positive characterization can we give to these postulated incorporeal substances? Can we say anything to differentiate such an incorporeal substance

---

[15]*Ibid.*, pp. 166-172.

from an imaginary, an unreal, a nonexistent substance? I end the present subsection of this paper by quoting two sentences of damning comment from Terence Penelhum's book *Survival and Disembodied Existence:*

> Beyond the wholly empty assurance that it is a metaphysical principle which guarantees continuing identity through time, or the argument that since we know that identity persists some such principle must hold in default of others, no content seems available for the doctrine. Its irrelevance . . . is due to its being merely an alleged identity-guaranteeing condition of which no independent characterization is forthcoming.[16]

The Way of the Astral Body

At this point, let us again review how far we have gotten. In the first section I described the enormous initial obstacle to any survival doctrine. In the second section I explained that I was here concerned only with personal survival, and how it is the first step that counts. In the third section I distinguished three possible ways of trying to proceed around or over that initial obstacle. In the present, the fourth section, we have been examining the theoretical difficulties which afflict these three possible ways. The great, and in my view insuperable, difficulties of the Platonic-Cartesian way, the assumptions of which have so often been taken for granted or even asserted as known facts, should now lead us to look with a new interest and respect at the way of the astral body.

In the context of this more sympathetic approach, it begins to emerge that many of those who have been thought of as—and who probably thought themselves—Platonic-Cartesians have really been believers in astral bodies. There is, for instance, some reason to think that the Latin Father Tertullian, who certainly held the soul to be corporeal, was also inclined to think of it as of human shape; and what is this but an astral body? See Chapter IX of his *de Anima,* in which he cites the visions of the good sister who saw "a soul in bodily shape . . . in form resembling that of a human being in every respect." Tertullian then goes on to argue that such an object must have a color, which could be no other than an

---

[16]T. Penelhum, *Survival and Disembodied Existence* (New York, Humanities Press, 1970), p. 76.

"etherial transparent one."[17] Or consider the British naval hero Lord Nelson, who took the fact that he sometimes felt twinges where the arm lost in battle should have been as evidence that there are, and we really are, souls. If this is evidence for anything, it is evidence for the assumptions not of the Platonic-Cartesian way, but of the way of the astral body.

Since we come to examine this notion of an astral body so soon after deploying the objection to the candidate notion of incorporeal spiritual substance, it will be easy to see what the problem for the protagonist is going to be. It is, obviously, to find some positive characterization for an astral body: such that an astral body really would be a sort of body in a way in which an imaginary body, or a nonexistent body, or an incorporeal body are not sorts of body; and at the same time such that the hypothesis that we have, or are, astral bodies is not shown to be false by any presently available facts. Confronted by this problem, the danger for the protagonist of an astral body view is that in his concern to avoid immediate falsification by presently known facts he may so qualify the nature of the body which he wants to hypothesize that it becomes in effect not a body, albeit elusive, but instead an incorporeal Platonic-Cartesian soul; and the whole burden of the previous subsection is to show why that is something to be avoided.

In principle these dangers could, I think, be escaped fairly easily. We should need only to postulate the detectability of astral bodies by an instrument of a kind not yet invented. But such an utterly arbitrary postulation would invite the comment made by Bertrand Russell in another connection: "The method of 'postulating' what we want has many advantages; they are the same as the advantages of theft over honest toil."[18] Such a drastic postulation would be warranted—or perhaps I should say is warranted—only if we thought—or think—that the survival evidence cannot be interpreted in terms of various ESP ongoings among ordinary corporeal people, and if we also believe—as I have been arguing that we should—that the Platonic-Cartesian way will not go. It would also be much

---

[17]A. Flew, *op. cit.*, pp. 91-93.

[18]B. Russell, *Introduction to Mathematical Philosophy* (London, Allen & Unwin, 1919), p. 71.

encouraged if evidence for levitating, apporting, and generally rip-roaring physical mediumship were better than it is.

CONCLUSION

Nevertheless, at the end of the day I am not myself inclined to make the sort of postulation required in order to proceed along the way of the astral body. This because I remain persuaded by the sort of considerations first deployed in E.R. Dodds' paper "Why I Do Not Believe in Survival,"[19] considerations later revised and reinforced by Gardner Murphy in his "Difficulties Confronting the Survival Hypothesis."[20] It still seems to me, that is, that what is presented as "the survival evidence" can be adequately, and there-fore better, interpreted in terms of normal and paranormal trans-actions among the living; and this without postulating any surviv-ing entities whether incorporeal or corporeal. If, however, I took the opposite view to that of Dodds and Murphy on this issue, as many do, then I should have to postulate some sort of astral body; and that notwithstanding the rather formidable difficulties indicated in the previous subsection. For these difficulties, unlike those of the supposed hypothesis of disembodied survival, do not necessarily reduce the proposed postulate to incoherence. My conclusion is, therefore, that if there is to be a case for individual and personal survival, what survives must be some sort of astral body; but that, in the present state of the evidence, we have no need of that hypothesis.

---

[19]E.R. Dodds, *op. cit.*
[20]G. Murphy, *op. cit.*

CHAPTER 24

PERSONAL IDENTITY AND SURVIVAL*

C. D. BROAD

B EFORE ENTERING ON A DISCUSSION of the possibility of a human
personality surviving, in some sense or other, the death and
destruction of the body with which it has been associated, I will
make one preliminary remark. The few contemporary Western
philosophers who have troubled to discuss this question seem generally to have taken for granted that survival of a human personality would be equivalent to its persistence *without any kind of
bodily organism*. Some of them have proceeded to argue that the
very attempt to suppose a personal stream of experience, without
a body as organ and center of perception and action, and as the
source of a persistent background of bodily feeling, is an attempt
to suppose something self-contradictory or at least unimaginable.
They have concluded that it is simply meaningless to talk of the
possibility of a human personality surviving the death of its body.
Their opponents in this matter have tried to show that the supposition of a personal stream of experience, in the absence of any
kind of associated organism, is self-consistent and imaginable. They
have concluded that it is possible (at any rate in the sense of self-
consistent and imaginable) that a human personality should survive the death of the body with which it has been associated.

I have two comments to make on this. One concerns both parties,
and the other concerns the second group of them.

(1) Of all the hundreds of millions of men in every age and
clime who have believed (or have talked or acted as if they be-

---

*Reprinted from the *Newsletter* of the Parapsychology Foundation, Inc., 1958, by
permission of the Foundation and the executors of the C.D. Broad estate.

lieved) in human survival, hardly any have believed in survival *without a body*. Hindus and Buddhists, e.g. believe in reincarnation either in an ordinary human or animal body or occasionally in the body of a non-human rational being, such as a god or a demon. Christians believe in survival with a peculiar kind of supernatural body, correlated in some intimate and unique way with the natural body which has died. Nor are these views confined to the simple and the ignorant. Spinoza, e.g. certainly believed in human immortality; and he cannot possibly have believed, on his general principles, in the existence of a mind without some kind of body. Leibniz said explicitly that, if *per impossibile* a surviving mind were without an organism, it would be 'a deserter from the general order.' It seems to me rather futile for a modern philosopher to discuss the possibility of human survival on an assumption which would have been unhesitatingly rejected by almost everyone, lay or learned, who has ever claimed seriously to believe in it.

(2) Suppose it could be shown that it is neither inconceivable nor unimaginable that there should be a personal stream of experience not associated with any bodily organism. That would be by no means equivalent to showing that it is neither inconceivable nor unimaginable that the personality of a human being should survive, in an unembodied state, the death of his body. Such survival would require that a certain one such *unembodied* personal stream of experience stands to a certain one *embodied* personal stream of experience, associated with a human body now dead, in those peculiar and intimate relations which must hold if both are to be counted as successive segments of the experience of one and the same person. Is it conceivable that the requisite continuity and similarity should hold between two successive segments of personal experience so radically dissimilar in nature as these two would seem *prima facie* to be? Granted that there might conceivably be unembodied persons, and that there certainly have been embodied persons who have died, it might be still quite inconceivable or overwhelmingly improbable that any of the former should be personally indentical with any of the latter.

"DISPOSITIONAL BASIS" OF PERSONALITY

We can now enter on our main question. It seems to me that a *necessary,* though by no means a sufficient, condition for survival is that the whole or some considerable part of the *dispositional basis* of a human being's personality should persist, and should retain at least the main outlines of its characteristic type of organization, for some time after the disintegration of his brain and nervous system. The crux of the question is whether this is not merely conceivable, in the sense of involving no purely logical absurdity, but is also factually possible, i.e. not irreconcilable with any empirical facts or laws for which the evidence seems to be overwhelming.

To ascribe a disposition to anything is in itself merely to state a conditional proposition of a certain kind about it. In its vaguest form the statement is that, *if* this thing were at any time to be in circumstances of the kind *C, then* an event of a certain kind *E* would happen in a certain kind of relation *R* to it. In its ideally most definite form it would assert or imply a formula, connecting each alternative possible determinate specification of *C* with a certain one determinate specification of *E* and of *R*. This ideal is often reached in physics, but seldom or never in the case of biological or psychological dispositions. But, whether the conditional proposition asserted be vague or detailed, we do commonly take for granted that there must be, at the back of any such purely conditional fact, *a categorical* fact of a certain kind, viz. one about the more or less persistent *minute structure* of the thing in question, or about some more or less persistent *recurrent process* going on within it.

Now it is easy to imagine a persistent minute structure in a human being considered as a *physical object.* It is also easy to imagine recurrent processes, e.g. rhythmic chemical changes, changes of electric potential, etc., going on in the minute parts of a human being considered as a *physical object.* But it is very difficult to attach any clear meaning to phrases about persistent *purely mental* structure, or to the notion of *purely mental* processes other than experiences of the various kinds with which each of us is familiar through having had them, noticed them, and remembered them. So it is not at all clear what, if anything, would be meant by ascribing to a human being, considered as a *psychical subject,* either a persistent purely mental structure or recurrent non-introspectable mental processes. Thus, it is also inevitable that we should take for granted that the dispositional basis of a human being's personality resides wholly in the minute structure of his *brain and nervous system* and in recurrent *physical processes* that go on within it. Not only is that supposition intelligible and readily imaginable in detail. It is also in line with the view which we take without hesitation and with conspicuous success about the dispositional properties of purely physical objects, e.g. magnets or chemical compounds. Moreover, it seems *prima facie* to be borne out by what we know of the profound changes of personality, as evidenced in speech and behavior, following disease or injuries in the brain.

Now, on this assumption, it seems plain that it is impossible for the dispositional basis of a man's personality to exist in the absence of his brain and nervous system and therefore impossible for it to persist after the death and disintegration of his body.

Unless we are willing to drop the principle that every conditional fact about a thing must be grounded on a categorical fact about its persistent minute structure or recurrent internal processes, there seems to be only one view of human nature compatible with the possibility of the *post mortem* persistence of the dispositional basis of a man's personality. We must assume some variant of the Platonic-Cartesian view of human beings. This is the doctrine that every human being is some kind of intimate *compound* of two constitutents, one being his ordinary everyday body, and the other being something of a very different kind, not open to ordinary observation. Let us call the other constituent in this supposed compound a "Ψ-component." It would be necessary to suppose that the Ψ-component of a human being carries some part at least of the organized dispositional basis of his personality, and that during his life it is modified specifically and more or less permanently by the experiences which he has, the training which he receives, and so on.

Now there are at least two features in the traditional form of the Platonic-Cartesian doctrine which need not be accepted and which we should do well to reject. (i) We need not suppose that a Ψ-component *by itself* would be a *person,* or that it would *by itself* be associated with a stream of experience even at the sub-personal level, such as that enjoyed by a rabbit or an oyster. It might well be that personality, and even the lowliest form of actual experience, requires the combination of a Ψ-component with an appropriate living body. The known facts about the intimate dependence of a human being's personality on his body and its states would seem strongly to favor that form of the doctrine. (ii) We need not assume that a Ψ-component would be *unextended* and *unlocated,* and have none of the properties of a physical existent. If we gratuitously assume this, we shall at once be in trouble on two fronts. (*a*) How could it then be supposed to have minute structure or to be the seat of recurrent internal processes, which is what is needed if it is to carry traces and dispositions? (*b*) How could it be conceived to be united with a particular living body to constitute an ordinary human being? If we are to postulate a 'ghost-in-the-machine'— and that seems to be the *conditio sine qua non* for the possibility of the survival of human personality—then we must ascribe to it some of the *quasi*-physical properties of the traditional ghost. A mere unextended and unlocated Cartesian 'thinking substance' would be useless and embarrassing for our purposes; something more like primitive animism than refined Cartesianism is what we need.

Nowadays we have plenty of experience concerning physical existents which are extended and in a sense localized, which have persistent structure and are the seat of rhythmic modulations, which are not in any sense ordinary bodies, but which are closely associated with a body of a certain kind in a certain state. One example would be the electro-magnetic field associated with a conductor carrying an electric current. Or consider the sense in which the performance of an orchestral piece, which has been broadcast from a wireless station, exists in the form of modulations in the transmitting beam, in places where and at times when there is no suitably tuned receiver to pick it up and transform it into a pattern of sounds. Perhaps to think of what may persist of a human being after the death of his body as something which *has experiences and is even a person,* is as if one should imagine that the wireless transmission of an orchestral piece exists, in a region where there is no suitably attuned receiver, in the form of *unheard sounds* or at least in the form of *actual sound-waves.* And perhaps to think that *nothing* carrying the dispositional basis of a man's personality *could* exist after the death of his body, is as if one should imagine that nothing corresponding to the performance of an orchestral piece at a wireless transmitting-station could exist anywhere in space after the station which broadcast it had been destroyed.

Any analogy to what, if it be a fact, must be unique, is bound to be imperfect and to disclose its defects if developed in detail. But I think that the analogies which I have indicated suffice for the following purpose. They show that we can conceive a form of dualism, not inconsistent with the known facts of physics, physiology, and psychology, which would make it not impossible for the dispositional basis of a human personality to survive the death of the human being who had possessed that personality.

Let us grant, then, that it is neither logically inconsistent nor factually impossible that the dispositional basis of a man's personality, or at any rate some part of it, might continue to exist and to be organized on its former characteristic pattern, for some time after the death of his body, without being associated with any other living body. The next question is whether there is any evidence (and, if so, what) for or against this possibility being realized.

The persistence of dispositional basis presupposes, of course, that ordinary human beings have the dualistic constitution which I have indicated. Now I think it is fair to say that *apart from* some of the phenomena which are investigated by psychical researchers, there is nothing whatever to support or even to suggest this view of human beings, and a great deal which seems *prima facie* to be against it. If, like most contemporary Western philosophers and scientists, I were completely ignorant of, or blandly indifferent to, those phenomena, I should, like them, leave the matter there. But I do not share their ignorance, and I am not content to emulate the ostrich. So I pass on to the next point.

THE DUALISTIC HYPOTHESIS

As to the bearing of the phenomena studied by psychical researchers upon this question, I would make the following remarks:

(1) To establish the capacity for telepathy, clairvoyance, or precognition in certain human beings, or even in all of them, would not lend any *direct* support to this dualistic view of human

nature. At most it would show that the orthodox scientific account of the range and the causal conditions of human cognition of particular things and events needs to be amplified, and in some respects radically modified. Since the orthodox scientific account is associated with a monistic view of the constitution of human beings, any radical modification of the former *might* involve rejecting the latter. But it is not obvious that it *must* do so. And it is quite certain that to postulate a dualistic view of the constitution of man does not by itself provide any explanation for such paranormal phenomena. At most it might be the basis on which an explanation could be built.

(2) What are described as 'out-of-the-body experiences' appear *prima facie* to be favourably relevant to the dualistic hypothesis. These are experiences in which a person seems to himself to leave his body, to perceive it from a position outside it, to travel to a remote place, and from a position there to view surrounding things, persons, and events. Such experiences become important for the present purpose, only in so far as the subject's reported observations can be shown to be correct in matters of detail, and when the details could have been perceived normally only by a human being occupying the position which the subject seemed to himself to be occupying. Even so, if such experiences stood by themselves, it might be wiser to interpret them in ways that do not presuppose dualism, though this might involve stretching the notions of telepathy and clairvoyance far beyond the limits shown by present evidence.

(3) From the nature of the case, much the strongest support for the dualistic hypothesis comes from those phenomena which seem positively to require for their explanation the persistence, after the death of a human being, of something which carries traces of his experiences and habits during life, organized in the way that was characteristic of him when alive. The phenomena in question are of at least two kinds, viz. cases of haunting, and certain kinds of mediumistic communication. The latter are the more important, being more numerous and better attested. I agree with Professor Hornell Hart in thinking that it is essential to consider the facts under headings (2) and (3) in close connection with each other. For the two together give a much stronger support to the dualistic hypothesis than the sum of the supports given by each separately.

I would add here that, if there should be any cases in which there is satisfactory empirical evidence strongly suggestive of 'reincarnation', they would be favorably relevant to the dualistic hypothesis. For suppose that there were evidence which strongly suggests that a certain man B is a reincarnation of a certain other man A. The most plausible account would be the following. A was a compound of a certain Ψ-component and a certain human body. When A died, the Ψ-component, which had been combined with his body, persisted in an unembodied state. When B was conceived, this same Ψ-component entered into combination with the embryo which afterwards developed into B's body. There would then be a unique correlation between B's personality and A's, by way of the common Ψ-component. For this is the dispositional basis of both personalities, and the modulations imposed on its fundamental theme by A's experiences may enter into the innate character of B. But there is no reason whatever why B should remember any of A's experiences, or why there should be even as much continuity between B's personality and A's as there is between the several personalities which alternate with each other in a single human being in certain pathological cases.

It is plain that, even if reincarnation were a fact, it would be only extremely seldom that any evidence would be available for the proposition that a certain human being B is a reincarnation of a certain other human being A. It is true that, with certain subjects under hypnosis, a skilled operator can by suitable suggestions evoke highly dramatic and detailed ostensible memories, purporting to refer to one or more past lives. (The best examples known to me are to be found in a book entitled *De hypnotiska Hallucinationerna* by a contemporary Swedish psychiatrist, Dr. John Björkhem.) But, unless such ostensible memories can be tested (which, from the nature of the case, is seldom possible), and shown to be veridical and not explicable by knowledge acquired normally, they provide no evidence for reincarnation.

My impression is that the notion of reincarnation seems strange and improbable to most people in the West, even if they accept the possibility of survival or believe it to be a fact. Yet it is, and has from time immemorial been, taken for granted in the Far East both by plain men and philosophers. Speaking for myself, I would say that it seems to me on general grounds to be much the most plausible form of the doctrine of survival, though I would not go so far as Hume, who said, in his essay *Of the Immortality of the Soul,* '. . . *Metempsychosis* is . . . the only system of this kind that philosophy can hearken to.'

Four Alternative Possibilities

Let us now take the persistence of the dispositional basis as an hypothesis, and raise the following question: What are the alternative possibilities as to the kind and degree of consciousness which might be associated during a period of disembodiment, with what I have called the "Ψ-component" of a deceased human being?

There seem to me to be at least the following four alternative possibilities:

(1) The Ψ-component might persist *without any experience whatever* being associated with it, unless and until it should again become united with an appropriate living organism.

(2) Either isolated experiences, or even a stream of more or less continuous experience, might occur in association with a disembodied Ψ-component; but the individual experiences might not be of such a nature, and the unity of the stream of experience might not be of such a kind and degree, that we could talk of *personality*. The consciousness might not reach the level of that of a rabbit or even that of an oyster.

(3) There might be a unified stream of experience associated with a disembodied Ψ-component, and this might have some, but not all, the features of the experience of a full-blown personality. We may think of it by analogy with what we can remember of our state when dreaming more or less coherently. Such a stream of experience, in order to be of the personal kind, must contain states of ostensible remembering, and some or all of these might be veridical. But it might be that all of them are rememberings of *post mortem* experiences, and that there are no states of ostensibly remembering any experience had by the human being in question *before* his death. In that case the *post mortem* unembodied personality would be as diverse from the *ante mortem* embodied one as are the alternating personalities of a human being suffering from dissociation. On the other hand, it is conceivable that such a

dream-like personal stream of experience might contain veridical ostensible rememberings of certain *ante mortem* experiences, just as our dreams often contain such rememberings of our earlier waking experiences. In that case it would be as legitimate to identify the *post mortem* unembodied personality with the *ante mortem* embodied one as it is to identify the dream personality and the waking personality of an ordinary human being.

(4) Finally, there might be a personal stream of experience associated with a disembodied Ψ-component, which was as continuous and as highly unified as that of a normal human being in his waking life. Here again there would be two possibilities. (i) The ostensible rememberings, contained in this personal stream of experience, might all refer to *post mortem* experiences; or (ii) some of them might refer to *ante mortem* experiences, and all or most of these might be wholly or mainly veridical. In either case there would be a full-blown personality associated with a disembodied Ψ-component. In the former case this would be completely dissociated from the personality of the deceased human being in whom the Ψ-component had been embodied. In the latter case there would be the following two alternative possibilities. (*a*) The personality associated with the disembodied Ψ-component might remember experiences had by the deceased human being in question, only as a human being in his waking states remembers isolated fragments of his dreams. (*b*) The disembodied personality might remember experiences had by the deceased human being, just as a human being in his waking state at one time remembers experiences had by him in his earlier waking states. In that case, and in that alone, could we say that the personality of the deceased human being had survived the death of his body, in the full sense in which one's waking personality is reinstated after each period of normal sleep.

Plurality of Personalities

We may sum all this up as follows. When a human being dies, at least the following alternatives (besides the obvious one that death is altogether the end of him) seem *prima facie* to be possible. (1) Mere persistence of the dispositional basis of his personality, without any accompanying experiences. (2) Such persistence accompanied by consciousness only at an *infra-personal* level. (3) Such persistence accompanied by a *quasi*-personal dream-like stream of experience, which may either (*a*) be completely discontinuous with the *ante-mortem* experiences of the deceased, or (*b*) have that kind and degree of continuity with them which a man's dreams have with his earlier waking experiences. (4) Such persistence accompanied by a full-blown personal stream of experience. This may either (*a*) be completely discontinuous with the *ante-mortem* experiences of the deceased; or (*b*) be connected with them only in the way in which one's later waking experiences are connected with one's earlier dream experiences; or (*c*) be connected with them in the way in which successive segments of one's waking experience, separated by gaps of sleep, are connected with each other.

Let us next consider the respective probabilities of these various alternatives, when viewed in relation only to admitted facts *outside* the region of psychical research. I should be inclined to say that, when viewed exclusively in that context, the alternatives which I have enumerated are in *descending* order of probability.

The most likely alternative (excluding for the present purpose complete extinction) would seem, from that point of view, to be mere persistence of dispositional basis, without any kind of experiences being associated with it. For we know that, when sensory stimuli acting on a man's body from outside are reduced to a minimum, he tends to fall asleep. And we know that, when in addition sensory stimuli from within his body are reduced to a minimum, his sleep tends to be dreamless. Now a disembodied Ψ-component would presumably be completely free from both. Yet ordinary human beings, who are, on the present hypothesis, compounds of a Ψ-component with a living human body, do have frequent periods of sleep which is to all appearance dreamless. The inference is obvious.

The least likely alternative, from the point of view which we are at present taking, would seem to be that the persistent dispositional basis should be associated with a full-blown personal stream of experience, connected with that of the deceased in the way in which successive segments of his waking experience, separated by gaps of sleep, were interconnected with each other. For we know that certain variations, which occur within the body and its environment

during the life-time of a human being, are accompanied by profound breaches in the continuity of his consciousness, e.g. falling
asleep, delirium, madness, alternations of personality. Now the
change involved in the death and dissolution of the body, with
which a Ψ-component has been united, must surely be more radical
than any that happens during its embodiment. So it might reasonably be expected to involve at least as radical a breach in the continuity of consciousness as any that has been observed during the
lifetime of a human being.

At this point the following questions may be raised. Some human beings have a *plurality* of personalities, which alternate with
each other. In the case of such a human being we may ask ourselves
the questions: If *any* of these personalities survive the death of the
body, *how many* of them do so? And, if not all do so, *which
ones* do?

This leads me to the following general reflection. The single
personality of the most normal human being is notoriously much
less stable and comprehensive than it may seem to others or even
to himself. The dispositional basis of it does not include by any
means all of his dispositions, inherited and acquired. It consists of
a predominant selection from that whole, much more highly organized than the rest, and organized in a certain characteristic way.
It might be compared to a single crystal, surrounded by a mass of
saturated solution, from which it has crystallized and in which it
floats. The total dispositional basis of a human being with two
personalities, which alternate with each other, might be compared
to a saturated solution which has a tendency to crystallize out,
sometimes at one and sometimes at another of two centers, and in
two different crystalline forms. Suppose now that the dispositions
of a human being are grounded in the structure and rhythmic
processes of a Ψ-component united with his body, and suppose
that this Ψ-component persists after his death and carries with it
the structural and rhythmic basis of those dispositions. It seems not
unreasonable to think that the Ψ-component, which had been
united with the body of even the most normal and stable human
being, would be liable to undergo a sudden or a gradual change
of internal structure and rhythm, a disintegration or a reintegration
on different lines, after its union with that body had been com-

pletely broken. These considerations seem to me to reinforce those already put forward for holding that straightforward survival of the personality of a deceased human being is antecedently the least likely of all the alternatives under discussion.

Another consideration which seems relevant here is this. The personal stream of experience of any ordinary human being has the following characteristic features among others. (i) It contains a core of bodily feeling, which generally changes but slowly in the course of one's life. (ii) Objects other than the body are perceived as from a center within the body, and as orientated about it at various distances from it. (iii) It contains experiences of making, carrying out, modifying, dropping, and resuming various plans of action, which involve initiating, controlling, and inhibiting bodily movements. (iv) In particular it contains experiences of speaking and writing, of listening to the talk of others, engaging in conversation with them, reading their writings, and so on. An extremely important part of the dispositional basis of any embodied human personality is the ability of organized dispositions to have such experiences and to initiate and control such bodily movements.

Now it is not very easy to believe that a set of organized dispositions, so intimately connected in origin and in exercise with the body and its functions, can be located in something other than the body and only temporarily connected with it. Let us, however, waive that difficulty. Let us suppose that a disembodied Ψ-component does carry with it specific modifications of structure or rhythm answering to such dispositions. Even so, it is plainly impossible that those dispositions should be manifesting themselves in *actual* speaking, writing or listening during a period of disembodiment. It is also impossible that there should be at such times experiences of *actually* perceiving from a bodily center, or of *actually* carrying out intentions by initiating and controlling bodily movements. Nor is it possible at such times that there should be a core of feeling *actually* arising from the body and its internal states and processes. But it would not be inconceivable that there should be a stream of *delusive quasi*-perceptual experiences, as of speaking, listening, reading, writing, doing and suffering, such as we have in our dreams. And it is not inconceivable that there might be a core of feeling or of imagery, qualitatively like that which one gets from one's body during one's lifetime, but not actually arising from an organism and its internal processes.

✻ TELEPATHY, CLAIRVOYANCE, MEDIUMSHIP

So much for the antecedent probalities of the various alternatives, when considered *without* reference to the phenomena studied by psychical researchers. Let us now introduce these into the background of our picture, and see what differences, if any, they make.

(1) I think that the fact that some human beings are capable of telepathic or clairvoyant cognition tends to weaken the otherwise strong probability that a Ψ-component, so long as it was unembodied, would merely persist without any kind of experience being associated with it. In order that a disposition may express itself in actual experience or action it needs to receive an appropriate stimulus. The appropriate stimuli for calling forth *normal* experiences in a human being are undoubtedly certain events in his brain and nervous system. Such stimuli presumably could not act upon a disembodied Ψ-component. Suppose, now, that we postulate a dualistic account of human beings; and that we admit, as we must, that they sometimes have telepathic or clairvoyant experiences. Then it would seem plausible to suggest that such experiences are evoked by some kind of *direct* stimulation of an embodied Ψ-component by the action of other Ψ-components, embodied or disembodied. Since this kind of action would not be mediated by the body, even in the case of an embodied Ψ-component, there is no reason why it should not continue to operate on a Ψ-component after it had ceased to be combined with a body. It might even operate much more freely under such conditions.

(2) Most of the well attested cases of haunting suggest no more than the persistence and the localization of something which carries traces of a small and superficial, but for some reason obsessive, fragment of the experiences had by a deceased human being within a certain limited region of space.

(3) Many mediumistic communications, which take the dramatic form of messages from the surviving spirit of a deceased human being, imparted to and reported by the medium's "control," obviously require no more radical assumption than telepathic cognition, on the medium's part, of facts known (consciously or un-

consciously) to the sitter or to other living human beings connected with him. But this kind of explanation seems to me to become intolerably strained in reference to some mediumistic phenomena.

Here I would call special attention to the many well attested cases, where the dramatic form of the sitting is direct control of the medium's body by the surviving spirit of a certain deceased human being, and where the medium speaks with a voice and behaves with mannerisms which are recognizably reminiscent of the alleged communicator, although she has never met him or heard or seen any reproduction of his voice or his gestures.* There are also cases in which it is alleged that a medium produces auto-matic script, purporting to be written under the control of the spirit of a certain deceased human being, and undoubtedly in his highly characteristic handwriting, although she has never seen, either in original or in reproduction, any specimens of his manu-script. I do not know whether any such cases are well attested; but, if they be, they fall under the same category as the direct-voice cases, some of which certainly appear to be so.

Now it seems to me that any attempt to explain these phenomena by reference to telepathy among the living stretches the word "te-lepathy" till it becomes almost meaningless, and invokes something under that name for which there is not a trace of independent evi-dence. *Prima facie* such phenomena are strong evidence for the persistence, after a man's death, of something which carries orga-nized traces of his experiences, habits, and skills, and which be-comes temporarily united during the seance with the entranced medium's organism. But they are *prima facie* evidence for some-thing more specific and very surprising indeed. For they seem to show that dispositions to certain highly specific kinds of *bodily* behavior, e.g. speaking in a certain characteristic tone of voice, writing in a certain characteristic hand, making certain character-istic gestures, etc., are carried by the Ψ-component when it ceases to be embodied, and are ready to manifest themselves whenever it is again temporarily united with a suitable living human body. And so strong do these dispositions remain that, when thus temporarily

---

*An elaborate account of such a case will be found in Vol. XXXVIII, Part 107, of the S.P.R. *Proceedings,* in an article by the late Mr. Drayton Thomas entitled "The Modus Operandi of Trance Communications."

activated, they overcome the corresponding dispositions of the entranced medium to speak, write, and gesticulate in *her own* habitual ways.

(4) Most of the well attested mediumistic phenomena which are commonly cited as evidence for the survival of a deceased human being's personality seem to me not to support so strong a conclusion. They fit as well or better into the following weaker hypothesis. Suppose that the Ψ-component of the late Mr. Jones persists, and that it carries some at least of the dispositional basis of his personality, including organized traces left by his experiences, his acquired skills, his habits. Suppose that a medium is a human being in whom the Ψ-component is somewhat loosely combined with the body, or in whom at any rate the combination does not prevent the body having a residual attraction for other Ψ-components. (We might compare a medium, in this respect, to an unsaturated organic compound, such as acetylene.) When the medium is in trance we may suppose that the persisting Ψ-component of some deceased human being, e.g. the late Mr. Jones, unites with the medium's brain and nervous system to form the basis of a temporary personality. This might be expected to have some of the memories and traits of the deceased person, together with some of those of the medium's own normal personality. But, unless the persistent Ψ-component has a personal stream of experience associated with it during the periods when it is *not* combined with the body of a medium, no evidence would be supplied at any sitting of *new* experiences being had, of *new* plans being formed and initiated, or of any *post mortem* development of the personality.

"THE WORLD AS IT REALLY IS"

Now it seems to me that the *vast majority* of even the best mediumistic communications combine these positive and these negative features. That is not true, I think, of quite all of them. Some few do seem *prima facie* to suggest the persistence of something which forms plans and initiates them between successive sittings.*

Of course, if the dispositional basis of a man's personality should

---

*The best of the cross-correspondence cases obviously fall under this heading. A useful collection of a variety of relevant instances has been published by Mrs. Richmond in a little book entitled *Evidence of Purpose*.

persist after his death, there is no reason why it should have the same fate in all cases. In some cases one, and in others another, of the various alternatives which I have discussed, might be realized. It seems reasonable to think that the state of development of the personality at the time of death, and the circumstances under which death takes place, might be relevant factors in determining which alternative would be realized. Obviously there might be many other highly relevant factors, which our ignorance prevents us from envisaging.

Again, it would be rash to assume that those Ψ-components of the deceased, for the persistence of which we have some *prima facie* evidence, are a fair selection of those which in fact persist. The nature, or the circumstances, or both, of the very few which manifest their continued existence, whether as ghosts or through mediums, may well be highly exceptional. Plainly, in the case of the vast majority of the dead, either they never had Ψ-components; or their Ψ-components have ceased to exist; or they have been reembodied either on earth or elsewhere, in human or in non-human bodies; or else they have lacked opportunity to communicate, or have failed (whether through lack of desire or of energy or of capacity) to make use of the opportunities which were available. For, if anything is certain, it is that the vast majority of dead men tell no tales and, so far as we are concerned, have vanished without trace.

In conclusion, I would say that I am inclined to think that those who have speculated on these topics have often oversimplified the subject in one or both of the following ways. In the first place, they have tended to ignore the discontinuities and abnormalities which are known to occur in the personalities of ordinary or pathological human beings. Secondly, in dealing with traces and dispositions, they have confined their attention to very narrow and old-fashioned physical analogies. I suspect that they tend to think of the dispositional basis of a personality by the old analogy of a ball of wax, on which experiences make traces, as a seal might leave impressions. It is plain that this analogy *must* be inadequate and positively misleading, even on a purely anatomical and physiological view of the facts of memory, of association, of heredity. *A fortiori* it must be hopelessly cramping to anyone who is trying to envisage a basis of dispositions which might persist after the death of a man's body.

Once we get outside this narrow sphere, and consider analogies with persistent vortices, stationary waves, and transmitting beams, we can envisage a number of interesting and fantastic possibilities. We can think of the possibility of partial coalescence, partial mutual annulment and reinforcement, and interference, between the Ψ-components of several deceased human beings, in conjunction perhaps with non-human psychic flotsam and jetsam which may exist around us. There are reported mediumistic phenomena, and pathological mental cases not ostensibly involving mediumship, which suggest that some of these disturbing possibilities may sometimes be realized. It is worth while to remember, though there is nothing that we can do about it, that the world as it really is may easily be a far nastier place than it would be if scientific materialism were the whole truth and nothing but the truth.

SECTION V
PSI AND SCIENCE

CHAPTER 25

INTRODUCTION

HOYT L. EDGE

Properly speaking, can parapsychology be considered a legitimate science? On the one hand, this question calls for a rather thorough knowledge of parapsychology, its content and its methods. On the other hand, this question calls for an adequate characterization of science—precisely what characteristics do we find in science, and does parapsychology fulfill them? A very basic condition of science, as Beloff points out, is an unremitting respect for truth, a condition that parapsychology surely fulfills. A second general characteristic of science is its use of empirical methods. Parapsychology, also, relies on observation. Indeed, it is the systematic observation of these unusual phenomena that has converted a once casual and haphazard collection of anecdotes into parapsychology. Further, the essential characteristic that separates this discipline from so called "occult" areas of thought is the reliance of parapsychology on empirical methods.*

A third characteristic of science is its quantitative nature. This, of course, varies according to the kind of science (natural or social), but both kinds are attempting to quantify their disciplines so far as the discipline will allow. There seems to be no question

---

*As an interjection, it is interesting to note that some people have questioned whether this characteristic of science (i.e. strict observation) has been too narrowly construed in the past. We have already seen Wheatley asserting that psi could be used to validate theories, although it is usually not thought to be able to. In this section, Tart (under "Observable Consequences") seems to agree with this view: "Thus a perfectly scientific theory may be based on data that have no physical existence." If this is the case, we would find psi being proved through traditional empirical methods, and then it could be used in an expanded view of what it means to be empirical. For another discussion of the possibility of a non-sensory-based science, confer the Feyerabend article found in the bibliography.

that, at least since the founding of J.B. Rhine's laboratory at Duke in the nineteen thirties, parapsychology has had as one of its main objectives the quantification of psi. Precisely how far parapsychology has advanced in this process, especially in light of its subject matter, its history, and its relatively recent attempt at quantification, is admittedly a subject for discussion; but there is no question that much progress has been made in this direction and that current workers in this field are constantly seeking to quantify their data as much as the discipline will allow at this point.

A fourth characteristic of science is the necessity for repeatability. In order to be accepted by the scientific community, the results of an experiment must be able to be replicated by others. Beloff discusses this basic aspect of science in his article and concludes that parapsychologists have not been sufficiently concerned about this aspect of their work. Indeed, some psi researchers argue that repeatability is simply not necessary. Others maintain that parapsychology has as much evidence of repeatability as some areas of psychology or even of astronomy, while still others contend that if a given experimental subject can repeat his performance over several experiments with the same researcher, the results are sufficiently corroborated—even if the subject should fail with another experimenter or lose his ability altogether. However, when one takes an overview of the issue, it seems obvious that most parapsychologists today are more concerned with repeatability than they were a half-dozen years ago and are taking steps to insure repeatability, both through their reporting of experiments and in their selection of kinds of experiments to undertake.

Finally, perhaps the most important characteristic of science is discussed by Murphy, who points out that it is not the business of science to collect disconnected "facts"; rather, it should aim at "solid facts," facts that fit into a conceptual scheme. As of yet, such a conceptual scheme or model has not been found for parapsychology. In suggesting how such a model might be constructed, Murphy discusses a set of seemingly isolated facts in terms of three theories of the mind-body connection. At this time, however, in this final sense of science, i.e. that the discipline must have a conceptual scheme into which its facts fit, parapsychology cannot yet be considered a science.

Is parapsychology, then, compatible with science? Meehl and Scriven argue that it is not incompatible with science, while Chauvin observes that, while in several ways parapsychology does not seem to fit in with the physics of today, that does not mean that it is incompatible with physics per se. First, psi may be compatible with "perennial physics" in that the physics of the future may be able to subsume psi into its theories and laws. Secondly, one cannot even say that psi contradicts present-day physics, for, even if we can discover the laws that govern psi, the present physical laws will be valid in their own domain, much as mechanical physics is true in its domain, although superceded in general by Einsteinean physics. Thus, just as plane geometry is true for planes but has been superceded by other geometries that give us a truer picture of the universe, contemporary physics (under which psi is not subsumable) can be considered as true, although it will be superceded by a future physics, which may explain psi in a law-like manner. Therefore, as Chauvin contends, an explanation of psi would not necessarily contradict contemporary physics but merely supercede it.

In contrast, Beloff points out that we ought not be too quick in trying to bring together parapsychology and other sciences, for the attempt to spiritualize physics or to physicalize the paranormal overlooks some very important distinctions. Also, Beloff asserts, there is nothing logically incoherent about dualism or dualistic interactionism, and in the end, this traditional view may be correct.

Approaching the problem in a different way, Shewmaker and Berenda take a rather radical position on the question of whether psi can be scientifically proved. Rejecting the position of Rhine and Soal, who argue that science will prove the existence of psi, Shewmaker and Berenda point out that science is in effect an abstraction of the world. Science is our way of understanding and controlling the world by utilizing certain abstract classification schemes, schemes which by their very nature cannot capture the entire nature of the world. According to Shewmaker and Berenda, the reason psi is incompatible with science is precisely because psi represents those events which are excluded by scientific classification schemes and abstractions. Thus, whether or not we can have a science of psi depends on whether or not we can have a science of the "unique," a solution which the two authors do not view as impossible. A concomitant issue not discussed by Shewmaker and Berenda, but one which we have already met in Chauvin's article, is whether the abstractions of science will not most likely be changed (in a "perennial science") to be able to include psi, not simply as data in a science of the unique, but within science's own future set of abstractions.

Of further interest in probing the complex relation between psi and science is LeShan's article, many points of which apply to several of the issues already considered in other sections as well, but which is of particular interest here because of his lucid discussion of the divergence between what he calls "Scientific Reality" and "Commonsense Individual Reality." As a further clarification, LeShan sets forth some noteworthy similarities between the Mystical and Clairvoyant Individual Realities. Just as he wants to say that neither the scientific nor the commonsense view of the world is wrong, so he wants to say that the mystical or the clairvoyant way of viewing the world is no more correct or incorrect than the scientific or commonsense way of viewing the world. Elsewhere in the monograph that this selection is taken from, LeShan says:

> Our view here is that perceiving reality in different—although equally valid—ways produces different possibilities of interaction with it. The Western cultural view of reality is seen, in this exploration, as valid. The mystical (and clairvoyant) view of reality is seen as equally valid. Neither is *more true* than the other. It depends on what you are trying to do that determines which is more effective. (p. 42)

In relating LeShan's position here back to that of Shewmaker and Berenda, one must conclude that all would agree that the abstractions of science are valid and useful for predicting and controlling some aspects of the world. But the mystical and clairvoyant views of the world (perhaps also abstractions?) are equally valid for their purposes, although LeShan admits that biologically, one could not survive very well using only the mystical or clairvoyant world view. In concluding his discussion, LeShan constructs a table contrasting the separate realities of an individual, using his sensory faculties on the one hand, and his clairvoyant faculties on the other.

The final article in this section is an attempt to provide a theoretical framework for the scientific investigation of Altered States of Consciousness. Such a framework is important, not only for psychology, but for parapsychology as well because there is much evidence to support the view that psi is manifested more readily in an altered state of consciousness—as one would guess from the previous article. Also interesting in relation to the LeShan article is Tart's argument that it would be possible to establish a science of altered states of consciousness—hence, perhaps possible to establish a science of the mystical and the clairvoyant experiences. For the present it might be easier than any other approach to make psi compatible with science in this way and keep working toward a general theory of psi which would subsume all the isolated facts under it and explain, if possible, the relationship of these facts to presently accepted physical facts.

CHAPTER 26

PARAPSYCHOLOGY AND ITS NEIGHBORS*

JOHN BELOFF

THE QUESTION I WISH TO DISCUSS is one that anybody who, like myself, tries to promote parapsychology within an academic setting is forced to consider; namely, "In what respects does parapsychology resemble and in what respects does it differ from any of the established sciences?" What I propose to do is to offer you my answer to this question. Briefly, my thesis will be that, with regard to what we may loosely call procedural questions—by which I mean the whole unwritten code of conduct that governs scientific discourse—there is, or there should be, no distinction whatever between parapsychology and any of the established sciences, be they physical, biological, or behavioral. With regard to the conceptual framework, however, within which the natural sciences have evolved, and more especially with regard to their physicalistic assumptions, there is a profound distinction between us and them, one which, so far as I can see, cannot be bridged. In order to develop this thesis I may, I fear, have to tread on some rather august toes. I trust, however, that the owners of these toes, if present, will not hold this against me. I do so, I can assure them, without malice.

To begin with, then, what is it that most unites us with our neighbors of the scientific community? I hope, an unremitting respect for truth. It is a solemn thought that science is the only realm of inquiry where universal consensus is attainable. Religion, philosophy, politics are based on faith, on opinion, on partisanship and tend to divide rather than unite mankind; art is dependent on

*Reprinted from *The Journal of Parapsychology,* 1970, by permission of the author and the editors. This paper was first presented as the dinner address at the Summer Review Meeting of the Institute for Parapsychology, August 28, 1969.

feeling and intuition, and these are personal experiences; science alone, being exclusively concerned with truth, is universal. This was not always so. One of the significant changes that took place when medieval science gave way to modern science was the renunciation of personal authority. More than ever, science required its experts and its men of vision, but the final court of appeal was henceforth to the facts. The development of scientific method was largely the attempt to reduce the personal bias in experiment, a bias which, because scientists are human, can probably never be completely eliminated. Parapsychology clearly has a long way to go before we can begin to speak of a consensus; but Dr. Rhine can, I think, be rightly credited with having made parapsychology a science by introducing a methodology which, in principle at least, is wholly objective.

And yet, there remains one lesson, it seems to me, that parapsychologists have still failed to learn. I refer to the problem of repeatability. One rule that science insists upon is that no new discovery be admitted to the general body of scientific knowledge until it has been checked and corroborated by some independent investigator. Only thus can we insure against the fallibility of the individual worker. In parapsychology, however, although we pay lip service to the principle of repeatability, we indulge in every manner of special pleading in order to cover up our failure to honor it. I could, were I so inclined, publish a fat anthology, culled from the pages of the parapsychological journals, of all the arguments I have read purporting to show that in parapsychology a repeatable experiment is either unnecessary or impossible. Now, there may well be excellent reasons why, in our field, reproducibility should prove so difficult to attain: the curiously elusive nature of the phenomena we study, the unconscious channels through which they operate, the subtlety of the variables involved in the effect, and so on. What is impermissible is to pretend that, unlike other scientists, *we* do not need to have our findings confirmed. For we cannot have it both ways; if we want to be treated on a par with the other sciences, then we cannot flout the very criteria that are used to distinguish genuine from pseudoscience.

It is merely frivolous to say, as I have heard it said, that astronomy, the most exact of all the sciences, deals with nonrepeatable events, for this ignores the fact than an astronomical observation can be corroborated at many different observatories. It also ignores the fact that astronomy is now so well integrated with physics that the two serve to buttress one another. It is a very different matter when, as in parapsychology, the observations are not only open to suspicion but lack any theoretical underpinning. The difference is well illustrated by considering what happens when something really unexpected does turn up in astronomy. Take for example the discovery of the quasars and of the still more recent pulsars. Neither of these new entities admits of a satisfactory interpretation in conventional terms, yet both are already firmly established facts of radioastronomy. How is this possible? The answer is that the relevant observations have been corroborated by all who are in a position to judge. I wish I could say the same of even a single psi phenomenon. Unfortunately, in parapsychology we labor under the double handicap of dealing with phenomena that are at once inexplicable *and* unrepeatable.

Does this mean that I reject the parapsychological evidence? By no means. As many of you will know, I am an incorrigible sheep, even among parapsychologists. Probably the catalogue of all the things that I manage to believe would shock some of the more staid and conservative among you. My credo would have to contain such oddly assorted names as Eusapia Palladino, Gilbert Murray, Stefan Ossowiecki, Ted Serios, and many others. But I accept them, not as scientific facts, but rather as historical facts, the distinction being that historical facts are necessarily unique and therefore nonrepeatable. And this applies equally to those cases in which the evidence is of the statistical variety, as in the standard controlled experiments we carry out in our laboratories. The fact that we are able to quote some approved level of significance does not automatically imply that our findings are scientific facts. To be that, they would first have to be confirmed by other workers in other laboratories. So long as they remain bound to some particular subject or experimenter performing under particular conditions on particular occasions, they remain just as much historical facts as any of the more bizarre and singular episodes that have found their way into the parapsychological literature.

In calling such cases historical facts, I am, I must point out, already going further than some philosophers would allow. Living in Edinburgh, I can never for long forget the name of David Hume; and it was Hume who insisted that no miracle should ever be believed, however good the evidence, since no human testimony could ever cancel out the antecedent improbability of an event that had to qualify as miraculous. Hume's advice has much to recommend it; but no rule, however sound, can logically dictate whether in a particular case we believe or disbelieve. We either do or we don't. As it happens, I have no option but to part company with Hume in favor of certain parapsychological miracles when I find that the only normal counterexplanations are even more incredible than the phenomena themselves. But Hume was astute enough to realize that if a miracle could be repeated, it would eventually compel belief, however much it might run counter to accepted laws. My plea to you today not to abandon the search for a repeatable experiment is, in effect, a plea to consummate the revolution which Dr. Rhine began more than thirty years ago and convert parapsychology from a historical science into a genuinely experimental science.

Yet, how far we still are from having learned this lesson is apparent when we examine certain pronouncements that have gone forth from this institute. Thus, in his Foundation Day address, "The Status and Prospect of Parapsychology Today," Dr. Rhine himself castigates psychologists who carry out psi experiments "on the assumption that if ESP is a genuine ability, it ought to be counted on to show itself in much the same way as memory or learning or subliminal vision"; and he goes on to remark, "What these many ill-conceived experiments do indicate is that psi cannot be dealt with in the absence of a research worker capable of producing it—that is, able to obtain results under adequately controlled conditions."[1] Now, I do not propose to question that what Dr. Rhine says here may well be true. Thus, it may well be that the successful outcome of a parapsychological experiment may be as much a function of the experimenter as of the subject. Following the work

[1] J.B. Rhine, "The Status and Prospect of Parapsychology Today," *Parapsychology from Duke to FRNM* (Durham, N.C., Parapsychology Press, 1965), p. 112.

of Rosenthal,[2] psychologists themselves have become very conscious of the so-called "experimenter effect." But if Rosenthal is
right, then it is our duty to isolate the relevant experimenter variables so that these too may be controlled. Does a successful experimenter have to have blue eyes and curly hair? It hardly matters
what the variable turns out to be only so long as we can specify it.
But if it remains at the level of a mere *je ne sais quoi,* then, I regret
to say, we are not yet an experimental science.

I wish to be scrupulously fair on this point. Dr. Rhine is undoubtedly correct in supposing that parapsychology has its own
special expertise and that those whose only training has been in
general experimental psychology are liable to make a hash of
things when they embark unthinkingly on some parapsychological
project. In science there is such a thing as sheer connoisseurship
and, as Polanyi has made abundantly clear, connoisseurship is not
something that can be communicated by any mere set of instructions; it can be acquired only by active participation in the field.
This is true in any speciality and it is no less true in parapsychology.
But, having said that, we must be careful how we use this argument.
If, by connoisseurship, we mean no more than the know-how that
enables one to design fruitful experiments, that is quite unexcep-
tionable. If, on the other hand, we mean some unaccountable
mystique that enables some individuals to elicit positive scoring
from otherwise "dud" subjects, then we have got to confess that
parapsychology is not a science after all but an art. Worse still, it is
beginning to look as if the good experimenter is going to be no
less rare than the good subject, in which case we shall be no better
off than we were before Dr. Rhine introduced his standard card-
guessing techniques which made it possible to test unselected
populations. At all events, the psychologists whom Dr. Rhine takes
to task when they fail to corroborate psi effects are merely paying
us the compliment of taking seriously our published claims. If we
have omitted to specify the critical variables, we cannot hold them
responsible if the experiment is a fiasco.

This concludes all that I now wish to say regarding the procedural aspects of parapsychology. My main point in this con-

---

[2]R. Rosenthal, *Experimenter Effects in Behavioral Research* (New York, Meredith
Publishing Co., 1966).

nection is that we must never make our weakness an excuse for demanding preferential treatment. I pass next to questions of substance. Here there will be a standing temptation to try and minimize the difference between ourselves and our neighbors, to pretend that we are not as subversive as we look, that we are not out to rock the boat, but that we are interested only in enlarging the frontiers of knowledge. There are, roughly, two main arguments that we may invoke at this juncture, and they start from opposite premises. On the one hand, we may argue that nothing but the relic of an old-fashioned materialism stands in the way of a complete rapprochement, that the boundary between the normal and the paranormal or between matter and mind has become so fluid that the modern sophisticated scientist need no longer feel scandalized by claims that would have shocked his Victorian predecessors. Alternatively—and this is more likely to be the line taken by those physical scientists who are attracted to parapsychology—we may argue that what we are concerned with essentially are certain obscure properties of the brain and that, as these become better understood and as science generally advances, they will find a natural explanation in keeping with the universal laws of physics and chemistry. The first of these arguments might be described as the attempt to spiritualize physics, the second as the attempt to physicalize parapsychology. Let us proceed to examine each in turn and see how it stands up to scrutiny.

To prove that everything is, in the last resort, mental, psychical or spiritual is the avowed aim of what philosophers call idealism. Its first exponent in modern European philosophy was the great Leibniz, who taught that atoms were really spiritual entities whose essence was to perceive rather than to occupy space. But it was, of course, Berkeley who put forward the first fully fledged idealist ontology which dispensed entirely with the concept of matter, in any objective sense, and made perception a kind of telepathic communication between an individual soul and an all-knowing deity. But Berkeley was writing in the noontime of the Enlightenment, and to his contemporaries he appeared mainly as a purveyor of elegant paradoxes. What gave idealism its initial impetus and brought it to the crest of its power was the romantic movement. The writers of the romantic epoch disliked both the mechanistic universe that Newton had bequeathed to them and the industrial civilization with which it had become closely associated. Hence the paradox that while, in the course of the nineteenth century, science became ever more powerful and materialistic, philosophy, as if by way of compensation, became ever more idealistic. This was true especially of Germany, the natural homeland of romanticism; but towards the end of the century even British philosophers succumbed to the lure of idealism and temporarily forsook their native empiricism. To those who had lost faith in revealed religion but found intolerable the thought of a vast, impersonal universe divested of purpose and meaning in which mankind existed as an accident of evolution, the assurances of idealist metaphysics provided an acceptable refuge. There were some, however, for whom a metaphysical solution of their religious perplexities was not enough, notably for the founding fathers of psychical research in England. It was precisely because they took science and scientific materialism seriously that they were determined either to establish the supernatural by scientific and empirical means or to abandon it once and for all as outworn superstition. It was, I suggest, this peculiar matter-of-factness and absence of dogmatism that is so salient a characteristic of the English outlook that made England rather than Germany or France the cradle of parapsychology.

In the course of this century, metaphysics came under fire from all directions and system-building became discredited, with the result that idealism as a philosophical school passed out of currency. Nevertheless, the attempt to rebut scientific materialism, or at least to draw its sting, has persisted. It can be found today in the works of philosophers who have little else in common, among existentialists as well as among adherents of linguistic philosophy. What this attempt usually amounts to is a refusal to grant to physics any prior claim to speak about the fundamental nature of the world. Physics, we are told, is but one specialized field of inquiry, one species of language game, and it cannot override the claims of other disciplines or of informed common sense. By talk of this kind, the bogey of reductionism is thought to be laid and, in particular, the autonomy of psychology preserved from the reductionist implications of brain physiology. Where exactly this leaves parapsychology is unclear because, for some reason, philosophers of this persuasion rarely seem to notice its existence.

Supporters of parapsychology sometimes take the line that modern physics is itself no longer materialistic and therefore no longer presents an insuperable barrier to an acceptance of the paranormal. This argument, I submit, is based on misunderstanding. What lies behind it is the undeniable fact that the concept of matter has indeed changed out of all recognition since late Victorian times. The search for fundamental particles lost its way, or so it looks to the layman, in a cloud of probability waves and suchlike mathematical abstractions, and meanwhile, energy rather than mass became the fundamental variable in physics. But I cannot see that this affords much comfort to the antimaterialist. Physics may have become exceedingly baffling, but this does not make it mystical. It has lost nothing of its precision; the conservation laws, which I take to be the core of physical theory, still stand; and, although various effects may now exist that were previously held to be impossible, this does not imply that anything is now possible or conceivable. The most, I think, that can be claimed in this connection is that scientists have become a lot more open minded than they once were.

So much, then, for the attempt to spiritualize the material realm. Of much greater interest, in my view, and of much more significance for the future of parapsychology is the converse attempt to physicalize the paranormal, for if it succeeded, if it even offered a moderate chance of success, it would, at one stroke, put an end to our isolation, so that instead of being regarded by our neighbors as hankering after a return to magic, we would forthwith take our place in the vanguard of science. For this reason, we should pay special attention to those scientists who have responded positively to the challenge of parapsychology by offering us, in however sketchy a form, physicalistic interpretations of psi phenomena. I would like especially to draw your attention to one such article by my friend Adrian Dobbs entitled "The Feasibility of a Physical Theory of ESP."[3] I am not convinced that Dobbs' theory is in fact feasible, but it is remarkable for its boldness and provides a salutary corrective to those who are inclined to dismiss physical theories of

---

[3]A. Dobbs, "The Feasibility of a Physical Theory of ESP," *Science and ESP*, J.R. Smythies, ed. (London, Routledge & Kegan Paul, 1967).

ESP out of hand. In this article he presents two separate theories, one a theory of telepathy, the other a theory of precognition. His theory of telepathy is based on a concept now current in quantum physics of particles with mathematically imaginary mass or energy. It transpires that such particles are not subject to the frictional loss of energy that applies to particles having real mass, but that they can interact with the latter. Telepathy, according to Dobbs, could be conceived of as an emission of a cloud of such imaginary-mass particles ("psitrons," he calls them), following upon some perturbation in the brain of the agent, which succeed in triggering off an overt response on the part of the receiver when they interact with certain "critically poised neurones" in the latter's brain. His theory of precognition is no less daring and revolutionary. It is based on the idea that a physical system at any given instant emits information relating to the possibilities of development that are inherent within it. This information is of a probabilistic nature only, so that what happens when a subject is said to precognize some event is that he somehow senses these objective probabilities, or "precasts," to use Dobbs' term. This theory is developed much more fully in his article "Time and ESP" in the *Proceedings of the S.P.R.*,[4] but here I am concerned with it only in its very broadest outline.

Before we try to assess the relevance of Dobbs' analysis, let us consider the general problem of precognition. Dr. Rhine, as you know, has frequently laid special stress on the fact of precognition as being our final guarantee that psi is necessarily of a nonphysical nature. Personally, I would have thought that this was a precarious position on which to take a stand in the light of the notorious controversies that have raged among philosophers of science on the nature of time ever since the advent of Einstein. No one denies that precognition is physically impossible from the point of view of classical physics; but that is partly because classical physics recognizes only a single dimension of time, so that the relationship of before and after between any two events is fixed and absolute. Even within classical physics there is room for argument as to the logical status of the principle that the cause must precede the effect, since the classical laws are completely symmetrical; but that is by

---

[4] H.A.C. Dobbs, "Time and Extrasensory Perception," *Proc. Soc. Psychical Rsch.*, Vol. 54 (1965), pp. 249-361.

the way. The situation is very different, however, if one introduces an additional time dimension; for it is not hard to understand intuitively, using the spatial analogy of a two-dimensional graph, that an event A might occur *before* an event B on time-dimension T_1 but *after* event B on time-dimension T_2. Now, according to Dobbs, Eddington in his posthumously published work *Fundamental Theory* of 1946[5] did, in fact, introduce a pentadic theory of space-time with the usual three dimensions of space but two dimensions of time; and this theory has since been shown to be consistent with all the recognized phenomena of relativity and quantum theory. Even more counterintuitive, perhaps, is the Feynman effect, the time reversal or backward flow of time, that is now postulated to hold for certain sequences of events at the quantum level.[6]

Of course, there are still a great many philosophical difficulties and paradoxes connected with the concept of precognition, as C.D. Broad has been at pains to show;[7] but the point I am making here is that we are never entitled to declare that a certain effect must be nonphysical just because it happens to be incompatible with a certain system of physics. There is, moreover, a further fact about precognition that calls for consideration. Aside from the spontaneous cases, whose evidential aspect is bound to be problematical, all the really strong evidence for precognition, so far as I know (i.e. experiments where the odds against chance reach astronomical proportions), involve small time intervals where the displacement is of the order of a few seconds only. I am thinking here of the celebrated Soal-Shackleton series and of the very recent work of Dr. Helmut Schmidt.[8] This makes it tempting to think that a fairly minor kink in space-time would do the trick.

Why, then, do I hold back? Why do I not gratefully accept the lead given by Dobbs and advocate a physicalistic approach to the problems of parapsychology? My answer is quite simple. For all

---

[5]A. Dobbs, *op .cit.*

[6]H.A.C. Dobbs, *op. cit.*

[7]C.D. Broad, "The Notion of 'Precognition'," *Science and ESP*, J.R. Smythies, ed. (London, Routledge & Kegan Paul, 1967).

[8]H. Schmidt, "Precognition of a Quantum Process," *J. Parapsychol.*, Vol. 33 (1969), pp. 99-108.

their ingenuity, such theories are really nonstarters. They concentrate on the energetics of the psi process while ignoring its even more intractable informational aspects. For the crux of the problem, as I see it, lies, not so much in specifying what kind of energy might surmount spatial and temporal distances or material barriers, but rather in explaining how it comes about that the subject is able to discriminate the target from the infinite number of other objects in his environment. Perhaps my point can best be illustrated with the help of an analogy. Imagine that sound waves were no longer attenuated with distance. It would follow that every conversation going on for miles around would be equally audible to you. But by this very fact, every conversation would be equally unintelligible. Because, of course, every sound would mask every other sound! By the same token, the closer the physicalists get to explaining the channel through which the subject receives information of the target, the harder it becomes to explain how the target is singled out from all the other potential sources of information. And on this crucial question, none of the physical theories, however imaginative or ingenious, seems to provide a clue. If telepathy were the only variety of ESP that we need to consider, the situation would not be so acute, since it would not be quite so difficult to conceive of two brains acting in resonance with one another; and, not surprisingly, most of the physicalists do concentrate on telepathy. But when we come to consider clairvoyance, as we must even if Dobbs prefers to ignore it, then the difficulty becomes so unfathomable that there seems no alternative but to declare that we are here confronted with a case of information transmission without physical mediation! In general, I have little sympathy with idealism; but I am forced to admit, as indeed Mundle has pointed out, that clairvoyance does become a shade less unintelligible in the sort of universe that Berkeley proposed.[9]

It follows, if I am at all on the right track, that we must abandon hope of a physical explanation of psi even if in doing so we alienate just those neighbors whom we would most like to cultivate. But having done so, we must not then attempt to keep our cake and eat it too. In other words, we must resist introducing a paraphysics

---

[9]C.W.K. Mundle, "The Explanation of ESP," *Science and ESP*, J.R. Smythies, ed. (London, Routledge & Kegan Paul, 1967).

to do the job for us. Let me illustrate what I mean by citing yet another Foundation Day address, this time the interesting talk by Dr. Rao entitled "The Place of Psi in the Natural Order."[10] Having established to his own satisfaction that ESP cannot involve *physical* energies of any description, he then proceeds to postulate a "hypothetical new energy" which "can now be studied as a problem in itself"; and soon he is talking blithely about "non-physical energetics," whatever that might mean. Similarly, Dr. Rhine, in his 1965 Guildhall Lecture in London, after disposing of the physicality of psi with special reference to his 1941 transcontinental precognition experiments in which the guesses were recorded one year ahead of the targets, insists, nevertheless, that "the characteristic mode of thinking of the natural sciences need not be abandoned."[11] Now, far be it from me to want to impose any kind of brake on free speculation in any field and in any direction, but I must confess that I do get worried when I come across expressions like "psi energy" or even "psi fields" that nowadays seem to pepper the parapsychological literature. That there may well be new forms of energy or new sorts of fields that have not yet been discovered is, of course, not in dispute. But to call them psi-this and psi-that sounds too much like begging the question. The concept of energy and the concept of fields of force are concepts that derive their meaning from physics, and tacking a prefix on them will not make them any the less physical. Consider the antiparticles about which physicists have been telling us in recent years. If there were, somewhere in the universe, a world of antimatter, its inhabitants would not be aware that it differed in any respect from our own world of matter; certainly no one would want to say that antimatter was in any sense nonphysical.

I think that the implicit argument that lies behind this prevalent confusion is as follows: Whatever psi may be, it is clearly something that is capable of interacting with the physical world. This indeed must be the premise from which we start, since there could be no parapsychology unless both the target and the response were, in the

---

[10]K.R. Rao, "The Place of Psi in the Natural Order," *Parapsychology from Duke to FRNM* (J.B. Rhine and Associates, Durham, N.C., Parapsychology Press, 1965).

[11]J.B. Rhine, "ESP: What Can We Make of It?," *J. Parapsychol.*, Vol. 30 (1966), p. 99.

first instance, physical facts. Now, anything that can interact with physical objects, so the argument proceeds, must itself be physical or, failing that, quasi-physical. Since we have demonstrated that psi is not physical in the conventional sense, let us call it quasi- or para-physical. Dr. Rhine, indeed, comes close to making this argument explicit when, in his 1966 address to the American Psychological Association, he has the following to say: "The very basic concept of the unity of personality is not in any way challenged thus far by any of the psi findings, since the presence of another type of energetic influence is recognized. The very interaction of this 'energy' with the known forces of the organism (as must be assumed to account for psi phenomena) rules out the hypothesis of any real dualism."[12] Yet this argument, I submit, involves a non sequitur. It does not follow from the fact that two processes interact *causally* that they are necessarily of the same nature or substance or that they obey the same fundamental laws. Despite much philosophical argument to the contrary, there is, as Ducasse has taken great pains to stress,[13] nothing *logically* at fault with the view of the mind-body relationship first advanced by Descartes, which was at one and the same time both dualistic *and* interactionist. Of course, there may be a good case for postulating other kinds of matter and other forms of energy—there is, indeed, plenty of precedent for doing so in the occult literature down the ages—but it would be unwise to complicate one's ontology in this way unless one had very strong grounds of a positive nature for doing so.

This brings me to the end of my discussion. I find, as so often, that what I have been saying is critical rather than constructive. I have nowhere committed myself to any particular view of psi. But perhaps this is only as it should be. The point is that we know so much by now about the physical world and the constitution of matter, but we are still so much in the dark about the nature of psi. In the circumstances, what else can one do but preserve an open mind? But this, I must add, is not as easy as it sounds. Few scientists are truly open minded; their whole professional training militates

[12]J.B. Rhine, "The Bearing of Parapsychology on Human Potentiality," *J. Parapsychol.*, Vol. 30 (1966), p. 253.

[13]C.J. Ducasse, "Minds, Matter and Bodies," *Brain and Mind*, J.R. Smythies, ed. (London, Routledge & Kegan Paul, 1965).

against it and keeps them safe within the confines of their precon-
ceptions. Perhaps we parapsychologists are the last true empiricists!
Parapsychology may not have much to show for itself vis-à-vis its
neighbors; but here, at least, is one virtue to which we can lay claim
and in which we should take pride. Let my parting message to you,
then, be simply this: Cultivate an open mind!

CHAPTER 27

ARE THERE ANY SOLID FACTS IN PSYCHICAL RESEARCH?*

GARDNER MURPHY

INTRODUCTION

IN A PRELIMINARY WAY, I will say at once that the following phenomena seem to me to be solidly established as facts in the field of psychical research:

First, telepathy, or the transmission, as Myers defined it, "of impressions of any kind from one mind to another, independently of the recognized channels of sense."[1]

Second, clairvoyance, or the direct perception of an object or objective event, again without the ultilization of the senses.

Third, precognition, or the perception of an idea or an event which is in a future time; in other words, telepathy or clairvoyance in which the perceiver is in the present time, but the event perceived is in future time; that is, looking into the future.

Fourth, retrocognition, symmetrical to precognition, or the perception in the present time of an object or event which is located in past time; that is, looking into the past.

Fifth, psychokinesis, of the voluntary movement of objects as a result of agencies not known to belong to those of the physically recognized energies; and closely related to this, the phenomena of

---

*Reprinted from *The Journal of the American Society for Psychical Research*, 1970, by permission of the author and the Society. (This paper is based on a lecture given by Dr. Murphy at a meeting of the Society held on January 27, 1969—Ed. [of *The Journal of the American Society for Psychical Research*])

[1] F.W.H. Myers, *Human Personality and Its Survival of Bodily Death* (London, Longmans, Green, 1903), Vol. I, p. xxii.

lights, sounds, odors, which are apparently produced by a dynamic which transcends our present knowledge of physics.

Closely parallel to all of these are phenomena appearing to indicate that the subject is acting upon physical reality in some indirect way, perhaps producing a phantasm or apparition of himself which manifests itself at a distance, or a physical effect which can ultimately be recorded by physical instruments, but not at present a part of the known physical system of energies.

But I wish to ask now whether any of these events are "solid" facts in another sense: in the sense in which the events that we find described in scientific textbooks are solid facts—that is, ordered within a conceptual system. Henry Margenau, Professor of Physics and Philosophy at Yale, is constantly insisting upon the difference between disconnected facts on the one hand and real science on the other, reminding us that the business of psychical research should not be with disconnected facts, but with facts which are scientifically coherent and meaningful.[2] I think that the series of realities which I have just described, the five broad categories of psychical phenomena, are still disconnected, and that in order to have real meaning they must be organized in an orderly way with reference to some systematic principles.

To get at this problem, I am going to make my own tentative effort to formulate three broad working schemata or principles that we ought to keep in mind; they are principles regarding the relations of mind and body. Of course, I did not "dream up" for this occasion these three classical schemata, for they were all well known to the Greeks and likewise to ancient India; but I am going to attempt to formulate them in such a way that they will be more serviceable for the purposes of psychical research, which must find its way to a sound conception of the relation of mind to body. I am inclined to think that every meaningful fact that we have uncovered in our investigations can be ordered in terms of one or another, or indeed all three, of these systems or models. And I am inclined to think that the task of psychical research transcends altogether the mere gathering of more and more facts and should comprise an effort to see whether the facts we now have support

---

[2]H. Margenau, "ESP in the Framework of Modern Science," *Journal A.S.P.R.*, Vol. 60 (July, 1966), pp. 214-228.

one another and are coherent within an intelligible system. I suggest that any solidly established fact tends to support one theory as against the other two theories which I shall describe, and I urge that all of you who have a research orientation keep pressing us to order our data so that they will support or refute one or another theory and lead us into greater conceptual clarity.

SYSTEMATIC POSSIBILITIES

The three systematic possibilities which I will now offer in capsule form are, first, classical monism as represented by Spinoza; second, classical dualism as represented by Descartes; and third, what I shall call the "etheric" theory, adapted more or less from the work of Myers and of Newbold, of whom I shall say more later.

Monistic Theory (Spinoza)

Spinoza argued that mental events and bodily events are completely parallel; for every mental event there is a physical event and for every physical event there is a mental event. Neither is "caused" by the other; both are aspects of the same ultimate reality and are considered by Spinoza to be "divine" attributes. According to this view, there cannot be a "relation" between mind and body because they are both simply aspects of one thing.

Dualistic Theory (Descartes)

Descartes put forward the theory of absolute dualism, which holds that mind and matter are eternally separable. He taught that motions terminating in the brain produced ideas in what he called the "unextended" mind, which he thought functioned through the pineal gland. It was as if the immaterial force of the mind comes in like an arrow, striking the pineal gland in such a way as to control the body. Descartes thought that if we are able to think of the soul clearly and perfectly without having to presuppose the concept of the body, and if we are able to think of the body clearly and perfectly without having to presuppose the concept of the soul, then this is a proof that we have two distinct beings or substances entirely independent of one another.

"Etherial" Theory (Myers-Newbold)

I am going to present the third, or "etherial," theory in a slightly novel manner. When I was a young psychical researcher, I talked with Professor W.R. Newbold at the University of Pennsylvania. Newbold was a distinguished philosopher, psychologist, and archeologist who had made studies of Assyriology and of the remarkable artifacts which had been dug up in the Near East showing the thought of the Assyrians and Babylonians long before the time of Christ. Newbold, who had had sittings with the celebrated Boston medium, Mrs. Piper, was deeply interested in psychical research and contributed a number of papers to the publications of the S.P.R. and A.S.P.R. He told me, as I understood him, that the main task of psychical research is to combine sound, modern scientific method with the ancient lore which has been forgotten. And one of the things that the ancients knew, he said, and that we ought to know today, is that it is never really a question of a simple dualism of mind versus body, but that there is a reality, so to speak, in between. There is a world, for example, of phantasms of ghosts, of hauntings, of ESP projections. These are not physical events— they do not leave a record on a photographic plate—but neither are they *solely* mental events. They seem to represent an interaction between our bodies and some unknown reality outside of time and space. I am trying to put this theory, first expressed to me by Newbold, into the form of what I am calling an etheric theory; it is something like, but not identical with, Myers' "metetheric" theory* put forward in *Human Personality*.[3] As I conceive it, there is a sphere of psychic events which is intermediate between the bodily sphere and a transcendent sphere; an apparition, for example, would be seen as something between a physical event and a transcendent event.

FORMING COHERENT SYSTEMS

Now, how can we bring such philosophical theories as these three into relation to our experimental results? I plead that we must turn the specific "hard facts" of psychical research into organized and meaningful systems such as these three mind-body theories require. I stress that we need to formulate theoretical systems and

---

*Myers defines the word "metetherial" as "that which appears to lie after or beyond the ether; the metetherial environment denotes the spiritual or transcendental world in which the soul exists."

[3]F.W.H. Myers, *op. cit.*, Vol. 1, p. xix.

then find which system is best supported by the kind of facts that we have.

Let us consider the first step that we will have to take as we get further data such as those of Osis, Schmeidler, Pratt, Ullman, and many others, systematizing their observations on long-distance telepathy or paranormal dreams, which they offer us a solid facts. What are some of the things that we will have to do to give such facts a coherent, meaningful form? We will have to show that these facts are related to other facts; that they form coherent systems; and that these systems of facts can be lodged within a larger theoretical framework, such as the mind-body theories that I have offered you. Can a new finding on long-distance telepathy, like the Osis-Turner studies of the effect of distance,[4] really be articulated and brought into relation to mind-body theory or some equally ambitious philosophical theory?

To illustrate the point, let us take the classic experiments of Brugmans and his associates[5] at the University of Groningen in the Netherlands. Since these experiments are so well known, I will merely remind you that the agents in an upper room in the University Laboratories were able to transmit letters and numbers to a subject sitting blindfolded in a black cage in a lower room. The possibility of sensory cues seems to have been adequately ruled out, and the results were hugely significant. This experiment is now being replicated in modified form at the A.S.P.R. This leads me to offer a challenge: If we get positive results, as Brugmans did, what can we do to show that these results have scientific meaning—that these evidences of telepathy are not mere flukes, but have an orderly place in nature relating to one of our mind-body theories? I would say that until this is done, the concept of telepathy hangs in the air, without having very much meaning.

WORKING PRINCIPLES

Fortunately, the experiments of Brugmans and his associates offer us three working principles which tie their results to those of

---

[4]K. Osis, and M.E. Turner, Jr., "Distance and ESP: A Transcontinental Experiment," *Proc. A.S.P.R.*, Vol. 27 (September, 1968), pp. 1-48.

[5]H.I.F.W. Brugmans, "Une Communication sur des Expériences Télépathiques au Laboratoire de Psychologie à Groningue. . . .," *Proceedings* of the First International Congress of Psychical Research (Copenhagen, 1922), pp. 396-408.

earlier experiments performed in Britain and France which bear on the question of the physical or mental conditions which facilitate the telepathic response.

First, there is the principle of relaxation. What has relaxation got to do with telepathy? We can say that in the telepathy experiments carried out by Warcollier[6] in Paris, in the early hypnotic experiments done in England under Gurney[7] and others, and in the hypnotic experiments done by Fahler[8] in Finland we have a converging line of evidence suggesting that relaxation both of mind and of body is a cogent preliminary experimental condition in relation to the elicitation of a telepathic result. Since mind and body vary concomitantly, this scores a point in favor of Spinoza's monistic theory. These experiments bind together several different kinds of relaxation and several different techniques for inducing relaxation. A generalized scientific principle begins to emerge. But it does not go far enough; it is just one point.

A second principle that begins to emerge from all these studies has to do with a "splitting" of the mind, or dissociation, by which it is possible for one part of the mind to be wholly fixated on a task while another part of the mind—perhaps a deep, unconscious part—is reaching out for telepathic contact. We have, in other words, the possibility that telepathy is an expression of a "split" condition of the mind, a condition which would probably interfere with most types of ordinary work, but which in the creative work of the artist seems to tie the psi process with the splitting process. As far as the evidence goes, it suggests that splitting occurs at the physiological level at the same time that it occurs at the psychological level. Score another point for Spinoza. But let us wait for more evidence.

Thirdly, evidence of the importance of motivation appears in almost all these studies; there seems to be a relationship between the degree to which a person is preoccupied with success and the degree to which he is capable of hitting the particular target de-

[6] R. Warcollier, *Experimental Telepathy* (Boston, Boston Society for Psychic Research, 1938).

[7] E. Gurney, "Recent Experiments in Hypnotism," *Proc. S.P.R.*, Vol. 5 (1888-1889), pp. 3-17.

[8] J. Fahler, "Parapsykologiska Experiment och Hypnos," *Serien Vetenskap i dag, Hbl.*, Vol. 15 (Helsinki, 1959), p. 4.

fined. This afternoon I was discussing with some of our young investigators the question whether this is a straight-line relationship; that is, whether we can always say that the greater the motivation, the greater the paranormal result. We can learn to find with new techniques just that degree of voluntary mobilization and degree of devotion to the task which, without making the subject too tense, will permit a steady and effective focusing upon the target. Clearly, this is a good lead, but definite results are not yet at hand.

Thus it would seem to me that we need to do more refined psychological, physiological, and mathematical analyses of all the variables involved before we can say that we have caught the essence of the favorable moment in which ESP occurs. We have clues sticking out at us, so to speak, from the underbrush. We have a few clues pointing in Spinoza's direction. A little later I shall refer to Tyrrell's study of apparitions[9] to find clues supporting the Myers-Newbold theory. I am afraid that the number of relevant variables is probably very large. Indeed, in our attempt at replication, we have usually tried to do over and over again what has been done before, forgetting that there are many favorable working conditions which have to be realized before the first study can be successfully repeated. We have a human situation of great complexity whenever psi phenomena appear. It isn't enough to take piecemeal bits of the total situation and hope that the results will reappear. It isn't enough merely to do what the experimenter said he did; he undoubtedly put much more into the experiment than he was able to make clear in his report. And our own difficult and arduous replication teaches us how complex the chain of interdependent relationships is which ties a paranormal result to the psychological conditions which predispose to it. I am asking for a great deal, I am afraid. But psychical research plods along slowly; maybe it can be speeded up by seeking the nature of science and of scientific theory-building and its testing.

TELEPATHY AND CLAIRVOYANCE

Suppose we should want to make generalizations about telepathic and clairvoyant phenomena (and retrocognitive and precognitive

---

[9]G.N.M. Tyrrell, *Apparitions* (London, Duckworth, 1953).

phenomena as well) which would all be coherent. There is almost none of this in psychical research. We can read in Rhine's first book[10] that the same conditions which assisted his subjects in telepathic results also assisted them in clairvoyant results; but for the most part, we don't know whether the working conditions that seem to be favorable for telepathy and clairvoyance are also favorable for precognition and psychokinesis. There is practically nothing in the literature which compares the working conditions for, say, psychokinesis and the working conditions for telepathy. We don't even know whether a person good at one type of paranormal task is good at other types of paranormal tasks, for we have not taken seriously the notion that the interdependence of many realities is what is required. It is not enough merely to give a certain type of result a name and say that it is one more case of psychokinesis; we must see this particular case of psychokinesis in relation to other cases of psychokinesis and also in relation to other types of psi phenomena.

It seems to me that, as we read the experimental reports in the journals, we are nearly always left with so-called hard facts in our hands and no idea what to do with them. They are like a series of facts that might be named by a geologist. The geologist might say, "I have some facts for you—there are mountains, there are rivers, there are oceans." But this is not geology, for it does not tell us what kinds of heat, or pressure, or erosion created these mountains and rivers and oceans. To say that the modern horse is descended from a little five-toed eohippus which lived millions of years ago is not evolutionary biology. It becomes evolutionary biology only when we can say what forces in nature favored bigger rather than smaller horses, and hoofed rather than five-toed horses, giving them power to survive in new worlds which the little eohippus did not confront. Are there dynamic laws of this sort, laws of development, in psychical research? Are there laws telling us what forces are at work over long periods of time and what results they produce? When we see a telepathic or a clairvoyant or a precognitive result, can we say anything about its developmental history? Are we conducting our experiments today in such a way as to permit us to

---

[10]J.B. Rhine, *Extra-Sensory Perception* (Boston, Bruce Humphries, 1964). First edition published in 1934.

decide between major constructions of reality? This is the kind of systematic effort which should ultimately give us "hard facts" in Margenau's use of the term.

Is all this too much to ask? I do not think so. Think of the thousands of studies of plants and animals which were done before the time of Darwin; that is, before the development of a sustaining theory. Can we, in psychical research, develop the systematic possibilities of the three theoretical mind-body constructions which I mentioned earlier? Can we develop these theories to a point where specific new experiments will decide between them—or, indeed, whether a fourth theory or an n*th* theory is better than the three that I defined? Can we find which gives the best fit to the recorded observations? How can we move, in our experiments, to transcend the question of looking for sheer facts and seek general principles?

Perhaps the trouble is that we fail to remember in psychical research that facts in nature do not really exist *except* in the form of *relations* between classes of events. Sunrises, for example, or eclipses, or the march of the seasons, are factual data arising from the relations between heavenly bodies that move, spin, and get in the way of one another. Barometers and thermometers go up and down and report changing relationships—not things intrinsic to the water or the mercury which are used for the measurements, but the systematic patterns of relationships between them. It may well be that in our efforts to understand the paranormal the relational system which ties the living individual to his environment has been neglected. It may well be, for example, that there is no such thing as clairvoyance within the individual mind, clairvoyance as an expression of just one person. It may turn out, in fact, that all psychic events are not only transspatial and transtemporal, but fully transpersonal as well; and that in this transpersonal world there are interpersonal relationships which we have ignored. It may be that all psi phenomena depend not upon the biological or psychological laws that describe the life of the individual, but upon transactions or relational systems which must be directly investigated in their own right.

Suppose we take Moss's recent observations[14] on the psychologi-

---

[14]T. Moss, "ESP Effects in 'Artists' Contrasted with 'Non-Artists'," *J. Parapsych.*, Vol. 33 (March, 1969), pp. 57-69.

cal openness of the individual as a factor which she says enables him to succeed in an extrasensory task. But it may well be that it is not the openness *in general* of the individual, but particular kinds of openness, or particular kinds of contact, that allow him, when working with another individual, to succeed in ESP. Perhaps the factors will come out more strongly and more meaningfully when they are stated in terms of the relationships between the subject, the agent, and the other persons who, together with the experimenter, comprise the experimental surroundings. If we could actually work out such a relational system, perhaps we would find that the "hard facts" of today are all facts relating to *systems* of events rather than to self-contained events.

ACTIVATION OF EXTRASENSORY PERCEPTION

In this matter of a shift of research emphasis from straightforward simple facts about behavior to facts about systems of relationships, I should like to refer to some ongoing research of Osis in which he factor-analyzed self-report items from psychological scales to determine how the items of these scales were associated with each other. He found that the items tended to cluster into five relatively clear-cut factors:

1. A feeling of openness and closeness to others, a lowering of the barriers between the group members.
2. A stillness, a state in which the mind is not active with thoughts and images.
3. A buoyant mood which is brought to the session.
4. A dimension of meaningfulness.
5. An intensification of and change in the individual's state of consciousness.[15]

We might do well to look at these five items and consider how we might evaluate them in relation to the way they may be associated with the activation of extrasensory perception.

It seems to me that the first item, a lowering of barriers between members of the group, is of importance in the sense that such openness is not an attribute of a single individual, but an attribute

---

[15]K. Osis, and E. Bokert, "Changed States of Consciousness and ESP," Paper read at the 12th Annual Convention of the Parapsychological Association (New York, September, 1969).

relating to the communication system that obtains between individuals. Indeed, a lowering of barriers between groups of persons is plainly something that is not anchored in the brain of one person, or the sum of all persons; rather, it is a form of mutual influence or potential communication between them. This illustrates what I mean by a relationship system.

The "stillness" of mind referred to in the second item is perhaps more difficult to define. It looks like a state of transition from one activity to another; a sort of emptying or clearing of the mind. This may be what Rhine has called "putting the mind on dead center," or what I have referred to as a "brown study" or state of abstraction. Perhaps it is not really a state as such, but the *transition* from an active to a passive state—a sort of "make-and-break" process—that is the critical preconditioning circumstance.

These same factors would probably also apply to the third item, the buoyant mood being based upon interpersonal relationships and, in any event, involving a capacity to bring a successful feeling pattern from one situation to another situation, thus involving a shift in figure and ground, or the "make-and-break" response.

As for item four, the "dimension of meaningfulness," this may again entail a figure-ground relationship, but we need to know more about it.

Item five, "an intensification of and change in the individual's state of consciousness," is exactly the point on which I would bear down most heavily. It is the *change*—whether of intensification or of qualitative attributes—that is the important and central fact, and this is plainly a matter of very complex field relationships.

I think, then, that in a strict sense there are no hard facts in psychical research—not at least until the term "hard facts" is thoroughly reconsidered and redefined. I do not believe that there is ever a "hard chunk" of telepathy, or even telepathy as an expression of someone's personal gift as such. I believe that telepathic contact can be identified as a form of perceptual response in which the individual is immersed for the time being in a new relationship with another human being. This is, of course, only a new way of saying something which has been familiar to psychical research for a long time. Yet there are two reasons for repeating it:

First, earlier statements about this, including my own, still seem very foggy and we need to keep struggling to make our meaning clearer.

Second, psychical research, all over the world and decade after decade, continues to be based almost entirely upon the effort to obtain more and more hard facts, solid replicable facts, solemnly placed within isolating cages which effectively prevent contact with the larger reality, the larger system of relationships that we need to see and use. However, it must be stressed that a few really *critical* facts may swing interpretations to one or another theoretical system.

ENVIRONMENTAL RELATIONSHIP

Let us look at a research program which might be based, like relativity theory, upon the attributes not of the experimental subject alone, but upon the attributes of a subject-environment relationship. Some possibilities follow:

First, interpersonal relations as they exist between subject, agent, and experimenter. This aspect has been stressed in the work of Schmeidler[11] and of Soal,[12] who studied the special psychological relationships obtaining between their subject-agent pairs. Much more intensive work of this sort is needed.

Second, a study of the life histories of subjects, agents, and experimenters as related to their psychic functioning. This need has long been recognized, but where do we go to find the developmental histories? Except for a few rather fragmentary autobiographies and biographies of special clairvoyants and mediumistic subjects, this literature is very feeble.

Third, experimental enrichment of the gift of paranormal communication: for example, learning how to use whatever limited powers one may have, as suggested by Tart,[13] and relating to the fact that we have overlooked the possibility of applying modern studies of the learning process as a way of enhancing extrasensory capacities.

Fourth, a study of cultural settings in which the paranormal is

[11]G.R. Schmeidler, "Telepathy and Resistance to It," *Journal A.S.P.R.*, Vol. 60 (July, 1966), pp. 207-209. (Abstract)

[12]S.G. Soal and F. Bateman, *Modern Experiments in Telepathy* (New Haven, Yale University Press, 1954).

[13]C.T. Tart, "Card Guessing Tests: Learning Paradigm or Extinction Paradigm?," *Journal A.S.P.R.*, Vol. 60 (January, 1966), pp. 46-55.

at home. We can all think of certain lands traditionally rich in psychic phenomena, but tragically little of the necessary cross-cultural investigation has actually been carried out.

Fifth, the attempt to formulate generalizations as laws, moving these laws into the realm of systematic body-mind theory. For we must not only find lawful contexts for paranormal events as they group themselves as illustrations of telepathy or clairvoyance or psychokinesis; we must also try to relate them to very broad general theories about mind and body, which I will now try to do.

TRANSITIONS IN PSYCHICAL PHENOMENA

I think that the generalizations which I have attempted to formulate hold broadly for all psychical phenomena. And I think that I can go further and say that these generalizations seem mostly to depend upon *transitions* from one state to another. For example, a deep relaxation leads to a break in which we are aware of the big difference between profound physiological relaxation and very intense and concentrated mental activity. I believe that these sudden transitions not only involve transactions between two or more observable events, but that they also involve transactions between one level of reality and another—or perhaps I should say between one *kind* of reality and another. This is certainly much easier to fit to the third theory (Myers-Newbold) than it is to the first theory (Spinoza), and almost impossible to fit to the second theory (Descartes).

There is almost no case of a sudden change of state, as in the altered state between great alertness and deep drowsiness, that does not remind one of the optimal states which have been discussed in the classical literature of psychical research—in *Phantasms of the Living*[16] or in *Human Personality*[17]—where we are given armfuls of cases which point to the importance of the change of state, particularly cases involving two or more persons as in the collective and reciprocal experiences.[18] All of this points strongly to the need

---

[16]E. Gurney, F.W.H. Myers, and F. Podmore, *Phantasms of the Living* (London, Trübner, 1886).

[17]F.W.H. Myers, *op. cit.*

[18]H. Hart and E.B. Hart, "Visions and Apparitions Collectively and Reciprocally Perceived," *Proc. S.P.R.,* Vol. 41 (1932-1933), pp. 205-249.

for devising experiments which will make the most of the sudden altered states of consciousness as a cardinal clue.

I think it becomes clear that we can no longer go on, as many investigators have, with simple generalizations as to conditions which favor one single phenomenon, or the appearance of this phenomenon in a single individual. If there really is an interaction of mental and physical processes, with mind remaining mind all the time and matter remaining matter all the time, do we not have an obligation to develop a meaningful bridge or meaningful conceptual schema which will carry us from one to the other? As I have suggested, the dualistic system of Descartes is probably the most difficult to apply to paranormal phenomena and the Myers-Newbold system the easiest. But the question arises: have we looked at the intrinsic limitations of these theories, and have we been ready to recognize the necessity for compounding new theories which will contain the advantages and not the disadvantages of the older theories?

CONCLUSION

Before I close, I would like to remind you of some further reasons why I think we would do well to take seriously the idea of a change of state, or change of level in the utilization of energies, which is involved in the Myers-Newbold theory. The physicists are constantly reminding us that the transition from one state to another involves the release of energy. When you burn a log of firewood, when you use a flashbulb, or when you strike a piano key, you shift from one kind of energy to another, and you can compute the amount of energy released all the way from the melting of a tiny bit of ice to the detonation of a hydrogen bomb. I am not saying, of course, that psychical "energies" are of any sort that physics now recognizes; in fact, the whole point is that they are remote indeed from the kinds of energy with which modern physics is dealing. But I am saying that the change of state, the change of level, and the manifestation of release of energy while making such transitions, stand out too obviously to be overlooked. This is what observers of paraphysical phenomena—raps, lights, movement of objects—have been telling us, and this is what the meaning of experimental psychokinesis seems to be. Perceptual phenomena also involve a kind of "detonation," a change of state, a precipitation of a new kind of response within the living organism. Ordinarily there is not enough sensory stimulation to trigger us into action, but under the conditions of high motivation, splitting of the mind, withdrawal from everyday preoccupations, and intense orientation toward distant reality, there may indeed be a sudden triggering of a response, a transition from one level or function to another. This accords well, so far as our fragmentary evidence goes, with the Myers-Newbold theory.

Let us take the well-known Larkin-M'Connel case and see what we can do with a rather typical type of apparition experience:

> The percipient was Lieut. J. J. Larkin, of the R.A.F., and the apparition was that of one of Lieut. Larkin's fellow officers, Lieut. David M'Connel, killed in an airplane crash on December 7, 1919. Lieut. Larkin reported that he spent the afternoon of December 7th in his room at the barracks. He sat in front of the fire reading and writing, and was wide awake all the time. At about 3:30 p.m. he heard someone walking up the passage. "The door opened with the usual noise and clatter which David always made; I heard his 'Hello boy!' and I turned half round in my chair and saw him standing in the doorway, half in and half out of the room, holding the door knob in his hand. He was dressed in his full flying clothes but wearing his naval cap, there being nothing unusual in his appearance. . . . In reply . . . I remarked, 'Hello! Back already?' He replied, 'Yes. Got there all right, had a good trip.' . . . I was looking at him the whole time he was speaking. He said, 'Well, cheero!' closed the door noisily and went out." Shortly after this a friend dropped in to see Lieut. Larkin, and Larkin told him that he had just seen and talked with Lieut. M'Connel. (This friend sent a corroborative statement to the S.P.R.) Later on that day it was learned that Lieut. M'Connel had been instantly killed in a flying accident which occurred at about 3:25 p.m. Mistaken identity seems to be ruled out, since the light was very good in the room where the apparition appeared. Moreover, there was no other man in the barracks at the time who in any way resembled Lieut. M'Connel. It was also found that M'Connel was wearing his naval cap when he was killed—apparently an unusual circumstance. Agent and percipient had been "very good friends though not intimate friends in the true sense of the word."[19]

---

[19]G. Murphy, "An Outline of Survival Evidence," *Journal A.S.P.R.*, Vol. 39 (January, 1945), pp. 3-4; E.M. Sidgwick, "Phantasms of the Living. . . .," *Proc. S.P.R.*, Vol. 33 (1923), pp. 151-160.

This apparition involved full perception through both visual and auditory modalities and it certainly involved a crashing type of experience in more than one sense. And we are reminded that apparitions are typically not slowly worked into our experience, but rather that they come to us with a "bang." I think that Shakespeare very fully understood this. You may remember that Macbeth, who was contemplating the murder of Banquo, is reaching out toward the dagger. "Here let me clutch thee," he says. He is not quite sure whether this is a so-called real or a so-called hallucinatory dagger. But he can't take hold and he decides that it is something from a "heat-oppressed brain," that he has been hallucinating. But does Banquo, when he appears in this scene, give any such impression? The stage directions are perfectly clear: "Enter Ghost!" And they are perfectly clear at the end of the scene: "Exit Ghost!" This crashes through; this is a change of state. And Macbeth pays tribute to this: immediately after the ghost has disappeared he says, "Why, so; being gone, I am a man again." He has gone through a moment of maximal sensitivity to a horrible paranormal impression and then is shaking it off. I don't think we could get clearer evidence of the change of state phenomenon, with tremendous release of energies. Lady Macbeth sees this with extraordinary clarity and helps Macbeth get out of the crowd. "Stand not upon the order of your going," she says. She realizes that she must get her husband out of this crisis as soon as possible.

I think this story beautifully illustrates the fact that with apparitions we are dealing with something that involves a true interaction, a true change of level, and a true alteration in energy relationships. After an intensive and extensive scholarly study of such cases, Tyrrell[20] declined to believe that apparitions are physical events which can leave a photographic or phonographic record. He did feel, however, that they represent a reality in time and space, conveyed both by sight and hearing to the senses and on to the mind of the percipient. This seems to be pretty close to what we would expect on the basis of the Myers-Newbold theory. There is, apparently, a sort of reality which is outside of the kind of time and space which we ordinarily know—a reality which we cannot touch

---

[20]G.N.M. Tyrrell, *op. cit.*

directly, but which we *can* touch through an intermediary. The apparition belongs to an "in-between" kind of reality.

An example of experimental telepathy which might fit the Spinoza theory but might also fit the Myers-Newbold model is the Brugmans-type experiment which is now being carried out in the A.S.P.R. laboratories if success is reached in the endeavor to raise the image level to the hallucinatory level. It will be interesting to see whether the physiological alterations, the splitting of the mind, and the development of special sensitivity which were helpful in Brugman's work will also be helpful in our own attempts at replication. I have already hinted that experimental psychokinesis seems to involve a relation between the world of the mind and the world of physical movement through sudden energy release.

Of course, I am not saying that the theory suggested by Myers and Newbold is correct. But I am saying that at this stage in psychical research we desperately need clear statements about alternative possibilities, and that the facts which we gather must be submitted to the acid test both of factual reality and of meaningful places in the world of what can properly be said to be known. There will be many mistakes made, but as I contemplate the many volumes on serious psychical research published by the English and American Societies, not even to count the world of books and the works of other lands, I ask whether the mere accumulation of more data is what we chiefly need. I think rather that what we need is the accumulation of systematic and orderly presentations of interlocking facts. One approach I have suggested is that we look at the three prominent mind-body theories which I have briefly described and that we test our empirical data against them to see which one gives the best fit. We shall have "hard facts" in psychical research only when we can relate our many observations to one another in a meaningful way and fit them all into a coherent system of ideas.

CHAPTER 28

COMPATIBILITY OF SCIENCE AND ESP*

PAUL E. MEEHL and MICHAEL SCRIVEN

A S TWO OF THE PEOPLE WHOSE COMMENTS on an early draft of George Price's article on "Science and the supernatural" he acknowledged in a footnote, we should like to clarify our position by presenting the following remarks.

Price's argument stands or falls on two hypotheses only the first of which he appears to defend. They are (i) that extrasensory perception (ESP) is incompatible with modern science and (ii) that modern science is complete and correct.

If ESP is *not* incompatible with modern science, then the Humean skeptic has no opportunity to insist on believing modern science rather than the reports about ESP. If modern science is *not* believed to be complete or correct, then the skeptic is hardly justified in issuing a priori allegations of fraud about experimenters even when they claim that they have discovered a new phenomenon that requires reconsideration of the accepted theories.

In our view, both of Price's hypotheses are untenable. Whatever one may think about the comprehensiveness and finality of modern physics, it would surely be rash to insist that we can reject out of hand any claims of revolutionary discoveries in the field of psychology. Price is in exactly the position of a man who might have insisted that Michelson and Morley were liars because the evidence for the physical theory of that time was stronger than that for the veracity of these experimenters. The list of those who have insisted on the impossibility of fundamental changes in the current physical

*Reprinted from *Science,* Vol. 123 (January 6, 1956), pp. 14-15, by permission of the authors and the American Association for the Advancement of Science.

theory of their time is a rather sorry one. Moreover, unhappy though Price's position would be if this were his only commitment, he cannot even claim that specifiable laws of physics are violated; it is only certain philosophical characteristics of such laws that are said to be absent from those governing the new phenomena.

It is true that Price attempted to give a specific account of the incompatibilities between ESP and modern science, rather than relying on Broad's philosophical analysis, but here the somewhat superficial nature of Price's considerations becomes clear. Of his eight charges, seven are unjustified.

1) He claims that ESP is "unattenuated by distance" and hence is incompatible with modern science. But, as is pointed out in several of the books he refers to, since we have no knowledge of the minimum effective signal strength for extrasensory perception, the original signal may well be enormously attenuated by distance and still function at long range.

2) He says that ESP is "apparently unaffected by shielding." But shielding may well have an effect: The evidence shows only that the kind of shielding appropriate to electromagnetic radiation is ineffectual; since detectors indicate that no such radiation reaches the percipient from the agent, this is scarcely surprising.

3) He says "Dye patterns . . . are read in the dark; how does one detect a trace of dye without shining a light on it?" The two most obvious answers would be by chemical analysis and physical study of the impression (which is usually different for different colors).

4) "Patterns on cards in the center of a pack are read without interference from other cards." The word *read* is hardly justified in view of the statistical nature of the results; however, this phenomenon is always used by parapsychologists as evidence against a simple radiation theory, which it is. But no simple radiation theory can explain the Pauli principle and one can no more refute it by saying "How could one electron possibly know what the others are doing?" than one can refute the ESP experiments by saying "How could one possibly read a card from the middle of the pack without interference from those next to it?" These questions are couched in prejudicial terms.

5) "We have found in the body no structure to associate with

the alleged functions." Even if true, this hardly differentiates it from a good many other *known* functions; and among eminent neurophysiologists, J.C. Eccles is one who has denied Price's premise.[1]

6) "There is no learning but, instead, a tendency toward complete loss of ability" a characteristic which Price believes has "no parallel among established mental functions." Now it would be reasonable to expect, in a series of experiments intended to show that learning does not occur, some *trial-by-trial* differential reinforcement procedure. Mere continuation, with encouragement or condemnation after *runs of many trials* can hardly provide a conclusive proof of the absence of learning in a complex situation. We ourselves know of *no* experiments in which this condition has been met and which show *absence* of learning; certainly one could not claim that this absence was established. Furthermore, *even if it had been established,* it would be very dangerous to assert that there is "no parallel among established mental functions." In the psychophysiological field particularly, there are several candidates. Finally, *even if it had been established and there were no parallel among mental functions,* there would be no essential difficulty in comparing it with one of the many familiar performances that exhibit no learning in adults—for example, reflex behavior.

7) "Different investigators obtain highly different results." This is the most distressingly irresponsible comment of all. ESP is a capacity like any other human capacity such as memory, in that it varies in strength and characteristics from individual to individual and in the one individual from one set of circumstances to another. The sense in which Rhine and Soal (Price's example of "different investigators") have obtained "highly different results" is when they have been dealing with different subjects or markedly different circumstances—for example, different agents; and exactly the same would be true of an investigation of, for example, stenographers' speed in taking dictation or extreme color blindness.

There remains only statistical precognition, which is certainly not susceptible to the types of explanation currently appropriate in physics: but then it is not a phenomenon in physics. Even if it were,

---

[1]Originally in *Nature* (1951), p. 168.

it is difficult to see why Price thinks that we properly accommodated our thought to the distressing and counterintuitive idea that the earth is rotating whereas we should not accept precognition. His test for distinguishing new phenomena from magic is hopeless from the start ("The test is to attempt to imagine a detailed mechanistic explanation") because (i) it is of the essence of the scientific method that one should have means for establishing the facts *whether or not* one has already conceived an explanation and (ii) it would have thrown out the Heisenberg uncertainty principle and action across a vacuum—that is, nuclear physics and the whole of electricity and magnestism—along with ESP.

Finally, Price's "ideal experiments" are only Rube Goldberg versions of the standard tests plus a skeptical jury. The mechanical contrivances would be welcome if only parapsychologists could afford them, and the jury is obviously superfluous because, according to Price's own test, we should rather believe that they lie than that the experiments succeed. However, in our experience, skeptics who are are prepared to devote some time and hard work to the necessary preliminary study and experimenting are welcome in the laboratories at Duke and London. Without the training, one might as well have (as Price would say) twelve clergymen as judges at a cardsharps' convention.

The allegations of fraud are as helpful or as pointless here as they were when they were made of Freud and Galileo by the academics and others who honestly believed that they *must* be mistaken. They are irresponsible because Price has not made any attempt to verify them (as he admits), despite the unpleasantness they will cause, and because it has been obvious since the origin of science that any experimental results, witnessed by no matter how many people, *may* be fraudulent.

CHAPTER 29

TO RECONCILE PSI AND PHYSICS*

RÉMY CHAUVIN

O NE OF THE ARGUMENTS USED by those who are unwilling to
accept the existence of psi phenomena is that the philosophical
implications of psi involve contradictions. Many parapsychologists
believe that psi research is directly opposed to the general direction
of scientific thinking of the last fifty years, particularly in regard
to the concepts of *mind* and *matter*. To quote Dr. J.G. Pratt,
". . . The battle over the past couple of centuries has certainly been
going strongly in favor of these philosophers and scientists who
would say that mind has no place at all." Some parapsychologists
think, on the contrary, that mind should be the prime concern,
and they would be glad to sacrifice matter.

My own position is that it would not be correct to say that if
psi occurs, the mind is primary and matter is secondary. There is
another way of reasoning. One might try to offer general definitions of words like "matter" and "mind"—definitions which physicists, psychologists, or parapsychologists, would all accept. This
would almost certainly be impossible and probably uninteresting.
The word "matter" is meaningless for the physicist; he is concerned only with protons, electrons, elementary particles, waves,
and trajectories. On the other hand, who is interested in mind
except the philosopher?—Is it the psychologist? Certainly not. He
studies memory, reasoning, attitudes, and emotions, but for him
the words "mind" and "matter" are only of philosophical interest,

---

*Reprinted from *The Journal of Parapsychology*, 1970, by permission of the author
and the editors. Dinner address at the Autumn Review Meeting of the Institute for
Parapsychology (September 13, 1968).

embedded in the dark clouds of metaphysics, useless for the scientists because they are vague and without precise meaning. The use of the terms would darken the light of scientific discussion.

But it is true that the evidence and conclusions of parapsychology (to divine signals in dark envelopes without using the sense of vision, to advance into the future by precognition, to act upon dice and elementary particles by psychokinesis without the intervention of any known physical force) do not seem to fit into the panorama of physics today. But we have absolutely no right to say that these facts contradict physical science—"perennial physics" as Aldous Huxley might have said. They disagree only with the physics of today. Every scientist knows that science in general, physics in particular, is very young and proceeding at a very fast evolutionary pace. With this everyone would agree, but few realize that this assertion may have very drastic consequences. That is, we cannot say what is possible and what is impossible—at least not for the future. Based on our present knowledge, we may be able to say something about today and perhaps about tomorrow—at least tomorrow morning. But it would be wrong to make a pronouncement that the inventory of natural forces in nature has been completed. For example, it has been discovered quite recently that quasars, while no bigger than medium-sized stars, fire as much energy as a whole galaxy. To the physicist and astronomer, however, the mechanism by which such energy is produced by quasars remains as obscure as the mechanism by which the sun produces energy was to the pilgrim fathers. But one cannot assert that what science does not know today will not be known next week. The rapid evolution of our scientific knowledge suggests that an open mind should be kept about matters that appear to be impossible by present standards.

But if it is said that the findings of parapsychology contradict the present laws of physics, what is the precise meaning of the word "contradict"? This is not clear, even in physics. The findings of Einstein do not contradict those of Newton, even if many people think they do. Rather, in Newton's scale and for Newtonian facts, Newtonian physics and astronomy were true and could be confidently used: Einstein uses another scale and considers other facts. In regard to parapsychology, then, we may affirm only that at the present time we do not know how to reconcile modern physics and psi. But we are not entitled to use the word "contradict." The existence of psi does not annul the laws of electrical currents, for on a proper scale and for the facts they regulate, they are true. But there may be other facts and other laws, not opposing these laws, but in addition to them.

It is true that we do not understand the way the nervous system acts to release psi. The instruments of modern physics have not been able, up to the present time, to detect any release of psi energy. But we are just as ignorant of the way the brain moves the body, and this ignorance does not disturb us very much.

If one is asked to extend his arm, he does it at once. In a fraction of a second his nervous system gives orders to contract *musculi extensores brachii* and to release *musculi flexores,* but his conscious (and for that matter, his unconscious) self ignores completely the "how" of what he has just done. Perhaps we will never know, at least not consciously, the precise way such movement occurs. It would even be false to say that it was learned in infancy, for what the infant learns is "to extend the arm" and not to contract *extensores* and to expand *flexores.*

So every day we use a power whose nature and mechanism we remain ignorant of, but a power we call our "will." This gives us the ability to order or arrange matter (even living matter)—to manage it. The exact way we manage it, we do not know, but at the same time we are not bothered by not knowing.

This is a process rather analogous to psi, and I am not the first one to remark on this. Who knows what we could learn if we had more knowledge of the nerve mechanism of the volitional act, or more exactly, of the relations between conscious will and its background of neural mechanisms? But this is a subject almost as obscure as psi.

What could psi change in psychology, in the biological sciences, in physics? In my opinion, it could change everything. This is why there is such a passionate reluctance by so many scientists to accept the findings of parapsychology—the fear of profound change. What change? I believe we are not far enough along yet to really answer this question, but there are two possible directions, as I see it. First, we could find if and where psi is localized or fits in the brain, measuring exactly the psi factor and controlling it eventually; or second, we might be compelled to conclude that psi escapes time and space entirely (and perhaps the precise measurements of science). In this case we would not be able to compare psi and other natural phenomena.

I think these two possibilities are before us. I would like the first to be the case rather than the second. The conclusions to be drawn would be revolutionary in either case.

CHAPTER 30

SCIENCE AND THE PROBLEM OF PSI*

KENNETH L. SHEWMAKER and CARLTON W. BERENDA

A MONG MISCONCEPTIONS CONCERNING SCIENCE, one of the most flagrant is the impression that it is the infallible mother of answers. Science, far from decimating one's decisions, multiplies possibilities and raises questions and issues which before had not been conceived.

Such a predicament faces many who are struggling with the "problem of psi," i.e. with the question of how we are to make sense of the data of parapsychology. This situation will serve for our present purposes as a paradigm for the exploration of the nature of the scientific commitment and for some of the problems which are basic to it. A limited number of the possible approaches to the problem will be considered, and a particular set of emphases will be pointed out which constitute, suggestively, a general direction for later developments.

THE PROBLEM

Psi phenomena are events which are not at present understood within the current scientific framework. Expressed another way, parapsychology is a *science* apparently incompatible with the whole family of other *sciences*. These phenomena appear to violate principles which are basic to our entire scientific mode of explaining all other physical and psychological phenomena. Yet they, no less than any other events, demand explanation.

Perhaps the most common treatment of the problem is to *wait*

---

*Reprinted from *Philosophy of Science,* 1962, by permission of the authors and the editors.

and see. Who knows but that another Newton or Maxwell will happen along and offer an explanation making psi as commonplace a scientific concept as gravitation or magnetism? This position may imply a simple faith that what is now *unexplained* will turn out to be understood after all within a relatively unchanged scientific framework. This is by no means an impossibility. It will be shown later that the developments most promising of an eventual satisfactory explanation of psi are taking place through the attempt to enlarge the deductive scope of present-day science.

What are we to do in the meantime? To some it may be enough simply to say, "We cannot now explain this. Perhaps someday we shall." Others, not so willing to hold their breath, feel compelled to offer a best possible explanation as of now. These days, those who say, *"Hypotheses non fingo,"* are scientifically mute.

How does one go about explaining phenomena which at first appear to contradict *accepted scientific* principles? How is this problem solved especially when the contradiction arises from an undertaking (parapsychology) which itself claims to be *scientific?*

APPROACHES TO A SOLUTION

We may approach such an issue as this by an appeal to criteria which are outside of science itself or by a reappraisal of the entire issue in the light of our theory of science.

In the case of our appealing to extra-scientific criteria, the argument would have it that as long as we take care not to let our surgeon's hand slip and cut a scientific artery we may feel safe to graft onto our body of science the healthy tissue of our own predilections.

In considering science as man's creation of his own world of explanation[1] we have often slighted the function which science serves in keeping man from constructing his world views in a purely autistic way.

Rogers[2] has effectively reiterated this point when he spoke of science as a way man has of avoiding self-delusion. Unamuno expressed the idea, perhaps a little baldly, by saying, "Science teaches us, in effect, to submit our reason to the truth and to know and

---

[1]A. Einstein, *Essays in Science* (New York, Philosophical Library, n.d.), pp. 2, 3.
[2]C. Rogers, "Persons or Science," *American Psychologist,* Vol. 10 (1955), p. 275.

judge of things as they are—that is to say, as they themselves choose to be and not as we would have them be."[3]

However it be expressed, science makes demands upon us, just as we make demands upon science, and, as Emerson[4] noted, side by side with man's *creativity* is the *discipline* which nature exercises upon him.

If the issue in question be an issue for science, and if science as we currently conceive it leads to a conflict, then we would do better to rephrase the question, to consider its appropriateness for science, or to reexamine our scientific structure itself, rather than shrugging our shoulders with a smile and putting our tongue in cheek.

ONTOLOGICAL ACCEPTANCE

In some ways unlike historic scientific struggles in the past, the issue of psi is seen by some as involving the very question of whether a certain class of phenomena occurs or not, more or less regardless of the theory which accounts for them.*

It is this very nature of the problem which has set the stage for quarrels over its *true existence,* and some have flatly affirmed that there is such a thing as psi, while others have as flatly denied that there is any such thing. On one aspect of this problem, Soal made the statement, "At present there is insufficient confirmation by experiment that non-inferential pre-cognition *really exists,* though there is a certain amount of evidence which suggests that this is a possibility."[5] On such points, Soal's suggestion is that we keep gathering in the *facts* until we have enough to be able to say whether or not it really exists, and then we can begin to formulate hypotheses on the basis of these facts.[6]

---

[3]M. Unamuno, *The Tragic Sense of Life,* trans. by Flitch (London, Macmillan, 1931), p. 197.

[4]R.W. Emerson, *The Complete Works of Ralph Waldo Emerson* (New York, Wise, 1921).

*In a sense, this is not entirely unique. For example, the issue of the phlogiston theory was similar on this point. There the issue was not whether there was burning but whether there was phlogiston. In the case of psi, the issue is not whether a given set of responses takes place but rather whether or not its occurrence demands or even justifies the postulation of psi.

[5]S.G. Soal and F. Bateman, *Modern Experiments in Telepathy* (New Haven, Yale, 1954).

[6]*Ibid.,* p. 345.

For such men, apparently science is what Aiken[7] might call a "noumenal cookie cutter," showing us what really is. For example, Carrington confidently affirmed, ". . . psychic phenomena undoubtedly exist, and their study will constitute a part of the science of the future."[8] Rhine himself stated, "Ideally we must all, laymen and scientist alike, look to the scientific way of solving problems as the only way of arriving at truth. There is no other dependable way known to man."[9]

For these men, science is evidently a mammoth fact-gathering program, and experimentation is its chief vehicle for discovering Truth. For Rhine, for example, scientific experimentation is analogous to opening one's eyes and seeing the truth. For him, it is perfectly obvious that psi exists: "That question [What are the prospects for scientific acceptance of psi?] we can answer with assurance, and the answer is: there is simply no alternative to acceptance."[10]

Soal makes such demands on the experimental situation that it would be by definition impossible to obtain any but positive results in demonstrating whether or not psi does *exist*.

> No scientific experiment can be repeated unless the relevant conditions remain the same. In a telepathy experiment two such conditions are the presence of a good subject, such as Pearce or Shackleton, and the presence of a suitable agent. It is absurd to insist as some scientists have done, that the same effects ought to be obtained when anyone else is substituted for Pearce or Shackleton.[11]

This apparently means that we can only perform parapsychology experiments with subjects who demonstrate psi phenomena. Yet the establishment of psi as a *real* phenomenon is said to rest on experiments and is purportedly so obvious to anyone who would take the trouble to "open his eyes and look" that there is no alternative to acceptance. There is indeed literally *no alternative* to acceptance if we grant such a prerequisite in the first place! If we consider the issue of psi as Soal and Rhine present it, the

[7]H.D. Aiken, *The Age of Ideology* (New York, Mentor, 1956).

[8]H. Carrington, *Mysterious Psychic Phenomena* (Boston, Christopher Publishing House, 1954), p. 152.

[9]J.B. Rhine, *The Reach of the Mind* (London, Faber and Faber, n.d.), p. 128.

[10]*Ibid.*, p. 126.

[11]S.G. Soal and F. Bateman, *op. cit.*, p. 52.

whole issue is either outside of science or else implies a naively realistic view of science. It involves the real existence of psi, which is purported to be established by experiments which, by definition, assure beforehand what the findings will be.

ONTOLOGICAL REJECTION

There are always those, of course, who can reject outright any such nonsense as psi. For the most part, unqualified and final rejection of psi involves the same kind of interpretation of psi and the nature of science as that of the realists who propose it as obviously true. This view takes the fact-gathering nature of science literally enough to reject psi on the grounds that it does not exist, regardless of one's enunciated philosophy of science (or lack of it). Skinner, for instance, was accused of attacking the ESP experiments of Soal without so much as having read them.[12] Scientific fervor of this sort quite generally has laid itself open to a good deal of criticism on the part of those who consider themselves scientists not so derelict as Skinner might think.

ACCEPTANCE AND SUPERNATURALISM

The problem which psi poses depends on the way we formulate the hypothesis of psi. Psi presents an unusual problem for the scientist when it is formulated so as to strike at the very foundations of science itself.

We can think of psi, for example, as something which is irretrievably beyond the scope of science, at least any *science* besides parapsychology. Psi, in this sense, is not only extra-scientific, it is supernatural and anti-scientific.

One is reminded at this point of Spiegelberg's criticism of supernaturalism. "The supernaturalist diagnosis presupposes an exhaustive survey of our natural knowledge. It furthermore requires human scientific omniscience as the basis for the inference to the supernatural. And even after that the inference amounts to an appeal to ignorance."[13]

If psi, as a case of *psychical phenomena,* is perceived as inher-

---

[12]*Ibid.,* p. 246.

[13]H. Spiegelberg, "Supernaturalism or Naturalism: A Study in Meaning and Verifiability," *Phil. of Sci.,* Vol. 18 (1951), p. 359.

ently beyond scientific explication, then it is, as Brown[14] expressed it, suicidal! As soon as a given instance or order of phenomena which we now relegate to parapsychology is explained on scientific grounds, it ceases to be the property of parapsychology, is no longer *psi* and becomes one more facet of psychology (or physics, as the case may be). As long as we hold this view of psi, we cannot, by definition, integrate it *as parapsychological* into our larger system of science, and if we were to accept psi (as so described) on any scientific basis, then we would indeed have a conflict between scientific commitments! For this reason, Parkes objects, ". . . the expression 'extra-sensory perception' is a singularly unfortunate one, in that it begs the question as to the nature of the phenomenon under discussion, and has a slightly supernatural or mystical connotation."[15]

DENIAL OF THE PROBLEM

There are those who, faced with the disastrous enigma of psi, are sent scurrying back under the skirts of Mother Science, perchance to find some grounds for predicting what *in fact* has already been observed.[16] This sort of attempt reminds one of the theologian who, after Darwin, proposes to show that the Scriptures have always very obviously supported evolution!

Despite the notable failure of attempts thus far to reevaluate psi by principles of the broader body of scientific concepts, this seems to be one of the most promising regions of eventual break-through.

One very promising step in this direction has been taken by McConnell.[17] It is his contention that the questions raised in connection with psi phenomena do not lie within the exclusive scope of physics or psychology. Consequently, he has undertaken to approach the whole question within the framework of what he has called *psychological physics,* an area which bridges the gap between *res extensa* and *res cogitans.* His approach thus involves a redefinition of the scope of the present bodies of scientific thought and

---

[14]Ciba Foundation Symposium on Extrasensory Perception, Wolstenholme and Millar, eds. (Boston, Little, Brown, 1956), p. 73.

[15]*Ibid.,* p. 235.

[16]*Ibid.,* p. 70.

[17]R.A. McConnell, "Psi phenomena and Methodology," *American Scientist,* Vol. 45, **no. 2.**

hence bears much promise for the successful extension of its deductive range.

ACCEPTANCE OF ACAUSALITY

Among those for whom psi presents especially difficult problems
are those who see in psi an inherently anti-causal principle. This is
related to, but not identical with, the impasse which results if we
think of psi as, by definition, anti- or extra-scientific. Here the problem is one of accepting along with psi a world view which is inherently acausal and basically not subject to our conventional ideas
of time and space. It involves, in many ways, a reconsideration of
whether the question of psi is appropriate to science, and it leads
to a reappraisal of science itself.

Take Martiny's definition as a starting point: "Psi may be defined as a psychological phenomenon characterized by an apparent
dislocation of the relations between cause and effect."[18]

In very few cases do those who are concerned with the acceptance of acausal principles[19] appear to recognize that the postulation of an acausal principle in the sense in which it is usually meant
implies a great deal about their conceptualization of causality itself.
To say, for example, that psi is something which is without cause
or which involves a dislocation of cause often involves being as
naive a realist as one who takes cause literally and supposes that
it has objective existence apart from the mind that thinks it. Even
those who would not admit to a position of a boldly stated realism
nonetheless appear to act in many ways as though this were their
implicit viewpoint.

If we take our laws literally, then indeed any apparent disruption
of them strikes us as a violation of Natural Law, and even to consider the possibility of this is to be no less naive then to believe in
pixies and wishing-wells. On the other hand, if we are not so easily
deluded by the formidable system of laws, which man has formulated, then the thought of such a possibility as psi is no more a
personal threat to ourselves, our world view, or our science than
the working hypotheses of atomic theory.

---

[18]*Proceedings of the First International Conference of Parapsychological Studies* (New
York Parapsychology Foundation, 1955), p. 170.
[19]*Ibid.;* C.G. Jung and W. Pauli, *The Interpretation of Nature and the Psyche* (New
York, Pantheon, 1955).

PSI AS FUNCTION OF THE UNIQUENESS OF EVENTS

There are a number of theorists whose approach to psi emphasizes the uniqueness of all events. In this framework, psi phenomena are not themselves any more *peculiar* than any of the manifold events to which we apply our explanatory categories. Albeit undetected, these phenomena may occur all about us, every day.

For example, Booth concluded, "Physical events are not the cause, but the expression of non-physical, presumably psychic tendencies. It is inherent in the nature of this situation that, generally, psychological relatedness goes together with physical proximity and that therefore the convergence of personalities is not expressed in the form of psi phenomena" (i.e. those *unusual* events we take special note of and call *psi*). "Cases in which the latter occur are always based on strong individual needs for communication in spite of physical distance.[20] This is the reason why spontaneous cases, if carefully enough examined, provide more impressive examples for the existence of psi than laboratroy experiments. In the latter the small deviations from chance illustrate that intellectual curiosity is very ineffectual in comparison to vital emotional needs."[21]

West[22] points out that ESP can be considered as taking place constantly, as participating in every real life occurrence, overlapping with everything else that might also be abstracted out and considered as analytically separate.

RE-EVALUATION OF THE PROBLEM AND OF SCIENCE

Once we begin to view the total context in which psi is embedded, we gain a new respect for its possible usefulness as a concept. We recall Frank's statement, "There is no science without oversimplification."[23]

Inasmuch as we are bound to the classificatory schemes and abstractions indigenous to our thought forms, we could expect that

---

[20]E. Lamar, Margaret Hobbs, and Helen Mull, "Friendship as a Factor in ESP," *Journal General Psychology,* Vol. 55 (1956), pp. 281-283.

[21]Proceedings of the First International Conference of Parapsychological Studies, *op. cit.,* p. 42.

[22]D.J. West, *Psychical Research Today* (London, Duckworth, 1954), p. 134.

[23]P. Frank, *Philosophy of Science* (Englewood Cliffs, New Jersey, Prentice-Hall, 1957), p. 43.

there would always appear unusual, apparently inexplicable events. That there are these *inexplicable* events may simply be an artifact of our imposing abstract classes upon the world we experience. This is not to imply that we simply do not have the correct abstractions but that we attempt to explain the world with abstractions at all.

Viewed from this perspective, psi is no longer some mysterious something we have been deluded into seeking. Psi, from this point of view, is the persistent remainder left over from our division of the world into abstract classes.

Notice that we can now consider psi itself as a class, an abstraction! Psi, in this sense, is to science somewhat as the imaginary numbers are to mathematics. We may even undertake to describe as best we can the ways we experience these *unusual* events. Whether this can itself be a *scientific* work is perhaps a moot question. For Eisenbud, psi is itself another of the long list of disconnections which are the raw empirical bone and marrow of science. His proposal, which would serve as his rebuttal to those who reject psi on grounds of parsimony, is that we take psi as the prototype of all such discontinuities and use what we know of human psychology as the grounds for *explaining the introduction of order!*[24]

PSI AND THE UNCONSCIOUS

In attempting to ascertain whether we can have a science of parapsychology and still define psi as we have, the issue quickly becomes whether we can have a science of the unique, to name at least one difficulty. One requirement of such a science would therefore be a system or language which does not necessitate abstraction, oversimplification, and the formation of classes. Such a system has already been described by Langer[25] and constitutes a nondiscursive symbolism, a presentational language.

Nondiscursive symbolism has already been used in the discussion of various art forms[26] and for communicating the psycho-dynamics of individual patients in the psychological clinic.[27]

---

[24]Proceedings of the First International Conference of Parapsychological Studies, *op. cit.,* pp. 51-52.
[25]Susanne K. Langer, *Philosophy in a New Key* (Cambridge, Mass., Harvard, 1951).
[26]Susanne K. Langer, *Feeling and Form* (New York, Scribner, 1953).
[27]C.W. Berenda, "Is Clinical Psychology a Science?," *Amer. Psychologist,* Vol. 12 (1957), pp. 727-728.

The use of such a system in psychodynamics seems to meet the demands for a language of the unique. In addition, there already exists a rich literature in psychology revealing the striking similarities between unconscious functioning and psi phenomena, for example the work of Ehrenwald,[28] Fodor,[29] and Fromm.[30] Fromm described unconscious functioning as the expression of a *forgotten language*:

> Symbolic language is a language in which inner experiences, feelings and thoughts are expressed as if they were sensory experiences, events in the outer world. It is a language which has a different logic from the conventional one we speak in the daytime, a logic in which not time and space are the ruling categories but intensity and association . . . Yet this language has been forgotten by modern man. Not when he is asleep, but when he is awake.[31]

There is a striking similarity between this description of the language of the unconscious and Booth's[32] description of psi phenomena, given above, particularly as to the importance of the dimension of emotional intensity. At this point, we can only speculate about the possibilities of exploring psi phenomena further using these principles.

We are already armed in the psychological clinic with the experience and the "measuring" devices necessary for the study of the unique personality, especially along dimensions appropriate to unconscious functioning, dimensions which seem no less appropriate to psi. The course to pursue would seem, therefore, to be a truly intense psychological study of the person or persons involved in any reported incident of psi, not simply to determine the personality types but rather *with the intent of a presentational understanding of the unique persons and the unique event.* This is to suggest that clinicians "gang-up" on one reported psi incident, as soon after the fact as possible, making use of any or all clinical devices at their command. Special attention might be paid to such

---

[28]Proceedings of the First International Conference of Parapsychological Studies, *op. cit.,* p. 47.
[29]N. Fodor, *New Approaches to Dream Interpretation* (New York, Citadel Press, 1951).
[30]E. Fromm, *The Forgotten Language* (New York, Rinehart, 1951).
[31]*Ibid.,* p. 7.
[32]Proceedings of the First International Conference of Parapsychological Studies, *op. cit.,* p. 42.

questions as: "What psychological meaning did the psi event have for this particular person at this particular time?" "What were the conditions of the interpersonal relationships at the time?" "What function did the psi event appear to serve for the persons involved?" Such an intense psychological study of any one psi event might provide us with the needed foothold in this apparently capricious, "tychistic" area.

Is it a contradiction in terms, however, to speak of explaining something while still saying it does not follow the usual categorical relationships? This issue is a familiar one in the psychological clinic. Here we use discursive language in *academically* explaining the workings of the unconscious, though we do not posit logic as a characteristic of the id level of functioning.[33] On the other hand, we often have recourse to a presentational language in *explaining* the psycho-dynamics of individuals!

The question of whether an undertaking such as clinical psychology can be considered a science has already been explored elsewhere by Berenda.[34] The relevancy at this point is whether it will be necessary or possible, after elaborating a nondiscursive treatment of psi, to proceed then to a discursive meta-language congenial to the main body of science.

To the extent to which this additional step is not taken, we would have a greater difficulty in defending the proposition that we are *explaining*. To that extent, we may be more nearly approaching a *knowing* which is apart from differentiation and categorization.[35]

We may cringe at the thought that there may always remain a kind of residue not covered by any consistent system of abstractions. Kierkegaard[36] would remind us, however, that there are two dreads common to man: the dread of possibility, which is the lack of necessity, but also the dread of necessity, which is the lack of possibility.

"We accuse the dreams of not making sense. And yet it is we

[33]S. Arieti, *Interpretation of Schizophrenia* (New York, Brunner, 1955), p. 205.

[34]C.W. Berenda, *op. cit.*

[35]B. Russell, *Mysticism and Logic* (Garden City, Doubleday Anchor, 1957).

[36]S. Kierkegaard, *Fear and Trembling,* and *The Sickness unto Death* (Garden City, Doubleday Anchor, 1955).

[37]E. Fromm, *op. cit.*, p. 9.

who have forced the 'sense' upon our waking state via our conventions of time, space, causality . . ."[37]

POSTSCRIPT

Some will no doubt call this a defeatist view, so far as science is concerned. That may well be, particularly as to science as it stands today. Nonetheless, the science that dies is the science that claims to have achieved its end or supposes that it ever will. Hence, Burns was able to say: "Philosophers in every age have attempted to give an account of as much experience as they could. Some have indeed pretended that what they could not explain did not exist; but all the great philosophers have allowed for more than they could explain, and have, therefore, signed beforehand, if not dated, the death-warrant of their philosophies."[38]

We have seen that the very problems we observe in psi arise from the specific way in which we conceive of psi and of science. If the issues be resolved within the scientific framework, we may expect to see changes not only in our concept of psi but of science as well. Rhine himself has said, "It is because it *does* fall well outside the present boundary of conventional science that ESP is a challenge to the science of today."[39]

[38]Susanne K. Langer, *Philosophy in a New Key*, p. 5.

[39]J.B. Rhine, "Comments on 'Science and the Supernatural'," *Science*, Vol. 23. no 3184 (1956), p. 12.

CHAPTER 31

INDIVIDUAL REALITIES:
COMMONSENSE, SCIENCE, AND MYSTICISM*

LAWRENCE LeSHAN

IT IS A TRUISM OF SCIENTIFIC investigation that one cannot speak meaningfully of *environment* without speaking of the organism involved. The organism is selective (as a function of its structure and experience) of the aspects of the environment with which it interacts. The environment, as it affects and is affected by the organism, cannot be described without knowing something of the characteristics of the organism. To speak, to a man born blind, of reproducing the colors of the sunset would ignore this fact. This point is rather clearly stated (or perhaps somewhat overstated) in the following quote by Aiken.

> [Before the nineteenth century, philosophers] . . . did not, on the whole, seriously doubt that there is a common, independent and objective reality which can to some extent be understood. Nor did they question whether there is an objective way of thinking about reality, common to all rational animals, which does not radically modify or distort the thing known. . . . The relation between man's thinking about reality and reality itself were thus regarded as a non-distorting relation of "correspondence."[1]

> Objectivity [in philosophy] in short, is now conceived of as inter-subjectivity. Inter-subjective norms are not agreed to by the members of a society because they are objective, but, in effect become objective because they are jointly accepted.[2]

---

*Reprinted from Lawrence LeShan, *Toward a General Theory of the Paranormal: A Report of Work in Progress,* by permission of the author and the Parapsychology Foundation, Inc., pp. 11-20, 57-61.
[1]*The Age of Ideology,* H.D. Aiken, ed. (New York, New American Library, 1956), p. 23.
[2]*Ibid.,* p. 14.

Sir Arthur Eddington has discussed this change, as it has affected modern physics, in some detail. He writes:

> The difference is most strikingly exhibited in modern quantum theory. According to the classical conception of microscopic physics, our task was to discover a system of equations which connects the positions and motions of the particles of one instant, with the positions and motions at a later instant. This problem has proved altogether baffling; we have no reason to believe that any determinate solution exists, and the search has been frankly abandoned. Modern quantum theory has substituted another task, namely to discover the equations which connect knowledge of the positions or motions at one instant with knowledge of the positions or motions at a later instant. The solution of this problem appears to be well within our power. . . . The introduction of probability into physical theories emphasizes the fact that it is knowledge that is being treated. For probability is an attribute of our knowledge of an event; it does not belong to the event itself, which must certainly occur or not occur.[3]

And Werner Heisenberg also makes this point when he writes:

> It was orginally the aim of all science to describe nature as far as possible as it is, i.e. without our interference and our observation. We now realize that this is an unattainable goal. . . . We decide, by our selection of the type of observation employed, which aspects of nature are to be determined and which are to be blurred in the course of our observation.[4]

The characteristics of an organism determine which characteristics of the environment can be perceived, responded to, and interacted with. It follows that if these characteristics of the organism change, it will then respond to and interact with an environment that is functionally different. In modern psychological parlance, it will then be in a different *life-space.*

The term *environment* clearly has special meaning conditioned by long usage. For this reason, we shall use the term *individual reality* (IR) to denote *those aspects of reality which the individual perceives, responds to, or interacts with.* We are not here concerned with the problem of the ultimate make up of reality.

We are making—to the best of our knowledge—only three as-

---

[3]A. Eddington, *The Philosophy of Physical Science* (Ann Arbor, Mich., University of Michigan Press, 1958), p. 50.
[4]W. Heisenberg, *Philosophic Problems of Nuclear Science* (Greenwich, Conn., Fawcett, 1966), p. 82.

sumptions about the nature of reality. These seem to be the least we can. They are:

1. That there *is* a subject-object differentiation: a separation between the individual and what is not the individual. That *something* is *out there*.
2. That reality has characteristics that can be abstracted. That individuals can respond to certain aspects of reality and not to others.
3. That multiple individuals exist. That there is more than one person in the cosmos.

These assumptions are common to all empirical exploration and we must use them here. If they are invalid, then all the rest of this paper is invalid. Unfortunately, the converse is not necessarily true.

Our concern is with those aspects of whatever is *out there* that constitute the *individual reality* (IR) of a specific individual. ("We must remember," wrote Werner Heisenberg in a famous statement, "that what we see is not Nature, but Nature exposed to our method of questioning.") The analogy of turning to different channels of a television set and thus responding to different aspects of one part of what is *out there* may not be too far fetched.

Each different IR has different possibilities of interaction. What IR the individual responds to determines how, and in what form, interaction between the two can take place.

There is a crucial question in this area that is rarely asked, since it is assumed that the answer is known. It is the central question of this paper. This is the question of the limits of the differences between IR's that can be selected. That is to ask: "If two IR's are interacted with by two individuals, how far can these IR's differ and on what parameters?" We might restate this by asking, "What are the possible limits of divergence between two IR's interacted with by two individuals?" It has been a general assumption that different IR's could only differ in a small number of ways. Parameters could be diminished or omitted (as in color blindness or in deafness), could be expanded (as in the special training of a tea taster or by highly motivated concentration on particular sensory stimuli), could be mildly restructured (as occurs when the sudden flash of insight shows a new relationship between facts and therefore new possibilities of action) and that is about all.

The phrase "and that is about all" implies that these differences are small ones; that these variations among the IR's are minor. Yet at first glance the variations appear to loom very large. The differences, for example, between the IR used by a man with his visual system and that of an eagle with his, between the IR used by a man's nose and that of a dog, between the IR of a biologist before Darwin's insight restructured the data and afterwards, seems very great. The same major differences appear if we contrast the IR of the musically untrained tone deaf individual with that of the trained musician with perfect pitch; the IR of the communication engineer before and after Marconi; or the IR of the psychologically rigid and constricted patient before and after successful psychotherapy.

With these large obvious differences, why is it implied that the variations between these IR's are minor? Simply because a large number of basic organizing principles remain the same in all of them, and it has generally been assumed that all IR's include them. These fundamental *principles* (*axioms, techniques of selection of attributes of the IR*) include the basic aspects of *reality* that we Westerners generally believe to be *objective, out there, real, unchangeable*. These are the aspects of reality upon which, most people believe, "all reasonable men can agree." Examples might include that matter is solid and real, that valid information about the world comes to us through the senses, that causes must precede effects in time, and that objects separated by space are different objects. These, and a variety of others, which people tend to believe, are basic in all IR's.

> C. D. Broad has discussed these—as he calls them—*basic limiting principles* in some detail. He says, "They form the framework within which the practical life, the scientific theories, and even most of the fiction of contemporary industrial civilizations are confined." In Broad's view, an event which violates one of these *basic limiting principles* must be defined as a *paranormal* occurrence.[5]

These *basic limiting principles* are aspects of a sort of generalized, Western-culture IR. (In effect, we might define their sum as the *commonsense* IR.) It is generally believed in our culture that

---

[5]C.D. Broad, *Religion, Philosophy and Psychical Research* (London, Routledge & Kegan Paul, 1953), p. 3.

all IR's include them insofar as the individual is sane and intelligent enough to conceive of them.

However, if we look carefully, we see that all IR's *do not* include these basic postulates. The mystic, for example, uses different axioms. One might try, in vain, to show how the overall pattern of the life of Ramakrishna or that of St. John of the Cross was based on such accepted *reasonable* principles as "valid information is received only through the senses" or "whatever exists has effects that in some way can be perceived through the senses." A great deal of historical material demonstrates clearly that individual *mystics*—living in different times and in different cultures—were reacting to, and writing of, a reality with quite different postulates and that they were in basic agreement on what these postulates were. Their perceptions were not purely individualistic and self-generating. They appear to have been responding to a specific IR. Evelyn Underhill, in her classic *Mysticism,* writes:

> The most highly developed branches of the human family have in common one peculiar characteristic. They tend to produce— sporadically it is true, and often in the teeth of adverse external circumstances—a curious and definite type of personality; a type which refuses to be satisfied with that which other men call experience, and is inclined, in the words of its enemies, to "deny the world in order that it may find reality." We meet these persons in the east and the west; in the ancient, mediaeval, and modern worlds . . . whatever the place or period in which they have arisen, their aims, doctrines and methods have been substantially the same. Their experience, therefore, forms a body of evidence, curiously self-consistent and often mutually explanatory, which must be taken into account before we can add up the sum of the energies and potentialities of the human spirit, or reasonably speculate on its relations to the unknown world which lies outside the boundaries of sense.[6]

And C.D. Broad has put it:

> To me the occurrence of mystical experience at all times and places, and the similarities between the statements of so many mystics all the world over, seems to be a significant fact. *Prima facie* it suggests that there is an aspect of reality with which these persons come in contact in their mystical experiences, and which they afterwards strive and largely fail to describe in the language of daily life. I should say that this *prima facie* appearance of objectivity ought to

[6]E. Underhill, *Mysticism,* 4th ed. (London, Methuen and Co., Ltd., 1912), p. 3.

be accepted at its face value unless and until some reasonably satisfactory alternative explanation of the agreement can be given.[7]

Bertrand Russell[8] has pointed up four basic characteristics of
the IR of the mystic. These are: 1) *There is a better way of gaining
information than through the senses.* 2) *There is unity of all things.*
3) *There is no reality to time.* 4) *All evil is mere appearance.* We
may not accept—as Russell does not—the validity of these postulates. Nevertheless, it is true that for many sincere and intelligent
men—whom we call mystics—they are part of the basic postulates
of their environment, and their possibilities and limitations of interaction with the IR are, in part, determined by these postulates.

The artist also often responds to a different IR. One may or may
not enjoy looking at a Picasso, a Chagall, or a Rouault painting.
Irrelevant to this, however, is the fact that if one seriously looks
at the painting, one knows that there is a validity and consistency
about it that is not based on the IR we live in, but on another.

The *primitive* (generally defined as an individual raised in a
non-Western, non-mechanical culture) also frequently uses quite
other postulates in the IR he interacts with. Thus he may not accept
the postulate that the two objects separate in space are *necessarily*
separate objects. He may believe that, although they have separate
spatial locations, they can form a functional unity, and that the
parts of this unity could interact in ways which appear impossible
to a Western-culture individual. The basic principle of sympathetic
magic—and whether or not it works in *our* IR (voodoo often *does
work* in his)—contradicts the principle of identity. The point is
not whether sympathetic magic works in whatever universe is *out
there,* but whether or not it works in a particular IR. In the typical
IR of the *primitive,* it does work. Although we may explain *how*
it works in terms of our IR, it works for quite different reasons,
according to the primitive individual.

Thus we come to the tentative conclusion that the individual
can live in different IR's and that these differences can produce
quite different possibilities of interaction between the individual
and reality. In order to begin to explore the possible limits of this,

---

[7]C.D. Broad, *op. cit.,* p. 242.
[8]B. Russell, *Mysticism and Logic and Other Essays* (London, Longmans Green, 1925),
pp. 8-11.

let us take one more example and examine it in slightly more detail. Let us contrast what might be called the *commonsense* IR (the IR generally used in everyday life in Western society), and what might be called the *scientific* IR (the IR of modern physics).

If, for the sake of examples, we contrast these two IR's insofar as they affect the possibilities of interaction between us and a bar of iron which is—let us say—buttressing a pillar, we can see that extremely different possibilities exist. In the scientific IR, we see it as a field of stresses, interspersed at wide intervals with foci of patterned, rapidly-moving electrical charges. With this view, we can calculate and predict such things as how long it will be before metal fatigue weakens the bar and the pillar collapses; how much pressure can be added to it until it buckles; and how it will resist the action of certain solvents and acids. With this IR (the IR of the physicist), however, it is extraordinarily difficult and complex to hang our clothes on it, or to admire its form and sheen, or to consider hammering it into a more artistic shape. We can do these things (since the commonsense IR is a special case of the physicist's IR), but we will have to work hard to accomplish them.

However, if we return to a *commonsense* IR, we see it as hard, solid matter of a particular color, and we can easily hang our clothes on it, etc. What we can *not* do (except in a crude rule-of-thumb, empirical, use-of-past-experience way) is to make predictions about metal fatigue or resistance to stress.

The *commonsense* and *scientific* viewpoints differ far more widely than is generally understood by the layman. One might take our commonsense basic postulate, that matter is solid and real. Henry Margenau recently said. "The atom has turned [through various discoveries in physics] into a series of singularities haunting space. That rather disposed of matter.[9]

In order to examine this matter further, let us see how Max Planck has described the concept of the particle in physics.

> Hitherto it had been believed that the only kind of causality with which any system of Physics could operate was one in which all the events of the physical world—by which, as usual, I mean not the real world but the world-view of Physics—might be explained as

---

[9]H. Margenau, *The Nature of Physical Reality* (New York, McGraw-Hill, 1950), p. 194.

being composed of logical events taking place in a number of individual and infinitely small parts of Space.

It was further believed that each of these elementary events was completely determined by a set of laws without respect to the other events; and was determined exclusively by the local events in its immediate temporal and spatial vicinity. Let us take a concrete instance of sufficiently general application. We will assume that the physical system under consideration consists of a system of particles, moving in a conservative field of force of constant total energy. Then according to classical Physics each individual particle at any time is in a definite state; that is, it has a definite position and a definite velocity, and its movement can be calculated with perfect exactness from its initial state and from the local properties of the field of force in those parts of Space through which the particle passes in the course of its movement. If these data are known, we need know nothing else about the remaining properties of the system of particles under consideration.

In modern mechanics matters are wholly different. According to modern mechanics, merely local relations are no more sufficient for the formulation of the law of motion than would be the microscopic investigation of the different parts of a picture in order to make clear its meaning. On the contrary, it is impossible to obtain an adequate version of the laws for which we are looking, unless the physical system is regarded *as a whole*. According to modern mechanics, each individual particle of the system, in a certain sense, at any one time, exists simultaneously in every part of the space occupied by this system. This simultaneous existence applies not merely to the field of force with which it is surrounded, but also to its mass and its charge.

Thus, we see that nothing less is at stake here than the concept of the particle—the most elementary concept of classical mechanics. We are compelled to give up the earlier essential meaning of this idea; only in a number of special border-line cases can we retain it.[10]

Hence, we have a case example of two IR's (the *scientific* and the *commonsense*) selected by a simple change in attitude, which differ—to a quite startling degree—in our possibilities of interaction with whatever is *out there* and with *reality*. Although these two IR's are different, we do not feel either is untrue. Illustrations such as those used by Eddington may help us, perhaps, to clarify this: "The physicist is not conscious of any disloyalty to truth when his

---

[10]M. Planck, *The Universe in the Light of Modern Physics* (London, George Allen and Unwin, 1931), pp. 24-26.

sense of proportion tells him to regard a plank as continuous material, well knowing that it is 'really' empty space containing sparsely scattered electric charges."[11]

Both are valid; either can be taken by the modern physicist, depending on his needs at the moment. He need only shift his attitude, and he is in a different IR with different possibilities and limitations of his interaction with it. To illustrate this—and to show how easily and automatically the shift from one IR to another can take place—we might repeat Eddington's charming example of the scientist who, ". . . is convinced that all phenomena arise from electrons and quanta and the like controlled by mathematical formulae [and who] must presumably hold the belief that his wife is a rather elaborate differential equation; but is probably tactful enough not to obtrude this opinion in domestic life."[12]

We do not speak here of the ultimate nature of reality (except insofar as we make the three assumptions referred to earlier)—a goal that Max Planck[13] has concluded is "theoretically unobtainable." (Indeed, Morris Rafael Cohen has put it, "The category of reality belongs not to science, but to religion."[14]) Rather, we are concerned with the problem of what can happen if we interact with different aspects of reality by shifting ourselves to different IR's; and how widely we can vary the IR's we interact with.

Having a brief glimpse of the fact that different IR's can give different possibilities of interaction between the individual and *reality,* let us now return to the IR of the mystic. This involves a set of axioms about the universe which—as was stated earlier—Russell has described as having four principles. (We might call them his "four theorems of the mystic experience.") These are: 1) that there is a better way of knowing than the senses, which, with reason and analysis are ". . . blind guides leading to the morass of illusion";[15] 2) that there is a fundamental unity and

---

[11]A. Eddington, *The Nature of the Physical World* (New York, Macmillan, 1931), p. 467.
[12]*Ibid.*
[13]M. Planck, *Where is Science Going?* (London, George Allen and Unwin, 1933), p. 15.
[14]C.C.L. Gregory and A. Kohsen, *The O-Structure: An Introduction to Psychophysical Cosmology* (Church Crookham, Hampshire, Great Britain, Institute for the Study of Mental Images, 1969), p. 16.
[15]B. Russell, *op. cit.,* p. 9.

oneness of all things; 3) that time is an illusion; and 4) that all evil is mere appearance.

William James, in his *Varieties of Religious Experience,* has also described four characteristics of the mystical experience: Ineffability, Noetic Quality, Transciency, Passivity. However, these are qualities described from *outside* the experience. (Thus ineffability—the inability of describing the experience in words—points to the reaction of the person in the *commonsense* IR to his past experience in the *mystical* IR.) Russell, on the other hand, describes the qualities from *inside* the experience (its *logic, axioms*) and therefore it is his description we will use here. As will be shown later, the qualities that Russell describes necessarily lead to those given by James, when we try to view the mystical IR from the vantage point of the commonsense IR.

It is perhaps easiest to continue to use the term *"mystic" to denote the individual who uses (at least at times) the IR we are describing.* The term itself has many connotations, some unfortunate, but it seems better to use it here rather than to invent a new word. In using it, we shall simply mean a person who sometimes interacts with the particular IR which Russell and James describe. No religious connotations are included in our use of this term. As we shall show, in a later section of this paper, the IR used by the *mystic* is essentially the same as that used by a person in a *peak experience,* by persons in certain ecstatic states, and in LSD or other hallucinogenic drug-produced conditions.

We now ask a basic question: What types of interaction with the mystical IR are possible if one embraces this viewpoint wholeheartedly? If one selects this IR, what can be done and what cannot be done in it?

Again it must be stated that we are not concerned here with a correlation between our viewpoint and the ultimate *truth* about *reality* but rather with what happens if our attitude is shifted from a *commonsense* one into a *mystical* one; if we use a mystical IR and live *as if* (in Vaihinger's sense) we live in a universe run on the laws of this IR.

What will occur *naturally* in this IR, what will we perceive, and what are the limits of our will and actions in it?

In the *commonsense* IR, certain things occur naturally and certain things cannot occur. We can accomplish certain things by our will and actions, and certain others (as altering the past or predicting the future when we do not know the variables involved) are forever impossible.

It is certainly clear that precognition and clairvoyance are impossible. They simply cannot exist in the world we commonly know and live in. Further, this picture we have of the everyday world is *clearly valid*. We have too many *successes* in our actions to dismiss it. We can predict the effect of actions and events too well to throw out our conceptual scheme. It works far too well to be false, and we know in our hearts that it is valid. And yet, precognition and clairvoyance *do* occur. We must do something about this paradox. Unfortunately, for the easy solution, we cannot solve the problem by a *discarnate entity* hypothesis. This simply pushes the paradox further away and conceals it. If we try the *spiritistic* answer, we are simply faced with the problem, "How can a spirit be precognitive and clairvoyant? How can *it* violate the laws of the cosmos?" The problem remains.

The fact, however, that one way of looking at reality is valid does not mean that another different way may not be equally valid. (There is an old poem about seven blind men and an elephant that has some relevance here.) It *is* valid to conceive of light as traveling in waves. It is *equally valid* to conceive of light as traveling in an entirely different—mutually exclusive—way, in particles. If you use only one concept, you can explain only one part of the data. You explain it well, but you need the other conception to explain, equally well, the other part of the data. Using both, we can understand a little more about the behavior of light.

The basic problem in understanding mysticism is not in the description of the cosmos given in this view; that is not too difficult to understand. It is the belief that this view of the cosmos cannot be valid, as it is contradictory to the—obviously true—everyday view of the world. If we look at it differently—that both may be equally true—we break through the difficulties. No longer are we constrained to try either to *explain* psi in terms of the everyday world, or else to discard it as untrue. We can *explain* it in terms of a concept of the cosmos in which it makes sense. We can *explain* everyday phenomena in terms of another concept of the cosmos. No paradox remains.

These ideas are not new, except perhaps in this form. They were made by others, notably perhaps Myers and Tyrrell. Indeed, as Western philosophy has been said to be a series of footnotes to

Plato, all psychical research seems to be developing as a series of footnotes to Myers!

TABLE OF COMPARISON OF THE SENSORY INDIVIDUAL REALITY (S-IR) AND THE CLAIRVOYANT INDIVIDUAL REALITY (C-IR) IN REFERENCE TO CERTAIN BASIC LIMITING PRINCIPLES

(S-IR)	(C-IR)
1. Objects and events separated in space and/or time are primarily individual and separate, although they may be viewed—in a secondary manner—as being related in larger unities.	Individual identity is essentially illusory. Primarily, objects and events are part of a pattern which itself is part of a larger pattern, and so on until all is included in the grand plan and pattern of the universe. Individual events and objects exist, but their individuality is distinctly secondary to their being part of the unity of the pattern.

This brings into clear focus the heart of the difference between the two IR's. This consists of the way one views a person, object, or event. If one sees its uniqueness, its isolation, its I-stand-alone quality; if one sees its this-is-a-so-and-so, its what-are-important-are-its-boundaries-and-cut-off-points quality, its this-is-where-it-ends-and-something-else-begins quality, one views it from the S-IR.

If, however, one sees as its most important characteristics its harmonious-relationships-to-other-parts-of-the-total quality, is part-of-a-pattern-that-is-part-of-a-larger-pattern quality, its field-theory quality, one views it from the C-IR.

Meister Eckhardt contrasts these two IR's when he writes: When is a man in mere understanding? I answer, "When he sees one thing separated from another." And when is a man above mere understanding? That I can tell you: "When a man sees All in all, then a man stands beyond mere understanding."[16]

It appears as if the other differences between the S-IR and the C-IR would follow logically from this difference.

---

[16] A. Huxley, *The Perennial Philosophy* (New York, Meridian Books, 1944), p. 57.

(S-IR)

2. Information comes through the senses, and these are the only valid sources of information.

3. Time is divided into past, present, and future and moves in one direction, irreversibly from future, through the now, into the past. It is the time of one-thing-followed-by-another.

4. An event or action can be good, neutral, or evil, although its consequences often cannot be seen until long after the event.

5. Free will exists, and decisions which will alter the future can be made. Action can be taken on the basis of will.

(C-IR)

Information is *known* through the knower, an object being part of the same unitary pattern. The senses give only illusory information.

Time is without divisions, and past, present, and future are illusory. Sequences of action exist, but these happen in an eternal now. It is the time of all-at-once.

Evil is an illusion, as is good. What is, *is* and is neither good nor evil, but part of the eternal, totally harmonious, plan of the cosmos which, by its very being, is above good or evil.

Free will does not exist since what will be *is,* and the beginning and end of all enfold each other. Decisions cannot be made, as these involve action-in-the-future, and the future is an illusion. One cannot take action, but can only observe the pattern of things.

6. Perception can be focused by the will in any desired direction, unless it is externally blocked, and thus specific knowledge acquired.

Perception cannot be focused, as this involves will, taking action, and action-toward-the-future, all of which are impossible. Knowledge comes from being in the pattern of things, not from desire to know specific information. Perception cannot be externally blocked since knowledge comes from being part of the All, and nothing can come between knower and known, as they are the same.

7. Space can prevent energy and information exchange between two individual objects unless there is a medium, a *thing-between,* to transmit the energy or information from one to the other.

Space cannot prevent energy or information exchange between two individual objects, since their separateness and individuality are secondary to their unity and relatedness.

8. Time can prevent energy and information exchange between two individual objects. Exchanges can only take place in the present, not from present to past or from present to future.

Time cannot prevent energy or information exchange between two individual objects, since the divisions into past, present, and future are illusions, and all things occur in the "eternal now."

As can be clearly seen from the above Table, a person cannot live fully consciously aware of the C-IR for any length of time. One would not survive biologically in this way for very long. To live completely consciously unaware of it, however, makes man less than he can be, and robs him of much of his potential. Perhaps the clairvoyant, with his ability to take the best from both modes of being, is closer to man's potential than the mystic or materialist who believes one mode is vastly preferable to the other.

It may be important to note that although we have described these two IR's as if they were completely separate and discrete, it is much more likely that we are dealing with a spectrum of IR's that each shade into the other, and that the descriptions given are merely convenient focal points on this range. Tidy compartments are easier to talk about than shades of grey and it may be permissible to do so for heuristic purposes, reality is rarely so neatly divided into sections.

In the S-IR, as we live in it in our everyday lives, there *are* relationships and patterns which make it possible for us to function effectively. This should not hide the fact, however, that these are secondary to our perception of unique objects and events. In this sense, the Western commonsense IR, the S-IR as we know it, is not the *pure* state at the extreme end of the scale, but rather a state near that end of the spectrum.

Similarly for the mystic, the C-IR, as he generally uses it, does not appear to be the extreme possible *pure* state, but a perceptual mode near the opposite end of the spectrum. Sub-patterns of events, and probably individual events themselves, are perceived, although these are distinctly secondary to the perception of larger patterns and harmonies. Lao-Tze divided Tao into the Tao of Heaven (T'ien Tao), the Tao of Earth (T'i Tao), and the Tao of Man (Jen Tao). All three are perceived in correspondence and harmony, but are nevertheless perceived as sub-patterns.

In the *pure* state of the C-IR, for which some mystics strive and which some say they have achieved, all specific contents and all events and sub-patterns vanish. This, however, seems as hard for most of us to conceive of as a *pure* S-IR state with *only* unique events and *no* relationships would be.

It also seems important to say here that I am much over-simplifying the mystical point of view. This viewpoint arises out of a profound study of the relationship of man and the cosmos; of man's being and potentiality for being. What I am doing in this monograph is analyzing one aspect of this study—its Weltbild, its concept of *this-is-how-the-universe-works*—but there is far more to serious mysticism than this.

For example, the special attitude brought by the mystic to the C-IR is *love* in its deepest and most profound sense. It is selflessness, a purity of heart and mind, a deep humility. When the Sufi poet Jalal-uddin Rumi writes: "The astrolabe of the mysteries of

God is love,"[17] he is expressing the mystic's way of entering into a union so complete with the harmony of the totality of the cosmos, that he apprehends it directly and fully. When I state here that the C-IR is the cornerstone of the mystic's Weltbild, I am writing of only one small part of what the mystic brings and offers to mankind. This cornerstone is what this monograph is concerned with, and I believe it is crucial to an understanding of the *paranormal,* but it must not be interpreted as *all* of mysticism. Books such as Huxley's *The Perennial Philosophy* can help illustrate more of the richness of the mystic's understanding than I can show in this work.

[17]A. Huxley, *op. cit.,* p. 206.

CHAPTER 32

STATES OF CONSCIOUSNESS
AND STATE-SPECIFIC SCIENCES*

CHARLES T. TART

B LACKBURN[1] RECENTLY NOTED that many of our most talented young people are "turned off" to science: As a solution, he proposed that we recognize the validity of a more sensuous-intuitive approach to nature, treating it as complementary to the classical intellectual approach.

I have seen the same rejection of science by many of the brightest students in California, and the problem is indeed serious. Blackburn's analysis is valid, but not deep enough. A more fundamental source of alienation is the widespread experience of altered states of consciousness (ASC's) by the young, coupled with the almost total rejection of the knowledge gained during the experiencing of ASC's by the scientific establishment. Blackburn himself exemplifies this rejection when he says: "Perhaps science has much to learn along this line from the disciplines, *as distinct from the content,* of Oriental religions" (my italics).

To illustrate, a recent Gallup poll[2] indicated that approximately half of American college students have tried marijuana, and a large number of them use it fairly regularly. They do this at the risk of having their careers ruined and going to jail for several years. Why? Conventional research on the nature of marijuana intoxication tells us that the primary effects are a slight increase in heart

*Reprinted from *Science,* Vol. 176 (June 12, 1972), pp. 1203-1210, by permission of the author and the American Association for the Advancement of Science. Copyright 1972 by the American Association for the Advancement of Science.
[1]T. Blackburn, *Science,* Vol. 172 (1971), p. 1003.
[2]*Newsweek* (25 January 1971), p. 52.

rate, reddening of the eyes, some difficulty with memory, and small decrements in performance on complex psychomotor tests.

Would you risk going to jail to experience these?

A young marijuana smoker who hears a scientist or physician talk about these findings as the basic nature of marijuana intoxication will simply sneer and have his antiscientific attitude further reinforced. It is clear to him that the scientist has no real understanding of what marijuana intoxication is all about.[3]

More formally, an increasingly significant number of people are experimenting with ASC's in themselves, and finding the experiences thus gained of extreme importance in their philosophy and style of life. The conflict between experiences in these ASC's and the attitudes and intellectual-emotional systems that have evolved in our ordinary state of consciousness (SoC) is a major factor behind the increased alienation of many people from conventional science. Experiences of ecstasy, mystical union, other "dimensions," rapture, beauty, space-and-time transcendence, and transpersonal knowledge, all common in ASC's, are simply not treated adequately in conventional scientific approaches. These experiences will not "go away" if we crack down more on psychedelic drugs, for immense numbers of people now practice various non-drug techniques for producing ASC's, such as meditation[4] and yoga.

The purpose of this article is to show that it is possible to investigate and work with the important phenomena of ASC's in a manner which is perfectly compatible with the essence of scientific method. The conflict discussed above is not necessary.

STATES OF CONSCIOUSNESS

An ASC may be defined for the purpose of this article as a qualitative alteration in the overall pattern of mental functioning, such that the experiencer feels his consciousness is radically different from the way it functions ordinarily. An SoC is thus defined not in terms of any particular content of consciousness, or specific be-

[3]An attempt to describe the phenomena of marijuana intoxication in terms that make sense to the user, as well as the investigator, has been presented elsewhere. See C. Tart, *On Being Stoned: A Psychological Study of Marijuana Intoxication* (Palo Alto, Science and Behavior Books, 1971).

[4]C. Naranjo and R. Ornstein, *On the Psychology of Meditation* (New York, Viking, 1971).

havior or physiological change, but in terms of the overall patterning of psychological functioning.

An analogy with computer functioning can clarify this definition. A computer has a complex program of many subroutines. If we reprogram it quite differently, the same sorts of input data may be handled in quite different ways; we will be able to predict very little from our knowledge of the old program about the effects of varying the input, even though old and new programs have some subroutines in common. The new program with its input-output interactions must be studied in and of itself. An ASC is analogous to changing temporarily the program of a computer.

The ASC's experienced by almost all ordinary people are dreaming states and the hypnogogic and hypnopompic states, the transitional states between sleeping and waking. Many other people experience another ASC, alcohol intoxication.

The relatively new (to our culture) ASC's that are now having such an impact are those produced by marijuana, more powerful psychedelic drugs such as LSD, meditative states, so-called possession states, and auto-hypnotic states.*

STATES OF CONSCIOUSNESS AND PARADIGMS

It is useful to compare this concept of an SoC, a qualitatively distinct organization of the patterning of mental functioning, with Kuhn's[5] concept of paradigms in science. A paradigm is an intellectual achievement that underlies normal science and attracts and guides the work of an enduring number of adherents in their scientific activity. It is a kind of "super theory," a formulation of scope wide enough to affect the organization of most or all of the major known phenomena of its field. Yet it is sufficiently open-ended that there still remain important problems to be solved within that framework. Examples of important paradigms in the history of science have been Copernican astronomy and Newtonian dynamics.

---

*Note that an SoC is defined by the stable parameters of the pattern that constitute it, not by the particular technique of inducing that pattern, for some ASC's can be induced by a variety of induction methods. By analogy, to understand the altered computer program you must study what it does, not study the programmer who originally set it up.

[5]T. Kuhn, *The Structure of Scientific Revolutions* (Chicago, University of Chicago Press, 1962).

Because of their tremendous success, paradigms undergo a change which, in principle, ordinary scientific theories do not undergo. An ordinary scientific theory is always subject to further questioning and testing as it is extended. A paradigm becomes an implicit framework for most scientists working within it; it is the natural way of looking at things and doing things. It does not seriously occur to the adherents of a paradigm to question it any more (we may ignore, for the moment, the occurrence of scientific revolutions). Theories become referred to as laws: people talk of the law of gravity, not the theory of gravity, for example.

A paradigm serves to concentrate the attention of a researcher on sensible problem areas and to prevent him from wasting his time on what might be trivia. On the other hand, by implicitly defining some lines of research as trivial or nonsensical, a paradigm acts like a blinder. Kuhn has discussed this blinding function as a key factor in the lack of effective communications during paradigm clashes.

The concept of a paradigm and of an SoC are quite similar. Both constitute complex, interlocking sets of rules and theories that enable a person to interact with and interpret experiences within an environment. In both cases, the rules are largely implicit. They are not recognized as tentative working hypotheses; they operate automatically and the person feels he is doing the obvious or natural thing.

PARADIGM CLASH BETWEEN "STRAIGHT" AND "HIP"

Human beings become emotionally attached to the things which give them pleasure, and a scientist making important progress within a particular paradigm becomes emotionally attached to it. When data which make no sense in terms of the (implicit) paradigm are brought to our attention, the usual result is not a re-evaluation of the paradigm, but a rejection or misperception of the data. This rejection seems rational to others sharing that paradigm and irrational or rationalizing to others committed to a different paradigm.

The conflict now existing between those who have experienced certain ASC's (whose ranks include many young scientists) and those who have not is very much a paradigmatic conflict. For example, a subject takes LSD, and tells his investigator that "You and I, we are all one, there are no separate selves." The investigator reports that his subject showed a "confused sense of identity and distorted thinking process." The subject is reporting what is obvious to him, the investigator is reporting what is obvious to him. The investigator's implicit paradigm, based on his scientific training, his cultural background, and his normal SoC, indicates that a literal interpretation of the subject's statement cannot be true, and therefore must be interpreted as mental dysfunction on the part of the subject. The subject, his paradigms radically changed for the moment by being in an ASC, not only reports what is obviously true to him, but perceives the investigator as showing mental dysfunction, by virtue of being incapable of perceiving the obvious!

Historically, paradigm clashes have been characterized by bitter emotional antagonisms, and total rejection of the opponent. Currently we are seeing the same sort of process: the respectable psychiatrist, who would not take any of those "psychotomimetic" drugs himself or sit down and experience that crazy meditation process, carries out research to show that drug takers and those who practice meditation are escapists. The drug taker or meditator views the same investigator as narrow-minded, prejudiced, and repressive, and as a result drops out of the university. Communication between the two factions is almost nil.

Must the experiencers of ASC's continue to see the scientists as concentrating on the irrelevant, and the scientists see the experiencers as confused* or mentally ill? Or can science deal adequately with the experiences of these people? The thesis I shall now present in detail is that we can deal with the important aspects of ASC's using the essence of scientific method, even though a variety of nonessentials, unfortunately identified with current science, hinder such an effort.

THE NATURE OF KNOWLEDGE

Basically, science (from the Latin *scire,* to know) deals with knowledge. Knowledge may be defined as an immediately given experiential feeling of congruence between two different kinds of

---

*Note that states of confusion and impaired functioning are certainly aspects of some drug-induced SoC's, but are not of primary interest here.

experience, a matching. One set of experiences may be regarded as perceptions of the external world, of others, of oneself; the second set may be regarded as a theory, a scheme, a system of understanding. The feeling of congruence is something immediately given in experience, although many refinements have been worked out for judging degrees of congruence.

All knowledge, then, is basically experiential knowledge. Even my knowledge of the physical world can be reduced to this: given certain sets of experiences, which I (by assumption) attribute to the external world activating my sensory apparatus, it may be possible for me to compare them with purely internal experiences (memories, previous knowledge) and predict with a high degree of reliability other kinds of experiences, which I again attribute to the external world.

Because science has been incredibly successful in dealing with the physical world, it has been historically associated with a philosophy of physicalism, the belief that reality is all reducible to certain kinds of physical entities. The vast majority of phenomena of ASC's have no known physical manifestations: thus to physicalistic philosophy they are epiphenomena, not worthy of study. But insofar as science deals with knowledge, it need not restrict itself only to physical kinds of knowledge.

THE ESSENCE OF SCIENTIFIC METHOD

I shall discuss the essence of scientific method, and show that this essence is perfectly compatible with an enlarged study of the important phenomena of ASC's. In particular, I propose that state-specific sciences (SSS) be developed.

As satisfying as the feeling of knowing can be, we are often wrong: what seems like congruence at first later does not match, or has no generality. Man has learned that his reasoning is often faulty, his observations are often incomplete or mistaken, and that emotional and other nonconscious factors can seriously distort both reasoning and observational processes. His reliance on authorities, "rationality" or "elegance," are no sure criteria for achieving truth. The development of scientific method may be seen as a determined effort to systematize the process of acquiring knowledge in such a way as to minimize the various pitfalls of observation and reasoning.

I shall discuss four basic rules of scientific method to which an investigator is committed: (i) good observation; (ii) the public nature of observation; (iii) the necessity to theorize logically; and (iv) the testing of theory by observable consequences; all these constitute the scientific enterprise. I shall consider the wider application of each rule to ASC's and indicate how unnecessary physicalistic restrictions may be dropped. I will show that all these commitments or rules can be accommodated in the development of SSS's that I propose.

OBSERVATION

The scientist is committed to observe as well as possible the phenomena of interest and to search constantly for better ways of making these observations. But our paradigmatic commitments, our SoC's, make us likely to observe certain parts of reality and to ignore or observe with error certain other parts of it.

Many of the most important phenomena of ASC's have been observed poorly or not at all because of the physicalistic labeling of them as epiphenomena, so that they have been called "subjective," "ephemeral," "unreliable," or "unscientific." Observations of internal processes are probably much more difficult to make than those of external physical processes, because of their inherently greater complexity. The essence of science, however, is that we observe what there is to be observed whether it is difficult or not.

Furthermore, most of what we know about the phenomena of ASC's has been obtained from untrained people, almost none of whom have shared the scientists' commitment to constantly reexamine their observations in greater and greater detail. This should not imply that internal phenomena are inherently unobservable or unstable; we are comparing the first observations of internal phenomena with observations of physical sciences that have undergone centuries of refinement.

We must consider one other problem of observation. One of the traditional idols of science, the "detached observer," has no place in dealing with many internal phenomena of SoCs. Not only are the observer's perceptions selective, he may also affect the things he observes. We must try to understand the characteristics of each individual observer in order to compensate for them.

A recognition of the unreality of the detached observer in the psychological sciences is becoming widespread, under the topics of experimenter bias[6] and demand characteristics.[7] A similar recognition long ago occurred in physics when it was realized that the observed was altered by the process of observation at subatomic levels. When we deal with ASC's where the observer is the experiencer of the ASC, this factor is of paramount importance. Knowing the characteristics of the observer can also confound the process of consensual validation, which I shall now consider.

PUBLIC NATURE OF OBSERVATION

Observations must be public in that they must be replicable by any properly trained observer. The experienced conditions that led to the report of certain experiences must be described in sufficient detail that others may duplicate them and consequently have experiences which meet criteria of identicality. That someone else may set up similar conditions but not have the same experiences proves that the original investigator gave an incorrect description of the conditions and observations, or that he was not aware of certain essential aspects of the conditions.

The physicalistic accretion to this rule of consensual validation is that, physical data being the only "real" data, internal phenomena must be reduced to physiological or behavioral data to become reliable or they will be ignored entirely. I believe most physical observations to be much more readily replicable by any trained observer because they are inherently simpler phenomena than internal ones. In principle, however, consensual validation of internal phenomena by a trained observer is quite possible.

The emphasis on public observations in science has had a misleading quality insofar as it implies that any intelligent man can replicate a scientist's observations. This might have been true early in the history of science, but nowadays only the trained observer can replicate many observations. I cannot go into a modern physicist's laboratory and confirm his observations. Indeed, his talk of what he has found in his experiments (physicists seem to talk about innumerable invisible entities these days) would probably seem

---

[6]R. Rosenthal, *Experimenter Effects in Behavioral Research* (New York, Appleton-Century-Crofts, 1966).

[7]M. Orne, *Amer. Psychologist*, Vol. 17 (1962), p. 776.

mystical to me, just as many descriptions of internal states sound mystical to those with a background in the physical sciences.

Given the high complexity of the phenomena associated with ASC's, the need for replication by trained observers is exceptionally important. Since it generally takes four to ten years of intensive training to produce a scientist in any of our conventional sciences, we should not be surprised that there has been very little reliability of observations by untrained observers of ASC phenomena.

Further, for the state-specific sciences that I propose should be established, we cannot specify the requirements that would constitute adequate training. These would only be determined after considerable trial and error. We should also recognize that very few people might complete the training successfully. Some people do not have the necessary innate characteristics to become physicists, and some probably do not have the innate characteristics to become, say, scientific investigators of meditative states.

Public observation, then, always refers to a limited, specially trained public. It is only by basic agreement among those specially trained people that data become accepted as a foundation for the development of a science. That laymen cannot replicate the observations is of little relevance.

A second problem in consensual validation arises from a phenomenon predicted by my concept of ASC's, but not yet empirically investigated, namely, state-specific communication. Given that an ASC is an overall qualitative and quantitative shift in the complex functioning of consciousness, such that there are new "logics" and perceptions (which would constitute a paradigm shift), it is quite reasonable to hypothesize that communication may take a different pattern. For two observers, both of whom, we assume, are fluent in communicating with each other in a given SoC, communication about some new observations may seem adequate to them, or may be improved or deteriorated in specific ways. To an outside observer, an observer in a different SoC, the communication between these two observers may seem "deteriorated."

Practically all investigations of communication by persons in ASC's have resulted in reports of deterioration of communication abilities. In designing their studies, however, these investigators have not taken into account the fact that the pattern of communication may have changed. If I am listening to two people speaking in English, and they suddenly begin to intersperse words and phrases in Polish, I, as an outside (that is, a non-Polish speaking) observer, will note a gross deterioration in communication. Adequacy of communication between people in the same SoC and across SoC's must be empirically determined.

Thus consensual validation may be restricted by the fact that only observers in the same ASC are able to communicate adequately with each other, and they may not be able to communicate adequately to someone in a different SoC, say normal consciousness.*

THEORIZING

A scientist may theorize about his observations as much as he wishes to, but the theory he develops must consistently account for all that he has observed, and should have a logical structure that other scientists can comprehend (but not necessarily accept).

The requirement to theorize logically and consistently with the data is not as simple as it looks, however. Any logic consists of a basic set of assumptions and a set of rules for manipulating information, based on these assumptions. Change the assumptions, or change the rules, and there may be entirely different outcomes from the same data. A paradigm, too, is a logic with certain assumptions and rules for working within these assumptions. By changing the paradigm, altering the SoC, the nature of theory building may change radically. Thus a person in SoC 2 might come to very different conclusions about the nature of the same events that he observed in SoC 1. An investigator in SoC 1 may comment on the comprehensibility of the second person's ideas from the point of view (paradigm) of SoC 1, but can say nothing about their inherent validity. A scientist who could enter either SoC 1 or SoC 2, however, could pronounce on the comprehensibility of the other's theory, and the adherence of that theory to the rules and logic of SoC 2. Thus, scientists trained in the same SoC

---

*A state-specific scientist might find his own work somewhat incomprehensible when he was not in that SoC because of the phenomenon of state-specific memory—that is, not enough of his work would transfer to his ordinary SoC to make it comprehensible, even though it would make perfect sense when he was again in the ASC in which he did his scientific work.

may check on the logical validity of each other's theorizing. We have then the possibility of a state-specific logic underlying theorizing in various SoC's.

OBSERVABLE CONSEQUENCES

Any theory a scientist develops must have observable consequences, and from that theory it must be possible to make predictions that can be verified by observation. If such verification is not possible, the theory must be considered invalid, regardless of its elegance, logic, or other appeal.

Ordinarily we think of empirical validation, of validation in terms of testable consequences that produce physical effects, but this is misleading. Any effect, whether interpreted as physical or nonphysical, is ultimately an experience in the observer's mind. All that is essentially required to validate a theory is that it predict that "When a certain experience (observed condition) has occurred, another (predicted) kind of experience will follow, under specified experiential conditions." Thus a perfectly scientific theory may be based on data that have no physical existence.

STATE-SPECIFIC SCIENCES

We tend to envision the practice of science as centered around interest in some particular range of subject matter, a small number of highly selected, talented, and rigorously trained people spend considerable time making detailed observations on the subject matter of interest. They may or may not have special places (laboratories) or instruments or methods to assist them in making finer observations. They speak to one another in a special language which they feel conveys precisely the important facts of their field. Using this language, they confirm and extend each other's knowledge of certain data basic to the field. They theorize about their basic data and construct elaborate systems. They validate these by recourse to further observation. These trained people all have a long-term commitment to the constant refinement of observation and extension of theory. Their activity is frequently incomprehensible to laymen.

This general description is equally applicable to a variety of sciences, or areas that could become sciences, whether we called such areas biology, physics, chemistry, psychology, understanding of mystical states, or drug-induced enhancement of cognitive processes. The particulars of research would look very different, but the basic scientific method running through all is the same.

More formally, I now propose the creation of various state-specific sciences. If such sciences could be created, we would have a group of highly skilled, dedicated, and trained practitioners able to achieve certain SoC's, and able to agree with one another that they have attained a common state. While in that SoC, they might then investigate other areas of interest, whether these be totally internal phenomena of that given state, the interaction of that state with external, physical reality, or people in other SoC's.

The fact that the experimenter should be able to function skillfully in the SoC itself for a state-specific science does not necessarily mean that he would always be the subject. While he might often be the subject, observer, and experimenter simultaneously, it would be quite possible for him to collect data from experimental manipulations of other subjects in the SoC, and either be in that SoC himself at the time of data collection or be in that SoC himself for data reduction and theorizing.

Examples of some observations made and theorizing done by a scientist in a specific ASC would illustrate the nature of a proposed state-specific science. But this is not possible because no state-specific sciences have yet been established.† Also, any example that would make good sense to the readers of this article (who are, presumably, all in a normal SoC) would not really illustrate the uniqueness of a state-specific science. If it did make sense, it would be an example of a problem that could be approached adequately from both the ASC and normal SoC's, and thus it would be too easy to see the entire problem in terms of accepted scientific procedures for normal SoC's and miss the point about the necessity for developing state-specific sciences.

STATE-SPECIFIC SCIENCES AND RELIGION

Some aspects of organized religion appear to resemble state-

---

†"Ordinary consciousness science" is not a good example of a "pure" state-specific science because many important discoveries have occurred during ASC's, such as reverie, dreaming, and meditative-like states.

specific sciences. There are techniques that allow the believer to enter an ASC and then have religious experiences in that ASC which are proof of his religious belief. People who have had such experiences usually describe them as ineffable in important ways— that is, as not fully comprehensible in an ordinary SoC. Conversions at revivalistic meetings are the most common example of religious experiences occurring in various ASC's induced by an intensely emotional atmosphere.

In examining the esoteric training systems of some religions, there seems to be even more resemblance between such mystical ways and state-specific sciences, for here we often have the picture of devoted specialists, complex techniques, and repeated experiencing of the ASC's in order to further religious knowledge.

Nevertheless the proposed state-specific sciences are not simply religion in a new guise. The use of ASC's in religion may involve the kind of commitment to searching for truth that is needed for developing a state-specific science, but practically all the religions we know might be defined as state-specific technologies, operated in the service of a priori belief systems. The experiencers of ASC's in most religious contexts have already been thoroughly indoctrinated in a particular belief system. This belief system may then mold the content of the ASC's to create specific experiences which reinforce or validate the belief system.

The crucial distinction between a religion utilizing ASC's and a state-specific science is the commitment of the scientist to re-examine constantly his own belief system and to question the obvious in spite of its intellectual or emotional appeal to him. Investigators of ASC's would certainly encounter an immense variety of phenomena labeled religious experience or mystical revelation during the development of state-specific sciences, but they would have to remain committed to examining these phenomena more carefully, sharing their observations and techniques with colleagues, and subjecting the beliefs (hypotheses, theories) that result from such experiences to the requirement of leading to testable predictions. In practice, because we are aware of the immense emotional power of mystical experiences, this would be a difficult task, but it is one that will have to be undertaken by disciplined investigators if we are to understand various ASC's.

RELATIONSHIP BETWEEN STATE-SPECIFIC SCIENCES

Any state-specific science may be considered as consisting of two parts, observations and theorizations. The observations are what can be experienced relatively directly; the theories are the *inferences* about what sort of nonobservable factors account for the observations. For example, the phenomena of synesthesia (seeing colors as a result of hearing sounds) is a theoretical proposition for me in my ordinary SoC: I do not experience it, and can only generate theories about what other people report about it. If I were under the influence of a psychedelic drug such as LSD or marijuana,[8] I could probably experience synesthesia directly, and my descriptions of the experience would become data.

Figure 3 demonstrates some possible relationships between three state-specific sciences. State-specific sciences 1 and 2 show considerable overlap.

The area labeled O_1O_2 permits direct observation in both sciences. Area T_1T_2 permits theoretical inferences about common subject matter from the two perspectives. In area O_1T_2, by contrast, the theoretical propositions of state-specific science number 2 are matters of direct observation for the scientist in SoC number 1, and vice versa for the area T_1O_2. State-specific science number 3 consists of a body of observation and theory exclusive to that science and has no overlap with the other two sciences: it neither confirms, denies, nor complements them.

It would be naively reductionistic to say that the work in one state-specific science *validates* or *invalidates* the work in a second state-specific science; I prefer to say that two different state-specific sciences, where they overlap, provide quite different points of view with respect to certain kinds of theories and data, and thus complement[9] each other. The proposed creation of state-specific sciences neither validates nor invalidates the activities of normal consciousness sciences (NCS). The possibility of developing certain state-specific sciences means only that certain kinds of phenomena may be handled more adequately within these potential new sciences.

---

[8]C. Tart, *op. cit.*

[9]N. Bohr, in *Essays, 1958-1962, on Atomic Physics and Human Knowledge* (New York, Wiley, 1963).

Interrelationships more complex than those that are illustrated in Figure 3 are possible.

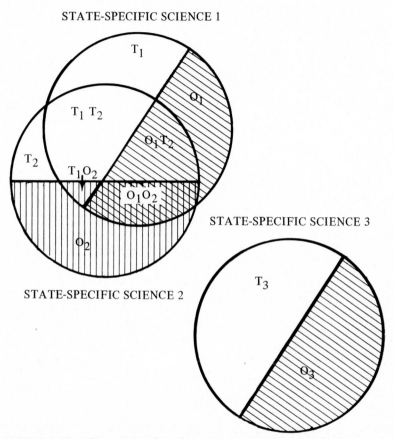

FIGURE 3. Possible relationships between three state-specific sciences. The area labeled O_1O_2 is subject matter capable of direct observation in both sciences. Area T_1T_2 consists of theoretical (T) inferences about subject matter overlapping the two sciences. By contrast, in area O_1T_2, the theoretical propositions of state-specific science number 2 are matters of direct observation for the scientist in state of consciousness number 1, and vice versa for area T_1O_2. State-specific science number 3 consists of a body of observation and theory exclusive of that science.

The possibility of stimulating interactions between different state-specific sciences is very real. Creative breakthroughs in NCS have frequently been made by scientists temporarily going into an

ASC.[10] In such instances, the scientists concerned saw quite different views of their problems and performed different kinds of reasoning, conscious or nonconscious, which led to results that could be tested within their NCS.

A current example of such interaction is the finding that in Zen meditation (a highly developed discipline in Japan) there are physiological correlates of meditative experiences, such as decreased frequency of alpha-rhythm, which can also be produced by means of instrumentally aided feedback-learning techniques.[11] This finding might elucidate some of the processes peculiar to each discipline.

INDIVIDUAL DIFFERENCES

A widespread and misleading assumption that hinders the development of state-specific sciences and confuses their interrelationships is the assumption that because two people are normal (not certified insane), their ordinary SoC's are essentially the same. In reality I suspect that there are enormous differences between the SoC's of some normal people. Because societies train people to behave and communicate along socially approved lines, these differences are covered up.

For example, some people think in images, others in words. Some can voluntarily anesthetize parts of their body, most cannot. Some recall past events by imaging the scene and looking at the relevant details; others use complex verbal processes with no images.

This means that person A may be able to observe certain kinds of experiential data that person B cannot experience in his ordinary SoC, no matter how hard B tries. There may be several consequences. Person B may think that A is insane, too imaginative, or a liar, or he may feel inferior to A. Person A may also feel himself odd, if he takes B as a standard of normality.

In some cases, B may be able to enter an ASC and there experience the sorts of things that A has reported to him. A realm of knowledge that is ordinary for A is then specific for an ASC for B. Similarly, some of the experiences of B in his ASC may not be available for direct observation by A in his ordinary SoC.

---

[10]B. Ghiselin, *The Creative Process* (New York, New American Library, 1952).

[11]E. Green, A. Green, and E. Walters, *Journal of Transpersonal Psychology*, Vol. 2 (1970), p. 1.

The phenomenon of synesthesia can again serve as an example. Some individuals possess this ability in their ordinary SoC, most do not. Yet 56 percent of a sample of experienced marijuana users experienced synesthesia at least occasionally[12] while in the drug-induced ASC.

Thus we may conceive of bits of knowledge that are specific for an ASC for one individual, part of ordinary consciousness for another. Arguments over the usefulness of the concept of states of consciousness may reflect differences in the structure of the ordinary SoC of various investigators.

Another important source of individual differences, little understood at present, is the degree to which an individual may first make a particular observation or form a concept in one SoC and then be able to reexperience or comprehend it in another SoC. That is, many items of information which were state-specific when observed initially may be learned and somehow transferred (fully or partially) to another SoC. Differences across individuals, various combinations of SoC's, and types of experiences will probably be enormous.

I have only outlined the complexities created by individual differences in normal SoC's and have used the normal SoC as a baseline for comparison with ASC's; but it is evident that every SoC must eventually be compared against every other SoC.

PROBLEMS, PITFALLS, AND PERSONAL PERILS

If we use the practical experience of Western man with ASC's as a guide, the development of state-specific sciences will be beset by a number of difficulties. These difficulties will be of two kinds: general methodological problems stemming from the inherent nature of some ASC's; and those concerned with personal perils to the investigator. I shall discuss state-related problems first.

The first important problem in the proposed development of state-specific sciences is the obvious perception of truth. In many ASC's, one's experience is that one is obviously and lucidly experiencing truth directly, without question. An immediate result of this may be an extinction of the desire for further questioning. Further, this experience of obvious truth, while not necessarily preventing

---

[12]C. Tart, *op. cit.*

the individual investigator from further examining his data, may not arouse his desire for consensual validation. Since one of the greatest strengths of science is its insistence on consensual validation of basic data, this can be a serious drawback. Investigators attempting to develop state-specific sciences will have to learn to distrust the obvious.

A second major problem in developing state-specific sciences is that in some ASC's one's abilities to visualize and imagine are immensely enhanced, so that whatever one imagines seems perfectly real. Thus one can imagine that something is being observed and experience it as datum. If one can essentially conjure up anything one wishes, how can we ever get at truth?

One way of looking at this problem is to consider any such vivid imaginings as potential effects: They are data, in the sense that what can be vividly imagined in a given SoC is important to know. It may not be the case that anything can be imagined with equal facility, and the relationships between what can be imagined may show a lawful pattern.

More generally, the way to approach this problem is to realize that it is not unique to ASC's. One can have all sorts of illusions, and misperceptions in our ordinary SoC. Before the rise of modern physical science, all sorts of things were imagined about the nature of the physical world that could not be directly refuted. The same techniques that eliminated these illusions in the physical sciences will also eliminate them in state-specific sciences dealing with non-physical data—that is, all observations will have to be subjected to consensual validation and all their theoretical consequences will have to be examined. Insofar as experiences are purely arbitrary imaginings, those that do not show consistent patterns and cannot be replicated will be distinguished from those phenomena which do show general lawfulness.

The effects of this enhanced vividness of imagination in some ASC's will be complicated further by two other important problems, namely, experimenter bias,[13] and the fact that one person's illusion in a given ASC can sometimes be communicated to another person in the same ASC so that a kind of false consensual validation

---

[13]R. Rosenthal and M. Orne, *op. cit.*

results. Again, the only long-term solution to this would be the requirement that predictions based on concepts arising from various experiences be verified experientially.

A third major problem is that state-specific sciences probably cannot be developed for all ASC's: Some ASC's may depend on or result from genuine deterioration of observational and reasoning abilities, or a deterioration of volition. Those SoC's for which state-specific sciences might well be developed will be discussed later, but it should be made clear that the development of each science should result from trial and error, and not from a priori decisions based on reasoning in our ordinary SoC's.

A fourth major problem is that of ineffability. Some experiences are ineffable in the sense that: (i) a person may experience them, but be unable to express or conceptualize them adequately to himself; (ii) while a person may be able to conceptualize an experience to himself he may not be able to communicate it adequately to anyone else. Certain phenomena of the first type may simply be inaccessible to scientific investigation. Phenomena of the second type may be accessible to scientific investigation only insofar as we are willing to recognize that a science, in the sense of following most of the basic rules, may exist only for a single person. Insofar as such a solitary science would lack all the advantages gained by consensual validation, we could not expect it to have as much power and rigor as conventional scientific endeavor.

Many phenomena which are now considered ineffable may not be so in reality. This may be a matter of our general lack of experience with ASC's and the lack of an adequate language for communicating about ASC phenomena. In most well-developed languages the major part of the vocabulary was developed primarily in adaptation to survival in the physical world.

Finally, we should recognize the possibility that various phenomena of ASC's may be too complex for human beings to understand. The phenomena may depend on or be affected by so many variables that we shall never understand them. In the history of science, however, many phenomena which appeared too complex at first were eventually comprehensible.

PERSONAL PERILS

The personal perils that an investigator will face in attempting to develop a state-specific science are of two kinds, those associated with reactions colloquially called a bad trip and a good trip, respectively.

Bad trips, in which an extremely unpleasant, emotional reaction is experienced in an ASC, and in which there are possible long-term adverse consequences on a person's personal adjustment, often stem from the fact that our upbringing has not prepared us to undergo radical alterations in our ordinary SoC's. We are dependent on stability, we fear the unknown, and we develop personal rigidities and various kinds of personal and social taboos. It is traditional in our society to consider ASC's as signs of insanity; ASC's therefore cause great fears in those who experience them.

In many ASC's, defenses against unacceptable personal impulses may become partially or wholly ineffective, so the person feels flooded with traumatic material that he cannot handle. All these things result in fear and avoidance of ASC's, and make it difficult or impossible for some individuals to function in an ASC in a way that is consistent with the development of a state-specific science. Maslow[14] has discussed these as pathologies of cognition that seriously interfere with the scientific enterprise in general, as well as ordinary life. In principle, adequate selection and training could minimize these hazards for at least some people.

Good trips may also endanger an investigator. A trip may produce experiences that are so rewarding that they interfere with the scientific activity of the investigator. The perception of obvious truth, and its effect of eliminating the need for further investigation or consensual validation have already been mentioned. Another peril comes from the ability to imagine or create vivid experiences. They may be so highly rewarding that the investigator does not follow the rule of investigating the obvious regardless of his personal satisfaction with results. Similarly, his attachment to good feelings, ecstasy, and the like, and his refusal to consider alternative conceptualizations of these, can seriously stifle the progress of investigation.

These personal perils again emphasize the necessity of developing adequate training programs for scientists who wish to develop state-

---

[14]A. Maslow, *The Psychology of Science: A Reconnaissance* (New York, Harper and Row, 1966).

specific sciences. Although it is difficult to envision such a training program, it is evident that much conventional scientific training is contrary to what would be needed to develop a state-specific science, because it tends to produce rigidity and avoidance of personal involvement with subject matter, rather than open-mindedness and flexibility. Much of the training program would have to be devoted to the scientist's understanding of himself so that the (unconscious) effects of his personal biases will be minimized during his investigations of an ASC.

Many of us know that there have been cases where scientists, after becoming personally involved with ASC's, have subsequently become very poor scientists or have experienced personal psychological crises. It would be premature, however, to conclude that such unfortunate consequences cannot be avoided by proper training and discipline. In the early history of the physical sciences we had many fanatics who were nonobjective about their investigations. Not all experiencers of various ASC's develop pathology as a result: indeed, many seem to become considerably more mature. Only from actual attempts to develop state-specific sciences will we be able to determine the actual SoC's that are suitable for development, and the kinds of people that are best suited to such work.*

PROSPECTS

I believe that an examination of human history and our current situation provides the strongest argument for the necessity of developing state-specific sciences. Throughout history man has been influenced by the spiritual and mystical factors that are expressed (usually in watered-down form) in the religions that attract the masses of people. Spiritual and mystical experiences are primary phenomena of various ASC's and because of such experiences, untold numbers of both the noblest and most horrible acts of which people are capable have been committed. Yet in all the time that Western science has existed, no concerted attempt has been made to understand these ASC phenomena in scientific terms.

---

*The ASC's resulting from very dangerous drugs (heroin, for example) may be scientifically interesting, but the risk may be too high to warrant our developing state-specific sciences for them. The personal and social issues involved in evaluating this kind of risk are beyond the scope of this article.

It was the hope of many that religions were simply a form of superstition that would be left behind in our "rational" age. Not only has this hope failed, but our own understanding of the nature of reasoning now makes it clear that it can never be fulfilled. Reason is a tool, and a tool that is wielded in the service of assumptions, beliefs, and needs which are not themselves subject to reason. The irrational, or, better yet, the *a*rational, will not disappear from the human situation. Our immense success in the development of the physical sciences has not been particularly successful in formulating our real knowledge of ourselves. The sciences we have developed to date are not very human sciences. They tell us how to do things, but give us no scientific insights on questions of what to do, what not to do, or why to do things.

The youth of today and mature scientists in increasing numbers are turning to meditation, oriental religions, and personal use of psychedelic drugs. The phenomena encountered in these ASC's provide more satisfaction and are more relevant to the formulation of philosophies of life and deciding upon appropriate ways of living, than "pure reason".[15] My own impressions are that very large numbers of scientists are now personally exploring ASC's, but few have begun to connect this personal exploration with their scientific activities.

It is difficult to predict what the chances are of developing state-specific sciences. Our knowledge is still too diffuse and dependent on our normal SoC's. Yet I think it is probable that state-specific sciences can be developed for such SoC's as auto-hypnosis, meditative states, lucid dreaming, marijuana intoxication, LSD intoxication, self-remembering, reverie, and biofeedback-induced states.[16] In all of these SoC's, volition seems to be retained, so that the observer can indeed carry out experiments on himself or others or both. Some SoC's, in which the volition to experiment during the state may disappear, but in which some experimentation can be carried out if special conditions are prepared before the state is entered, might be alcohol intoxication, ordinary dreaming, hypno-

[15]J. Needleman, *The New Religions* (New York, Doubleday, 1970).

[16]C. Tart, *Altered States of Consciousness: A Book of Readings* (New York, Wiley, 1969).

gogic and hypnopompic states, and high dreams.[17] It is not clear whether other ASC's would be suitable for developing state-specific sciences or whether mental deterioration would be too great. Such questions will only be answered by experiment.

I have nothing against religious and mystical groups. Yet I suspect that the vast majority of them have developed compelling belief systems rather than state-specific sciences. Will scientific method be extended to the development of state-specific sciences so as to improve our human situation? Or will the immense power of ASC's be left in the hands of many cults and sects? I hope that the development of state-specific sciences will be our goal.

[17]*Ibid.*

BIBLIOGRAPHY

By no means exhaustive, this bibliography does contain most of the works in philosophy of parapsychology published in English since 1940, and a few of earlier date. Some of the works listed do not explicitly refer to parapsychology, but nonetheless deal with philosophical problems relevant to it. Also cited are several non-philosophical works whose theoretical or speculative approach to problems of parapsychology makes their inclusion desirable. And in addition, for readers wishing to begin or extend an acquaintance with parapsychological research itself, we offer at the front of the bibliography (Part A) a list of thirty informative books and articles that promise to help those in search of reliable introductions and surveys.

PART A

Ashby, R. H.: *The Guidebook for the Study of Psychical Research*. New York, Weiser, 1972.

Ducasse, C. J.: *Paranormal Phenomena, Science, and Life after Death*. New York, Parapsychology Foundation, 1969, pp. 17-36.

Edmunds, S.: *Miracles of the Mind: An Introduction to Parapsychology*. Springfield, Thomas, 1965.

Gudas, F. (Ed.): *Extrasensory Perception*. New York, Scribner, 1961.

Heywood, R.: *Beyond the Reach of Sense*. New York, Dutton, 1961. (Originally *The Sixth Sense*. London, Chatto, 1959.)

Knight, D. C. (Ed.): *The ESP Reader*. New York, Grosset, 1969.

Koestler, A.: *The Roots of Coincidence*. New York, Random, 1972, Ch. 1.

McConnell, R. A.: *ESP Curriculum Guide*. New York, S&S, 1971.

Murphy, G. (with L. A. Dale): *Challenge of Psychical Research*. New York, Harper and Brothers, 1961.

Pierce, H. W.: *Science Looks at ESP*. New York, NAL, 1970.

Pratt, J. G.: *ESP Research Today: A Study of Developments since 1960*. Metuchen, Scarecrow, 1973.

Rao, K. R.: *Experimental Parapsychology: A Review and Interpretation*. Springfield, Thomas, 1966.

Rhine, J. B.: *New World of the Mind.* New York, Sloane, 1953.

―――――: *The Reach of the Mind,* rev. ed. New York, Sloane, 1960.

Rhine, J. B., and associates: *Parapsychology from Duke to FRNM.* Durham, Parapsych Pr, 1965.

Rhine, J. B., and Pratt, J. G.: *Parapsychology: Frontier Science of the Mind,* rev. ed. Springfield, Thomas, 1962.

Rhine, L. E.: *ESP in Life and Lab: Tracing Hidden Channels.* New York, Macmillan, 1967.

―――――: *Hidden Channels of the Mind.* New York, Sloane, 1961.

―――――: *Mind over Matter.* New York, Macmillan, 1970.

Roll, W. G., et al. (Eds.): *Research in Parapsychology 1972.* Metuchen, Scarecrow, 1973.

Ryzl, M.: *Parapsychology: A Scientific Approach.* New York, Hawthorn, 1970.

Schmeidler, G. (Ed.): *Extrasensory Perception.* New York, Lieber-Atherton, 1969.

Schmeidler, G.: Parapsychology. In *International Encyclopedia of the Social Sciences.* New York, Macmillan and Free Pr, 1968, pp. 386-399.

Sinclair, U.: *Mental Radio,* rev. 2nd printing. Springfield, Thomas, 1962.

Thouless, R. H.: *Experimental Psychical Research.* Baltimore, Penguin, 1963.

―――――: *From Anecdote to Experiment in Psychical Research.* Boston, Routledge & Kegan, 1972.

Ullman, M., and Krippner, S. (with A. Vaughan): *Dream Telepathy.* New York, Macmillan, 1973.

Wallace, K.: Looking into psi. *The New Yorker,* March 14, 1959, pp. 122-145.

West, D. J.: *Psychical Research Today.* London, Duckworth, 1954.

White, R. A., and Dale, L. A. (Compilers): *Parapsychology: Sources of Information.* Metuchen, Scarecrow, 1973.

PART B

Anderson, M. L.: The relations of psi to creativity. *Journal of Parapsychology, 26:*277-292, 1962.

Angoff, A. (Ed.): *The Psychic Force: Essays in Modern Psychical Research.* New York, Putnam, 1970.

Ayer, A. J.: Carnap's treatment of the problem of other minds. In Schilpp, P. A. (Ed.): *The Philosophy of Rudolf Carnap.* La Salle, Open Court, 1963, pp. 269-281.

―――――: Chance. *Sci Am, 213:* no. 4, 44-54, 1965.

―――――: The concept of a person. In *The Concept of a Person and Other Essays.* New York, St. Martin's Pr, 1963, pp. 82-128.

―――――: ESP. *The Listener, 90:*375, 1973.

Beloff, J.: *The Existence of Mind*. London, MacGibbon and Kee, 1962, Ch. 7.

————: Explaining the paranormal. *Journal of the Society for Psychical Research, 42*:101-114, 1963.

————: The mind-body problem as it now stands. *Virginia Quarterly Review, 49*:251-264, 1973.

————: Parapsychology and its neighbors. *Journal of Parapsychology, 34*:129-142, 1970.

————: Parapsychology as science. *International Journal of Parapsychology, 9:* no. 2, 91-97, 1967.

————: *Psychological Sciences*. New York, B&N, 1973, Ch. 8.

————: What are we up to?. *Journal of Parapsychology, 28*:302-309, 1964.

Bergson, H.: *Matter and Memory* (translated by N. M. Paul and W. S. Palmer). London, Allen & Unwin, 1910.

————: Presidential address. *Proceedings of the Society for Psychical Research, 27*:157-175, 1914-15.

Besterman, T.: On the impossibility of proving survival. In Ayer, A. J. (Ed.): *The Humanist Outlook*. London, Pemberton, 1968, pp. 241-247.

Binkley, R.: Philosophy and the survival hypothesis. *Journal of the American Society for Psychical Research, 60*:27-31, 1966.

Bridgman, P. W.: Probability, logic, and ESP. *Science, 123*:15-17, 1956.

Brier, B.: Magicians, alarm clocks, and backward causation. *Southern Journal of Philosophy, 11*:359-364, 1973.

Broad, C. D.: The antecedent probability of survival. *Hibbert Journal, 17*:561-578, 1919.

————: Autobiography [and replies to Ducasse and Flew]. In Schilpp, P. A. (Ed.): *The Philosophy of C. D. Broad*. New York, Tudor, 1959, pp. 3-68, 774-786, 794-796.

————: Dreaming, and some of its implications. *Proceedings of the Society for Psychical Research, 52*:53-78, 1959.

————: *Ethics and the History of Philosophy*. New York, Humanities, 1952, *passim*.

————: The experimental establishment of telepathic precognition. *Philosophy, 19*:261-275, 1944.

————: Foreword. *Enquiry, 1:* no. 1, 4, 1948.

————: A half-century of psychical research. *Journal of Parapsychology, 20*:209-228, 1956.

————: *Human Personality and the Possibility of Its Survival* (Foerster Lecture). Berkeley, U of Cal Pr, 1955.

————: In what sense is survival desirable?. *Hibbert Journal, 17*:7-20, 1918.

————: *Lectures on Psychical Research*. New York, Humanities, 1962.

————: *The Mind and Its Place in Nature.* London, Kegan Paul, 1925, Section D.

————: The notion of "precognition." In Smythies, J. R. (Ed.): *Science and ESP.* New York, Humanities, 1967, pp. 165-196.

————: *Personal Identity and Survival* (Myers Lecture). London, Society for Psychical Research, 1958.

————: Phantasms of the living and of the dead. *Proceedings of the Society for Psychical Research, 50*:51-66, 1953.

————: The phenomenology of Mrs. Leonard's mediumship. *Journal of the American Society for Psychical Research, 49*:47-63, 1955.

————: The philosophical implications of foreknowledge. *Proceedings of the Aristotelian Society, Supplementary Volume 16*:177-209, 1937.

————: Philosophical implications of precognition. *The Listener, 37*:709-710, 1947.

————: *Religion, Philosophy and Psychical Research.* New York, Harcourt, 1953, Section I.

————: Science and psychical phenomena. *Philosophy, 13*:466-475, 1938.

Broad, C. D., Price, H. H., et al.: A tribute to Curt John Ducasse 1881-1969. *Journal of the American Society for Psychical Research, 64*:131-160, 327-342, 1970.

Bucke, R. M.: *Cosmic Consciousness: A Study in the Evolution of the Human Mind,* 24th printing. New York, Dutton, 1967, *passim.*

Burt, C.: The implications of parapsychology for general psychology. *Journal of Parapsychology, 31*:1-18, 1967.

————: *Psychology and Psychical Research* (Myers Lecture). London, Society for Psychical Research, 1968.

Campbell, K.: Materialism. In *The Encyclopedia of Philosophy.* New York, Macmillan and Free Pr, 1967, vol. 5, pp. 179-188. (See "Parapsychology" section of article, pp. 185-186.)

Carington, W.: *Matter, Mind and Meaning.* London, Methuen, 1949.

————: *The Meaning of "Survival"* (Myers Lecture). London, Society for Psychical Research, 1935.

————: *Telepathy: An Outline of Its Facts, Theory and Implications.* London, Methuen, 1945.

Carnap, R.: Replies and systematic expositions. In Schilpp, P. A. (Ed.): *The Philosophy of Rudolf Carnap.* La Salle, Open Court, 1963, pp. 859-1013. (See p. 876.)

Chari, C. T. K.: ESP and "semantic information." *Journal of the American Society for Psychical Research, 61*:47-63, 1967.

————: ESP and the "theory of resonance." *British Journal for the Philosophy of Science, 15*:137-140, 1964.

Chauvin, R.: To reconcile psi and physics. *Journal of Parapsychology, 34*:215-218, 1970.

Corrective Psychiatry and Journal of Social Therapy. Vol. 12, no. 2, 1966. (Special issue on ESP.)

Crookall, R.: *Intimations of Immortality.* London, J. Clarke, 1965.

Dean, E. D.: Parapsychology and Dr. Einstein. *Proceedings of the Parapsychological Association,* 4:33-56, 1967.

————: Techniques and status of modern parapsychology. *Science,* 170:1237-1238, 1970.

Dodds, E. R.: Why I do not believe in survival. *Proceedings of the Society for Psychical Research,* 42:147-172, 1934.

Ducasse, C. J.: Broad on the relevance of psychical research to philosophy. In Schilpp, P. A. (Ed.): *The Philosophy of C. D. Broad.* New York, Tudor, 1959, pp. 375-410.

————: Broad's lectures on psychical research. *Philosophy and Phenomenological Research,* 24:561-566, 1964.

————: Causality and parapsychology. *Journal of Parapsychology,* 23:90-96, 1959.

————: *A Critical Examination of the Belief in a Life after Death.* Springfield, Thomas, 1961.

————:*Is a Life after Death Possible?* (Foerster Lecture). Berkeley, U of Cal Pr, 1948.

————: Knowing the future. *Tomorrow, 3:* no. 2, 13-16, 1955.

————: Life after death conceived as reincarnation. In *In Search of God and Immortality: The Garvin Lectures,* Boston, Beacon Pr, 1961.

————: *Nature, Mind, and Death.* La Salle, Open Court, 1951, esp. Part IV.

————: Paranormal phenomena, nature, and man. *Journal of the American Society for Psychical Research,* 45:129-148, 1951.

————: *Paranormal Phenomena, Science, and Life after Death.* New York, Parapsychology Foundation, 1969.

————: Patterns of survival. *Tomorrow, 1:* no. 4, 2-14, 1953.

————: The philosophical importance of "psychic phenomena." *Journal of Philosophy,* 51:810-823, 1954.

————: Physical phenomena in psychical research. *Journal of the American Society for Psychical Research,* 52:3-23, 1958.

————: Science, scientists, and psychical research. *Journal of the American Society for Psychical Research,* 50:142-147, 1956.

————: Some questions concerning psychical phenomena. *Journal of the American Society for Psychical Research,* 48:3-20, 1954.

Dunne, J. W.: *An Experiment with Time,* 3rd ed. New York, Hillary, 1958.

Eccles, J. C.: Hypotheses relating to the brain-mind problem. *Nature,* 168:53-57, 1951.

Ehrenwald, J.: Human personality and the nature of psi phenomena. *Journal of the American Society for Psychical Research,* 62:366-380, 1968.

————: *Telepathy and Medical Psychology.* London, Allen & Unwin, 1947.

Eisenbud, J.: Some notes on the psychology of the paranormal. *Journal of the American Society for Psychical Research, 66*:27-41, 1972.

Eysenck, H. J.: Personality and extrasensory perception. *Journal of the Society for Psychical Research, 44*:55-71, 1967.

Fechner, G. T.: *The Little Book of Life after Death* (translated by M. B. Wadsworth; introduction by W. James), 4th ed. Boston, Little, 1904. (First published 1836 under pseudonym "Mises.")

Feigl, H.: Physicalism, unity of science and the foundations of psychology. In Schilpp, P. A. (Ed.): *The Philosophy of Rudolf Carnap.* La Salle, Open Court, 1963, pp. 227-267, *passim.*

Feyerabend, P. K.: Science without experience. *Journal of Philosophy, 66*:791-794, 1969.

Fisher, R. A.: The statistical method in psychical research. *Proceedings of the Society for Psychical Research, 39*:189-192, 1929-31.

Flew, A. (Ed.): *Body, Mind, and Death.* New York, Macmillan, 1964, *passim.*

Flew, A.: Broad and supernormal precognition. In Schilpp, P. A. (Ed.): *The Philosophy of C. D. Broad.* New York, Tudor, 1959, pp. 411-435.

————: Coincidence and synchronicity. *Journal of the Society for Psychical Research, 37*:198-201, 1953-54.

————: Immortality. In *The Encyclopedia of Philosophy.* New York, Macmillan and Free Pr, 1967, vol. 4, pp. 139-150.

————: Is there a case for disembodied survival?. *Journal of the American Society for Psychical Research, 66*:129-144, 1972.

————: *A New Approach to Psychical Research.* London, Watts, 1953.

————: Precognition. In *The Encyclopedia of Philosophy.* New York, Macmillan and Free Pr, 1967, vol. 6, pp. 436-441.

————: "The soul" of Mr. A. M. Quinton. *Journal of Philosophy, 60*:337-344, 1963.

Freud, S.: *Studies in Parapsychology.* In Rieff, P. (Ed.). New York, Collier-Macmillan, 1963.

Fuller, J. G.: *The Great Soul Trial.* New York, Macmillan, 1969.

Garrett, E. J. (Ed.): *Does Man Survive Death?.* New York, Helix Pr, 1957.

Gauld, A.: *The Founders of Psychical Research.* New York, Schocken, 1968.

Good, I. J. (Ed.): *The Scientist Speculates.* New York, Basic Bks, 1962.

Green, C.: *Lucid Dreams.* Oxford, Institute of Psychophysical Research, 1968.

————: *Out-of-the-body Experiences.* Oxford, Institute of Psychophysical Research, 1968.

Gregory, C. C. L., and Kohsen, A.: *Physical and Psychical Research: An Analysis of Belief.* Reigate, England, Omega, 1954.

Hansel, C. E. M.: *ESP: A Scientific Evaluation.* New York, Scribner, 1966.

Hardy, A.: Biology and psychical research. *Proceedings of the Society for Psychical Research, 50*:96-134, 1953.

————: *The Living Stream: Evolution and Man.* London, Collins, 1965, Lecture IX.

Hare, M. M.: *Microcosm and Macrocosm.* New York, Julian Pr, 1966, *passim.*

Hart, H.: Creative discussion in psychical research: a rejoinder to Professor Wheatley. *Journal of the American Society for Psychical Research, 61*:72-75, 1967.

————: *The Enigma of Survival.* Springfield, Thomas, 1959.

————: Psychical research and the methods of science. *Journal of the American Society for Psychical Research, 51*:85-105, 1957.

————: *Toward a New Philosophical Basis for Parapsychological Phenomena.* New York, Parapsychology Foundation, 1965.

Haynes, R.: *The Hidden Springs: An Enquiry into Extra-sensory Perception.* London, Hollis & Carter, 1961.

Hesse, M. B.: *Forces and Fields: The Concept of Action at a Distance in the History of Physics.* London, Nelson, 1961, pp. 96, 98, 293, 295-303.

Heywood, R.: *Beyond the Reach of Sense.* New York, Dutton, 1961, Appendix.

Huxley, A.: *The Doors of Perception and Heaven and Hell.* Harmondsworth, England, Penguin, 1959. (*The Doors of Perception* originally published 1954, *Heaven and Hell* originally published 1956, both by Chatto & Windus, London.)

International Journal of Neuropsychiatry. Vol. 2, no. 5, 1966. (Special issue on ESP.)

Jacks, L. P.: The theory of survival in the light of its context. *Proceedings of the Society for Psychical Research, 29*:287-305, 1916-17.

Jaffé, A.: *Apparitions and Precognition: A Study from the Point of View of C. G. Jung's Analytical Psychology.* New Hyde Park, Univ Bks, 1963.

————: *From the Life and Work of C. G. Jung* (translated by R. F. C. Hull). New York, Har-Row, 1971, *passim.*

James, W.: see Murphy, G., and Ballou, R. O. (Eds.).

Johnson, R. C.: *The Imprisoned Splendour.* London, Hodder, 1953.

Jung, C. G.: *Synchronicity: An Acausal Connecting Principle* (translated by R. F. C. Hull). In Jung, C. G., and Pauli, W.: *The Interpretation of Nature and the Psyche.* New York, Pantheon, 1955, pp. 1-146.

Kneale, M., Robinson, R., and Mundle, C. W. K.: Is psychical research relevant to philosophy? [symposium]. *Proceedings of the Aristotelian Society, Supplementary Volume 24*:173-231, 1950.

Kneale, W. C.: Broad on mental events and epiphenomenalism. In Schilpp, P. A. (Ed.): *The Philosophy of C. D. Broad.* New York, Tudor, 1959, pp. 437-455.

Koestler, A.: *The Roots of Coincidence.* New York, Random, 1972.

Kooy, J. M. J.: Space, time, and consciousness. *Journal of Parapsychology, 21*:259-272, 1957.

Lamont, C.: *The Illusion of Immortality.* New York, Philos Lib, 1950.

Le Clair, R. (Ed.): *The Letters of William James and Théodore Flournoy.* Madison, U of Wis Pr, 1966, *passim.*

LeShan, L.: *The Medium, the Mystic, and the Physicist.* New York, Viking Pr, 1974.

————: *Toward a General Theory of the Paranormal: A Report of Work in Progress.* New York, Parapsychology Foundation, 1969.

Lewy, C.: Is the notion of disembodied existence self-contradictory?. *Proceedings of the Aristotelian Society, 43*:59-78, 1942-43.

Lilly, J. C.: Inner space and parapsychology. *Proceedings of the Parapsychological Association, 6*:71-79, 1969.

McConnell, R. A.: ESP and credibility in science. *American Psychologist, 24*:531-538, 1969.

————: ESP research at three levels of method. *Journal of Parapsychology, 30*:195-207, 1966.

McCoy, J. O.: Parapsychology and inter-scientific dependence. *Journal of the Foundation for Research in Parapsychology, 1*:75-87, 1961.

McCreery, C.: *Science, Philosophy and ESP.* Hamden, Archon Bks, 1967.

Mace, C. A.: *Supernormal Faculty and the Structure of the Mind* (Myers Lecture). London, Society for Psychical Research, 1937.

MacKinnon, D. M., and Flew, A.: Death [two papers]. In Flew, A., and MacIntyre, A. (Eds.): *New Essays in Philosophical Theology.* London, SCM Pr, 1955, pp. 261-272.

Margenau, H.: ESP in the framework of modern science. *Journal of the American Society for Psychical Research, 60*:214-228, 1966.

Marshall, N.: ESP and memory: a physical theory. *British Journal for the Philosophy of Science, 10*:265-286, 1960.

Meehl, P. E., and Scriven, M.: Compatibility of science and ESP. *Science, 123*:14-15, 1956.

Meerloo, J. A. M.: *Hidden Communion: Studies in the Communication Theory of Telepathy.* New York, Garrett Publications, 1964.

Mehlberg, H.: *The Reach of Science.* Toronto, U of Toronto Pr, 1958, pp. 72, 116-117, 342.

Miller, G. A.: Concerning psychical research. *Sci Am, 209:* no. 5, 171-177, 1963.

Moncrieff, M. M.: *The Clairvoyant Theory of Perception.* London, Faber, 1951.

Montague, W. P.: *The Chances of Surviving Death.* Cambridge, Harvard U Pr, 1934.

Morris, R. L.: An experimental approach to the survival problem. *Theta,* nos. 33-34, 1971-72 (pages unnumbered).

Mundle, C. W. K.: Does the concept of precognition make sense?. *International Journal of Parapsychology, 6*:179-198, 1964.

————: ESP phenomena, philosophical implications of. In *The Encyclopedia of Philosophy.* New York, Macmillan and Free Pr, 1967, vol. 3, pp. 49-58.

————: Professor Rhine's views about PK. *Mind, 59*:372-379, 1950.

————: Some philosophical perspectives for parapsychology. *Journal of Parapsychology, 16*:257-272, 1952.

————: Strange facts in search of a theory. *Proceedings of the Society for Psychical Research, 56*:1-20, 1973.

Murphy, G.: Are there any solid facts in psychical research?. *Journal of the American Society for Psychical Research, 64*:3-17, 1970.

————: A Caringtonian approach to Ian Stevenson's *Twenty Cases Suggestive of Reincarnation. Journal of the American Society for Psychical Research, 67*:117-129, 1973.

————: A comparison of India and the West in viewpoints regarding psychical phenomena. *Journal of the American Society for Psychical Research, 53*:43-49, 1959.

————: Difficulties confronting the survival hypothesis. *Journal of the American Society for Psychical Research, 39*:67-94, 1945.

————: Field theory and survival. *Journal of the American Society for Psychical Research, 39*:181-209, 1945.

————: Lawfulness versus caprice: is there a "law of psychic phenomena"?. *Journal of the American Society for Psychical Research, 58*:238-249, 1964.

————: The natural, the mystical, and the paranormal. *Journal of the American Society for Psychical Research, 46*:125-142, 1952.

————: An outline of survival evidence. *Journal of the American Society for Psychical Research, 39*:2-34, 1945.

————: The place of parapsychology among the sciences. *Journal of Parapsychology, 13*:62-71, 1949.

————: The problem of repeatability in psychical research. *Journal of the American Society for Psychical Research, 65*:3-16, 1971.

————: Psychical research and personality. *Journal of the American Society for Psychical Research, 44*:3-20, 1950.

————: Psychical research and the mind-body relation. *Journal of the American Society for Psychical Research, 40*:189-207, 1946.

————: Psychological aspects of studies in extrasensory perception. *International Journal of Parapsychology, 3:* no. 1, 37-55, 1961.

————: Psychology and psychical research. *Proceedings of the Society for Psychical Research, 50*:26-49, 1953.

Murphy, G., and Ballou, R. O. (Eds.): *William James on Psychical Research.* New York, Viking Pr, 1960.

Murray, G.: Presidential address. *Proceedings of the Society for Psychical Research, 29*:46-63, 1916.

Myers, F. W. H.: *Human Personality and Its Survival of Bodily Death,* 2nd ed. New Hyde Park, Univ Bks, 1954.

Nash, C. B.: Physical and metaphysical parapsychology. *Journal of Parapsychology, 27*:283-300, 1963.

————: The unorthodox science of parapsychology. *International Journal of Parapsychology, 1:* no. 2, 5-23, 1959.

Nayak, G. C.: Survival, reincarnation, and the problem of personal identity. *Journal of the [Indian] Philosophical Association, 11*:131-143, 1968.

Odegard, D.: Disembodied existence and central state materialism. *Australasian Journal of Philosophy, 48*:256-260, 1970.

————: Persons and bodies. *Philosophy and Phenomenological Research, 31*:225-242, 1970.

Osis, K., et al.: ESP over distance: research on the ESP channel. *Journal of the American Society for Psychical Research, 65*:245-288, 1971.

Owen, A. R. G.: *Can We Explain the Poltergeist?.* New York, Garrett-Helix, 1964.

Payne, P. D., and Bendit, L. J.: *The Psychic Sense,* rev. ed. London, Faber, 1958.

Penelhum, T.: Personal identity. In *The Encyclopedia of Philosophy.* New York, Macmillan and Free Pr, 1967, vol. 6, pp. 95-107.

————: Personal identity, memory, and survival. *Journal of Philosophy, 56*:882-903, 1959.

————: *Survival and Disembodied Existence.* New York, Humanities, 1970.

Phillips, D. Z.: *Death and Immortality.* London, Macmillan, 1970.

Pratt, V.: The inexplicable and the supernatural. *Philosophy, 43*:248-257, 1968.

Price, G. R.: Science and the supernatural. *Science, 122*:359-367, 1955. (See also Price, G. R.: Apology to Rhine and Soal [letter]. *Science, 175*:359, 1972.)

————: Where is the definitive experiment?. *Science, 123*:17-18, 1956.

Price, H. H.: Apparitions: two theories. *Journal of Parapsychology, 24*:110-128, 1960.

————: *Essays in the Philosophy of Religion.* New York, Oxford U Pr, 1972.

————: The expressive theory of the mind-body relation. In Dommeyer, F. C. (Ed.): *Current Philosophical Issues: Essays in Honor of Curt John Ducasse.* Springfield, Thomas, 1966, pp. 121-126.

————: Foreword. *Enquiry, 1:* no. 2, 4, 1948.

————: Haunting and the "psychic ether" hypothesis: with some preliminary reflections on the present condition and possible future of psychical research. *Proceedings of the Society for Psychical Research, 45*:307-343, 1939.

————: Mediumship and human survival. *Journal of Parapsychology, 24*:199-219, 1960.

————: A mescaline experience. *Journal of the American Society for Psychical Research, 58*:3-20, 1964.

————: Parapsychology and human nature. *Journal of Parapsychology, 23*:178-195, 1959.

474   *Philosophical Dimensions of Parapsychology*

——: Psychical research and human personality. *Hibbert Journal,* *47*:105-113, 1948-49.

——: Some objections to behaviorism. In Hook, S. (Ed.): *Dimensions* *of Mind.* New York, New York U Pr, 1960, pp. 79-84.

——: Some philosophical questions about telepathy and clairvoyance. *Philosophy, 15*:363-385, 1940.

——: Survival and the idea of "another world." *Proceedings of the Society for Psychical Research, 50*:1-25, 1953.

Price, H. H., and Broad, C. D.: The philosophical implications of precognition. *Proceedings of the Aristotelian Society, Supplementary Volume* *16*:211-245, 1937.

Price, H. H., Ducasse, C. J., et al.: see Garrett, E. J. (Ed.).

Progoff, I.: The role of parapsychology in modern thinking. *International Journal of Parapsychology, 1:* no. 1, 5-16, 1959.

Quinton, A. M.: The soul. *Journal of Philosophy, 59*:393-409, 1962.

Randall, J. L.: Psi phenomena and biological theory. *Journal of the Society for Psychical Research, 46*:151-165, 1971.

Ransom, C.: Recent criticisms of parapsychology: a review. *Journal of the American Society for Psychical Research, 65*:289-307, 1971.

Rao, K. R.: The bidirectionality of psi. *Journal of Parapsychology, 29*:230-250, 1965.

——: Consideration of some theories in parapsychology. *Journal of Parapsychology, 25*:32-54, 1961.

——: *Mystic Awareness: Four Lectures on the Paranormal.* Mysore, India, U of Mysore Pr, 1972.

——: *Psi Cognition.* Tenali, India, Tagore Publishing House, n. d. (author's preface dated 1957).

Rees, D. A.: The meaning of "survival." *Analysis, 12*:94-98, 1951-52.

Reiser, O. L.: *The Integration of Human Knowledge.* Boston, Sargent, 1958.

——: A theory of extrasensory perception. *Journal of Parapsychology, 3*:167-193, 1939.

Rhine, J. B.: The bearing of parapsychology on human potentiality. *Journal of Parapsychology, 30*:243-258, 1966.

——: Comments on "Science and the supernatural." *Science, 123*:11-14, 1956.

——: The experiment should fit the hypothesis. *Science, 123*:19, 1956.

——: *Extra-sensory Perception,* rev. ed. Boston, Humphries, 1964.

——: On parapsychology and the nature of man. In Hook, S. (Ed.): *Dimensions of Mind,* New York, New York U Pr, 1960, pp. 74-78.

——: Parapsychology and man. In Laszlo, E., and Wilbur, J. B. (Eds.): *Human Values and the Mind of Man.* New York, Gordon, 1971, pp. 3-20.

——: Psi and psychology: conflict and solution. *Journal of Parapsychology, 32*:101-128, 1968.

————: The science of nonphysical nature. *Journal of Philosophy, 51*:801-810, 1954.

————: Some guiding concepts for parapsychology. *Journal of Parapsychology, 32*:190-218, 1968.

————: *Telepathy and Human Personality* (Myers Lecture). London, Society for Psychical Research, 1950.

————: What do parapsychologists want to know?. *Journal of the American Society for Psychical Research, 53*:3-15, 1959.

Richet, C.: *Thirty Years of Psychical Research*. New York, Macmillan, 1923.

Robertson, L. C.: The logical and scientific implications of precognition, assuming this to be established statistically from the work of card-guessing subjects. *Journal of the Society for Psychical Research, 39*:134-139, 1957.

Rogo, D. S.: Three approaches to the teaching of parapsychology. *Parapsychology Review,* January-February, 1972, pp. 5-8.

————: *The Welcoming Silence.* Secaucus, Univ Bks, 1973.

Roll, W. G.: ESP and memory. *International Journal of Neuropsychiatry, 2*:505-521, 1966.

————: *The Poltergeist.* Garden City, Nelson Doubleday, 1972.

————: The problem of precognition. *Journal of the Society for Psychical Research, 41*:115-128, 1961.

————: The psi field. *Proceedings of the Parapsychological Association, 1*:32-65, 1957-64.

————: Survival research: problems and possibilities. *Theta,* nos. 39-40, 1-13, 1974.

Roll, W. G., et al.: What next in survival research? [symposium, edited by C. J. Ducasse et al.]. *Journal of the American Society for Psychical Research, 59*:146-166, 186-210, 309-337, 1965.

Russell, B.: Do men survive death?. In Sayers, D., et al.: *The Great Mystery of Life Hereafter.* London, Hodder, 1957, pp. 19-27.

Ryzl, M.: ESP, the universe, and man: some theories and considerations. *Psychic, 1:* no. 4, 18-22, 1970.

Salter, W. H.: *Zoar: The Evidence of Psychical Research concerning Survival.* London, Sidgwick & Jackson, 1961.

Saltmarsh, H. F.: *Foreknowledge.* London, Bell & Sons, 1938.

Schiller, F. C. S.: *Riddles of the Sphinx,* rev. ed. New York, Macmillan, 1910.

Schmeidler, G., and McConnell, R. A.: *ESP and Personality Patterns.* New Haven, Yale U Pr, 1958.

Scriven, M.: The compleat robot: prolegomena to androidology. In Hook, S. (Ed.): *Dimensions of Mind.* New York, New York U Pr, 1960, pp. 113-133.

————: The frontiers of psychology: psychoanalysis and parapsychology.

In Colodny, R. G. (Ed.): *Frontiers of Science and Philosophy.* Pittsburgh, U of Pittsburgh Pr, 1962, pp. 79-129.

————: Modern experiments in telepathy. *Philosophical Review, 65*:231-253, 1956.

————: New frontiers of the brain. *Journal of Parapsychology, 25*:305-318, 1961.

————: Some theoretical possibilities in psi research. *Journal of the Society for Psychical Research, 39*:78-83, 1957.

Scriven, M., et al.: Physicality and psi: a symposium and forum discussion. *Journal of Parapsychology, 25*:13-31, 1961.

————: Responses to the forum on physicality and psi. *Journal of Parapsychology, 25*:214-218, 1961.

Servadio, E.: Telepathy and psychoanalysis, *Journal of the American Society for Psychical Research, 52*:125-133, 1958.

Shaffer, J.: Mind-body problem. In *The Encyclopedia of Philosophy.* New York, Macmillan and Free Pr, 1967, vol. 5, pp. 336-346.

Shewmaker, K. L., and Berenda, C. W.: Science and the problem of psi. *Philosophy of Science, 29*:195-203, 1962.

Sidgwick, H.: Presidential addresses. *Proceedings of the Society for Psychical Research, 1*:7-12, 65-69, 245-250, 1882-83.

Sloman, A.: New bodies for sick persons: personal identity without physical continuity. *Analysis, 32*:52-55, 1971-72.

Smart, B.: Can disembodied persons be spatially located?. *Analysis, 31*:133-138, 1970-71.

Smythies, J. R. (Ed.): *Brain and Mind.* New York, Humanities, 1965.

————: *Science and ESP.* New York, Humanities, 1967.

Soal, S. G., and Bateman, F.: *Modern Experiments in Telepathy.* London, Faber, 1954.

Spencer Brown, G.: *Probability and Scientific Inference.* New York, Longmans, Green, 1957, *passim.*

Stanford, R. G.: Parapsychology and the method of science. *Journal of the Foundation for Research in Parapsychology, 1:* no. 1, 11-22, 1961.

Stevenson, I.: An antagonist's view of parapsychology. A review of Professor Hansel's *ESP: A Scientific Evaluation. Journal of the American Society for Psychical Research, 61*:254-267, 1967.

————: Carington's psychon theory as applied to cases of the reincarnation type: a reply to Gardner Murphy. *Journal of the American Society for Psychical Research, 67*:130-146, 1973.

————: *Twenty Cases Suggestive of Reincarnation.* New York, American Society for Psychical Research (*Proceedings,* vol. 26), 1966.

Stevenson, I., and Roll, W. G.: Criticism in parapsychology: an informal statement of some guiding principles. *Journal of the American Society for Psychical Research, 60*:347-356, 1966.

Strawson, P. F.: *Individuals.* London, Methuen, 1959, Ch. 3.

Swiggart, P.: A note on telepathy. *Analysis, 22*:42-43, 1961-62.

Tart, C. T. (Ed.): *Altered States of Consciousness.* New York, Wiley, 1969.

Tart, C. T.: States of consciousness and state-specific sciences. *Science, 176*:1203-1210, 1972.

Thalberg, I.: Telepathy. *Analysis, 21*:49-53, 1960-61.

Thouless, R. H., and Wiesner, B. P.: The psi processes in normal and "paranormal" psychology. *Proceedings of the Society for Psychical Research, 48*:177-196, 1946-49.

Tietze, T. R.: The final frontier: some perspectives on survival. *Psychic, 3:* no. 1, 8-13, 1971.

Tischner, R.: *Telepathy and Clairvoyance* (translated by W. D. Hutchinson). New York, Harcourt Brace, 1925.

Toynbee, A., et al.: *Man's Concern with Death.* New York, McGraw, 1969.

Tyrrell, G. N. M.: *Apparitions,* rev. ed. London, Duckworth, 1953.

————: The *modus operandi* of paranormal cognition. *Proceedings of the Society for Psychical Research, 48*:65-120, 1947.

————: *The Nature of Human Personality.* London, Allen & Unwin, 1954.

————: *The Personality of Man.* Baltimore, Penguin, 1947.

————: *Science and Psychical Phenomena.* London, Methuen, 1938.

Van Over, R. (Ed.): *Psychology and Extrasensory Perception.* New York, NAL, 1972.

Van Over, R., and Oteri, L. (Eds.): *William McDougall, Explorer of the Mind: Studies in Psychical Research.* New York, Garrett-Helix, 1967.

Vasiliev, L. L.: *Mysterious Phenomena of the Human Psyche* (translated by S. Volochova). New Hyde Park, Univ Bks, 1965.

Wade, N.: Psychical research: the incredible in search of credibility. *Science, 181*:138-143, 1973.

Walker, K.: What can survive?. *Newsletter of the Parapsychology Foundation, 6:* no. 4, 3-5, 1959.

Walker, R.: Parapsychology and dualism. *Scientific Monthly, 79:* no. 1, 1-9, 1954.

Warcollier, R.: *Mind to Mind* (edited by E. K. Schwartz and translated by Mrs. J. B. Gridley et al.). New York, Creation Age Pr, 1948.

Warner, L.: Is "extra-sensory perception" extra-sensory?. *J Psychol, 7*:71-77, 1939.

Wheatley, J. M. O.: Is telepathy a faculty?. *International Journal of Parapsychology, 7:* no. 2, 117-133, 1965.

————: Knowledge, empiricism, and ESP. *International Journal of Parapsychology, 3:* no. 1, 7-23, 1961.

————: Love, telepathy, survival: reflections on Professor H. H. Price's *Essays in the Philosophy of Religion. Journal of the American Society for Psychical Research, 67*:295-303, 1973.

————: The necessity for bodies: an appreciation of Professor Terence Penelhum's *Survival and Disembodied Existence. Journal of the American Society for Psychical Research, 66*:321-328, 1972.

————: Notes on guessing. *Journal of the American Society for Psychical Research, 64*:286-295, 1970.

Whiteman, J. H. M.: Quantum theory and parapsychology. *Journal of the American Society for Psychical Research, 67*:341-360, 1973.

Wolstenholme, G. E. W., and Millar, E. C. P. (Eds.): *Ciba Foundation Symposium on Extrasensory Perception*. Boston, Little, 1956.

INDEX

479